LIBERTY AND POWER 1600–1760

LIBERTY IN AMERICA
1600 TO THE PRESENT

VOLUME ONE

Liberty and Power
1600-1760

Oscar and Lilian Handlin

A Cornelia & Michael Bessie Book

HARPER & ROW, PUBLISHERS, New York
Cambridge, Philadelphia, San Francisco, London
Mexico City, São Paulo, Singapore, Sydney

FIRST EDITION

Designer: Sidney Feinberg

This book was set in 12-point Bembo by The Haddon Craftsmen, Inc., ComCom Division, Allentown, Pennsylvania, and printed and bound by The Haddon Craftsmen, Inc., Scranton, Pennsylvania.

Library of Congress Cataloging-in-Publication Data

Handlin, Oscar, 1915–
  Liberty and Power, 1600–1760.

"A Cornelia & Michael Bessie book."
Includes bibliographical references and index.
Contents: v. 1. Liberty and power, 1600–1760.
1. United States—Politics and government. 2. United
States—History. I. Handlin, Lilian. II. Title.
E183.H32 1986   973   85-45997
ISBN 0-06-015617-1 (v. 1)

86 87 88 89 90 HC 10 9 8 7 6 5 4 3 2 1

TO THE MEMORY OF
LEON BOMBACH

CONTENTS

PREFACE

The second half of the twentieth century began amidst conditions that seemed to assure the future of liberty in the United States and in the world. A war recently concluded destroyed the despotisms that threatened Europe and Asia; historic empires released the grips upon their colonies; racist feelings subsided; equality became an objective widely subscribed to; and technology promised to create the abundance to solve the age-old problems of want. Confidence did not long endure, however. In actuality, wars sputtered around the globe; the area of freedom contracted instead of expanding; and pervasive uneasiness spread about the worth of goals many people had long taken for granted.

The irony of excessive expectations and excessive disappointments formed the background against which this book was written. Both the high hopes and the gloom about the future sprang from a failure of understanding about the nature of liberty and its relation to human experience. This volume and its successors will, we believe, throw light upon the social, cultural, and personal factors conducive to the development of liberty, not simply as an idea, but also as a condition of life. Although we trust that the discussion will have a larger relevance, we confine our analysis to the United States—a unique case, no doubt, but one that offers instructive insights for all countries in modern times.

Yet to understand the history of liberty in the United States we found it necessary to push the story back in time to a moment before such an entity existed. The process by which the United States came to be spanned an era of more than a century and a half from the initial settlements to the dawn of a national consciousness, and bore an intimate relationship to the development of liberty.

The first settlers were not free by virtue of having planted themselves in a wilderness state of nature. To become free they had to move beyond the palisades where they long huddled in fear. Somehow they did so and acquired the ability to act, to exercise the will, although the ways of organizing power brought from Europe proved inappropriate in the new setting. Hence, we had to trace the modification in transplanted institutions required by the new scale of distances. Command and obedience were not the same in a land of immense spaces as in the limited Old World. We sought the mechanisms by which force in America came to depend on consent—on the authority of some to deliver orders, on the willingness of others to obey. Without forethought, by trial and error, the fledgling societies developed rules and rule-making bodies that permitted action in an acceptable fashion. With force most effective when local and immediate rather than when applied from a remote central source, a new kind of community took form, one more dependent upon voluntary decisions than upon compulsion and reflecting the great differences in origins and in circumstances of the population.

By the eighteenth century the pluralistic communities of the New World had become home to a distinctive personality type. We trace the evolution through the changing forms of religious worship and of church organization and through the modifications effected in family relations. By 1760 those developments had produced a recognizable American character—rude, assertive, prone to risky innovation, trusting calculation above habit, and detached from the drain of traditional ties. That character found scope for self-expression in the growing economy. Fed by abundant resources, the productive system provided an ample field for the activities of enterprising men and women with results that transformed the social system.

Slowly the Americans became aware of their national identity, the product of the same political, cultural, and social forces that made them aware of the meaning of liberty. They had discovered that the freedom of each depended on the enjoyment of rights that did not emanate from a grant or from the provisions in the clauses of ancient documents but rather had developed as aspects of the way of life of the people who claimed them and who protected them by participation in the exercise of power.

More than two centuries later, those still concerned about liberty might well ponder the significance of that discovery.

OSCAR HANDLIN
LILIAN HANDLIN

Cambridge, Massachusetts

THE ISSUE

Why wish to be free?

The question long seemed hardly worth asking, therefore remained unanswered.

Ever since Rousseau, perhaps since Locke, Western people assumed that humans, from birth, innately craved freedom. The history of liberty consisted of a succession of external efforts to impose restraints, fended off by men and women who battled in defense of what was naturally theirs.

Was it so? In the 1980s, the question is more than ever worth asking, for not all the evidence points in an affirmative direction. And if not, then analysis of the history of liberty calls for quite another approach.

At another time and at another place, an Inquisitor launched the accusation:

> You went into the world with some promise of freedom, which men in their simplicity and their innate lawlessness cannot even comprehend, which they fear and dread—for nothing has ever been less endurable to human society than freedom! When the people, like a flock of sheep in the barren desert, offered to follow you forever if you would but turn the stones into bread, you rejected the offer. "What sort of freedom is this," you thought, "if it is bought with loaves of bread? Man does not live by bread alone."

It is not through contempt of man but through comprehension of his nature that I remind you that ages will pass and mankind will proclaim in the wisdom of science that there is no crime and, therefore, no sin, but that there are only hungry people. "Feed them first and then demand virtue of them!"—that is what they will inscribe on their banner.

Grim warnings echoed down through the century that followed:

"In the end they will lay their freedom at our feet and say, 'We don't mind being slaves as long as you feed us!' They will at last realize that there cannot be enough freedom and bread for everybody, for they will never, never be able to let everyone have a fair share. You promised them bread from heaven, but, I repeat again, can it compare with earthly bread in the eyes of that always vicious and always ignoble race of man?"

The Inquisitor's admonitions arose from awareness of factors in human nature of which Americans rarely wished to take cognizance. The New World's image of free individuals, shaping their own destiny in their own way, blocked out the alien message:

"Man's universal and everlasting craving . . . can be summed up in the words, 'Whom shall I worship?'" But man seeks to worship only what is incontestable, so incontestable that all can at once agree to worship it all together. For the chief concern of those miserable creatures is to find something that all believe in, and the absolutely essential thing is that they should do so ALL TOGETHER. This need for UNIVERSAL worship is the chief torment of every man individually and of mankind as a whole from the beginning of time.

Humans therefore have no real wish for freedom, the Inquisitor insisted:

Men have no more agonizing anxiety than to find someone to whom they can hand over with all speed the gift of freedom with which the unhappy creatures are born. They will remember the horrors of confusion to which freedom brought them. Freedom, a free mind and science will lead them into such a jungle and bring them face to face with such insoluble mysteries that some of them, the recalcitrant and the fierce, will destroy themselves; others, recalcitrant but weak, will destroy one another, and the rest, weak and unhappy, will come crawling to our feet, and will cry aloud: "Yes, you

were right, you alone possess this mystery, and we come back to you
—save us from ourselves!"

Americans denied the validity of the accusation. Long before the
utterances of the Grand Inquisitor saw print, New World people acted
in a fashion that rejected his charges. They demonstrated that some
humans did not crave an object to worship and that some did not fear
freedom.

Refusing to choose between bread and liberty, they insisted they
could have both. They wanted the power to act alone and felt an urge
to decide autonomously. This book explores the sources of that urge.

Confidence sprang in part from consciousness of the country's great-
ness. The United States, said Woodrow Wilson in 1913, was incompara-
bly great in its material aspects, in its wealth, in the diversity and sweep
of its energy, in its industries, and in its limitless enterprise. It was also
very great in its moral force. Nowhere else in the world had noble men
and women exhibited more striking forms of sympathy and helpfulness
and counsel in their efforts to rectify wrong, alleviate suffering, and set
the weak in the way of strength and hope.

Awareness of strength, comfort in the capacity to act, and faith in
the future did not dull sensitivity to shortcomings. Far from it. Americans
were quick at self-flagellation: with the good had come the evil; with
riches, inexcusable waste. Wilson mourned the squandering of what
might have been used and the failure to count human costs—of lives
snuffed out, of energies overtaxed and broken. The deadweight and
burden of it all fell pitilessly the year through on men, women, and
children whose groans came up out of the mines and factories and out
of every home where the struggle had its intimate and familiar seat.
Wilson found something crude and heartless and unfeeling in the haste
to succeed and be great. Willing to "let every man look out for himself,
let every generation look out for itself," his countrymen reared the giant
machinery so that only those who stood at the levers of control had a
chance to look out for themselves. Heedlessness and the hurry to be great
by 1913 had obscured the standards of justice and fair play, and few
remembered that policy ought to serve the homeless as well as the most
powerful.

The consciousness of deficiency, however, was no cause for questioning basic assumptions: Americans, when Wilson spoke, had not budged
from the certainty that they could have bread as well as freedom. They

could, he said, look upon the good with the bad, the debased and decadent with the sound and vital. Their duty was to clean and to restore, to correct the evil without impairing the good, to purify and humanize every process of human life without weakening or sentimentalizing it. The use of reason and the will to be good would correct shortcomings, the results of human failings rather than inherent in human nature. The ability to perceive deficiencies implied the ability to do something about them. Americans thus affirmed that they could have bread and freedom, success and salvation. That, the essence of their dream, denied the validity of the Grand Inquisitor's charge.

Was it a delusion? Or did some unique quality of time and place grant those fortunate people exemption from the ominous outcome in the Grand Inquisitor's grim warning? The pages that follow confront the issue.

The analysis will not escape persistent personal and social questions. Why do people wish to be free? Those who escape to the open frontier wistfully drag with them the trappings and restraints from which they flee. Those who insist upon the right to participate in politics prove apathetic in its use once granted. Do they really want the condition of freedom, or does the attraction lie in the desire—in the process of securing it?

Why does a society that highly praises individuality and reason nevertheless drift frequently toward group solidarity, conformity, and communion? Cherishing dissent, it nonetheless often punishes deviance and offers scope to discrimination, then turns itself to the immense task of extirpating all forms of group prejudice.

What has been the relationship of freedom to the other values of life? Liberty was only one among several goals Americans cherished, not all of them compatible either among themselves or with freedom: mobility and the pursuit of happiness, perfectability and property, competition and family solidarity.

Freedom carries with it obligations—for decisions, for choices, and for unexpected experiences. It threatens routine and order, breeds change, conflict, and insecurity. Yet some men and women seek it in preference to the comfort of unvarying habit, to the certainty of infallible authority, to the peace of a rigid system that admits no questions and holds each individual in place.

The human personality can grow in one direction or another. It can develop traits of character that reach toward liberty or toward stability as the social environment encourages it to unfold in one fashion or another. The relationship of the seed to the soil, of the individual personality to the society, is the subject of this book.

We therefore seek the materials for answers not in philosophers' theories, nor in the policies of governments, but in the experiences of people's daily lives; not in legislation or judicial decisions, but in administration and informal personal and communal actions. Focus on the way of life of a people in all its complexity requires a shift of attention away from particular events and incidents to developments over long spans of time, although not to the abuse of chronology. It requires also the incorporation of political and constitutional, as well as economic, social, and cultural trends, into a unified narrative.

We have not written a political or economic or cultural history, although we have dipped into those and other fields for illustrations. We are well aware that each of the incidents and statements here drawn together was specific to a particular moment and place; and we have been sensitive to the uniqueness of each. We know, too, that we traverse more than a century and a half crowded with drastic changes in Europe as well as in America which multiply the difficulties of seeing the era as a whole. But we have shaped these intractable materials within a long chronological span, encompassing areas as diverse as Georgia and Maine, in the hope of discerning large patterns of thought and behavior that explain the discovery of liberty in a newly settled land.

In the beginning was the void, into which seventeenth-century Europeans hastened, driven by earthly fears and demonic dreams, torn away from the familiar settings that formerly set limits upon the employment of force and prevented the relapse to savagery everyone feared. Here, when the traditional European ways of mobilizing power failed, the transplanted explored other means. For a century and a half, down to the 1760s, their slow quest for stability suffered repeated interruptions. Power, locally based and exercised through integrated communities, required frequent reinforcement through consent by individuals who recognized that they enjoyed rights and bore obligations. In doing so, they became independent well before 1776.

Liberty was not the goal toward which the Europeans becoming Americans set forth but a continent inadvertently discovered in the search for another destination.

LIBERTY AND POWER 1600–1760

I

POWER, 1600

POWER IN THE WORLD of 1600 meant above all the force of arms. Memory of times recent and remote permitted no one, high or low, to forget the ultimate persuasiveness of the sword. Rarely could the peasant raise eyes from the furrow without noting the distant crenelated towers of the rulers. Stout walls no longer offered burghers a sense of security, for no city could withstand an artillery siege. Ecclesiastics knew that respect for their vestments did not extend to their persons, as John Alen, archbishop of Dublin, discovered in 1534 when minions of the Lord Offaly dragged him out of bed and dashed out his brains. Nor could the aristocracy relax; feuds extended from generation to generation so that blood blotted the pages of every genealogical record. Bishop Leslie noted of the Scots that "the greater of degree and the nobler of blood they were," the more eager to be first to set upon the enemy and the more likely to lose their lives. At Flodden (1513) James IV along with twelve earls, fourteen other lords, and at least one member of every important Scottish family fell victim to the savage English forces. At the battle of Al Kasr Alkebir (1578), three kings lost their lives. A century later, a traveler in Scotland noted the gentlemen's houses built like castles—"they being so treacherous to one another, that they are forc'd to defend themselves in strongholds."[1]

Even apart from the threat of foreign foes, hardly a royal head rested secure; those raised high could easily sink low if their grip slackened. Jealous contenders sniffed out any hint of weakness that might vacate a throne; in 1580, seven pretenders jostled for the crown of Portugal, and

1

the English succession was far from clear after the death of Henry VIII. Then, too, unruly divines warned their majesties that the "laws of God and Nature" allowed liberty-loving subjects to imprison and depose their princes for their enormities and to execute them, if need be. Queens, too, had had their heads chopped off, the Duke of Buckingham warned Henrietta Maria, wife of Charles I. He had in mind Mary Queen of Scots; but the roster of distinguished names that mounted the block included a Buckingham, a Surrey, a Somerset, an Arundel, Sir Thomas More, and Thomas Cromwell. In a time of plots and conspiracies, security was a prize no one possessed.[2]

The force of arms was not the only form of power in 1600. In a society increasingly accustomed to cash transactions, the ability to exact payment for goods, to reward services with wages, and to make or withhold loans, put means of control into the hands of merchants, employers, bankers, and usurers. The payment of 222,000 crowns in 1564 assuaged English grief at the loss of Calais six years earlier. Spiritual force also exerted compulsive pressure. Though the idea of hell was changing, Europeans still assumed that only the threat of eternal punishment kept potential transgressors in line; and a society concerned with salvation, fearful of damnation, armed bishops with the weapon of excommunication, preachers with the force of denunciation. When John Knox informed her that subjects had the right to disobey monarchs in religious matters, Mary Stuart protested unavailingly that she would thereby become responsible to the sovereign people.[3]

But ultimately naked force decided. In 1599 Richard Price assembled the men of Cardiganshire in the church, surrounding them with five-hundred armed family partisans. When the services ended, four justices of the peace proclaimed a comortha (the traditional custom of free benevolence for victims of misfortune) for Price's benefit, threatening those who refused to contribute with impressment for military service in Ireland. Price collected £100, and then had his wife initiate a similar comortha among women—augmenting his income by £200.

Warfare in the sixteenth century counted among its victims not only the fighting men slain but also those who yielded their lives to disease. Of the 3,400 troops the Earl of Essex led to France in 1591, only 800 returned. And the brutality affected not just those who bore arms but everyone, spreading from the fields of battle to the towns and villages, to the accompaniment of ceaseless wailing, of unremittent suffering. Ill-paid or unpaid soldiers picked the countryside clean, in gentlemanly disdain of the fate of the huddled plebeians. And in the wake of war famine spread, with the dead lying in the ditches, their mouths all colored green by eating nettles, dock, and all things they could tear from the ground.[4]

New features added to the terror. Gunpowder, devilish if not actually more lethal than the blade, professional troops who valued the opportunity for looting and booty over chivalric codes, and religious fervor that justified the slaughter of unbelievers imparted a frightful quality to the fighting. A horrible carnage preceded the sack and conflagration when the Spaniards took Saint Quentin from the French on August 27, 1557. That day, the victors butchered every human being, stripping the women lest they conceal treasure, then slashing them with knives. In the streets strewn with corpses, hands, limbs, and trunks mingled among the bricks and rafters of the houses. The killing, plundering, and burning lasted three days and nights, while dismembered bodies, gnawed by dogs or blackened by fire, polluted the summer air. On August 29 King Philip ordered the 3,500 surviving women driven out of the city into French territory. The slaughters at Valenciennes in 1562 and at Mechlin in 1572 were so horrible that a survivor could say nothing: his hair stood on end "not only at recounting, but even at remembering the scene." No one reckoned the massacred in more remote places—in Stockholm (1520), Novgorod (1570), Moscow (1571), or Cartagena (1586).[5]

Religious differences envenomed conflict. In 1555–1556, during the reign of Mary I in England, three hundred people met death by burning at the stake for conscience' sake, and the number would have risen but for the expense of that edifying procedure. Everywhere, from Ireland in the west to the eastern marches of the Continent, massacre was an incidental feature of warfare, among believers as against heretics. With an uprising in Cumberland suppressed, Henry VIII ordered the Duke of Norfolk, "without pitie or respect," to execute "a good number of the inhabitantes of every town, village and hamlet" either by "the hanging of them uppe in trees" or "by the quartering of them, and the setting of their heddes and quarters in every towne, great and small" as a "ferefull spectacle" to assure obedience. Queen Elizabeth rejoiced at the massacre of the six hundred men in the garrison of Smerwick after their surrender. As a matter of course, Tudor and Cromwellian statesmen, having cold-bloodedly calculated the cost of exterminating the whole Irish population, abandoned the idea because of the price.[6]

Peace was not a time of quiet. The watchful Deity, wrathful and unpredictable, legitimized the pleasure the righteous took in the suffering of the guilty. An eye for an eye, the rule of vindictive justice, fueled endless border conflicts and turned cities into scenes of butchery and daily fights. The taste for blood, not otherwise sated, fed upon rough sports —baiting bears and bulls, cockfighting.[7]

Familiarity with violence made torture a usual technique of persuasion, and particularly where suspicions of Satanism or witchcraft stoked hostility against the accused. Dr. Fian (John Cunningham), charged with having aroused the wind that made the royal passage from Denmark stormy, first confessed under pressure, then retracted, thus enraging James VI of Scotland (later James I of England). The king ordered the bones of the culprit's legs broken into small pieces in the boot, an iron device employed for the purpose. James then suggested that a pair of pincers, called in Scottish a *turkas,* pull the nails from all the prisoner's fingers, into each of which were thrust two needles, even up to their heads. Dr. Fian's insistence upon his innocence proved how deeply the devil had entered into his heart.[8]

James considered some of his subjects "utterly barbares," but was no fool, and was certainly learned. He knew all about poisons; about witches, how they evoked worship; and about the phenomena of possession; about demons, about familiars, about innocent surface appearances and hidden evils. Dr. Fian's denial conformed to the king's expectations; the torture was an end in itself, not an instrument of justice.[9]

The English common law excluded the use of torture; but, the Lord Chancellor explained in 1606, exorbitant offenses were not subject to the ordinary course of law, which the extraordinary powers of the crown could always supersede. Gory devices extracted confessions for commonplace crimes also, their use limited not by compunction or sympathy but by doubts about reliability. Too often, the weakling gave whatever answer the questioner desired while stouthearted criminals maintained silence, whatever the pressure.[10]

Merciless punishment awaited the guilty. In good conscience Sir Thomas Smith boasted (1583) that England did not use "cruell torments" in capital cases, just hangings with the corpses left to rot in the air. Felons dangling by the roadside were as common a sight inland as pirates dangling at the water's edge; and hundreds of crimes led to the gibbet—carrying horses into Scotland, letting out ponds, hunting by night with painted faces, digging up boundary stones, and concealing the death of a bastard child, among others. The most heinous crimes, Smith explained, called for penalties more severe than the gallows. Treason and offenses akin to it—as the murder of a husband by a wife or of a master by a servant—deserved a horrid fate. Death then came in various guises—swiftly, as by decapitation or strangulation; more slowly, as by burning or boiling alive; most leisurely, as by *peine fort et dur,* during which gradually added weights crushed the embers of life. Burnings and quarterings in public ceremonies also edified onlookers. On September 20, 1586, Anthony Babington and others were drawn on hurdles to St. Giles in the Fields, London, for protracted execution. They were strangled but brought down alive, their bodies cut open slowly, castrated, and carved apart over a period of hours during which the savage crowd could hear their groans. Offenses judged not so serious exposed their perpetrators to retribution of lesser degree though of equal brutality. The whipping post, the branding iron, the pillory, the stocks, and the ducking stool, everywhere at hand, displayed the force always available to correct wrongdoers.[11]

The grisly sense of humor that moved the Scottish Earl of Huntly to roast alive two captured cooks from an enemy clan showed the cheapness of life, the familiarity with death, the absence of any impulse to squeamishness. What better way to refute the allegation that he had been devoured by lice or, like Herod, by worms, then publicly to expose the body of John Pym, who had died of cancer. James I, a passionate hunter, thought it unfair to kill the prey with bullet or arrow; he followed after the hounds who brought the deer down, then slit its throat, opened its belly, played with its blood, and pranced into the open cadaver. He celebrated the birth of his son (the future Charles I) in part by dismemberment of the carcass of the disloyal Earl of Gowrie. Not the dramatic massacres, when rage or hatred spread through whole districts; not even the devastating plagues, when London lost a quarter of its residents, or Genoa three-quarters; nor yet the prolonged famines that emptied whole regions—the casual acceptance of brutality was not the product of adjustment to such extraordinary instances, but rather of day-to-day experience in an era when life expectancy at birth was well below thirty, when the maimed, the disfigured, and the crippled were the commonplace sights of every community, and when starvation and disease, cutting an ample swath among the poor, at least lessened the financial burden of relief.[12]

Power—visible, familiar—affected all human life. Violence, or the implied threat of it, governed the relationship of parents and children, of husbands and wives, of buyers and sellers, of priests and communicants. Soldiers held Louis XIII down (until the age of nine) while his nurse whipped the royal buttocks, in accordance with his father's instruction that nothing in the world was better to deal with obstinacy or misbehavior. A spaniel, a woman, and a walnut tree, ran the doggerel, the more they are beaten, the better they be. Seventeenth-century Europeans knew from their own experience, from their contacts with other peoples, and from past history, the decisive qualities of the fist, the cudgel, the sword, and the gun. The state, Thomas Hobbes understood, was only "organized force."[13]

Personal security therefore ranked high in the scale of sixteenth-century values. The threat of impressment hung over every able-bodied man: those who heard Richard Price's order in Cardiganshire knew that the whims of the mighty could well dispatch anyone to distant regions with little likelihood of return.

Only those so mean as to own nothing worth taking, so repulsive as to escape the ravisher's attention, so feeble as to be incapable of labor, could disregard the encompassing violence. Whoever valued even a mite of his own worried about its protection and sought freedom from concern about the hostile use of force. Yet few Europeans possessed weapons or knew to how to use them—not the peasants or craftsmen, and rarely the merchants. The gentry did command arms and skill and so too did the bandits, Whilliwhaes, gallowglasses, rufos, ruffians, bravos, and condottieri who spread terror along country roads or the lanes of the towns. But they were more likely to increase rather than abate the anxieties of others.[14]

Hence people sought the shelter of a group or gladly yielded obedience in exchange for protection, accepting rules as binding in the hope of being done unto as they did to others. For the same men and women habituated to the pervasiveness of violence also clung to the traditional Christian belief in the sacredness of life and hence of death. Those mortal bodies—flayed, pierced, mutilated—housed more than spurting blood and crumbling bones. Within the walls of flesh, however abused, immortal spirits also resided. No European could long forget that the object on rack and gibbet was a creature in God's image and that an element of holiness inhered in its destruction as in its creation.

Something sacred therefore adhered to the use of force. Punishment was not a covert event but a ceremonial occasion visible to all, not as observers, but as participants. A hanging was educational, a warning; it also acknowledged personal and social failure. This act involved a whole group and not just the executioner and the culprit. Power, employed on behalf of society, a whole greater than the sum of its parts, justified violence, endowed it with respect as well as fear. Force thus employed differed from that exercised by an individual—any individual—inherently tyrannical, subject to caprice, and likely to give rise to injustice.

The sword ceased to be a means of oppression, became an instrument of justice, when wielded not on behalf of a person but of some larger entity. Thus employed it created authority, legitimated power, maintained order, and encouraged self-restraint as against violence, litigation as against private vendettas. "Revenge," wrote Edward Coke, "belongeth to the magistrate." Whoever killed another in a duel was guilty of murder; for such "insolent persons" presumed to "frame a law and commonwealth to themselves, as if they had power to cast off the yoke of obedience to peace and justice." Force, explained a handbook for English justices, was utterly forbidden, "but being used in the maintenance of law, and with the warrant of law, it is allowed, for that maintaineth the peace of the realm." And indeed litigation increased as the resort to physical retaliation declined.[15]

Most men and women found themselves group members by virtue of birth or marriage, and never considered an alternative, for it was hardly thinkable that one alone would long survive in sixteenth- or seventeenth-century society. Any person's liberty hinged upon the shelter some association provided, for only within it could society maintain a balance. "As on the lute," the Earl of Strafford explained, "if anything be too high or too wound up, you have lost the harmony, so here the excess of prerogative is oppression, of a pretended liberty in the subject disorder and anarchy."[16]

From the circumstances of their old lives, the first European colonists in the New World understood the need to distinguish force used for brute personal ends from that used in the administration of justice, the one a product of passion, the other an expression of law; the one wielded by an individual out of impulse and on his own account, the other applied by authority according to defined procedures. Political power enabled neighbors to live quietly with one another so that all might serve God in holiness and righteousness. Without government, mankind could not be preserved. "The rich would oppress the poor and the poor seek the destruction of the rich; the mighty would destroy the weak and the great fish eat up the small. And so one seeking the destruction of others, all would at length be undone."[17]

By the end of the sixteenth century jurists and legal theorists in Europe had heaped up a great body of ideas about the meanings of the terms *law, authority,* and *procedures;* and intricate formal systems bound officials and courts into the apparatus of the evolving centralized state. That some matters lay beyond the reach of earthly authorities, that law was supreme even as against royal will, that government functioned in part by the consent of the governed, and that extreme cases justified tyrannicide were ideas with a long history. Indeed, blame for the excesses of wicked rulers, properly called tyrants, who made people their game and prey, rested on those who did not protest against the use of deceit, force, and cruelty. The good subject did no evil; but the better one prevented injustice and refused to make or consent to wicked laws. The magistrate, bridle reins in hand, had to be wary lest abuse of authority lose him subjects—not subjection, for they would yield obedience though nothing remained to them but prayers and tears, but the best part of them, their affections. Despite general assent to those ideals, the plea of necessity still permitted the crown to override restraints, as when the Privy Council directed gaolers to disobey writs of habeas corpus. When Sir John Smythe ventured to argue that no subject could be commanded to go out of the realm in Her Majesty's service, he found himself imprisoned for an indefinite period (1596), as did Robert Tallboys for questioning her authority to levy money. Some ideas, institutions, and problems of limits on power would cross the ocean to get implanted in the New World.[18]

However qualified, the rule of law in 1600 did not imply the existence of a single uniform code, even in realms as centralized as England and France. Vestiges of Christian and pagan, Teutonic, Celtic, and classical ways of thinking, expounded by the keepers of folk memory like the Irish Brehons, permeated judgments of right and wrong, of good and evil, of innocence and guilt. The sheriff, the coroner, the county, and the hundred courts sprang from communal traditions, with roots hundreds of years in the past. The honors and baronies, the courts leet and other franchises with medieval origins, coexisted with the justices of the peace and of the Assize, "the King's eyes and ears," according to James I. In London and in some outlying districts, local chieftains or bands ruled their liberties, or autonomous enclaves, without external interference, in a fashion somewhat analogous to that of the Italian city-states from which the term derived. Even within the scope of royal justice, where the common law provided recourse to a reasoned pattern of precedents, variation by region, place, and status often nullified the general rule, as the Star Chamber, the councils of the North and of Wales, the Chancery, the Court of Requests, and the Admiralty encroached upon the general jurisdiction. And quite separate systems governed marriage, divorce, inheritance, ecclesiastical and mercantile affairs, and the Cornish stannaries or tin mines.[19]

In day-to-day relations, justice presented a more intimate guise. But rarely did such folk as migrated deal with the awesome magistrates; the more usual encounter involved a clerk or a bailiff, frequently venal, who grasped at pence for his pain in serving and suppressing writs. Since fees for services paid the salaries of these officials—and indeed of judges as well—a hint of corruption tainted all their activities. Under these circumstances, *freedom from* required *power to*. Freedom from fear, from assault, or from spoliation depended not on an abstract, impersonal justice but rather on the power to protect person and property and to be able to act without hindrance or restraint. And since no individual—not even the greatest—wielded total power, none enjoyed total freedom. Apart from the completely powerless and therefore completely unfree—like the English and Scottish colliers, salters, and coalbearers bound to their work for life—all, according to their station, held some power and therefore some degree of freedom. The people of 1600 used the three words as synonyms—*freedom, liberty,* and *privilege*—because all depended on some measure of power.[20]

Most individuals could attain a share of power only by accepting the obligation of mutual defense. No doubt, each householder preferred to bar his door and shutter his windows at rumors of slaughter and murder in the neighborhood. The failure to resist and punish the same, a great scandal and defamation of the town, induced Edinburgh to order every merchant and craftsman to keep at hand one ax for each servant and to come at once to assist the provost and bailiffs, on pain of fine or imprisonment (1529–1531). Justice, like defense, was thus a communal responsibility. Inhabitants of the hundred where a robbery occurred were liable for damages unless they raised the hue and cry and captured the criminal within forty days; and though many wrongdoers were vagrants, they could not be tried where caught but only back in the place where the offense had occurred. Where there was no common power, there was no law, where no law, no justice, any more than in war, where force and fraud were the cardinal virtues and notions of right and wrong had no place.[21]

Justice, being personal rather than abstract, depended as a matter of course on the verdict of peers. The jury had developed out of ancient tribal and medieval practices of compurgation, by which kin or neighbors swore to the truth or falsity of statements in a trial. In 1600 it had become less often an instrument for protecting the accused than a means of communal action. Now expected to render judgment, the jurors could pass upon facts at issue not by virtue of their skill in assessing the evidence, but because they were likely to know about characters and events, as observers or through the rumors that passed current among neighbors. Opinions and prejudices counted as much as the exhortations of the royal justices. Corruption and intimidation might well distort the verdicts; and some jurors refused to see at all, or saw but through their fingers (1582). Still the best hope of arriving at a correct decision was to draw upon the knowledge of the group acquainted with the contending parties or possible lawbreakers.[22]

Furthermore, the community possessed, as the individual did not, means to apprehend criminals and sanctions to enforce judgment. Here the sheriff raised his posse, and the local militia or train band, though not a formidable fighting force, mobilized the available power of the district. By setting limits beyond which the transgression of norms invited retaliation, the community defined right and wrong; and it used force when habit and tradition did not suffice. People therefore had to belong and had to conform. Those who did not were suspect; slipping through the bounds of institutions and controls left them unrestrained, potential criminals, dangerous to others.

Weak reeds standing alone offered no resistance to any passing breeze. Bound together they acquired strength. Even when the disparity of actual power was greatest, unity provided some protection. The most brutal lord, secure among his retainers, became aware of surly looks, knew that mischief in the dark and arsonous flames might undermine his authority, and proceeded with caution.

Seventeenth-century settlers in America expected to belong to such groups as they had known in the homes they had left. They brought from the Old World a recollected sense of organization, within which every-one fitted into a precisely defined place. Not the individual in detachment but the community of which he or she was a part was the meaningful social unit. And life's hazards in the unfamiliar wilderness increased the dependence.

The way in which position in a community defined status and charac-ter took concrete forms in memory. Settlement brought together people of diverse origins, each with a distinctive pattern of organization. But in retrospect, a few general features stood out. Most colonists could recall the rustic village, a setting for homes, for worship, for labor, and for justice. The experience of others ran back to towns, denser clusters of people governed by charters that assigned rights and obligations to the denizens. The power of the great independent trading cities of Venice, Genoa, and the Hansa was in decline. But smaller places with no political aspirations throughout western Europe clung to communal ways, as in Dundee, which wakened at sunrise to the sound of the hautbois and went to bed at sundown to bagpipe and drums. In all municipalities, artisans and merchants formed guilds, as the clergy and nobility did estates. Every being belonged somewhere, had to belong somewhere, for the commu-nity integrated all aspects of human life—political, religious, and eco-nomic.[23]

Hermits and such lived alone, isolated in solitude, exposed to Satan's wiles and unprotected except by the poverty and ugliness that put them beneath the notice of thieves and marauders. But other men and women had to cling together lest they become the prey of strangers and of each other. Together they could do better what was more difficult to do apart.

Communities helped cope with every aspect of existence. The village or the town mobilized the force to hold off or negotiate terms with intruding outsiders, and also punished or set limits about the acts of deviants. Those who belonged together worshiped together and together marked the calendar's ritual events. Agreements determined the appropri-ate use of common fields, the appropriate time to sow and to reap, the appropriate prices of commodities and of labor, the appropriate standards of production. When loss of its court occasioned disorder "in breach of Christian charity and peace" at Shrewton in Wiltshire (1596), the parson drew up seventeen bylaws to which all subscribed at a town meeting.[24]

Family and community sustained one another, reinforcing each other's discipline. In the household the emotional ties of husbands and wives, of parents and children, deepened from awareness that together

they earned their daily bread, that together they held property for trans-
mission from generation to generation. Home, the setting for the cycle
of birth, marriage, and death, also provided training in the skills of later
life, instruction in duties toward others and an intimate circle for daily
religious communion.

No person could forget that status hinged upon identification with
the family, or that the whole network of relationships within it existed
in the context of the community that supported them and that they
supported. Each one belonged with others as a particular in a general
whole, without which work and worship, order and culture, would
collapse. Concern with reputation, fear of shame, and suits for slander
reflected the importance of these little worlds to their inhabitants. The
comprehensive, integrated community was the norm among sixteenth-
century Europeans, who carried it to the New World in the seventeenth
century. On both sides of the ocean it remained an attractive ideal on into
the eighteenth century.

When the sixteenth century drew to a close, Europeans had scarcely
learned to organize power on a larger scale than that of the local community. Scotland went for a whole year (1560–1561) without a government
and was hardly the worse for it. But the wider legal and political concepts
of kingdom and empire had already taken hold. Since feudal times, people
understood the hierarchical structure of legitimate power emanating from
a single source, the crown, and reaching down through successive levels
to the local magnate. The royal justice administered through the royal
courts preserved the kingdom's order. An interlocking chain connected
the throne through sheriffs and judges to the magistrates in town and
justices of the peace in the countryside, so that the sentence handed down
or order given was a mandate delivered by authority of the crown. "The
King's Majesty, by his Dignity Royal, is the principal Conservator of the
Peace within His Dominions," proclaimed a handbook. The administration of all justice and all jurisdictions was initially his; "and afterwards
by and from him only was the Authority derived and given to others."[25]
Law fashioned the links of the chain. The command given, the
judgment rendered, expressed not the random will of an individual but
an opinion fashioned by precedent or by legislation derived from the
crown, the source of all authority. And that understanding of law carried
over across the ocean to the colonies. Lord Baltimore instructed the
commissioners he appointed in Maryland (1666) to fulfill the functions

usually carried out by justices of the peace in England—including prosecution of "all manner of felonies, witchcrafts, enchantments, sorceries,
magic arts, trespasses, forestallings, ingrossings and extortions."[26]

In seventeenth-century practice the voice that stated the law and
uttered commands was invariably that of one of the local gentry. Though
but an agent of the king, whose commission he held, such a person
commanded respect and fear by virtue of family, wealth, or estate as well
as by position, and thus preserved social order and provided sanctions for
the wishes of the remote figure in Westminster or Paris. Therefore the
king was not entirely free in choosing to whom to delegate power. Low
persons, mean in purse and lacking retainers, would not elicit obedience,
no matter what sealed papers they held and, indeed, might evoke a habit
of defiance. Without private local territorial power, a justice of the peace,
warden, or sheriff had little authority. It was only prudent to nominate
men of status, great landowners or chiefs of clans, whose position reinforced that of the crown, while royal favor added luster to their
strength.[27]

In England and in most of Europe the gentry still asserted their will
where it mattered to them, but had developed an effective accommodation with the crown. Ordinarily, they arrayed their power not in opposition but in alliance with the royal government. They thus shaped an
articulated structure in which each community controlled its own affairs
though tied by legal and personal connections to the source of authority.
The tightened controls that accompanied the growth of the centralized
states hardly affected this consistent hierarchical pattern.[28]

In 1600 wealth brought some Europeans other forms of power. Trade
along the familiar routes to the Mediterranean and overseas through the
oceans enriched substantial families and furnished the basis for a thriving
patrician urban culture. Great merchants, dissatisfied with their lavish
baroque houses and impatient with the restrictive guilds and the traditional oligarchies, considered municipal posts a thankless burden and
sought political power outside the city. In some places bribery and the
liberal use of money to buy office offered a means of exercising influence.
But the more attractive approach to the gentry lay in the purchase of a
country estate or marriage into one; and that method had the additional
attraction of a pleasant rural life and escape from illness-ridden cities.[29]

In the final analysis, force, tending to fragmentation, remained in the
hands of the successors of the feudal nobility—either the holders of great

estates able to put in the field a fighting band of followers and servitors, or the mercenary contractors paid to protect commercial towns. Gentry by virtue of birth, wealth, or favor also controlled the local militia, raised the regiments, and formed the officer corps in the nascent armies of various princes. Such forces were, as yet, temporary and provisional. They served in wars conducted by one state against another, sometimes by one baron against another, when there need be no restraint upon pillage, looting, and destruction. They recognized no limits to the force used against outsiders or to protect municipalities from invasions. But they were not so useful within the realm when the prince sought the obedience —not the slaughter or impoverishment—of the populace, a point already made in Machiavelli's comments on mercenaries. These standing forces did not in themselves provide an effective instrument of internal control in the absence of viable techniques for using a large professional body of fighting men against the members of a society to regulate local behavior.[30]

Power thus disposed did not arrive at a state of equilibrium. Disputed boundaries and inheritances, failed court intrigues, or simple envy, pride, greed, and pugnacity created opportunities for conflict. Little spurts of violence, sputtering feuds and local battles, and the ruthless carnage of great wars lowered the life expectancy of the nobility and of the lesser gentry, and extinguished many an ancient line in the sixteenth century. In the end those who survived, tired of the endless bloodshed, longed for intervals to enjoy the Renaissance life of leisure, build great houses, lay out woods and gardens, and even compose lines of poetry. They gladly yielded up the responsibilities of power so long as that did not diminish their own privileges.

Europe's feudal past and its hierarchical habits of thought established the king as the ultimate repository of power. The authority of each officeholder derived from him; and each acted as though the monarch's grace were personally present. True, the king had been but the first among equals. True also, most of Europe's crowns in the seventeenth century rested upon heads but recently risen to the royal dignity. Tudor, Stuart, Orange, Bourbon, and Hohenzollern were the designations of upstart frontier families that earned their positions by ruthless brawling, judicious alliances, shrewd bestowal of favors, and the skilled choice of ministers. They developed more centralized states to establish their primacy over the local wielders of power. Judges, sheriffs, tax gatherers, and other administrative officers formed a communication and command network that extended from the royal court throughout the kingdom. The effective appointees, as earlier, could apply power in their own district and elicited obedience by virtue of their own status. Whether recruited from the aristocracy or ennobled for service, they owed their loyalty, like their place, to the king.

Centralizing tendencies varied in strength from kingdom to kingdom, but everywhere gained force from the religious role of the monarch. Even much earlier, with power dispersed and fragmented, the king was somewhat more than the first among peers. Religious attributes altogether distinct from the feudal role endowed him with a position of unique importance and respect, the Anointed One sacred in person and Defender of the Faith. Even the feeble monarch, a childish Edward or Louis, for instance, who controlled but little force, radiated majesty. In the name of the king! That formula proclaimed that every legitimate use of power derived from the sovereign. Positioned at the apex of a hierarchy, the supreme lawgiver validated every form of authority in the church as in the government. His or her right to use violence derived from God and gave legitimacy to the law. Bestowed on subordinates within the state, it made permissible the use of force and even the taking of life.

The relationship of king to subject was not only more remote, but of quite another kind, than that of landlord to tenant or of gentry to retainer or of nobleman to commoner. In *Calvin's Case* (1608), Sir Edward Coke explained that the tie of monarch to subject grew out of the natural order of the world. Divine in origin, like the relation between parent and child, it was personal, perpetual, unchanging, indissoluble, and involved reciprocal duties. Besides, kingship was useful apart from the qualities of a particular ruler, a thing men made for quietness' sake to avoid confusion; and whatever faults appeared were due to evil advisers.[31]

In the seventeenth century the faith endured, although rebellion cost a king not only his crown but his head. Britain and the Netherlands briefly tried to administer a government without a throne, and both failed. The American colonists acquiesced during the interregnum, promising to be true to the Commonwealth of England without king or House of Lords and ordering all writs issued "in the name of the keepers of the liberty of England by authority of parliament" (1652). The English Protectorate ended not in conflict with the royalists, but in a desire for restoration out of the felt need for a sacred sovereign to control the application of power.[32]

Although Europeans did not challenge the concept of monarchy, they did reflect upon its nature. Through decades of turmoil while dynasties rose and fell and fundamental religious issues remained undecided, subjects earlier taken for granted called forth heated discussion. Anointment, unchallenged as a concept while administered through the Catholic See of Peter in Rome, evoked bitter debate after the Protestant Reformation set some states spinning away and left dissenting minorities in others. In the absence of the certainty once provided by a verification that ran back through the centuries to biblical times, bold thinkers raised questions not about monarchy as such, but about the relationship of the royal prerogative to government. To James I (1609) the matter was simplicity itself: "The State of Monarchie is the supremest thing upon Earth: For Kings are not onely Gods Lieutenants upon earth, and sit upon Gods throne, but even by God himselfe they are called gods." On the other hand, George Buchanan, his former tutor in Scotland, wrote that princes, while divinely chosen, ruled by the will and for the good of the people—quite a different understanding. In the course of the resolution of that difference of opinion, James's son and heir would lose his head.[33]

Visible reality, as the sixteenth century closed, belied royal pretensions to divine election. That the king, bejeweled and draped in lavish stuffs, should waste scarce resources was perhaps expected of a being shielded from mundane concerns. But the corruption rippled outward from his person, as when his peregrinations with a vast retinue of retainers imposed upon reluctant hosts the obligations of hospitality that denuded the countryside. The sale of public office and bribery, while expected, uncovered the mortal flesh beneath the robes and qualified the respect and deference of inferiors for superiors. When James I shifted control of the state from one homosexual favorite to another, all Britons felt the consequences. Costly masques and unrestrained orgies flaunted the poisonous fruits of impurity at the apex of society. Nor was the church safe with the crown its head; not long before, the Stuarts in Scotland had chosen their mistresses from noble families and had invested their bastards as child-ecclesiastics.[34]

Honest, sober men and women in all walks of life who respected or feared the county sheriff, the local justices of the peace, the robed magistrates on the bench, and the imposing bishop who ordained the parish priest did not doubt that the king's majesty established order in society; for all who wielded power derived authority from the crown, either directly or by rank in a fixed hierarchy. The monarch was indispensable to rein in brute violence and forestall the horrid war of person against

person. And yet the evidence of reality revealed the danger of unrestrained power even in royal hands and made converts to Buchanan's
views.

Individuals therefore remained warily on guard lest the force mobilized to preserve order turn against them. Whatever happened among the
mighty, peasants, artisans, fishermen, and traders thought of themselves
in relation to the local community, membership in which offered protection against abuse of power so long as each kept to the rules. Anyone not
connected with a group could not be certain of protection in person or
property. Security lay in being with others, so that all could defend their
privileges. Together, the community of which each was a part could
assemble the power to shelter their liberties against abuse.

In 1600 visible deviations from the norm intruded upon many a
landscape. Individuals always moved about and some remained ever
unfixed. No community invariably bound its members to a fixed place
in space or in the social order. The frowns and favors of fortune pulled
some down and permitted others to rise in status. Although social lines
remained in place, an occasional exceptional one strayed over or across
them. Then too, marriage and opportunities for hire and service caused
some shuffling about; and now and again, wanderers passed through the
towns and villages. Beggars, pilgrims, peddlers, Gypsies and Jews, itinerant craftsmen and other strangers provided Europeans with glimpses of
outsiders going their own ways in their own groups, governed by codes
of their own. The numbers increased, so that the English had to extend
the statute against rogues and vagabonds to counterfeits, that is, to English
or Welsh people who called themselves Egyptians, "disguising themselves
by their apparel, speech, countenance or other behaviour." They were
felons all to be sent to the gaol.[35]

In the sixteenth century more important deviations appeared. A sense
of times out of joint nagged at people's consciousness. "The hed agreth
not to the fete, nor fete to the handys, no one parte agreth to the other"
—laymen against clergy, commons against nobility, subjects against rulers. Every man was for himself and no man for all—a Hell without order
one could well call it.[36]

In 1600 numerous people in fact lived outside integrated, comprehensive communities. Complex social, economic, and religious forces had
detached them from recognized social forms and values. Expansion,
religious dissent, and economic displacement had spread disorder

throughout Europe. The self-contained, static community, unchanging through the generations, its population constant and unaltered in character or number, still existed as an ideal. But reality ever more often departed from it.

Western Europeans had long aggressively expanded the boundaries of their settlements. The Crusades had expressed in one form the itchiness for distant horizons; feudal wars and the advance along the eastern and northern marches, another. Trading enterprises out of the towns and the efforts of some land-hungry villages to bring new lands under cultivation followed from the desire to push boundaries outward. Proselytization, the urge to bring overseas infidels or nearby savage strangers into the faith, also turned attention outward. Expansion, however, involved a contradiction between the effort to increase numbers by bringing in outsiders and the desire to maintain the self-contained community by excluding strangers with recognizable differences.

Religious dissent cut some individuals adrift. The sense of belonging that infused both faith and group membership faded when some worshiped in ways not those of the others; without communion, the community weakened. Schisms and heresy had often in the past troubled Western Europe; but the Protestant Reformation had graver consequences, for it challenged the authority of the Supreme Pontiff in Rome and arrayed anointed monarchs against one another. Lacking guidance, individuals relied on the dictates of their own conscience whether they wished to or not. In the villages discipline generally held; but in the towns novel forms of faith, diffused by print and preaching, loosened ties to existing groups.

Military force, inadequate to restore unity, only deepened the insecurity of life and property. Endemic wars, great and small, erupted spasmodically across the countryside according to a pattern unpredictable by common men and women. The clash of arms, though usually brief, required preparations and maneuvers that cruelly interfered with the lives of civilians compelled to provision the troops, find them lodgings, and look aside while trampled fields and pillaged storehouses wasted the labor of months. And in periods of peace, when the size of armies shrank, dismissed soldiers and even officers wandered about, themselves unsettled, unsettling others. The Elizabethan poor laws provided only a few with meager pensions, not enough to make them stable elements in society.[37]

In the sixteenth and seventeenth centuries dramatic economic displacements also unsettled many European communities. Geographic and demographic changes, and alterations in trade routes and in manufacturing and agricultural technology prevented substantial parts of the population from remaining where they were. The shift away from traditional forms enclosed in great landed estates common fields that whole villages had once used, while merchants took control of marketing the goods fabricated in the households of artisans and husbandmen. Cut adrift and left without bargaining power, such people accepted whatever terms a master offered—generally a year's service in return for maintenance and perhaps for a small sum of money or some clothing at the term's end. Entirely subject to the master's discipline, the servant at the close of that period had no alternative but to sign on again, if the master would have him. The Statute of Apprentices (1563) provided for the sale at public auction of anyone without a master.[38]

The sense of helplessness nudged the displaced into motion. People swarmed in the land, "as young bees in the hive," so there was "hardly roome for one man to live by another," lamented the English preacher, urging his flock to depart (1609). Many longed to escape from this life without hope. Displaced peasants and craftsmen and their children thronged the highways. But only in the crowded metropolis of London could placeless people escape oversight and the penalties of the Statute of Apprentices. The influx from the countryside rapidly pushed London's population upward despite disastrous fires, persistent disorders and plagues, and despite the laws that attempted to limit its size. Artisans who could no longer find customers, journeymen without masters, and husbandmen without land to till separated themselves from the community and drifted to the cities or aimlessly wandered the highways.[39]

Large and increasing numbers did not belong in the early seventeenth century, but unsettling social forces did not in themselves diminish the attractiveness of the community. Even the displaced whose situation had ceased to be normal clutched at the ideal as more stable folk did. This remained the most desirable form of social organization; and the policy of all Western states aimed to preserve such communities as were still intact and to restore those that were not.

In the marches, where power flickered but feebly, the difficulty of exercising control deeply influenced community life. Monarch after monarch wrestled with the problems of applying authority at a distance, of enlisting the loyalty of the cutthroats who could use force, of cajoling the support of rising families, of shaking off the dubious in decline. Regions remote from the center of authority, those on the border between one kingdom and another, or those isolated by difficult terrain, suffered from endemic disorder. There was no keeping track of pastoral folk who followed their flocks and herds from one district to another. Thievery, murder, and rape therefore plagued Ireland, Wales, the Scottish frontiers, and the neighboring English shires. In Durham (1488), "the rude and beastlie people with great violence set upon" the Earl of Northumberland and "furiouslie and cruellie murthered both him and diverse of his household servants." The people of Orkney and the Shetlands, quite ignorant of royal authority, obeyed "foreign and uncouth laws" of their own. Henry VIII (1552) thought that by garrisoning the borders and buying off the leaders he had tamed the wild Irish and brought that "nation from rude, beastly, ignorant, cruel and unruly infidels, to the state of civil, reasonable, patient, humble, and well-governed Christians." For two centuries, his successors would discover how wrong he was.[40]

In these regions, kinship was the basic communal bond, and clans alone offered protection to their members. The O'Neills and O'Donnells, the Scotts and the Armstrongs and other chieftains, when they were not fighting the king's men, busily fought one another. The "brutall custome of deadlie" feuds, long the elemental instrument of justice, all too often became the cloak for crimes and enormities, especially theft, slaughter, fire-raising, and the ravishing of women.[41]

These arrangements, spilling over as they did into nearby towns, offended the concepts of order that prevailed in Edinburgh and Westminster, and they threatened security by opening invasion routes to French and Spanish enemies. Yet there were no easy remedies. The good bishop of St. Davids, anxious to curb the sexual immorality stimulated by the mountain air, excommunicated two hundred persons in 1570—but to no avail, because the sheriff would not serve the writs. Such conditions called for extraordinary measures, government by a council that exercised judicial and also military power. And when the extension of royal authority checked the number of feuds, litigation took their place, for it was easy, for a trifling cause, to vex a neighbor with a malicious suit.[42]

Self-constituted communities of another sort roved the seas, lurked along the roads, and prowled the lanes of town. In the liberties of London, no one knew who ruled. There and elsewhere, bands of highwaymen, beggars, and pirates, led by their own officers and governed by their own laws, seized the power of defense and attack without authority. Other wanderers moved together in companies of pilgrims and players, traders and tinkers and Gypsies. Settled outsiders did the same. In London, Paris, Antwerp, Seville, Lyons, and Geneva, the Florentines, Lombards, Venetians, Lucchese, the Hansa merchants, and the Jews lived in their own quarters as nations or plantations subject to their own controls. Europeans had also learned to set up permanent self-governing trading stations in more distant places—in Russia, Turkey, and North Africa—and in time along the Gold and Ivory Coasts, at Goa, Cochin, and Calicut in India, at Macao in China and at Nagasaki in Japan, usually with the consent of local rulers, but using force if needed. All these associations held together by the will of their members and the tolerance of governments that treated them as groups. They offered but fragile assurance against internal dissent or external assault.[43]

The more fortunate associations for centuries had sought the shield of legitimacy through recognition by the crown. The grant of a privilege or liberty gave the recipient the power that the less favored lacked. A royal charter turned a borough, a college, or a guild into a body politic and corporate, with a life and identity of its own, able to act as a unit and to govern and tax its own members through its own elected officials. The device, available to whoever gained the king's favor, was adaptable to a variety of circumstances. It would prove particularly important in the North American settlements that ultimately became the United States.

In 1600 the English, French, Dutch, Swedes, and Spaniards stood poised for an assault on the frontier in the as yet unsettled part of North America. They expected to take with them such liberties as they possessed at home. None were totally free. But all enjoyed that degree of freedom proportional to their status in the community which they expected to transfer with them. To be free required power that came with membership in a group. Without power there was no freedom—whether for colliers or salters, for placeless servants, convicts, or prisoners of war, whether Europeans, Slavs, Africans, or Indians.

The Europeans who came voluntarily to America, among them the displaced people who formed a significant part of the armies that extended Europe's influence in the world, held the same idea of power as those who stayed at home, and sought to reconstruct communities similar to those they had left. However, migration altered communities and therefore also altered the relationship of individuals to them, so that the web of ways of using power changed. Those who participated in the process casually assumed that all the old arrangements would cross to the New World with them; quickly distance and the new environment required drastic innovations. The restructuring of communal life in response to new conditions reallocated power. Individuals taken out of their communities by migration vainly imagined that they could restore the forms of home, and people who had lived altogether outside the old order imagined they could come within it. And as the settlers recast their lives, they created new institutions and gave new forms to the use and the concept of power. Power, formerly an element in community cohesiveness, now with communal instability became an instrument for refashioning the world.

Peering forth, those about to leave could only dimly discern the distant destination. Whatever fevered dreams or lurid fears set them in motion provided no foreknowledge of what that far country held in store for them. But in departure, they knew, they abandoned the only security available in a world of chance and violence. Only slowly would they learn that they had forever lost the whole community of town and village; and that each alone would have to seek other ways to seize and hold the wraith of liberty.

I I

SPACE, 1600–1690

THE RESIDENTS OF PROVIDENCE, Rhode Island, were not alone in expressing the need for government in the wilderness. Few contemporaries matched them in aversion to restraints. But it was plain to them in 1641 that men who continued to resist order would rob one another not only by stealth, "but openly, in public, justly or unjustly, according to their wills." Aware that only wild creatures could love the liberty of the woods, Europeans tried in the New World to recreate familiar communities that could impose the restraints that differentiated men from beasts. Only small, exceptional groups succeeded. The corrosive effects of American space frustrated those intentions and redefined the social order.[1]

Europe in 1600 did not lack space. But it seemed to. The continent was far from overcrowded, but seemed so—how much, its residents did not fully realize until they encountered a totally different relation of people to place in the New World.

Imaginations formerly exercised in an older environment adjusted with difficulty to novel conditions. Everywhere at home, the visions of Europeans fell upon horizons closed in by known landmarks or by defined frontiers—not only at the remote marches across which total strangers held sway but also at the nearby boundaries of counties, baronies, estates, communes—all barred off, unavailable, already appropriated by others. Comfort in closeness offset the confining quality of narrow boundaries. Sight of the neighboring village was a reminder both of the limits of this one and of the proximity of the next. Still, where one ended, the other began, creating an impression of fullness—with the few intervening areas blocked off in forests, marshes, or wastes, all equally unavailable. While there was still plenty of uncultivated land, landlords easily found tenants and increased rents when new leases were available. They strove to conserve what they had and attempted to consolidate scattered holdings. The result in 1600 was a familiar patchwork landscape marking off manors, parishes, and communities.

Economic changes heightened the sense of crowding. In the long term, population did not grow dramatically in the sixteenth and seventeenth centuries. Periods of increases alternated with intervals of decline, so that the general tendency over time evened itself out. But individuals could not wait for the long run. In the decades when numbers mounted, younger sons found no portions to inherit and servants found no masters to take them on. A worldwide depression late in the sixteenth century coinciding with a rise in the cost of living added to the hardships of ordinary people which government enactments did little to mitigate. The trends toward conversion of arable land to pasture and toward enclosure of the common fields, and the shift of some handicrafts from town to country, steadily increased the number of placeless.[2]

The difficulty of reaching across distance added to the impression of lack of space. High transportation costs confined most goods to local markets. To dispose of surpluses, even a few miles away, peasants had to carry panniers slung across their shoulders or use carts or pack horses that moved laboriously over roads not much improved since Roman times— unless washed out by floods or encroached upon by neighbors. Communications, though bounded by the reach of the walking man or the galloping horse, still depended upon emissaries because the messenger validated the authenticity of the message; and most dealings required face-to-face encounters—in government, in business, and in the church. In England it took a royal agent eight days to cover one hundred miles; and justices of the assize moved cumbersomely about with their great retinues. Although the smallness of European space left much of the population of the kingdom or country within a few days' reach of one another, that only strengthened the sense of narrow confines.

Lands of closed horizons narrowed ambitions, so that thoughts ran within circumscribed bounds. Nothing in the world could "be without banks and bottom, but the Lord himself." The ruler, warned a poet, was not to covet imperium nor to seek domination of strange nations, but was to be content to defend his realm against invasion. Traders were to conduct their businesses in authorized locations; everyone who moved was suspect. Men of wisdom did agree that the "end why all men be create" was to maintain "the public state in the country where they shall be."[3]

Enters a new word—EXPLORE, find out, uncover what had been hidden. The languages receive it; people speak and write it in awareness that out there in space promises lie concealed; and in that consciousness the thought glimmers of alternatives to the narrow, known, closed world. In choice, hope lies.

Visionaries again and again reached out beyond the horizons, tempted sometimes by science, sometimes by faith, sometimes by dreams, to burst the bonds of reality. So the Portuguese pushed out from the Madeira Islands down the African coast, ever farther south until they rounded the Cape and moved on to the Far East. So too, Christopher Columbus (1451–1506) conceived the idea of a westward voyage to where he imagined a terrestrial paradise awaited him, its divinely appointed discoverer. With one hundred and twenty men in three tiny ships, he landed in the New World, discovering a continent until then unknown to Europeans, but gaining little for himself.

The heaven on earth that eluded Columbus was familiar from the folktales current in Western Europe. John Mandeville's *Travels* had described the land of Prester John, close to paradise, the hills of gold, the trees that bore meal, honey, and wine. Imaginings of a new world occupied many minds as they did Gonzalo's—a country without trade or magistrates, without riches or poverty, without servitude or contracts, where

> . . . all men idle, all;
> And women too; but innocent and pure.
>
> (Shakespeare, *The Tempest*, II, i)

Apocalyptic visions also tantalized earnest readers of the gospels. Ambiguous though they seemed to the unenlightened, the prophecies uttered a clear command to a chosen few. The Revelation of John, with its allusion to a New Jerusalem, to a heaven on earth, pointed directly to the land providentially kept vacant for God's missioners. John Winthrop (1558–1649), a lawyer of Suffolk, the Yorkshireman William Bradford (1590–1657), and Samuel Gorton (1592–1677) saw each his own instructions to plant an outpost in New England. A century later Count Nikolaus Ludwig von Zinzendorf (1700–1760), persecuted in his native Saxony, sought refuge for his Moravian followers in Pennsylvania.[4]

Some merchants also nursed dreams. On the surface these hardheaded calculating types carefully reckoned out the ounces and pence, their eyes sternly fixed on the balance between receipts and expenditures. But the view from the countinghouse reached out to ships battling the distant seas, and in that gaze imaginings were born. The crusaders, having discovered the inestimable sweetness of sugarcane, carried the taste back to Europe, where a market developed that Italian traders satisfied. Then the bold decision to take the risk—not to import the sugar, but to raise it—in Sicily, in Madeira, later in America. Certainly it was simpler to buy the finished product from the Levant in the familiar fashion. Yet the temptation, not simply for profit but for daring the novelty, drew merchants on to organize estates, recruit a labor force, and risk fortunes on suitable weather in strange places.[5]

For a century English traders had moved far from their coasts. Robert Thorne's father had sailed to North America in 1502, while his son, domiciled in Seville, traded with the Canaries and the West Indies. John Rut, busy fetching the king's wine from Bordeaux, took across the Atlantic seventy men, including artisans with tools, to explore the coast. In 1530 William Hawkins, having found the way to South America, brought home a Brazilian chief for the king. And every war or pretext of war encouraged privateers and pirates to seek the quick rewards of battle.

Such an adventurer, Thomas Smythe (1558–1625) of London, spread his affairs around the world—in the East Indies, in Russia, in Virginia, and in voyages to discover the fabled Northwest Passage, all reflecting new spatial possibilities. Uniting business and politics, he used his government connections to serve his commercial interests, and success in trade earned him the support of the court. He could therefore lay hands on capital for big deals—from other traders whom fortune left funds for investment, and also from little people persuaded by his prestige to risk their hoardings. Into the Virginia Company he drained the enormous sum of £200,000, in the hope of harvesting a profit in the limitless space of North America.

Men of another sort stood ready to execute the schemes visionaries conceived. "Big Guts," as the Indians named Johan B. Printz (1592–1663), made an impressive figure. A master of profanity, whose voice commanded authority even among those who did not understand his language, he carried his four hundred pounds with dignity. Son of a Swedish village pastor, destined to follow his father's calling, Johan studied in Germany, but in 1620 enlisted in a regiment of mercenaries on their way to Italy. Combat attracted him more than contemplation, and five years of fighting made him a professional soldier. In 1625 he entered the service of his own king, rising rapidly from one command to another during the Thirty Years' War until he lost the city of Chemnitz in 1640. To recoup his fortunes, he came in 1643 to the shores of the Delaware as governor of New Sweden, where, to his dismay, obstinate settlers demanded wider rights than those granted men in the ranks.[6]

John Smith (1579–1631) was another. Born in Lincolnshire and apprenticed to a merchant, he rejected the settled life of buying and selling and joined the "rascals," men with ambitions but no resources other than their swords. Taken prisoner while fighting the Turks in Hungary, held in Constantinople as a slave, Smith wandered about Europe and ultimately returned to England no better off than he had been before, though now he knew what he wanted—to acquire a gentleman's estate. Across the ocean a whole world awaited the daring. Smith joined the Virginia Company's first expedition and became a member of the council. More perceptive than Printz, he understood the importance of friendly relations with the Indians, of explorations of the interior, and of agriculture, and undoubtedly saved the colony from starvation in the winter of 1608–1609. His books later helped attract new settlers, but he never acquired his great estate. It mattered little; your true knight venturer, avid for honor, plunder, glory, power, romance, ever sold away competent certainties to purchase, along with danger, excellent uncertainties.[7]

The adventurers, like the visionaries, could not appraise the New World's spaces accurately because they depended on Old World standards of measurement. Even Smith failed to assimilate the implications of a boundless wilderness, wedded as he was to narrower concepts. In 1682 William Penn turned for advice to Sir William Petty, a founder of the Royal Society and the ablest statistician of his time, who predicted that Pennsylvania in fifteen hundred years would be as fully peopled as England then was, and advised as an ample allotment the grant of seven acres a soul.[8]

The unpredictable transatlantic crossing reinforced the sense of tightness of space and confirmed traditional units of measurement. The vessels that carried the Europeans west had grown slightly in the century after Columbus had assembled his armada of three craft—240 tons among them—but were still neither swift nor commodious. In 1620 one hundred pilgrims made their two-month voyage to Plymouth in the 180-ton *Mayflower,* neither the largest nor the smallest vessel to carry settlers; and always space set aside for crew, for supplies and cargo adequate for a journey of three months or even six, diminished the room for passengers. The tedium of the voyage and the dangers from pirates were "lions in the way" of those who made the crossing. Not all who embarked survived. Of those who sailed with Sir George Yeardley in 1619, thirty-seven died, including two children born aboard ship. The *Jonathan,* a year later, more fortunate in its speedy six-week crossing, still lost sixteen of its two hundred passengers; and in 1623 Lady Wyatt arrived in a vessel "so full of infections that after a while we saw little but throwing folkes ouer board." The want of cleanliness between decks caused putrefaction of blood and bred a disease much like the plague. The more fell sick, the more they annoyed and poisoned their fellows.[9]

Difficult communications continued to remind settlers of the empty space around them. Even in 1690, the sea remained the preferred mode of travel in the absence of a road network. By uncertain trails through the hazardous forest, it took days on end to get from New York to Philadelphia or Boston; and even Worcester and New Haven were a considerable distance away from each other. Travelers generally chose to go by some coastal vessel, although that often required long waits and risks attendant on the vagaries of weather.

The inescapable space unsettled the survivors. Whether they had started from some East Anglian or Finnish village, from a London lane, or from the African jungle, they had come a long way before they finally found the hut in the clearing that they would call home. And the course of the journey had more than once compelled them to adjust to strange settings, on the road to port, in the tiny tumbling ships and in the virgin forest. They would never regain the stability enjoyed by those who lived and died in the places of their birth. The colonists learned to be wary, to take nothing for granted, to depend on themselves. Their inner disturbance imparted a turbulent quality to existence.

The New World, by reversing the conditions of the old, normalized the situation of the visionaries. Between Florida and Maine in 1607 only scattered handfuls of indigenous people occupied the soil; and no towns or villages marked off a pattern Europeans recognized. Space welcomed the new arrivals, afforded them opportunities to make of the land what they wished, free from old restraints. And the condition was permanent, affecting not the first comers only but generation after generation able to reach beyond the line of settlement, wherever it was, to glimpse the ever renewed promise of space. Hendrik Williams and three others in 1677 each requested the right to take up three hundred acres of new land, at home a baronial estate. In seventeenth-century Lincolnshire only 11 percent of holdings extended over more than twenty acres, and more than 61 percent to fewer than five; and a mere 7 percent were freeholds. Nevertheless, the petition posed no problem. The New Castle, Delaware, court agreed because the supply was ample.[10]

At first, fear of the unknown inhibited any inclination to move away. The golden haze through which Europeans regarded the paradisiacal New World dissolved upon contact with actuality, which revealed no field for heroics, no figures from classical antiquity; only immense emptiness concealing the advantages of abundant land. John Rory later enjoyed the crystal rivers and odiferous woods, but at his first coming in 1619 "the solitary uncouthness of this place compared unfavorably with those partes of Christendom and Turkey" he knew. Others too recognized that the dangers of the unfamiliar called for prudence. The wilderness, a vast chaos, resembled a lawless world where greedy and furious men persecuted and devoured the harmless and innocent, as the wild beasts pursued and devoured the hinds and roes. The situation called for more than customary caution. Roger Williams had heard of many English lost in the trackless forests, as he himself often had been. The magnitude of the settlers' task was indeed frightening. "They had now," William Bradford remembered, "no friends to welcome them, nor inns to entertain and refresh their weatherbeaten bodies, no houses or much less towns to repair to." They had to improvise everything, for nothing familiar existed—not roads or bridges, not churches or homes, not law or custom.[11]

The presence of Indian tribes elicited further fear. From beyond the stockades, attacks erupted in the long series of wars that kept the colonies on edge. In 1647, in the concern for defense, Rhode Islanders ordered settled places to keep a vigilant eye on outlying trading houses and outlawed drunkenness and gaming in order "to propogate *archery,* which is both manlike and profitable." The colony also regulated the response to danger: three muskets "distinctly discharged and a herald appointed to go speedily through the town and cry Alarum, Alarum, and the drum to beat incessantly." The penalties of space sometimes included greater regimentation than Englishmen had experienced at home.[12]

Perhaps indeed "God's name be praised for ever and ever," at the massacre of 347 Virginians in 1624, which the survivors believed provided just cause to destroy the Indians by any means. Meanwhile, dealings with natives more at home in the American spaces called for prudence. The Indians, even when allied with the French, were a pitiful enemy, could they "be brought to fight fairlie, but the wood, swamps and bushes" made them vexatious. And initially at least, they proved better able to take advantage of the land than the Europeans.[13]

Attitudes were long ambiguous: fear and loathing mingled with attraction, with a desire for fair dealing and with a wish for credit in heaven for bringing the true faith to the heathen. Conversion was the object, John Rolfe wrote in explaining why he wished to marry Pocahontas (1614). Roger Williams in 1637 urged a kind reception for Pequots who voluntarily entered a community—have houses and goods and fields given them—lest they "go to the enemy or turn wild Irish themselves." A year later, Plymouth executed three Englishmen for murdering an Indian. Massachusetts in 1642 rejected Connecticut's plea for war against "the savages," arguing that it would be dishonorable to fight while "upon treaty." The Puritans also restored arms taken from the tribesmen, "for although we saw it was very dangerous to us, that they should have guns, &c. yet we saw not in justice how we could take them away, seeing they came lawfully by them, (by trade with the French and Dutch for the most part)." Settlers then paid for land acquired; and the Talbot County Court in 1664 ordered John Boone to make reparations for the corn taken from an Indian and for the beating he gave him. A few years later the New Amsterdam director general and council warned all inhabitants who owed anything to an Indian for wages or otherwise to pay, lest the aggrieved recover their remunerations by improper means. Virtually every colony enacted laws to regulate Indian relations, but the vastness of space made evasion easy and enforcement difficult.[14]

The fear was not only of the Indians, however; an enemy lurked within also, for the Devil was most dangerous when people lived in solitude. Since salvation was a communal enterprise, isolation put the soul in jeopardy. Unknown impulses might lead the unwary astray, as they did young Thomas Granger of Duxbury, who confessed to buggery with a mare, a cow, two goats, five sheep, two calves, and a turkey—all identified and slaughtered before his eyes in advance of his own execution. Distinctions between right and wrong blurred without the intrusion of nosy neighbors to clarify issues. Cases less self-evident were therefore no less puzzling. Unexplained deaths, for instance: rumor found John Winchester guilty of murdering his wife, although he adduced evidence that he was as kind to her as any man could be. Did a tree fall on Mr. Tilghman's servant and beat his brains out or was it a blow from a stick? The Maryland jury, examining the body of Samuel Yeoungman, suspected murder from the deep depression in his cranium; but it could well have been accident or simple negligence. Isolation hid the answers. The Duke of York's Laws (1676), noting that the private burial of servants and others gave occasion to much scandal by the uncertainty of discovering whether murder had been committed, forbade interment other than in an established graveyard and only after three neighbors had viewed the corpse.[15]

With the passage of time, fear of the wilderness subsided, revealing the attractions of the virgin land. The untouched stands of timber impressed Englishmen who had left a deforested country and now found plentiful material for building and for fuel. The Indians noted that the settlers in New England, having burned up the wood in one place, were fain to remove to a fresh location; and in Virginia the planters, having exhausted the soil in one plot, casually shifted to another. There and elsewhere, earlier marriages, a rising birthrate, and declining mortality also encouraged expansion.[16]

Instead of repelling them then, the wilderness tempted people to move apart. Inevitably, the opportunity to spread out, to go off, to start anew, sapped the capacity for discipline and weakened efforts to establish communities such as those known at home. For if individuals could set up for themselves at will, then each could be self-governing, heedless of the standards of others. Only a tight, familiar group would know, as Flushing, New York, did, that Carel van Brugge and Charles Bridges were one and the same person, whose name changed for political convenience. Stable settlements identified troublemakers like James Fewox and Peter Middleton in advance of possible mischief and they could see to it, as the law provided, that no person alter or remove known landmarks. In the absence of control picaresque characters drifted about. The Pilgrims suspected, but could not be sure, that Sir Christopher Gardner, who turned up with a "comely young woman whom he called his cousin," was actually an agent of their enemy. Much later the people of Princeton, New Jersey, could not guess that the eloquent revivalist was the notorious Tom Bell, equally adept at burglary, counterfeiting, and preaching (1741). Luke Barington, which may have been his name, kept school and may have been a Methodist preacher or perhaps a Jesuit priest; he may have had noble ancestry, or was perhaps an escaped servant, but languished in the Kingston jail in 1742.[17]

When settlers became familiar with the trackless forest, the dangerous beasts, and the strange human residents, they ventured ever farther away —out of reach, attending more to present profit than to safety and seeking only to please their humors and fancies. An early suggestion (1619) for a ban on the movement of anyone more than twenty miles from his dwelling got nowhere. The emptiness, ever renewed as each advance revealed the land available beyond, drew people on and expanded the remoteness from authority. In vain the Duke of York's Laws (1676) ordered officers to seize strangers or persons unknown until proven free men, hoping thereby to quiet complaints about servants who ran away from their masters. Nor were Virginians able to prevent the escape of fugitives by closing their borders. The sheltering distance offered all a refuge. Scattered dispersedly in households, far from neighbors and out of the eyes of the magistrates, too many settlers lived like libertines, responsible to no community. To exasperated local officials space was a burden; for liberty it was a boon.[18]

Space implied dispersal; yet efforts to supervise population movements rarely checked migration or protected the interests of those who stayed behind. Virginia and, later, Maryland were unable to restrain settlers who chose to move away. Only the New England colonies succeeded for a while, or at least so their envious neighbors believed. Unavailingly, the director general and council of New Amsterdam ordered everyone to "move closer together in villages, neighborhoods and hamlets" like those of Plymouth or Massachusetts, places spared the murders, killing of cattle, and burning of houses that afflicted people who lived apart. As late as 1766, the areas of America taken up and settled in the New England manner seemed the solid strength of the colonies.[19]

Elsewhere neither common origin nor attempts to preserve inherited traditions offset the centrifugal forces. Habit was not enough to hold a group together. To no avail, his instructions urged Governor Printz to keep the Swedish language free of foreign words, to call rivers, streams, herbs, and woods by Swedish names, and to preserve old manners and customs. Printz's inability to obey testified to the corrosive effects of space. The Germans led by Francis Daniel Pastorius or the inhabitants of the Welsh Tract in Pennsylvania preserved their ethnic identity but did not long enjoy the liberty to try cases before their own judges and juries, though they wished but to live together as a civil society in a gospel order and not to entangle themselves with laws in an unknown tongue.[20]

The religious motives that moved both the English separatists who came to Plymouth in 1620 and the Puritans who arrived in Massachusetts Bay a decade later proved somewhat more effective in withstanding the challenges of space. The initial migration to New England consisted of many whole families and congregations, including clergymen, lawyers, and merchants with comfortable estates, a balanced cross-section of the population of England. Accepting the need of discipline "to prevent a world of disorders, and many grievous sins and sinners," both the Pilgrims and the Puritans applied to their settlements strict codes enforced by power, as well as by the threat of eternal damnation. To knit together the whole population so that none would pursue his own ends, but all labor for the common good, they also tried to draw in the outlying people who lived under no government. To the same end, a measure of 1655 required every family to live within a half mile of the meetinghouse. Legislation aimed to limit the settlement of new areas in an ordered sequence, and for a time encouraged the supervised movement of whole groups rather than allowing individuals to scatter where they would. William Penn later (1681) hoped to do the same in Pennsylvania, without more success. When no other means served, the Puritans purged off the incorrigible. The difficulty of maintaining social order made them extremists. Living in an extended crisis, they believed that any relaxation of vigilance would incur the danger of total disaster. They tolerated no dissent out of fear that the poison of error not immediately counteracted would corrupt the whole society. Altogether apart from theological considerations therefore, the Pilgrims and Puritans banished Thomas Morton, Roger Williams, and Anne Hutchinson and persecuted the Quakers who appeared in the Bay Colony between 1656 and 1660. They burned heretical books and punished idleness, drunkenness, violations of the Sabbath, gambling, and swearing. Civil and religious sanctions aimed to hold together a self-contained community.[21]

Yet the New England settlement changed dramatically within a generation, yielding to forces that altered all American communities.

Where space was abundant, people drifted away, guided by their own inclinations. The banished, if they survived, set up their own utopias only to confront problems similar to those earlier persecutors had faced. Not everyone agreed on the definition of the common good, and tight-knit groups came apart in space. As a result new settlements sprouted with little supervision. In the early eighteenth century Colchester, Connecticut, and other new towns drew their inhabitants from many scattered parts of New England. Sooner or later also intruders appeared, wondering more successfully than Thomas Morton had why there could not be space for all, since there was "Elbow roome for more than were in all the Land" and no need to contend for space for their cattle.[22]

In time therefore New England went the way of the colonies to the south, although not as far, for the small town, ideally six miles across, survived. It could not however isolate itself from disruptive forces. Internal instability and the unfamiliar environment prevented the Puritans from preserving the integrated community without unexpected changes. Mournfully in 1644 William Bradford reviewed the effect on Plymouth, "left, like an ancient mother grown old and forsaken by her children." Thus, "she that had made many rich became herself poor."[23]

Those who planned the American colonies could not solve the political problem of mastering vast spaces, distant, largely unexplored, their potential untapped and lacking population. The early planters and investors knew well the hazards of voyages across the great seas; at first hand or in the accounts of explorers they also learned the perils of wilderness life. Participation in such enterprises might even threaten all they had by exposing them to liability for debts, as for a time seemed likely to happen to the underwriters of the Muscovy Company. Considering all the pitfalls, none would stake their lives or their property, defenseless on the ocean or in the forest, without arming themselves with power to deal with existence at a distance from home.[24]

Europeans in 1600 had considerable experience in providing security for remote areas where the force of law was weak.[25] The English marches along the frontiers with Wales and Scotland for generations had suffered from thievery and violence. To cope with culprits who easily slipped out of reach by crossing the borders into refuges unsafe for ordinary officials, and also to assume administrative and judicial jurisdiction in the exposed regions, councils led by a president or a warden mobilized extraordinary military power. Command over strategically placed castles and manpower levies upon the local clans and feudal lords supplied the force needed to hunt down criminals.[26]

The English could not apply the same methods to Ireland, a much more difficult land cut off by sea, broken up by impenetrable bogs, and sparsely populated by nomadic clans. The "ancient and lovable" customs of the Welsh and Scottish borders supplied no precedents for dealing with the Irish, or with the residents of the highlands and the outer islands of Scotland, also "utterly barbarians, without any sort or show of civility." Those difficulties, which marked settlement in America as well, called for different arrangements. To Walter Raleigh and other promoters of ventures on both sides of the Atlantic, the solution lay in planting cities that would engender civility and decency. Such plantations within a short time would reform and civilize the best inclined, rooting out or transporting the stubborn. The problem was to devise a means of doing so.[27]

Again and again old and inappropriate precedents molded ideas about colonization. Avarice for distant riches, ambition for dynastic glory, piety for the spread of the true gospel turned the thoughts of kings, councillors, courtiers, and merchants in the same direction: grant a royal favorite the privilege and the presumptive profit of ruling a vast though remote domain under the suzerainty of the crown. Then leave him the obligation to carry the enterprise forward.

In 1600 English memories were fresh of two ill-starred efforts to create great feudal estates in America. Sir Humphrey Gilbert (1537–1583) never lost the taste for battle, the pull toward danger, the stubborn belief in a Northwest Passage to the Orient's riches. Having made his mark fighting in Ireland and France, he received from Queen Elizabeth a patent to found colonies, but went down in a storm on the way back to seek reinforcements for a meager settlement in Newfoundland. His half-brother Sir Walter Raleigh (1554–1618), no more fortunate, lived longer only to lose his head on the block. A poet and a brawler, he too put in time in Ireland, did well raiding the Azores and South America, and pursued his own Eldorado in Guiana. But his settlement on Roanoke Island disappeared in the wilderness (1591) for reasons never known. Daring and courage were not sufficient for success.[28]

Another pattern of government for distant spaces joined economics and politics and enlisted the ambitions of the crown, the gentry, and the merchants. The king contributed authority, the merchants capital, the nobility influence, and the gentry administrative personnel. Valuable privileges from the government, adequate funds, and sufficient manpower established large-scale enterprises at once royal in derivation and voluntary in participation, bearing the approval of the king with members enrolled of their own wills.

To protect their ships at sea and their goods at the destination, merchants engaged in a common line of trade with a distant place associated in companies, much as they had in the old guilds. The term *company* thus reflected both a military and a commercial enterprise which could last for one voyage or for several.

Time revealed the advantages of continuity. A permanent organization could erect buildings overseas to store and protect the goods of its members, and make rules in the general interest. A royal charter transformed the associated individuals into a body politic and corporate, like the municipal corporations and universities. The charter also bestowed some powers of government—the rights of perpetual succession, of electing officers, of holding property, of using a common seal, and of making and enforcing bylaws—and often, in addition, a monopoly. From 1550 onward the number of such regulated companies in England grew rapidly for trade with Russia, the Baltic, Morocco, the eastern Mediterranean, Africa, and India. This was the model for the plantations planned in Ulster and for those of the Gentlemen Adventurers of Fife.[29]

After 1600 a significant Dutch innovation, quickly copied by others, established a joint stock, pooling the members' investments, which the corporation managed as a unit and out of which it paid profits. Members or freemen acquired shares by contributing either capital or services. They met regularly to do business as a general court, while between meetings elected directors or selectmen managed their affairs. In this form, English, Dutch, French, and Swedish corporations became involved in the settlement of North America.

In well-developed cities like Constantinople, European corporations housed the staff in a compound or factory, while the local society supplied all they needed. On the coast of Africa or in Ireland, however, where the company had to seek its own provisions and also defend itself against hostile nomadic clans, it built a plantation—a stockaded little town with houses, gardens, and storehouses.[30]

Success depended on power and military organization. The ever-present hazards of distance, of weather, of pirates, and of unfriendly governments, as well as danger from the people among whom the company did business, required a fighting man in command. The president or governor, prepared for barter or for battle, held supreme authority over company affairs and over his charges—soldiers to protect the settlement, clerks to conduct its trade, and artisans to keep its property in repair. Preferably a gentleman of good education and integrity, and possessed of a sufficient fortune so that he would not unduly rob the company, he had "a kinde of Regall power" broad enough to execute the laws and punish offenders. Enterprises of this sort founded the English plantations at Jamestown, at Plymouth, and on Massachusetts Bay, the Dutch on the Hudson, the Swedish on the Delaware, and the French in Canada.[31]

The promoters expected these commercial ventures to yield gold and other precious commodities, like similar enterprises in other parts of the world. But since the power to act by incorporation was a privilege, pleas for charters stressed the great advantages to the whole kingdom: conversion to the true faith of the indigenous residents; production of such valuable crops as sugar; and relief from dependence upon such expensive imports as tobacco. Hence too the appeals for charitable assistance in the hard first decades of settlement.[32]

Space would deny the promoters their profits and would reshape the broader goals of colonization. The chartered trading corporation functioned effectively in Asia, Africa, and in some parts of America. In the area that ultimately became the United States, only New Netherland did well enough to hold on for a while. The West India Company, strong, rich, and experienced, used New Amsterdam as a center for its Caribbean trading enterprises and provided markets for its tenants' produce. Elsewhere, disruptive forces appeared as soon as settlement took form, for, in respect of space, Jamestown and Boston differed drastically from Constantinople and Goa: too much for too few people.

Shortages led to starving times; in Massachusetts, "it was not accounted a strange thing in those days to drink water" in the absence of milk or beer. Not a few in Charlestown's first year found shelter only in empty casks. Many who arrived in the summer died of fevers, just as others who arrived in winter died of scurvy, especially "the poorer sort, whose howses and bedding kept them not sufficiently warm nor their dyet sufficiently in heart."[33] Disease, unfamiliar foods, and inclement weather weakened the survivors; and enemies, real or imagined, human and animal, threatened all. Prolonged crises called for drastic regulation. Virginians, for a time at least, had fewer political and civil rights than their English contemporaries. The brutality of commanders stirred bitter resentment. Some passengers out of the *Abigail* who "died in the streets at

Jamestowne" lay there until the hogs ate the corpses, the government caring of nought but "extortinge upon the people." The residents of that settlement considered themselves "so miserable that the happiest day that ever some of them hoped to see was when the Indians had killed a mare, they wishing while she was boiling that [Governor] Sir Thomas Smith was upon her back in the kettle."[34]

Individuals provoked by need demanded exceptions from the rules. In Virginia, once the crisis passed, people wanted to labor for themselves instead of for the company. Those who worked for "halves," their expectations disappointed, ran into debt or lost their crops while hunting. Some died of melancholy; others made for the distance. Once familiar with the wilderness, the aggrieved treated it as a resource to which they could escape from the narrow gothic stockades. As discipline slackened, unwillingness to respect power hastened the disruption of the community. The process was slower in New England than to the south; in Massachusetts, a generation passed before the authority of the Puritan magistrates weakened. But weaken it did, even there.[35]

Space and the character of the people were alike inimical to corporate communities. Everywhere the plantations were but at the edge of an immense emptiness. Here were no surface resources to be carried away without effort, nor yet an indigenous populace to be set toiling for the advantage of conquerors. The whole area from Georgia north to Maine, whether early in 1600 or in 1760, offered up no riches except those that labor would bring forth; and the indigenous population was not exploitable. In the absence of any sense of material values, the Indians, few in number and elusive in the wilderness, made neither effective yeomen nor satisfactory servants. Holding all things in common, they lacked the incentive to strive. God sometimes gave them fish or flesh, noted Roger Williams, yet they were content without; and whatever came in they readily shared with friends and strangers. The settlements could draw on no labor force except that induced or forced to come from overseas. Furthermore, the wilderness soon represented opportunity to malcontents; and in time any who sought to improve their own condition could do so.[36]

The promoters indulged in dreams of great feudal estates or of corporate plantations yielding riches equivalent to those the Portuguese had won in Brazil and the Spaniards in Mexico and Peru. Always in the thinking of Virginians, and even of Puritans, envy mingled with hatred of the cruel, unmoral Catholics. From the thriving bases in Bahia, Recife, Havana, Vera Cruz, Cartagena, and Lima, those merchants could despoil numerous natives, find gold, silver, and pearls, and raise sugar.[37]

Alas, by contrast, the only riches the soil of New England and Virginia produced were those hard work extracted from it, by people accustomed to labor with their hands. The need, John Rolfe wrote in 1619, was for carts and plows, and skillful men who knew how to use them. Whoever came for worldly ends that could live well enough at home would soon repent. In the first half century the high death rate, the low life expectancy, and the shortage of childbearing women heightened the sense of the sparsity of population in contrast to the abundance of land. In this vast emptiness, a shipload of homeless youngsters or of a hundred marriageable maidens transported in the hope that wives and families would pin the settlers down made little difference. It was not enough to suggest that every male child, "being the onely hope of a posterity," receive a share of land. The promoters had to attract outsiders —not shareholders in the stock of the Virginia Company, not the saints of Plymouth or the converted church members of the Massachusetts Bay, but others of another, humbler sort. Yet immigration declined after 1640. Except for the religiously motivated great Puritan migration of the 1630s, no stream of newcomers arrived.[38]

Company promoters learned only slowly that successful colonization in North America required a novel relation of people to place. When their immediate response—force—failed, they reverted to earlier feudal forms in the hope of stiffening discipline. To salvage its enterprise, the Virginia Company created particular plantations, granting individuals baronial privileges, in the expectation that they would people and police their holdings. Having succeeded in a similar scheme in Ireland, William Newce thus received the title of Knight Marshall (not General as he had requested), and other concessions, for undertaking to transport a thousand persons to the colony at his own expense. The patroonship in New Netherland was designed to serve the same end. The results, according to the *True State of Virginia* (1620), reduced the rigor of martial law and established a laudable form of just government.[39]

The *True State* exaggerated, to say the least. The clusters of private privilege proved more trouble than they were worth. Knight Marshall Newce died two days after his arrival in the New World, and the ragged, sickly laborers who came with him fared poorly. To attract settlers, the recipient of another grant, Captain John Martin, relaxed controls, peopling his territory with vagabonds, bankrupts, and other disorderly persons. The New Netherland patroonships worked out somewhat differently but no more successfully.[40]

In vain, the Virginia Company cajoled the settlers: the wealth and happiness of each rested upon the common good. "We have absolute power derived from his Majesty," but prefer just this once to appeal to the love of the colony rather than to command its obedience (1620). No response. The losses piled up and burdens accumulated—huge debts, clamorous investors demanding a share of nonexistent profits, high death rates, religious squabbles, mismanaged assets, and then too petitions from widows for compensation for past services of their spouses, a patent for making artificial wine, requests for land grants, disputes over fishing rights and over control of the tobacco trade and of lotteries, crimes, and illicit relations with Indians. The company in London was remote and the council in Virginia met rarely and with indifferent attendance. After a dissident faction in 1623 demanded that the crown take over, judicial proceedings a year later vacated the charter and converted Virginia into a royal province. The Virginia Company became one of the first casualties of the American environment.[41]

The dissolution of the Virginia Company by no means settled the issues of colonial government or of the economy in America. Though the chartered company provided a mechanism for the Puritan migration to Massachusetts, it did not attract either the investors or the settlers a successful plantation required. And no alternative appeared that could join power sanctioned by the crown to voluntary features that would draw in the needed population.

In forming new settlements in Maryland, Pennsylvania, New Jersey, and Carolina (for which John Locke composed the constitution), the English resurrected an older pattern adapted from European frontier experience, where order depended upon regalities, baronies, and private jurisdictions. The grants to the Duke of York of the former Dutch possessions and to the Georgia trustees followed somewhat the same form. None of the proprietary colonies worked out as expected, however—any more than the company had or than royal provinces would.

Europeans in America assumed that law depended on power derived hierarchically from the crown. Legitimate force could have none but a royal source, which made magistrates viceregents of God. The Virginia Company, knowing it was "not fitt that his Majesty's servants should be governed by any other lawes than by such as shall receive influence of life from his Majesty" (1620), compiled a collection of orders and constitutions, particularly necessary "in regard to the farr distance of the colony." But while the company tried to resolve the uncertainties in its jurisdiction that prevented it from punishing offenses committed overseas or even from controlling its government, others accused it of usurping royal power. Captain John Bargrave, its gadfly in its dying years, objected that encroachments upon the king's sovereignty produced a condition of extreme liberty worse than extreme tyranny. No one disagreed with Bargrave's basic premise, that all rulers required some token of authority, and that the only source of that authority was the crown; common wisdom regarded that hierarchical order as the panacea for all evils. When the Civil War for a time snapped the lines of legitimacy, a meeting in Rhode Island (1652) wanted whoever was then in power in England to invest and appoint a governor, which might induce refractory persons "to yield themselves over as unto a settled government." All authority came from England, they reasoned, regardless of who was in charge there. So strong was this sentiment that even the accidental omission of the king's name on a warrant raised scruples about obeying in the town of Oyster Bay, New York (1670). However, space and distance, in shaping the actual experience of those who peopled America, introduced profound ambiguities into these ancient assumptions about power.[42]

Once the settlers learned that neither gold nor other easy means of enrichment lay within reach, they confronted the need to produce some staple commodity highly valued in overseas trade. The precious articles were well-known: iron and timber from the Baltic, silk and glass from Italy and central Europe, furs from Russia, fish from the North Sea, and tobacco and sugar from the Spanish colonies. Trade with the Indians might yield beaver skins; but it would take more than that to justify the vast sums poured into the colonies; and unfortunately, the gentlemen soldiers and clerks of the plantation were useless in the field or the workshop. Promoters had to recruit skilled artisans, seamen for fishing, and husbandmen to raise tobacco and also the food to sustain the settlements. Among the craftsmen thus brought to Virginia were some foreigners—Swedes, Poles, Dutchmen, Frenchmen, and Italians. But such people did not readily migrate, despite efforts to counteract slanderous reports of bad news with promotional literature that described the abundant resources and the salubrious climate of the New World. Nor did repeated assurances that "any laborious honest man may in a shorte time become riche in this country" attract substantial groups. Servants were long not to be had except at high cost.[43]

Europe did not suffer from the same dearth of servants. In the countryside, no better fate awaited landless people who lacked even a claim to a humble cottage than service to the gentry and the substantial yeomen. In the towns, the unskilled without capital or connections sought masters among the merchants and artisans. Since the demand for rentable land outdistanced the supply, they competed for employment against people once householders on their own; and not all found places. Those who did not swelled the ranks of the vagabonds. Peasants and craftsmen, displaced by shifts of industry and agriculture away from traditional forms, thronged the highways, homeless, drifting through the villages, congregating uncounted among the superfluous multitudes of London, the population of which soared from 93,000 in 1563 to 500,000 in 1660, despite the devastating plague of 1603, the fire of 1625, and the law of 1580 reenacted twelve times that forbade it to grow. These were not beggars or rogues, but poor widows, fatherless children, and tenants driven to poverty by mischance. Among them were once-prosperous yeomen who had failed after having done their best. Desperate enough to hazard any risk, they responded to suggestions (1622) for emigration: Let us not straiten one another, "seeing there is a spacious land, the way to which is through the sea."[44]

Lack of the means to pay for the crossing was not long an obstacle. With land abundant and people scarce, enterprisers found ways to get labor to the soil. John Bargrave's abortive scheme of 1623 made grants and titles available in return for bringing men over. Virginia and then other colonies offered a headright of fifty acres to anyone who paid for a passage—his own, or that of anyone else, including persons who had agreed by indenture, in accordance with English practice, to serve for a term of years. For the price of a crossing, therefore, the planter acquired the additional acreage and also the labor of an indentured servant. Placeless people signed on, some skilled, some unskilled, if not for the New World's attractions then for fear of the statutes against common idle men and women that might force them into hopeless bondage at home. In Virginia, the headrights acquired a value of their own, and in time one man sold them to another as commonly as the land itself. The system steadily increased the number of hands in the colonies.[45]

In 1690 those who brought in Africans and Indians, boys, girls, and women were also eligible. The lucrative trade tempted evil-minded persons to spirit some youths and maidens away, while others, having received money and clothes, complained that they were carried off without their consent. Governor Printz warned against abuses; otherwise, "no others would desire to come here." Although the difference in legal status was long unclear, a distinction appeared between servants who arrived of their own will, in anticipation of future freedom, and those taken involuntarily, whose bondage was indefinite in duration.[46]

Servile elements formed an increasing percentage of the labor force, well over half of that of the southern colonies. Although some 2 percent of the population of the British Isles came to North America by the middle of the seventeenth century, the settlements were thus not simply a cross-section of that or of any European country.

A heterogeneous population injected into empty space created explosive conditions for the exercise of power and therefore for liberty. A political system dependent at home on the orderly exercise of authority flowing from recognized sources along visible lines through defined emissaries could not be recreated in a distant space, remote from the king, whose few scattered representatives lacked the familiar paraphernalia of power. Nor could that system long survive in an environment without the social classes through which power had passed downward and outward and through which individuals had defined their rights and privileges in relation to others above and below them.

Migration and dispersal having sapped their cohesion, communities could no longer compensate for the disorganization of customary power. The colonies lacked the elements to hold individuals together since those who sought to restore the European world of village and town were often placeless types before their departure. Such people, who had sometimes belonged to no communities at home, had only their own interests to pursue. The contract or indenture meant little to them, and many, having overcome fear of the forest, ran away, took refuge beyond the line of settlement or joined the Indians with little fear of recapture.

The feel of a sword, or even a club, in hand altered many an outlook on power, dissolving meekness, stoking audacity. Coming down the hill near Rensselaerswyck, Jacob Lambertsz accosted the director (1651). "You carry a sword?" he asked. "I do, too, if you are an officer, I am one also." Unpunished japery, irreverent behavior, bold threats against "the blood and lives of the Honorable members of this Court," revealed the unraveling of the web of respect that had once held government together (1697).[47]

Out there, near Dudley, Massachusetts, one Gardiner, who had left two wives in England and was cohabiting with a third, spied the men sent to take him and fled northward—to perish of hunger and cold, the governor hoped (1631). Up in Saco, Maine, the outrageous, lawless, and impervious John Bonigliton molested local fishermen despite a reward of £20 for anyone who would bring him to Boston, dead or alive (1658). Their vexatious counterparts in other colonies offered an ever-present challenge to orderly life.[48]

The presence of rootless people in empty space forced subtle adjustments on the conception of law and, in time also, of liberty. No one could long wield local power without easing unnecessary frictions and without lessening the lure of the wilderness; by small, often imperceptible steps, those who wished to govern moved gradually to closer definitions of privileges and obligations. Once the early travails of settlement ended, military regimentation gave way to measures protecting individuals against unscrupulous exploitation in the hope of establishing voluntary attachments to the community and its general welfare. Simple accommodations aimed to attract population, as when the Virginia Company, to prevent competition for labor, forbade any practice that might entice away tenants or servants; and to ensure fair treatment, required written contracts deposited with it and gave the masters' obligations to servants precedence over all other debts.[49]

The spacious wilderness complicated every attempt to transfer a legal system from Europe. It was all very well for William Pynchon, respected and feared, overlord of his district, to name commissioners to hear civil and criminal cases in Springfield, Massachusetts, "they being destitute of any magistrates" (1652); and certainly the colonists wanted order with the law written down, not dredged up from the fickle memories of judges and jurors. But the discouraging social context frustrated the clear intention—to surround a trial in Jamestown or Albany with the precision, pomp, and dignity of London or Amsterdam. Instructions to Virginia's governor (1609) asked him to beget reverence for the authority of his office by using appropriate forms and insignia and by a guard to command respect. He was also to impress upon the populace the gravity of the laws, "the fountaine thereof" being His Majesty's pleasure. Cecil Calvert wanted Maryland officials set off from the people by wearing habits, medals, or ribbons (1670). Even much later Georgia insisted that judges wear their robes and wigs—tattered, besmirched, and infested with vermin as they were—despite the heat and humidity (1737). Pretend as the officers would, however, the rude huts were not palaces, nor the planters courtiers. The Virginia instructions therefore also asked the governor, in making judgments, to act upon the natural right and equity of issues rather than upon the niceness and letter of the law. The expressed wish recognized the difficulties of the problems but offered no formula for solving them.[50]

Realism long continued to blunt the edge of abstract principle and foster accommodation. Plymouth reassured the inhabitants of the Kennebec River, required to take an oath of fealty, that it did not expect "strict obseruance of euery thing peculiare to" its laws, but would allow them liberty to do what "may best conduce to their welfare." Governor Printz received instructions to administer according to Swedish law, but also to fit the usages "of this most praiseworthy kingdom to the new conditions," with much left to his own discretion (1642). The Swedes had little choice —their warrior governor, weak in the knowledge of law and shaky in Latin (having more often held the musket and pistol in his hands than Tacitus and Cicero), lacked trustworthy subordinates to carry out their orders. The Dutch authorities knew that conditions in New Netherland were not like those in the fatherland or in kingdoms and republics with well-established laws and fundamentals. In their little settlement composed of folk of different nations, many things occurred for which there were no rules or examples and which therefore had to be left to the governor's discretion (1651). Toward the end of the century, under more stable conditions, Charles Carroll advised the Maryland council of the need for greater latitude than in England, "because some of our judges and some of our juries," used in the absence of more knowledgeable men, "do often times judge according to the affection or disaffection they have for the person plaintiff or defendant, and not according to the merit of the cause or the law."[51]

Uncertainty clouded every matter, petty or serious. The baker had skimped on the weight of bread in New Amsterdam; did one judge him by the custom in Holland? Did it amount to treason when William Harris asserted that conscience would not allow him "to yield subjection to any human order"? The Rhode Island court, uncertain about the relevant laws, submitted the case to London (1657). Abraham Man, dissatisfied with the ruling in a New York case of slander (1681), appealed to

England and then threatened to leave the colony altogether. Repeatedly cases without precedent required speedy decision, yet an inquiry addressed across the Atlantic might take six months or more for the return of an answer. Printz complained that years passed without a message from the miserly fatherland, which also refused him an entertainment budget. Hesitancy about the speedy use of power, improvisation, and unpredictable or eccentric outcomes enabled malcontents to cast aspersions upon the government, even upon "the most temperate and juste that ever was in this country, too milde indeed" for those whom unwonted liberty made insolent (1619). Moreover, ambiguously phrased laws and orders, susceptible to "acute distinctions [and] metaphysical Reasons," and the lack of assurance about where authority rested, inhibited any effective action.

Disorders erupted in the town meetings of even settled places, like Dorchester, Massachusetts (1645), when obstreperous settlers insisted on having their own way whatever the rules. All too often the governed wondered who was in charge, as when squabbling officers undermined the discipline of their troops or as when it took a long process of persuasion to induce the military commander not to oust the New Castle court from its meeting place because he needed a stable for his horses (1678). Two decades later (1700), the inhabitants of Piscataway, New Jersey, nailed shut the doors of the meetinghouse, assaulted the sheriff, and told the judge that the house was the town's and the justices had nothing to do with it.[52]

Europeans associated power with solemnity and deference. The Star Chamber in 1603 had warned all men not to complain in words against any magistrates, "for they are Gods." Not in the New World, where "the much honored Justices of the Peace, as you call yourselves," were told, "Pray consider we are men like yourselves, made of the same earth." In the new spaces, all was provisional and tempting to irreverence. Told that the evidence he proffered was not Law, Robert Holden boldly replied that "it was Law and he would make it Law." Thomas Hynson, an influential Puritan in Kent County, Maryland, entered the court to dry something he had written at the fire and commented, "Now wee are in his Majesty's dog house" (1661). And often, the language roughened. Cornelis Teunissen Bosch openly threatened "to wipe his ass" with an ordinance that interfered with his activity (1659). Seabank Hog (no lady, she) said that the governor of New Hampshire and the rest of the gentlemen were a crew of miserable curs. "As for John Tuften, she said, she could take down his breeches and whip his . . ." (1684). At the county meeting in Elizabethtown, New Jersey, Samuel Carter (no gent, he) "in an insolent and contemptious manner railed and disowned the authority and power of the court," calling the president rascal and "bidding him Kiss his arse" (1700).[53]

The low repute of authority crept forth from behind the obsequious language of addresses to the crown. In 1646 the Massachusetts deputies, all obsequiousness, readily admitted that, by wisdom and experience, the great council in London was "farr more able to proscribe rules of government, and to judge of cawses, than such poor rustickes as a wilderness can breed up." Then the poor rustics went on the explain that "considering the vast distance between England and these parts," judgments made in London "could neither be so well grounded, nor so seasonably applied" as those made on the spot. A generation later, their successors, fearful for their charter's future, prostrated themselves at King Charles's royal feet, begging his favor, "as the high place you sustain on earth doth number you here among the gods, so you will imitate the God in heaven in" maintaining the cause of the afflicted. But the address went on to reject the royal plan for reorganizing the government and to threaten to move out of his reach. That attitude also produced a willingness to circumvent or violate inconvenient regulations by smuggling and contraband trade. As a matter of course, those who could learned to avoid the payment of fines or taxes. The New Castle court in 1677 informed Governor Andros that it would be difficult to collect "unlesse your honor Resolves to send souldiers to assist the Sheriffe," the people having already made their mutinous disposition clear. Admonished that he intruded in territory of the Swedish crown, Lamberton, a New Haven merchant, threw the warning "into the air and paid no attention to such things." Sadly William Penn reproached the council of his holy experiment (1698) for condoning illicit commerce. "Also that you doe not only wink but imbrace pirats," so that "there is no place more overrun with wickedness, sins so very scandalous, openly committed in defiance of law and virtue."[54]

Governing officials proved singularly reluctant to use their ample power to punish crime. Judgments were far less severe than in Europe, although magistrates enjoyed plenary authority. Often indeed, a harsh verdict was set aside in an expression of leniency. Governor William Kieft of New Amsterdam blustered at the shooting death of an innocent bystander (1644). This was "mutiny and manslaughter . . . not to be tolerated or suffered in countries where justice is maintained." A court-martial sentenced the guilty to be shot as an example to others, but then pardoned them. The Virginians who took arms and ammunition to the Indians or who stole a woman prisoner or a calf (1617)—acts punishable by death—all had their sentences commuted. The court at Rensselaers-wyck first ordered punishment (though less severe than in the fatherland), then forgave culprits who abused the patroon's steeds, which they left cold and hungry before the doors of tavernkeepers and which out of pure mischief they raced past the director's door (1648). The New Amsterdam baker condemned to refrain from his trade for six weeks, for short weight (1661), had the penalty canceled. In the same town (1660), the defendant fined 1,200 guilders for saying the magistrates were only fools and simpletons had the judgment reduced to 190 guilders, which he refused to pay. William Ballantine, fined and sentenced to an hour in the pillory with his ear nailed to the post and then cut off for counterfeiting the seal of the packer (1661), escaped with an intact ear and a reduced fine upon the plea of his wife. Robberd Hutchinson of Delaware, found guilty of larceny (1679), deserved execution, but the court decided instead on thirty-nine lashes. Ellinore Moline, forgiven her contemptuous words against the government, finally received her long-overdue whipping after frequent repetitions of the offense. New Hampshire in 1640 set severe penalties for sedition and treason; but two years later punished Thomas Wright with only a fine of twenty shillings and loss of his privileges as a freeman. Even Captain Henry Spelman, who slandered the Virginia governor in front of the Indians (1619), thus putting "the whole colony in danger of their slippery designs"—a crime punishable by death—was only demoted; and "he, as one that had in him more of the Savage than the Christian," showed neither remorse nor gratitude to the assembly for its leniency.[55]

Colonial magistrates were not more humane than those of Europe. Far from it. Considerations of another order moved them. Perhaps they found mitigating circumstances in the unfamiliar wilderness setting. More likely, difficult conditions of life forced upon them a different way of calculating the worth of an individual—better bend the law a bit, over-look minor deficiencies in weight, than lose a baker and have no bread. When several slaves killed one of their number (1641)—a crime against God and their masters—the authorities, unwilling to decimate their labor force, allowed the gang to choose one for the gallows by lot; but when the rope broke, a pardon allowed them all to return to work. The crew that filched goods from a captured prize (1648) got off because there were very few men around and the vessel prepared for another voyage. The constant shortage of labor, the need to attract more newcomers into the empty spaces, the reluctance to spare anyone from a sparse group: these inner pressures weighed heavily on every settler. And then no one could be sure of anything at such a remote distance, away from king, bishop, all sources of authority; better to rely on local decisions than on communications that left answers months or years away.

Every effort to recreate European social or political restraints therefore failed, for without the hierarchical structure that in the Old World sustained communities, meshed all groups into one social fabric, and integrated them with the monarch, power became simply force exercised locally by whoever held it. Other ways would have to sustain communities to secure the freedom of their members.[56]

The passage of time brought some stability to the colonies. In 1690 no uncertainties about sovereignty remained. The elimination of the Dutch and the Swedes had made the whole coast British, and the Glorious Revolution had brought England such calm in government as it had not enjoyed for a century past. For better or worse, the subjects in America knew with whom they had to deal.

Space in plenty remained, but increased population gave the coastal areas a settled character. The seventeenth century would close with almost 300,000 people in the colonies. The grandchildren of the first settlers in many places approached a majority of the residents. Men and women who had never known Europe at first hand, who felt at home in the New World, grew up under familiar conditions that shaped the context of their personal and social relations. Yet the influence of space endured—and not only because the emptiness of the ever-present west continued to beckon restless people who compared the limited present with the boundless future. More important, the experience with open distances in the seventeenth century left a permanent impress upon American institutions.

Almost from the start, and on into the eighteenth and nineteenth centuries, power slipped into local hands. The charter of 1643 had given the inhabitants of the Providence Colony, which included Providence, Portsmouth, Newport, and Warwick, the authority to govern themselves according to English law, "so near as the nature and constitution of the place will admit." But in 1649 the town of Providence, inconveniently remote from the others, split apart, the better "to provide for the ease and liberty of the people." In Massachusetts, groups dissatisfied with one jurisdiction simply petitioned to belong to another. By the time Pennsylvania took form, the Provincial Council understood the importance of precise bounds of counties, so that people would know where they belonged in order to answer their duties and so that judicial proceedings would fall to the appropriate local court.[57]

Improvisation and informality followed upon fragmentation of the power to govern. The few law books at hand—mostly those of Sir Edward Coke and Michael Dalton—could not answer every question. In the absence of clear guidelines, experience and local needs supplied the rules. The Duke of York's Laws (1676) authorized particular towns to promulgate such peculiar constitutions as were necessary to their welfare in matters that concerned only themselves, and also to arbitrate small causes rather than use the courts. Juries gained confidence and expanded their authority, as Judge Nicholas Moore discovered (1685). When he excluded a person from jury service in New Castle a wrathful neighborhood charged him with "assuming to himselfe an unlimited and unlawful power"; and the uproar persuaded the council to bar him from any future place of responsibility. Nine years later, the assembly warned justices of the peace and judges not to act contrary to juries or to "the dissatisfaction of the countrie." Most places set the dates of meetings to accommodate the local needs of an agricultural population.[58]

Accommodation indeed was the key to successful government. A selective emigration had brought to America an unusual proportion of visionary, ambitious, or displaced people disposed to test the limits of the society they left; and in the New World space weakened corporate communities and scattered apart individuals and families in pursuit of their own interests. Such people sought not what later generations called liberty, but what *they* called liberty—that is, security and power. In the wilderness, they still valued order; and to maintain it they would construct new communities operating by rules to which they gave their own consent.

Later in the eighteenth century, the unusual cohesive Moravian experience threw light on the more usual experience of fragmentation. The

Moravians used space, as others did not, to form a community integrated in worship and in economy, and therefore retained enough internal strength to resist forces that pulled others apart.

Led by Count Nikolaus Ludwig von Zinzendorf, the Moravians began to arrive from Saxony in 1741 and established themselves at Bethlehem, Pennsylvania, and Salem, North Carolina. There they remained, carrying on their way of life, economy, and religion as they had in their homeland—that is, they adhered to the norm recognized by most colonists, who attempted to do the same but failed. The Moravians and a few other sects did not fail because a clear conception of purpose enabled them to transfer the instruments of power to their new homes and to use space, as others did not, to form an integrated community.[59]

Moravian cohesiveness was a product of qualities uncommon in the colonies. The self-selected members, having voluntarily joined the sect, formed a body of the totally committed, consistently unified by custom and faith. Their laws centralized control over the modes of production and strictly regulated family life, requiring, for instance, general group approval for all marriages. Distinctive religious beliefs and also distance separated them from outsiders; persecution gave them cohesiveness; and migration into a totally strange environment compelled them to accept rigorous discipline lest they perish. Pressure from the organized community and the threat of eternal damnation assured obedience.

Space in the New World shielded the Moravians and enabled them to stand apart and whole, and to escape the conflicts that might have developed had they settled in a district already inhabited. The members were free insofar as no external compulsion forced them to enter the group or to remain. But once in, each surrendered individual choice. A cooperative community required subordination of the person to the collectivity.

The contrast between the freedom to enter a group and that to make individual decisions intruded into every aspect of colonial experience. All settlements aimed at the same communal objectives. The Moravians attained their goal; others developed in quite another direction. Yet the Moravians paid a price for success, for in gaining stability, they lost the opportunities hidden in the New World's emptiness. By contrast, the failures reaped unexpected rewards, for the inability to reestablish Old World forms forced them to reach out for liberty in surprising fashions.

Emptiness, at first frightening, now revealed itself as opportunity; and liberty became a tool for its use. Ready-made designs brought over by planners and schemers did not match the unimaginable contours of continental space. But that space proved malleable in the hands of nimble, daring people willing to risk departures beyond the limits of what the past deemed possible.

III

CONSENT AND CONTENTION,

1600–1760

ALL THOSE PEOPLE adrift in space nevertheless found novel means of association. Wherever they came to rest, they longed for the security associated in their old homes with time-honored restraints now forever gone. Neither kinship, nor shared place of birth or residence, nor yet adherence to a common faith would supply the cement to hold them together, but rather voluntary decisions to unite their individual interests.[1]

Power dispersed and exercised locally and the inability to fix rules created conditions that required recurrent improvisation to adjust recollections of the law to unexpected circumstances. The ability of some to command depended on the willingness of others to obey, that is, on consent, accorded willingly or unwillingly. Definitions differed from place to place, but however varied the features, the forms of consent everywhere fell into a common framework.

Few colonists were even vaguely familiar with the idea given currency in the seventeenth century by Thomas Hobbes (1588–1679) and John Locke (1632–1704) that government derived its authority from the consent of the governed. The forty-four years that separated the dates of birth of the two thinkers helped explain why one described life as nasty, brutish, and short while the other used more kindly adjectives. But both located the ultimate source of the state's right to use force in the individual who assented to be ruled, in implicit contradiction to the hierarchical order deriving legitimacy by divine right from the monarch.

The American settlers, not themselves theorists, reached a similar position in the experience of establishing order in the wilderness. They knew at first hand the inadequacies of solitary life in a state of nature, and promptly sought the blessings of civil society. Those terms, abstractions to a European, to the colonists described reality. But lacking a precise general understanding of the issue, they floundered from one expedient to another as they met specific problems. Reacting to a situation that left power localized and informal, they unwittingly developed representative assemblies, not like the estates of the Old World, not even like the quite exceptional English parliament, but grounded on individual consent.[2]

Migration had brought to America disproportionate numbers of people uprooted by economic and social pressures. The flow increased between 1690 and the middle of the eighteenth century, with the newcomers more diverse than earlier: Africans imported as slaves to toil on the plantations and in the cities, convicts grabbing at another chance, English and Irish yeomen and artisans in search of opportunities, and substantial groups of Germans, Scots, and Scotch-Irish. As before, sprinklings of merchants, clerics, and officials appeared. In addition, a steady flow of redemptioners, indentured servants from the continent of Europe and from Britain, reflected the workings of an organized transatlantic system to recruit labor, waxing in the peaceful 1720s and 1730s, waning when warfare at sea cut the flow.

Abstract political considerations did not intrude on the consciousness of the colonists, old or new; they faced other, more urgent problems. In Europe, the concept of consent had borne only narrow practical meanings. Status by birth and the surrounding network of institutions determined choices, so that subtle linkages circumscribing the capacity to act limited personal options. Born and baptized into a parental church, destined by family for a calling or type of work, bound by place to political obligations, each individual occupied a position in the community dictated by uncontrollable circumstances.

In a few areas authentic transactions required personal consent, as in the affirmation of the partners during the rite of marriage. Margaret Kebell of Staffordshire, forcibly abducted by Roger Vernon, thus carried her case to the Council in Star Chamber, which annulled her marriage. On the same grounds Elsjen Jans successfully appealed to the New Netherland authorities (1642). The idea of contract implied agreement also in buying and selling, in accords to hire or to borrow, and in surviving vestiges of feudal and manorial relationships which affected the use of much land and the operations of government.[3]

Membership in associations based on a voluntary decision to join, rather than on cooption by birth, inheritance, or status, likewise depended on consent. University affiliation thus rested on an agreement, explicit or implicit, to fulfill certain obligations in return for the benefits of participation. Those were also the terms under which people joined bodies politic and corporate, created by royal charters and able to hold property, to sue and be sued, and to enforce rules. Guilds and boroughs were also corporations, as were the joint stock companies engaged in overseas trade. Members—merchants who became investors and planters who became settlers—subscribed in return for the gain expected from the ventures. The Virginia and Massachusetts corporations thus rested upon two contractual relationships, that with the crown and that with their members. The first balanced rights and privileges with responsibilities. The second involved the mutual obligations of company and participants. In the New World even more than in the Old, the charter provided a reference point by which to judge the governing body, as if its right to rule derived not only from the crown but also from the consent of those who accepted the conditions of association.

The concept of consent extended to the confraternities of established churches and other voluntary religious associations founded by communicants who accepted common discipline to work toward common ends.[4] The Puritans tailored the concept to the Calvinist pattern by emphasizing the centrality of faith to salvation; election by God, for reasons only dimly knowable, predestined the saints to heaven, the sinners to hell. Their church, as a sometimes persecuted sect, but also as an article of faith, rested on a voluntary covenant among the saints, twofold in nature— among the converted members, and between each and God—to live in ways that manifested their election.

Solemn ritual added significance to every affirmation of consent in the form of an oath that provided religious sanctions for the undertakings of the contract. Delinquents then faced not only civil penalties but also the burden of sin. Fallible mortals might later seek to wiggle out of assumed obligations, but did not enter upon them lightly. Such agreements before witnesses—whether to marry or to hire, whether to buy or to sell—implicated God and the community. The open confession of faith in front of the entire congregation testified to the Puritan's readiness to bear the double yoke of God's will and of the congregation's sanctions.[5]

In practice, the association of consent with status often converted a voluntary into a hereditary group, as when membership in confraternities, guilds, and municipal corporations passed from generation to generation within the same family. The act of joining remained voluntary, but in effect usually open only to those eligible by birth or position. Even membership in Puritan congregations eventually acquired hereditary features through the halfway covenant.

Displacement and migration softened the power of prescription and emphasized consent, for many who moved had no set place within the community and only imperfectly knew the forms they were attempting to establish. Having left rounds of customs, habits, and beliefs associated with familiar places and occupations, they had a whole world of new connections to form. Unexpected choices arose all along the way— during the journey by land, the voyage by sea, and the settlement in a strange environment. Even the involuntary servants, and much more so those who came of their own accord, had to make decisions; and in the process, consent acquired novel dimensions, still not formal or theoretical but actual.

The institutional developments of the early seventeenth century linked consent to the exercise of power. Virginia, Plymouth, and Massachusetts began with dissimilar governments; Maryland, Connecticut, Rhode Island, Pennsylvania, and Carolina—formed later—differed among themselves and from the earlier colonies. New Hampshire, New York, New Jersey, Delaware, and Georgia were each unique. To that extent there was no American political system. Yet government in all the provinces nevertheless acquired common features.

The drastic upheavals in the British constitutional order, following one upon another in the seventeenth century, exerted little effect on the internal organization of the colonies. Bitter religious quarrels and the long struggle of country and court in Parliament led in 1649 to the execution of Charles I and his replacement by a protector. An uneasy interval after Oliver Cromwell's death, the Stuart Restoration of 1660, and finally the Glorious Revolution of 1688 inaugurated a long period of stability in the royal line and in the British parliament. However significant colonizing ventures were in the evolution of the Country party or in the later schemes of court favorites, events in England provided but a distant backdrop for responses to the pressure of space on the local use of power across the Atlantic.[6]

The Virginia settlement began as a joint stock company under a corporate charter that provided for an annual meeting in London at which investors elected a board of directors or general court. A governor (at first called president) ruled on their behalf in America with the aid of an appointed council. After fewer than twenty years the arrangement proved ineffective and a royal administration replaced the company. Such the Old Dominion remained in the eyes of the law for a century and a half. But other more important changes effectively reshaped its political order.

Distance and dispersal early undermined the Virginia Company's capacity to govern. Settlement did not cluster as planned in one post, Jamestown, but instead dotted an extensive area. No one challenged the authority of the governor; but the lack of channels through which to exercise power at a distance blunted his influence. The company in London was too remote to help. Unsure of its own powers, it compared itself to a parliament and yet shrank from the suggestion that it tax the goods of the planters "without their consent first."[7]

On the particular plantations and in other remote places, power lay fragmented in the hands of individuals able to mobilize force in train bands or militia by virtue of wealth, amount of land, numbers of servants, support of an absentee proprietor, or respect in the neighborhood. "Hundred" and "town," inappropriate English terms, applied to units that the company feared would escape control, a matter significant in the future allocation of land grants. Besides, Virginia would have no recourse if unlicensed intruders simply established themselves in the vast domains to which it had title. Accepting reality in 1618, the company sought to organize space by instructing the governor to divide the colony into "four Cities or Borroughs," administrative entities modeled after their English counterparts. That designation reflected the continued desire to cluster people in "convenient Multitudes," that is, in compact, manageable settlements. Particular plantations, "placed stragglingly in divers places," weakened the colony; united in one body corporate, all would thrive together under the same law.[8]

The company's wishes did not halt dispersal, and to stimulate investment and immigration it had to concede that people would live where they wished. Less than a year later it allowed a group of adventurers "to erect and build an incorporated Towne with liberty to frame and make orders, ordinances, and constitutions." In 1620 it extended the privilege to all who brought over tenants or servants. It denied (1623) that it was a company of merchants for managing trade and insisted that its purpose was to settle people in uninhabited territory, without infringing anyone's liberty—none of which forestalled the loss of its charter. Nor did the transition to royal government after the company's dissolution strengthen the center; indeed, efforts to do so then slackened. In 1634, threatened by attack, Virginia set apart eight counties "to be governed as the shires in England," with lieutenants in each "to take care of the warr against Indians," and with sheriffs to be elected, also as in England. The number of counties increased thereafter, along with the growth of population. At their monthly courts, the commander and commissioners decided suits, resolved controversies, and transacted any business of concern to the district. Here power rested on into the eighteenth century, reflecting local reality, for those who met here could mobilize force, give effect to decisions, and consent to be governed. In other colonies, too, power dribbled away to little local pools of practical authority.[9]

Among the patents the Virginia Company issued in the eagerness to attract newcomers was one to a group of Puritan separatists, residents of Leiden in the Netherlands, who planned to come to America and inadvertently settled in New England. Blundering seamanship, inept management, and stubborn insistence upon personal judgment made consent a necessity; in addition, the concept of covenant bore weighty theological as well as political connotations for them as for other Calvinists. While they accepted the magistrate as viceregent of the king and of God, the Pilgrims also believed that only covenanted people, that is, church members, could choose the magistrate. Always a minority in Britain, Puritans became the dominant majority in New England and strongly influenced the structure of its government.

The company that settled Plymouth applied these views when the *Mayflower* approached land far north of the area in which its patent was valid. Lacking either a title to the soil or the authority to govern, the passengers nevertheless wished to ensure order in their society. Governor Bradford later recalled warnings in mutinous speeches that when the few strangers aboard ship "came ashore they would use their own liberty, for none had power to command them." To employ force to govern, the Pilgrims needed the consent of the eligible participants, and therefore entered upon a social contract to form a society and to live by agreed-on rules.[10]

In Plymouth, as in Virginia, the solvent of space loosened ties among settlers; even pious families, devoted to the community, moved apart and began to manage their own affairs. The governor and assistants could hardly resist with their own legitimacy in question. Instead they perforce authorized Duxbury and other places to govern themselves, referring to them, not altogether appropriately, as towns, the smallest units of English local government.

The neighboring, much larger Massachusetts Bay colony responded to local pressures in the same fashion. On the surface, little distinguished its charter from those of other joint stock corporations. The document envisioned a single settlement governed by the usual board or general court. But it omitted any reference to the place of meeting, usually London in other charters. When the great migration brought the Puritan founders to Boston, they carried with them the charter and ultimate authority over the plantation. No more than the rulers of the other colonies, however, could the Bay magistrates resist the tendency to dispersal and the formation of separate towns; and to maintain some semblance of order they too recognized reality.

Elsewhere in New England the issue never arose. Hartford, New Haven, Providence, and the clumps of population to the north sprang up without direction or control through the decisions of the settlers, who formed governments of their own accord and only later worried about legitimacy.

In all the colonies, Dutch as well as English, proprietary as well as royal, the underlying problem was the same. Whatever title, privileges, and instructions the governor brought with him, he had to take account of the wishes of the settlers, who held local power. There was no controlling their territory without involving them as active participants.

English administrators sought to make their authority effective through methods long customary on the Welsh and Scottish marches and in Ireland: by assembling local dignitaries to receive their consent to apply general rules throughout the areas they dominated. These ad hoc conclaves, summoned at irregular intervals, aimed to strengthen royal authority, as Sir John Davies explained with reference to Ireland. Twenty-five years had gone by without a meeting when he wrote in 1613; and in eighty-nine years under the Tudors the Irish parliament had assembled but seventeen times. Sir John hoped that more frequent sessions would develop loyalty to the crown.[11]

In 1619 the governor of Virginia of necessity turned to the same device, as his successors also would. The body they called together met not annually or at regular intervals but discontinuously. Nevertheless when the governor's commission in 1624 omitted any reference to further meetings, the assembly petitioned for a revival with all its former privileges.[12]

Had Virginians troubled to do so, they would have found it hard to define those privileges. The title sometimes used, "House of Burgesses," offered no clue, for the name reflected the old expectation that settlement would cluster in urban places. In any case, the Virginia body differed from the board that directed municipal or trading corporations in England. Fearing that the insolent populace "would shake off all government and there would be no living among them," it preferred to share authority with London (1619, 1621). It had no formal prescribed area of competence, although it did insist (1624) that the governor "shall not laye any taxes or impositions uppon the colony, theire landes or commodities otherwise than by the authoritie of the General Assembly, to be levied and imployed" as it directed. The assembly was not just a legislature although it did make laws, which however did not always have statutory effect but were sometimes reenacted or forgotten after a few years. The assembly also conducted trials, performed executive chores, and dealt with any business the governor brought before what was, to begin with, simply a gathering of influential men for consultations about the maintenance of order. Those summoned came not by virtue of any right to be there but rather because the local power they controlled gave value to their advice.[13]

Forty years passed between the 1620s and the 1660s before the Virginia Assembly established its nature. A selection process that varied from place to place and time to time long made its composition unpredictable. Occasionally, the governor's writ named a person who thereupon attended. At other times, the justices of the county court or the vestry of a parish chose a delegate. Often, the person who went the year before, or a few years earlier, simply went again. It made little difference. Attendance was more a burden than a privilege; and schemes such as those of John Bargrave (1623) for a more systematic mode of election found no support.[14]

In an effort to forestall its own demise, the Virginia Company in 1623 claimed credit for the successful reforms of 1619. The discontented and mutinous, it announced, now lived in peace and tranquillity. A "Democraticall forme" had provided "the most just and most profitable and the moste apt means" to increase the wealth of the plantation and of the king. The disingenuous and inaccurate plea did not prevent the dissolution of the company. But the assembly survived, and its counterparts appeared in other colonies.[15]

The spontaneous formation of governments by consent, a practice born of necessity, continued into the eighteenth century. Wherever legitimate lines of authority from the crown proved inadequate, the settlers subjected themselves to rule in ad hoc arrangements. The sequence revealed the salient relation to power. First came the county, town, or parish, where effective force resided; only then did the assembly knit the smaller units together. The true test of government's effectiveness came in the implementation of its orders and in the vital decisions affecting daily life; and those occurred at the local level.

Distinctive patterns of settlement shaped the links between central and local power in New England. At first a small group of leaders assumed that they would manage matters as they had in the course of migration. All the freemen in the colony could attend the general court if they wished and nod approval of the selection of magistrates who were assumed to serve for life, as had been the practice in other English corporations. John Cotton explained (1634) that no magistrate ought "to be turned into the condition of a private man without just cause," any more than the magistrates could "turn a private man out of his freehold &c." without public trial. Within five years the Massachusetts people had rejected that view and within a decade had turned the general court into a representative assembly. Meanwhile, the controlled movement of population and the prompt formation of churches and towns created political institutions that acted as channels of communication with the colonial government. The composition of the assemblies in New England therefore escaped the uncertainties of Virginia—the town meetings designated the representatives, not usually by a choice among competing candidates, but by recognizing a person of status and position, most often an influential landowner or wealthy merchant who commanded power and prestige in the neighborhood. Attendance here as elsewhere was a burden; and the one appointed was likely to continue in the position year after year, almost as a matter of course. Rhode Island and Connecticut elected governors in the same fashion.[16]

In Connecticut, Rhode Island, and New Hampshire, local governments took form in advance of legislation or of any legitimizing authority. From the onset of settlement, continuing on to successive frontier communities, they did so by undertakings, like the Mayflower Compact, to consent to be governed. The people of Dover, New Hampshire (1640), thus voluntarily agreed to combine into a body politic, the more comfortably to enjoy "the benefit of his Majesty's laws, together with all such laws as shall be concluded by a major part of the freemen of our Society, in case they be not repugnant to the laws of England." The inhabitants and the town officers of Exeter, New Hampshire, took oaths to submit to rule and be ruled "according to the will and word of God and such wholesome laws and ordinances as shall be derived therefrom by our honored Rulers and the lawful assistants, with the consent of the people."[17]

Massachusetts for a time sheltered the New Hampshire towns; and those of Connecticut and Rhode Island federated and ultimately secured recognition of their legitimacy. Throughout New England the assemblies, in time, without authorization, assumed the right to charter subdivisions. When there were enough "men of good ability" around, as in Hull (1647), Massachusetts authorized them to "carry on the affayres of a towne." The presence of nine families in Prescott (1653) was sufficient justification for similar action; and John Eliot's plea earned Indians the same liberty (1654). The Rhode Island General Assembly in 1649 granted the residents of Providence "a free and absolute charter of civil incorporation" to rule themselves "by such a form of civil government as by voluntary consent of all, or the greater part of them, shall be found most suitable to their estate and condition." The murky question of the validity of such charters long remained unanswered.[18]

Later, after the Restoration, crown officials decided that Massachusetts had no authority to organize governments in New Hampshire. But they did not act without sending commissioners to win over the towns. The people who favored continued affiliation with the Bay charged the emissaries with "secret seducing the Ignorant and ill affected"; and Massachusetts sent its own commissioners to hold the population's loyalty (1665). For the time being the old affiliation endured. And when New Hampshire in 1679 became a royal province governed by a president and council, the English authorities accepted the need for a general assembly, which, however, they vainly imagined would act only on laws proposed by the president.[19]

Maryland and New York arrived at the same legislative destination by somewhat different routes. In 1632 a charter gave Lord Baltimore a substantial tract detached from northern Virginia in the form of a palatinate or large feudal barony. He thus acquired not only land, but also complete and almost absolute powers of government, subject only to appeals to the crown. He planned a development in which great estates called "honours" or "baronies," dependent on the lord proprietor, would carry with them the right to rule their tenants. Each new baron was to settle manors with peasants who would toil for their sustenance and his advantage. A city at St. Mary's would house free artisans and traders, also obligated to Lord Baltimore, who expected to attract to America Catholics irked by religious restraints in England. A governor appointed by the proprietor would rule with the advice of the freemen when consulted. But there would not be many freemen to consult—only the barons and the burghers of St. Mary's.

The plan never worked. The Virginians protested as soon as they got wind of the proposal to take away part of their territory. Although the Privy Council rejected their remonstrance and left them an unwelcome neighbor, individuals from across the border continued to intrude upon Lord Baltimore's domain. William Claiborne, a shrewd and enterprising adventurer, thus conducted a profitable trading operation with the financial support of some London merchants and with a Virginia license to settle Kent Island (1629) within Maryland's patent. The effort to oust Claiborne led to decades of controversy, and other boundary disputes also irritated relations among the colonies, as did differences in domestic legislation.

In America feudal privileges and obligations commanded little respect. When the court leet met (1670), it found that the lord of the manor had not even provided the elementary instruments of justice—stocks, pillory, and ducking stool. The rights bestowed by the crown remained idle words on paper in the absence of force on the spot to compel obedience; and the proprietor could find that force only among loyal, subservient settlers. Yet newcomers would not be peasants on baronies when they could as readily be freeholders in Virginia. Before long, Maryland adopted a land system similar to that of Virginia. The governor granted smaller manors of a thousand to three thousand acres without feudal trappings, and in time made headrights available to settlers. Counties took form as in Virginia, with courts to manage local affairs and do justice. In 1635 the proprietor, "out of grace," also summoned an assembly for advice and approbation.[20]

To attract yeomen Lord Baltimore diluted the Catholic character of the province. Besides, the necessity of defending his claims made him sensitive to Protestant opinion in England; and he also feared that the Jesuits already in Maryland might become a power in their own right. In 1641 he therefore extended the statute of mortmain to Maryland, to prevent the accumulation of great tracts by religious orders. Relationships with the settlers remained a problem, however, for they often disregarded the proprietor's wishes. And in England, the Long Parliament was about to begin the sessions that would end in civil war.

Baltimore was therefore in no position to resist demands for concessions. The freemen, more numerous than originally contemplated, met more often and claimed greater authority. In 1648 the proprietor appointed a Protestant governor; a year later a Toleration Act assured freedom of religion to all Christians; and in 1650 the assembly became an elected body of representatives, meeting regularly and separately from the council and with the power to initiate as well as approve bills.

Although grievances against the proprietor provoked other conflicts in the 1650s, the province by then had a stable, far from feudal political order. The assembly spoke for the landholders, the council for the owners of great estates, and the governor for the proprietor. Except for one difference—that, in Virginia, the governor was the agent of the crown —the two Chesapeake colonies had developed identical forms of government. The fact that one had started as a trading company and the other as the domain of a feudal lord was less important than the common conditions both encountered in America.

New Netherland moved in the same direction, despite its urban and Dutch character. The governors, William Kieft and Peter Stuyvesant, military types accustomed to having orders obeyed, learned New World procedures the hard way. In 1641 Kieft asked the burghers to select a council of twelve men to assist him in controlling the Indians. They, however, opposed military action and also requested a share in the government, even in administering justice and levying taxes. Dissolving the presumptuous body, the headstrong governor embarked upon a vicious and costly little war against the Indians, and in 1644 the need for revenue compelled him again to consult the populace, this time through a council of eight. Stuyvesant did no better. Toward the end of the 1650s, when peace with Spain drained Dutch interest in New Netherland, the West India Company granted New Amsterdam a municipal government (1658). After it fell to the English, the colony adopted the same political institutions as other colonies and so, in time, did later settlements in Pennsylvania, Carolina, and Georgia. New York City received a new municipal charter in 1730, and other cities, like Williamsburg and Norfolk, Virginia, and Baltimore, Maryland, became bodies politic and corporate or boroughs as a matter of course.[21]

As population increased, as settlement spread away from the first posts, and as assemblies acquired regular form, the people in outlying areas sought to share power through representation. Participation in the affairs of the central government ceased to be a burden shirked and became a right sought. With stability came interconnectedness, greater mutual dependency, and broader benefits from control of the central government. That authority, once almost as remote as England and equally irrelevant to local needs, acquired a new status and also became a source of possible profits. While local power continued to decide most matters affecting the colonists' lives, the growing importance of the wider jurisdiction created new balances between the centers and the peripheries.

The New England town, itself a corporate entity, demanded and secured representation, as the only force able to apply coercion and implement the assembly's rules. In Rhode Island, town meetings reviewed General Assembly laws and disapproval by a majority of the freemen annulled any measure. No other colony went that far. But everywhere local objections could impede or nullify orders from the center.[22] Representation, valued in the abstract, sometimes lay unused when inconvenient —a sheathed weapon. The bother of a long journey and of a stay away from home moderated enthusiasm for participation; and the expectation that delegates bring with them lists of the ratable estates in their towns for assessment and taxation often extinguished interest in the privilege. In 1734–1735, 52 out of 149 places entitled to send representatives in Massachusetts failed to do so, yet only 5 were fined.[23]

The town's virtual autonomy troubled the assemblies. Some members chosen proved profane and immoral. The Massachusetts magistrates in 1634 vetoed the election of the inferior sort; and the House of Representatives in 1656 rejected Richard Nason, the unsuitable deputy from Kittery, and ordered the courts to punish those who had voted for him.

So too in 1715 the House judged John Randall unworthy and reprimanded Rochester for "sending a person of such an ignominious character to represent them." Ultimately, however, the assembly, like the governor and the crown, needed local power to govern by consent. Though jealous of the right to pass on the qualifications of members, it acquiesced in popular choices more often than not.[24]

In New York and the colonies to the south the issue of representation sparked continued contests between the older eastern and the newly settled western regions. Without such a clear unit as the town, endless quarrels erupted over numbers and boundaries as population spread. In North Carolina, for instance, the older counties each sent five men to the assembly, the newer ones only two. In due course, when the latter achieved a majority, a law equalized the representation of all; the older counties then refused to send anyone and instead dispatched an agent to England to regain their former rights. As a result, while county courts sat as usual, the assembly between 1746 and 1751 represented only the newer counties.

Outside New England, the governors sought to limit the assembly's power through the council, a small body they appointed on behalf of the crown or proprietor to give advice in executive matters. In Virginia its members, designated commissioners, were to model themselves on the English justices of the peace, in the hope that they would form a pliable link to local power. In other provinces also the same intention prevailed when the assembly took form in the last quarter of the seventeenth century, for the governors long regarded that body as a provisional arrangement thrust upon them by the necessities of settlement. Since the council was not representative and its members came from the uppermost social groups, it stood for the hierarchical view of the governing authority and became the counterforce to the assembly. Through it the influence of the crown and its colonial allies offset the influence of consent.[25]

In Massachusetts, where down to 1684 the council in effect chose the governor, collaboration was even closer than elsewhere; and so it remained after that date when the colony became a royal province. In Rhode Island and Connecticut also, the elected governor usually worked closely with the council.

The need for careful maneuver among forces in uncertain balance complicated the tasks of government already out of equilibrium by reason of distance from the source of power. Solicitude for the interests and opinions of the social groups entrenched in assemblies, councils, or localities affected the resolution of every issue, as did the need to satisfy remote imperial officers.

Governor, council, and assembly locked horns over finances, patronage, privilege, and the right to create new subdivisions—counties, towns, precincts—the units of local power demanded by the expansive spread of population away from the original centers of settlement. During the English interregnum (1649–1660), with no king in authority, the assemblies expanded their power; that in Virginia thus declared itself the representative of the people, endowed with "the supreme power of the government of this country." As a result the governors later had to struggle for position. Of course, unbounded expressions of loyalty to the crown united all ranks and parties, whatever unhappy differences existed among them. Never any prince reigned more absolutely in the hearts of the subjects. Nor would anyone suggest that a governor designed to introduce any arbitrary power or to invade the liberties of the people (1705). The effusive declarations did not blunt the edge of conflict. To the assertion of royal prerogative by the North Carolina governor in 1733, the assembly responded by reaffirming the birthright of British subjects to be governed by laws of their own making, a right confirmed by charters. "These constitutions" were "evidence of the compact and agreement" between the proprietors and the people of North Carolina, confirming their natural right. It was not credible that a "most gracious sovereign" wished to deprive the poor people of North Carolina of privileges allowed to and enjoyed by the neighbouring colonies.[26]

The arguments ever more insistently referred to charters as constitutions based on compact and drew analogies between the assembly and the House of Commons. At first the comparisons were procedural, as when Massachusetts adopted the custom of enacting no bill that had not been thrice read and debated (1657). But in time (1695) a Pennsylvanian argued that his poor province should "proceed in some sense in a parliamentarie way" by withholding approval of any money bill until the end of the session to be sure of respect for the people's privileges.[27]

Year after year, the participants in politics fought it out. The governors, infuriated by dependence on grudgingly voted grants, demanded fixed and stated salaries; the assemblies, aware of the power of the purse, explained, as Massachusetts did in 1717, "that considering our Constitution," it would "not be for his Majesty's Service, nor for the good advantage of his subjects" to agree, although expressing willingness to provide annual sums "according to our Ability." Twelve years later, in the same running battle, the House added "Magna Charter" to the sources validating its position. Little irritants added to the bitterness—over whether the attorney general was to be appointed or elected, over rumors spread by ill-minded persons of the sale of office by the governor, over the adjournment by the assembly for three days, an act the governor told the members revealed they were "weary of the Liberties of your country."[28]

The same issues surfaced in Virginia, in addition to disputes over auditing finances, over presentation to benefices in the established church, and over judicial appointments. The colony divided: "county's friends" and "governor's friends"; and Governor Spotswood charged that "a Cataline Crew of Male contents" conspired to secure his removal. The assembly had evoked that response by accusing him of lavishing vast public sums on his house, of insisting upon the right to patronage, and of unsettling land titles by stringent collection of quitrents. Most offensive, it sent an agent to London to represent its views, a practice other colonies would also follow, thus bypassing the governor as a channel of communication.[29]

However acrimonious their debates, the governor and assembly had room in which to maneuver, for they were only two of the elements involved in political confrontations. Royal officials and proprietors, remote in London, still required reassurance and conciliation—their wishes could not be disregarded indefinitely. Moreover the governor and the assembly sometimes discovered common interests, especially in dealing with outsiders. The threat that New York might swallow up their colony in 1693 united the governor and assembly of New Jersey against a common enemy. Six years later, Newark and other towns complained about the cowardice and sloth of Governor Jeremiah Basse and his subversion of the assembly. The Virginia council and assembly in 1714 joined forces in the effort to avoid new taxes by dipping into royal reserves to replenish provincial resources. The council and governor generally worked together, but not always. In 1692 the Carolina proprietors took from the council sole power to propose laws to prevent "obstructions to the dispatch of publique Affairs in the way of parliaments or asemblyes." Disputing the assembly's claim that it was like the House of Commons and therefore enjoyed exclusive control over money bills, the Virginia council plaintively pointed out in 1711 that it lacked the privileges of the House of Lords.[30]

Much depended on the character of the governor. Armed with powers of patronage and with some privileges to bestow, although far less than a minister in Britain, he was pivotal in these transactions, especially when he also commanded persuasive rhetoric. Governor Spotswood declared himself as great a patriot as anyone in the country when he pointed out Virginia's perilous state in 1711—"the treasury entirely exhausted, the publick credit utterly ruined," and an Indian treaty to be complied with. By withholding support, he added, the assembly exposed itself to the censure of all mankind and the rage of heaven—an argument he used again in 1715.[31]

As colonial government acquired more stable forms, political rivalries exposed the need to define limits of participation. Power, exercised locally and unified only through the assembly, posed the question of who would wield it. The assembly itself was but an imperfect body, ill defined in character and procedures and unclear about whom it represented. In the early days, any group could enter upon a covenant—consent to be governed—and thereby form a body politic. But representation in the assembly changed the meaning of consent. Each new place accorded a seat affected the balance among those already there, as the old North Carolina counties learned. And when numbers increased so too did the importance of deciding who had the right to participate in the emerging polity.

Not everyone, of course! Not everyone wanted to share the responsibilities of power, of holding office, or even of voting. George Sheppard of Providence owned land enough to give away for public purposes, but claimed he was unfit for decision making, unable to deal with weighty affairs. Much better, he believed, simply to submit to the wholesome orders others made (1660s). In addition to those who opted out, whole categories of persons could not claim to participate. Every sort of dependent, the member of someone's household, was unfree, incapable of entering fully upon a civil or political contract—among them servants, slaves, children, wives, and the feeble-minded.[32]

Among the rest of the populations, other distinctions controlled the degree of participation. The origin of some colonies in corporate companies transferred to the New World exclusive criteria of membership. Freedom in a corporate body was a privilege extended to the qualified; and as a matter of course the distinction between inhabitants and freemen was transferred to Virginia and Massachusetts. A reform plan for Virginia (1623) recommended a sharp line between those "free of our soyle and trade onely" and those "that are citizens and free of our government." None of these little self-defined societies conceded to every individual the right to consent, to become members, and to share community power.[33]

In a small colony, Plymouth, the old comers continued to set themselves apart from others. But the distinction between inhabitants and freemen faded, not simply with the dissolution of the companies, nor yet in response to any challenge to theory or objection in principle, but rather from practical difficulties in confronting the realities of local power in remote places. The Massachusetts General Court in Boston (1642) thus gave all the inhabitants of Piscataquack who were formerly free "liberty of freemen in their severall townes to manage all their towne affairs," and allowed each town to send a deputy to the General Court "though they be not at present church members." In 1647 inhabitants not freemen were allowed to serve on juries and to vote for selectmen in towns that wished them to do so. In effect, every settled community member could participate; and generally the status of freeholder—ownership of landed property—was evidence enough: a minimal qualification in view of the ease of acquiring holdings. Lack of even that minimum in some places was no bar to voting, the governors frequently complained. Governor Spotswood of Virginia sadly noted (1712) "a defect in the constitution which allows to everyone tho but just out of the condition of a servant, and that can but purchase half an acre of Land an equal vote with the man of the best estate in the country." In 1736 a corrective law aimed at frauds to multiply votes by leasing small and inconsiderable parcels for feigned considerations in order to protect the property qualification, but with dubious success.[34]

In New England after the first generation, church membership diminished in importance as an additional qualification. Puritans did not consider every resident eligible to join the covenant, only the converted; and only those armed with an appropriate certificate from the minister had enjoyed political privileges. In 1646, the deputies still insisted that the liberties and privileges of the charter extended only to those the governor and company thought fit to receive in fellowship. But that year they allowed all who served to vote for military officers. And other compromises soon appeared. The halfway covenant extended the privilege to children of church members who had not experienced conversion; respectable and influential individuals who led exemplary lives and worshiped with their neighbors thus became fully eligible. Massachusetts finally recognized the trend when it extended the franchise to all freeholders. In 1690 the General Court reduced the amount of property required and also eliminated the need for a minister's certificate. Similar adjustments to actuality operated in Maryland and other colonies.[35]

Property qualifications for voting and for holding office persisted everywhere, in part because the royal instructions insisted upon them, in part because the colonists did not object. Office was in any case a burden, as Abraham Delamontage complained (1713) when he was chosen constable of Harlem by a single voice—that of his predecessor, the only inhabitant to turn up at the election. A few years earlier, the governor of Virginia, distressed by the discovery that gentlemen he appointed sheriffs felt free to refuse, recommended enactment of a law to make service obligatory. Nothing happened. The governor of New Hampshire (1684) punished obstreperous legislators by appointing them constables. Even an annual salary of £100 did not help Philadelphia find a mayor; Alderman Morris in 1747 went into hiding to evade notice of his election. Only people with leisure or with expectations of personal gain or glory bothered to seek office or vote unless some unusual event stirred up the district. Those who proved willing found multiple jobs on their hands, as did Richard Sikes of Springfield, Massachusetts, a farmer and selectman who also swept the meetinghouse and rang the bells for marriages, funerals, and other occasions.[36]

Much depended on local circumstances. In some New England towns a single family or a few magnates held sway year after year; in others respectable yeomen formed opinion and managed affairs, and vigorous protests brought dictatorial moderators to heel. Characteristically, Springfield annually gave five men the power to do whatever was necessary for the benefit of the town, but with the proviso that the generality of the town could overrule them. Virginia repeatedly tinkered with the mode of electing burgesses (1646–1670), sometimes broadening the suffrage, sometimes narrowing it out of fear of tumult. In eighteenth-century South Carolina, elections held in Anglican churches supervised by wardens in effect excluded outsiders, while in North Carolina, Governor George Burrington indignantly observed (1733) that the requirement that only freeholders vote, though always inserted in the writs, carried no weight in practice.[37]

Consent did not require actual participation by everyone—only the potential for involvement. Nor did consent depend on consensus. In ordinary times, the powerful and influential governed. Some were high, others low; some ruled, others acquiesced. For a while, the colonists agreed that magistrates existed on a higher plane than the rest of the populace; that, as John Winthrop put it, they were to speak and the people listen. Consent therefore implied agreement, but agreement to obey. It did not imply the right to disobey or not to consent, just as the right to vote did not carry with it the right to elect inappropriate representatives. The concept of consent was thus analogous to the Puritan's relationship with God, or the Englishman's to the crown. The covenanter was not free to strike terms or bargain, but could only acknowledge God's majesty and power. So too in Europe consent did not mean that subjects had a right to select whomever they wished as king or that all could choose which statutes to accept. From Machiavelli Europeans had learned that the chief merit of the people lay in their characteristic tendency to benign passivity. An act of Parliament, explained Sir Thomas Smith (1583), was the whole realm's deed, of which no man could justly complain, "but must accommodate himselfe to finde it good and obey it." For every Englishman, from the prince to the person of lowest degree, was understood to be present, in person or by proxy. "And the consent of Parliament is taken to be everie mans consent."[38]

In the New World, however, the actualities of power altered the concept's meaning. Apart from self-contained groups like the Moravians, who passed through the process of migration unchanged, so that individuals continued to conform to established rules of thought and behavior, the colonists inferred from the ability to consent the ability also not to consent and thereby shifted the understanding of authority. "In the name of the king"—the phrase still evoked respect; and the right to command still derived hierarchically from the crown, but the individuals affected had also to wish to obey. Those who ruled learned the importance of developing support in ever wider circles. Only some made decisions; but the whole town came to meeting, and just listening implicated everyone in the process of government. Freemen, among them yeomen and artisans, voted and acquired a growing sense of involvement, growing agreement on the importance of participation. The governors still commanded, but through experience learned to explain, to argue coherently, to mobilize followers in order to elicit obedience. In areas of sparse settlement, authority thinned out; but even in sizable cities with legal procedures and courts in place, officials could not take order for granted, could not puff themselves up, take themselves too seriously. The habit of derision easily punctured pride of office. Came Richard Kelsick, Esquire, mayor of Norfolk, Virginia, complaining that several people "set up in the house of Richard Scott a Negro Man Slave named Will . . . and did there elect and chuse the said Slave as Mayor, that they seated him and drank to him as Mr. Mayor," an indignity "and a great Insult offered to him the said Mayor, the Recorder, Aldermen and Common Council of this Borough" (1755). Whatever satisfaction an apology brought altered no attitudes.[39]

And everywhere, repeated statements that members of the general court or House of Burgesses were agents representing the will and reflecting the consent of the people, however circumscribed at the moment, implanted significant implications in the consciousness of the populace. In 1682, when William Penn introduced the constitution for his colony, he explained, "Any government is free to the people under it (whatever be the frame) where the laws rule and the people are a party to those laws . . . for liberty without obedience is confusion, and obedience without liberty is slavery."[40]

By the last quarter of the seventeenth century, the colonies had developed stable political institutions grounded in consent. But having emerged from a Hobbesian rather than a Lockean state of nature, they then embarked upon an era of contention instead of concord. People ceased to obey reflexively. Alternatives presented themselves. Yes or no? This course or that? Why? Opinions and interests differed so that resolutions were not always peaceful. For a century intermittent conflicts tested the durability of the polity and its capacity to expand liberty by satisfying the wishes of ever more individuals.

The turmoil surrounding the Glorious Revolution of 1688 paradoxically showed that the political system had arrived at an equilibrium. Despite the constitutional adjustments that followed the restoration of Charles II, the removal of James II, and the ascent of a new ruling house; despite also internal political upheavals, colonial governments remained intact, able easily to incorporate New Netherland as New York and to make room for Georgia. Rebellions, armed conflicts, and shifting political alliances did not alter basic forms. Force rested in the hands of the governor representing the crown or proprietors, the council he designated from among the great landowners, and the assembly that expressed the wishes of those who wielded local power. That balance endured and individual liberty steadily expanded because contention more often erupted in political than in military tests of strength. Little alliances and alignments appeared, similar to, although not the same as, those in England, and differing from place to place in accord with the social, religious, and ethnic factors that governed the distribution of power. In Pennsylvania the Quakers and the Germans joined forces; in Connecticut divisions came over paper money, land policy, and revivalism. In New York Indian policy and the fur trade were the polarizing forces. In Virginia new families rose to political prominence, while in Massachusetts the power of the founders waned. Gradually political mechanisms accommodated the changes.[41]

Events in England occasionally raised fears that developments beyond local control would disturb fragile institutions, newly planted and not yet sturdy enough to resist external shocks. Far across the ocean, sudden shifts in policy or personnel might tamper with the charters on which all rights rested, might alter established boundaries as the Dominion of New England attempted to, or might proclaim all laws provisional, dependent on validation in London, thus undermining the security of property. The jittery colonists warned the king (1664) that imposing greedy courtiers upon them would force his poor subjects to seek new dwellings or faint under intolerable burdens. The royal commissioners' complaints against Massachusetts (1665) unwittingly gave substance to those suspicions. The commissioners objected to the pretensions of the General Court, to the links between church membership and the right to vote, to extravagant land claims, to the college that produced religious and political schismatics, to the readiness to style the colony a "free state" or "common wealth," even to the un-English appearance of Boston. They warned against Puritan tactics to weary the king and his secretaries: "seven yeares they can easily spin out by writing and before that time a change may come." Even before the ascent of James II, therefore, fears sprouted of devious oligarchical plots to grab off monopolies, to knit the empire into an uncomfortable embrace, even to assure the dominance of Catholicism.[42]

Fears of another sort also troubled the colonists who shared the power to govern. Stories lingered of events in the 1640s, when mobs in London terrified the king and the House of Lords, and in Naples, under the fisherman Tomasso Massaniello, brought an imperial viceroy to terms. Here, remote from the sources of authority, every cluster of force threatened order. "Till matters come to a settled government," wrote Roger Williams (1681), "no man is ordinarily sure of his house, goods, land cattle wife children and life. Hence is that ancient maxim it is better to live under a tyrant in peace than under the sword, or where everyman is a tyrant." Massachusetts feared (1646) men of unquiet spirits who insinuated the notion that many were secretly discontented with the government, and emboldened others to sedition "in confidence of so many thousands redy to joyne with them." To prevent disturbances by unlawful assemblies, New Hampshire (1683) and other colonies forbade "any public meeting about any town business" without leave from the justices of the peace.[43]

Even before 1688, and intermittently thereafter, colonists resisted measures contrary to their interests, but drew back when order was in danger. Turbulent outbreaks tested political authority seriously, but not to the point of irreparable damage.

In 1676 Nathaniel Bacon, a young English gentleman living in Virginia and a member of the council, impatient with delays in protecting frontier settlers, led an armed band against the marauding Pamunkey Indians. Governor Berkeley's objections resulted in open rebellion, which collapsed when Bacon fell ill and died. Berkeley restored order by hanging those of his opponents who could not flee. "The old fool had killed more people in that naked country than I have done for the murder of my father," Charles II is reported to have commented. Similar issues lay behind the uprisings by the Clifts in Maryland and by malcontents in other colonies.[44]

Dissension came to a head in 1688, when uncertainties about where power actually resided after the Glorious Revolution permitted men with grievances to express their discontent openly. Massachusetts had received news of James II's departure with delight. It promptly sent Governor Andros packing and the old Puritan families resumed control. The Dominion of New England—James II's grandiose plan for centralized control—died peacefully without ever acquiring significant local support.

Elsewhere the transition was more complex. New Hampshire, having become a royal province, continued to suffer from the uncertainties that had plagued it in the past—concern about land titles, lingering loyalties to Boston, and worry about the inconvenient enforcement of the Navigation Acts. In 1683 the assembly refused to concur in any measure it did not originate and claimed the power to appoint judges. Mumblings against the governor spread—he subverted juries, imprisoned people without due cause, presumed to legislate without the assembly. "He came for money and money he will get, and if he gets it you know who must lose it, and how miserable must our condition be." Edward Gove, a wealthy Hampton yeoman, set the people up to rebellion, challenging the validity of the governor's commission. "His sword was drawn and he

would not lay it down." But seized and sent to England for a while, Gove
subsided.

The revolution of 1688 and the abrupt departure of Governor Andros
kindled these flammable materials. There seemed no government or authority. The towns on their own sought to find an orderly way but could
not agree out of suspicion of their neighbors' designs. Whereupon the
Portsmouth people petitioned to return to the oversight of Massachusetts;
and Exeter, Dover, and Hampton agreed, despite fears of the heartburn-
ings and disobedience sure to follow (1689).[45]

In the end, a compromise of sorts ensued. New Hampshire reverted
to its separate status as a royal province under governor, council, and
assembly, "the three branches together making the laws." Those chosen
for office were to be "men of Estate and ability, and not necessitous
people, or much in debt," and only freeholders could vote (1692). A
practical stratagem softened potential resistance from people who still
looked to Boston: New Hampshire's chief executive for the next quarter
century was the same individual as the governor of Massachusetts.[46]

Andros had also ruled New York, where a violent conflict followed
his downfall; and open rebellion, for a time, exposed the stakes of the
struggle for power. On one side were the established mercantile and
landowning families. On the other were malcontents led by Jacob Leisler,
a German who had come to New Amsterdam in 1660 at the age of
twenty. Having married into one of the leading Dutch families, he had
grown rich through trade in fur, tobacco, and wine, and in the 1680s was
one of the colony's wealthiest men, a captain of the militia and a deacon
of the Reformed Church. Leisler feared an attack by the French papists
and their Indian allies, and he had quarreled with the dominant merchants.
The crisis gave him the opportunity to move into a place of power.

In June 1689, with a band of armed followers, he seized the town's
fort and proclaimed William and Mary the rightful sovereigns. For
twenty months, Leisler ruled New York, bestowing upon himself the
successive titles of captain, commander in chief, and lieutenant governor.
He summoned an assembly to enact laws, collected taxes, and recruited
forces to suppress internal opposition and to fight the Indians and the
French.

But the royal authorities, unwilling to let an upstart assume power
however loyal he professed to be, dispatched troops under Governor
Henry Sloughter to settle matters. After a two-month siege, Leisler
yielded; and Sloughter hanged him as a traitor on May 16, 1691. Yet

many New Yorkers believed that Leisler's conviction had been unjust; and more than a decade later, they persuaded the assembly to vote an indemnity to his heirs.

None of these rebellions was simply a struggle for individual power; each attracted substantial followings. They expressed no hostility to royal authority and affirmed their loyalty to the crown, their desire for legitimacy, and their wish to strengthen legality. Leisler sincerely feared that the supporters of James II might hand the colony over to the Catholic French. But more general considerations also moved the insurgents and revealed the points at which consent broke down.

The colonists knew the importance of privilege as a stake of government, one of the channels through which political power generated economic rewards. The only question was—for whom? Loose organization and decentralization complicated the answer. The king had delegated power to the governor; but back in their own counties, Bacon and Leisler also had power; and so too did the New Hampshire townsmen. The efforts of influential groups around the governor to monopolize the important prizes primed the excluded to violent protest. Contests for privilege among individuals, factions, or interests usually transpired in the vestry or town meeting, in sessions of the assembly or council, or behind the scenes in discussions among the leading men. Now and again the competition verged on insurrection.

The outbreaks involved related issues. In Virginia and New York, the governors refused to take vigorous action against the frontier Indians. Berkeley was so much their friend that he would not suffer anybody to hurt one of them, despite the losses of great stocks of cattle and of many men, women, and children. The hesitancy sprang not from affection for the red men nor from scruples about the justice of ousting them, but rather from a desire to protect the fur trade, supplied by the Indians and threatened by the advance of agriculture and the destruction of the forests. Those who profited by that trade lived a safe distance away and shrugged off complaints from the wilderness. By contrast, Indians posed obstacles to people along the frontier, who eagerly favored advances that would give them more space and raise the value of their holdings. In both New York and Virginia the fur trade was also a valuable political prize. Bacon and some of his supporters suspected that Berkeley's tolerance toward the Indians masked plans for a monopoly that would exclude all but the governor's friends from the business. Leisler and his allies based in Schenectady suffered losses when the province restricted the trade to the Albany merchants. A law that confined the right to bolt grain to New York City also damaged his interests, for he owned a mill in Suffolk County. Monopolies of every sort, granted under the guise of regulation, divided those favored from others.[47]

Land itself was an object of contention. Abundant space did not ease the competition among eager speculators who understood the possibilities of appreciation from the growth of population. The governors granted away immense tracts, but squatters already settled did not peacefully vacate their places in response to the claims in a strange piece of paper. In addition, jurisdictions disputed in the past, as in New Hampshire, left titles derived from them open to question. On through the 1750s an uncertain boundary provided cover for the conflict of tenants and land-ords along the eastern frontier of New York.

In Maryland, Pennsylvania, and New Jersey conflicts erupted over the rights of the proprietors to quitrents provided for in the original land grants. The recalcitrant settlers quibbled over terms and objected to an arrangement that seemed to make proprietors both landlords and rulers. The absentees lived it up in England and expected American husbandmen to pay for their luxurious tastes. Resentment festered, then boiled over. Distance and local power made collection difficult. The inhabitants of East New Jersey (1700), while professing loyalty to the crown, protested against the proprietors "who under pretence and colour of having bought the government with the soile," ejected several persons "under pretence of quitt rent." Aggrieved by the loss of even a few working days at harvest time, the people accused the proprietory agents of drinking the health of the deposed King James—an indication that it was not for the country's benefit or in the royal interest that those officials continue in office. The proprietors, in response to those complaints, perceived a plot and requested royal support lest the settlers "set up a government of their own." William Penn, the pragmatist, ever for taking what he could get, advised agreement "by an easy and engageing way," knowing "that ½ loaf is better than no bread." His counsel was: "Friends—if in the consti-tution by charter there be anything that jarrs—alter it. If you want a law for this or that, prepare it." Consent, Penn implied, could best be secured by allowing the widest possible latitude of action to meet unforeseen local circumstances.[48]

His less perceptive successors opposed the settlers' demands head-on and tried to elicit consent by force. In response the Pennsylvanians not only continued to object to quitrents, but also sought to tax the proprietor's vast unoccupied lands, especially to meet wartime expenses in 1755. "Our Lord Proprietary, though a subject like ourselves, would send us out to fight for him, while he keeps himself a thousand leagues removed from the Danger . . . This is not merely vassalage, it is worse than any vassalage . . . ; it is something we have no adequate name for; it is even more slavish than slavery itself."[49]

Eruptions of violence over more specific issues exposed the fragility of consent. A drought that left Massachusetts short of wheat (1710–1713) raised questions about the morality of exports and profiteering. Samuel Sewall believed it was poor judgment to send large quantities away in times of scarcity, in line with Scripture: He that withholds corn, the people will curse him. God's people, though they brought themselves into straits by their own fault, yet God pitied and helped them. His minister, however, said "with much fierceness they were not God's people but the devil's. . . . There was corn to be had, if they had not impoverished themselves by rum." Whether greed, drink, or the drought were at fault, no one bothered to decide. God's or the devil's, people took matters into their own hands, cut the rudder of a ship about to carry off food, and broke open a warehouse in the Boston Common, hoping to find more corn.[50]

In 1700 Samuel Burwell, accused of begetting a bastard child, refused to provide the security demanded for its maintenance. When the Elizabethtown, New Jersey, court ordered the constable to take Burwell into custody, his supporters pulled the judges off the bench, tore their hats and wigs, broke their swords, and freed the prisoner. Asked by what power they demanded his release, Burwell's friends "held up their clubbs and said that was their power." Similarly, much good it would do the governor of Pennsylvania to urge Philadelphia magistrates in 1726 to suppress more effectually the town's frequent riots and disorderly practices; obligations that weighed heavily on English municipalities applied lightly to America.[51]

Nor did Lord Granville succeed in dealing with his responsibilities in North Carolina. Granville's tenants, infuriated by his surveyor's outrageous charges and shady dealings, "combined together in traitorous conspiracies and committed several riots and routs" (1759–1760). Indignant petitions to the Board of Trade in London followed, but, the North Carolina House complained, no effectual steps checked the licentious extravagances. On the contrary, some of the tenants' principal leaders and conductors, elected magistrates and honored with militia commissions, displaced distinguished gentlemen, depriving courts of influence and rendering liberty and property precarious—so ran the complaints of those formerly in control.[52]

Yet the little societies did not fall apart. Although the potential for violence persisted, clubs and muskets usually remained at home, most stored grain survived intact, and those charged with fathering illegitimate infants usually contributed to their support. On a broader level, the politics of consent eased contention over grave social, economic, and religious issues. Land grants, monopolies, taxation, and other economic matters continued to divide the politically active, as did social and religious policy. In the course of prolonged debate, people defined their interests with reference to these questions; taking sides, they formed coherent political groups, at least when it came to specific decisions. The desperate possibility of armed resistance remained. But stability brought with it a preference for resolution in the give-and-take of the assembly over the uncertain fortunes of the brawl.

The charter was a reference point by which the colonists resolved conflicts among themselves and with the officials in England. In June 1661, Massachusetts, disturbed about the effects of the Restoration, appointed a committee to discuss the liberty and duty of the colonists and thereby to beget unity while observing due obedience unto the authority of England. The committee reported that the patent, under God, the main foundation of their civil polity, established the governor and company as a body politic vested with power to make freemen, who in turn had the right to choose annually a governor, deputy governor, assistants, and their representatives or deputies. Together, these possessed the legislative and executive power to govern in all matters concerning "ecclesiasticks and in civils," without appeal, except in the case of laws repugnant to the laws of England. Any imposition from abroad would infringe upon their rights. A grudging proclamation of loyalty to the king, however, forbade any person to drink his majesty's health, "which he hath special forbid." Massachusetts was not to have its way. Flattering comparisons of Charles II to King David got it nowhere. An adjustment, after more than a quarter century of negotiation, finally established a royal governor and extended the power of the London authorities, but nevertheless brought the province a new charter.[53]

New York, Maryland, and Pennsylvania had no company charters in their pasts. There the extensive prerogative of the crown or proprietor left colonists no recourse in resisting abuses but appeals to the uncertain rights of Englishmen. Nevertheless there too the holders of local power asserted themselves through the assemblies despite efforts to hold them in check. In 1669 the governor of Maryland rejected the assembly's analogy to the House of Commons; and in 1675 the Virginia House of Burgesses petitioned in vain for incorporation. On the other hand the mainland assemblies would not acquiesce as Jamaica did in the rule that they could act only on laws drafted by the king. And New York's Charter of Liberties and Privileges (1683) vested supreme legislative power in the governor, council, and "the people," a term for the assembly indignantly questioned by the Lords of Trade in London.[54]

After the Restoration, ties to the mother country grew closer and a growing army of bureaucrats in London and overseas maintained oversight over the colonies. But English forms and procedures did not shape government in America. Local power prevailed. Long experience in dealing with internal problems accustomed colonists to think of government as a means of attaining their own ends, particular or general. Profuse professions of loyalty did not quite conceal the underlying reality. "His Majestye [has] nothing to do here," said Daniel Gookin of Massachusetts (1681), "for we are a free people of ourselves." Few colonists went as far as he, but experience showed that the crown lacked force adequate to say him nay. Subjects pushed too hard took to arms and only the militia or other force on the spot could assert control. Generally the governors' efforts to manipulate the assemblies through patronage politics after the English manner came to nothing; the representative assemblies contained no places for rotten boroughs.[55]

Indeed, with time the assemblies grew more zealous in defense of their prerogatives, scrutinizing with care the governor's use of allies to influence opinions or elections. One of the perennial confrontations in Virginia (1715) exposed the issues and exemplified the rhetoric. The House of Burgesses wished to arrest two justices who refused to certify grievances addressed to it. It protested that evil persons, enemies to peace and tranquillity, had falsely insinuated that the people had been called together in a riotous manner and demanded help from the governor lest erosion of its power leave it nothing but shadow and name. The council thereupon intervened, claiming that, as the upper house, it should have received all communications. The governor used the occasion to request additional appropriations and to warn against interference with his right to appoint justices—an intention the burgesses disavowed. The governor dissolved the contemptuous house, but not before scolding it for wasting time and money, for claiming "greater power than ever the commons of England pretended to," for heeding "the giddy resolves of the illiterate vulgar in their drunken conventions," for rudeness to the king's representatives, for seeking to defraud His Majesty of quitrents, for a militia law unfair to the poor, and for appointing committee chairmen unable to spell or write common sense.[56] However furious the combat, the contestants returned to another session and another trial of will.

Free people lived by the law, but law was that to which they consented, written by their assemblies and enforced by judgments not of an alien court but of their own juries, in all cases, civil and criminal. In response to the externally imposed Court of Admiralty, North Carolinians in 1730 stamped about the courthouse, set up two mock judges, and drove away the aliens.[57] The troublesome New Jerseyites from Elizabethtown, in the course of an interminable controversy with the proprietors, rejected a jury "chosen by the said Proprietors or their creatures." They protested even more vigorously when partial and arbitrary judges overturned a favorable verdict in 1696. Thomas Maule of Salem insisted on the right to a trial at home before a jury of his equals and won acquittal despite a biased charge from the judge. "Look well to your work," he exhorted those in whose hands his fate rested, "if you miss doing me justice the fault will lie on your part, for these my accusers on the bench are but clerks, to concluding your work with Amen."[58]

To prevent the manipulation of inadequate, servile, or dependent juries, colonists insisted they be drawn from the vicinage, with the exception perhaps of convicts already convicted before transportation from Britain. Nor did the provincials accept English practice as binding. The South Carolina House refused Governor Glen's request for a minimum property qualification for jurors and instead disqualified only insolvent debtors, heedless of Glen's strictures on the "vanity and weakness" of trying to improve the British constitution.[59]

Swagger as they would, however, all those free people were not content to rattle around in space by themselves. Force could not regulate the whole of life. Many must often have echoed the sentiments of William Penn (1700), who wished there were no need of any government, which only man's degeneracy made necessary. Government was not an end but a means, serving what was good for all as a body politic.[60]

Consent had become more than a ceremonial ritual, more than a means of negotiation among peers and estates. In the strange New World taking form across the Atlantic, the people making much of their freedom, who expected consent to enter into all transactions between rulers and ruled, learned that the right to say *yea* or *nea,* to choose one way or another, called for hard decisions, for which habit and tradition were inadequate guides. Challenged to think new thoughts, the settlers grew contentious in accord with their divided interests. Conflicts, sputtering across the decades, demonstrated the limits of compulsion, the utility of resolving issues by agreement.

In the absence of the corporate community that migration and dispersal had destroyed, there was, however, no certain means of knowing what was good for all. While struggling ineffectively to reconstruct what could not be restored, men and women out of necessity hit upon another way of doing things more in accord with their being free.

I V

COMMONWEALTHS,

1600–1760

SEVENTEENTH-CENTURY COLONISTS defined the function of the state as did Europeans: service of the common ends of its subjects; it did for all what each could not do individually. Defense against external enemies, self-preservation, and maintenance of order justified the use of power and enlisted the support of significant social groups.

Each individual had particular interests. But a general, common interest comprehended them all, one sometimes identified with the crown, sometimes with such abstractions as the country or the people. The new centralized states, sustained by dynastic power and by the economic and political ideas of mercantilism, viewed themselves as custodians of the common interest; and by the end of the century a coherent body of ideas explained that they ruled not an aggregate of individuals but a society that was more than the sum of its members—a commonwealth or republic. The term *body politic* often served as a metaphor for the interdependence of all elements in the society. "You are not onely naturally membres of one bodi, with the pore creatures of this realme, but also by religion you ar membres of the same misticall body of Christ, whoe is the heade of vs all (his membres)." Frequent references to society as a great family or corporation pushed the analogy further. "A family is a little commonwealth," John Winthrop said, "and a commonwealth is a great family." Sir Thomas Smith (1583) indeed traced the origins of all polities to the family.[1]

People associated in transient or provisional hosts for purposes of their own; but free men, united by common accord and covenant for their conservation in peace or war, formed a commonwealth. They did not thereby merge into an undifferentiated whole. The term *commonwealth* did not imply unity in any utopian sense, as it had for Sir Thomas More. Individuals retained their identity and their particular interests, and worked for their own ends, except insofar as a common purpose animated them. The corporate communities of the Old World policed the line established by tradition and habit between what was individual and what was common; and the Moravians continued to do so. But the more general dissolution of integrated communities in the New World opened a long, difficult process of redefinition in the social order, in religion, in family life, and in the economy.[2]

Since the New World was a blank paper, the schemes inscribed on it initially emphasized common interests. Many a ship sets to sea, wrote Roger Williams, and there was no doubt of the obligation of all passengers to help in its protection. Nor was there at first any doubt among those huddled within the palisades of Jamestown or Plymouth. The hazards of crossing the ocean, of planting communities in the wilderness, of threats from the Indians and from French and Spanish neighbors, reminded all of the need for unity and common defense. Garrison conditions persuaded the population that the welfare of the whole encompassed that of the individual.

The sense of mission that animated the colonists from the start and never entirely disappeared fortified the feeling of unity. The obligation to convert the unconverted as a prelude to the great drama of salvation that constituted universal history had been deeply entrenched in European thought since the Crusades. Now the task had passed to the American plantations. "Offend not the poor natives," John Cotton entreated; "as you partake in their land, so make them partakers of your precious faith; as you reap their temporalls, so feed them with your spirituals: win them to the love of Christ, for whom Christ died."[3]

The awareness of a religious significance to their migration animated even the odds and ends of settlers who came to the Chesapeake colonies. It was a firm article of faith among the New England Puritans. John Winthrop explained that they had crossed the ocean to build a city upon a hill, a model saints everywhere would emulate. Roger Williams reflected (1643) that God in his wisdom and power had separated from Europe, Asia, and Africa such a mighty, vast continent as America and thereby presented the elect an opportunity to form a community based on divine will as reflected in the Scriptures. The significance of this enterprise ran far beyond the personal welfare of its participants. Cosmic in nature, this was a decisive event in a drama that began with the Creation and would culminate in the approaching millennium.

The hardships of settlement did not diminish faith in the mission—indeed, proved its vitality. Every setback tested God's chosen people, gave evidence of his special providence. The more difficulties beset the settlements, the more conviction it required of the correctness of the mission. "Come, behold the works of the Lord, what desolation He has made in the earth," exclaimed a woman, her house destroyed, her family massacred in the Indian attack on Lancaster, Massachusetts (1675). That enduring faith in the importance of the enterprise sustained awareness of the common elements in the society.[4]

Migration, however, altered the relationship of the individual to the community—at first to the company, colony, or province in general, then to the town, county, or parish locally. The adjustment called forth new social institutions.

The Virginia plantation at the start rested on a common purpose not compatible with individual property or with trade by merchants on their own accounts. The corporation owned everything, established the settlement, and engaged in commerce, seeking profits through a joint stock. The interests of the organization subsumed those of all the participants. In New Netherland, the Dutch West India Company did the same.

Yet common purpose disintegrated—more quickly in some places than in others, but in time everywhere. The cargoes remained yet unloaded from the earliest ships when seamen and settlers took to selling goods to the Indians; and the temptation to unauthorized dealings persisted through the whole history of both companies. Individuals also insisted on the personal ownership of land, and the hard-pressed colonies had to yield them the privilege. As a result, people pursued their own objectives in their own way, no longer bound by the original corporate structure. The concessions essential to the settlement's survival steadily eroded the sense of common purpose.

In the proprietary colonies, the process was swifter. Their grants treated Baltimore and Penn as feudal overlords. The interests of such overlords hardly seemed identical with those of the people, who regarded them as landlords making obnoxious demands for quitrents. The Marylanders, too busy gathering their crops, in 1649 refused to act upon complicated proposals from Lord Baltimore in England and suggested that his lordship send no more such bodies of law, which served no other end than to stir up suspicion, jealousy, and dislike. William Penn explained that he intended everything in the Charter of Liberties of 1683 "for the Good and Benefit of the Freemen of the Province." But debates in the assembly revealed divergent views of what that benefit might be. The commonwealth concept seemed inapplicable to Maryland and Pennsylvania, where the proprietors' prosperity curtailed the welfare of the residents.[5]

Puritan influence gave developments in New England a different form. Both Plymouth and Massachusetts began as joint stock corporations, but the joint stock never amounted to much and quickly disintegrated. Yet common purpose for a time remained, not economic in character but nonetheless providing a focal point of organization. John Cotton (1630) had cautioned those who departed for America to go "with a public spirit, looking not on your own things only, but also on the things of others" in a spirit of universal helpfulness.[6]

The Puritans however knew better than to rely on such injunctions; they insisted also upon obedience to authority in a tight community. Love and grace no doubt would generate the spirit of universal helpfulness; but security and order imposed on society immediate demands of their own. The magistrates refused to allow anyone to reside alone or away from the center of settlement. Concerned because Joseph Ramsden lived remotely in the woods, exposing his family to great hardships, perils, and inconveniences, Plymouth ordered him to move into some neighborhood (1652) and threatened to pull down his house when he still remained apart four years later. So too, the Watertown selectmen warned James Hollon (1672), who lived without family government and misspent his time in idleness, that unless he found himself a master in a fortnight's time, they would provide one for him. John Cotton's effort to codify Massachusetts law even forbade an heir who had inherited distant land to move more than a mile from the meetinghouse.[7]

Nevertheless, in New England also the concept of community, whether based on helpfulness or on power, changed as the economy made place for private initiative and as settlement spread out. Plymouth accepted some newcomers not among the original Pilgrim band, persons who seemed able "to govern themselves with meet discretion." The colony "saw not how peace would be preserved without so doing." Yet the invasion of strangers jeopardized the delicate balance Puritans sought between diligence in mundane business and deadness to the world.[8]

The second generation further upset the balance. Distinctions appeared between the first comers and later arrivals. The discipline of the town meeting and the church held some forms intact, but Richard Mather warned (1657) that worldly affairs might so drain the life and power of religion "that nothing thereof should be left but only the external form, as it were the carcass or shell, worldliness having eaten out the kernel, and having consumed the very soul and life of godliness." Individual differences diluted the concept of community as New England settlement pushed into the interior, to the distress of those concerned about the impact on the church.[9]

In all the colonies, the commonwealth conception endured through the eighteenth century. But it acquired a meaning detached from the integrated community. Necessity compelled people to explore, ad hoc, new modes of living together in a society in which not all members were alike, and which could not eliminate differences among them. Furthermore, Pennsylvanians openly claimed, and other colonists implied, that they were due "greater Privileges than they had Enjoyed in their native Countreys." Such people in such a society would yield personal preferences to the common good only voluntarily.[10]

Practical problems required responses, some based on recollected European precedents, others improvised. No abstract theory described those reactions; they evolved empirically through adjustments to unexpected conditions, often awkwardly, sometimes with great difficulty, occasionally after disturbing conflicts, usually based on contract and consent. In the process the obligation of society to advance not merely the aggregate of interests but some common interest transcending those of individuals acquired a new form.

The ability to give general communal purposes priority over personal ones depended on the sanctions available—more in the Puritan colonies, less elsewhere, none as extensive as in the enclosed, self-contained settlements of the Moravians. Where individuals, to some degree, asserted their own interests, the colonists met with but qualified success in the efforts to maintain communal control of religion and the church, or to organize family life according to the old norms, or to prevent changes in the productive system. Yet chaos did not follow. Though the American environment sapped the common purpose as at first conceived, the unexpected outcome was a set of compensating adjustments.

New Englanders again and again reexamined the limits of the community whenever they considered the common fields that remained at their disposal. The first settlers of each town had allocated to each family as arable land only a small portion of the area within its limits. The rest stayed in reserve—to be granted to new settlers or divided among the old when needed, or for use in common as grazing meadows or forests, in accord with Old World practice. But very early, fresh arrivals revealed the value of the undivided lands. Once increased population raised the price of corn and cattle, William Bradford noted in 1632, there was no longer any holding the Pilgrims together. "No man now thought he could live except he had cattle and a great deal of ground to keep them, all striving to increase their stocks. By which means they were scattered all over the Bay quickly." The question then arose, whether to give tracts away to the newcomers or to increase the holdings of the old inhabitants or to sell some off for the benefit of all. With the passage of time, the answer ever more frequently favored those already established.[11]

Towns, unwilling to share their resources, jealously narrowed entry against outsiders. Watertown, Massachusetts, having required the consent of the freemen before any foreigner from England or another plantation could set down among them (January 1635), before the end of the year decided that an excess of inhabitants put the town "in danger to be ruinated" and therefore ordered that access to the commons or undivided lands be only by purchase. Three years later the town forbade the sale or exchange of town lots to any foreigner, but only to "Freemen of the congregation. It being our reall intent to sitt down there close together." And three years later the restrictions were further strengthened.[12]

Newcomers did not seem to deserve the same property rights as the original planters and their heirs, but had to purchase them. Dedham in 1659 thus used tax lists to apportion its common lands to the proprietors who, for years thereafter, could sell their cow commons to others. The proprietors of the common fields became a separate body, distinct from the town. A generation later, the Dedham people who planted Deerfield in the west received their grant "in propryetie" as joint owners, while newcomers were inhabitants only.[13] Conflicts between commoners with rights and inhabitants without rights persisted, so that the colony court had to fix an equitable judgment between them, as in the case of Marblehead (1674). Newer communities, like Colchester, Connecticut, at first granted away their lands by a town vote, then in time decided that the matter "be wholey and solely in the power of the propriters" (1714), a difference that gained importance as the supply of unused tracts shrank.[14]

Common needs persisted, even among freeholders perched each on his own holding. Simple prudence required joint action for security and order, for defense against external threats and against lurking dangers from the elements. The whole community had to resist Indian attacks and join in precautions against marauding wolves. Everyone with a lot in town had to contribute labor to cutting brush (1672); everyone with a share in the general enclosure had to contribute to fencing it according to proportion (1635); everyone had to pay local taxes, locally voted— although the mode of setting equitable assessments required prolonged discussion. Five years or more Springfield, Massachusetts, expended in considering the matter (1655–1660). Land certainly counted, but by acreage or value? Buildings, but merchandise held for trade? Livestock, and if so, by age or by weight?[15]

Order depended on firm controls as well as on cooperation. The corporate community bred intolerance of every form of deviant behavior, ruling as it did all aspects of life. Each public body must be purged of rotten humors, wrote a sixteenth-century Puritan poet, "els wyll it decay, as do the bodyes naturall, When rotten humours haue infected them." So Plymouth refused to associate with Rhode Island in order to "keep ours from being infected by them" (1642). And Rhode Island made the purpose of its own laws plain: "No inferior shall rise against his superior" lest stability fail. The colonists valued discipline out of fear that wrong behavior by some would destroy the health of all, even in a land where sin was narrowly looked into and severely punished. The apparent fragility of communities increased the need for order imposed by force. Men's lusts were sweet to them, held in check only by godly magistrates. Leniency, John Cotton explained, was "a mercilesse mercy," for to pity the incurably contagious was not to pity the hundreds of souls threatened by infection.[16]

The punishment of evildoers as a means of law enforcement occupied all magistrates worried by standards loosened under wilderness conditions. The more difficult the task became, the more determined were the authorities to enforce the letter of their laws. Legislation, with its minute attention to detail, reflected the effort to regulate morality and acceptable behavior. New Jersey's Governor Basse in 1698 indulged in wishful thinking when he asked justices of the peace, sheriffs, and constables to put into force an ordinance that forbade "cursing swearing immoderate drinking sabbath breaking and all sorts of lewdness and prophane behavior in word or action" in the hope that "by religious and virtuous carriage and behavior of everyone in his respective station and calling all heats and animosities and dissentions may vanish." William Penn's more realistic charter and laws defined the machinery of justice. Courts would be open and justice "neither sold, denied or delayed." Persons of all persuasions would freely appear in their "own way and according to their own manner," their pleadings, processes, and records to be short and in English, and of such "an ordinary and plain character that they may be understood and justice speedily administered."

Banishment, for a time, was the most economical means of ridding a community of actual or potential wrongdoers. In the 1630s Massachusetts called attention to itself by shipping off dissenters, a procedure authorized by its charter and one to which Parliament also resorted in England. But the practice lapsed when the exiles made trouble in London and when the boundaries among the provinces proved porous. Fines, whippings, the pillory and the gallows provided a full array of alternatives.

Each colony established jails, usually to hold suspects for trial, sometimes for incarceration of the incorrigible undeterred by other punishments. In advance of his time, Penn suggested (1682) that prisons serve as workhouses for the rehabilitation of felons, vagrants, and loose and idle persons. But cost proved an insurmountable obstacle to this reform. Usually authorities contracted with a keeper, more interested in his own gain than in the welfare of his charges. In the 1730s, riots in Boston's jail called attention to the abuse of power by Zechariah Trescott; and a legislative investigation led to his dismissal. In 1748 Rawlins Lowndes asked South Carolina to establish a secure jail; he was tired of having criminals lodged in his home, from which they frequently escaped.[17]

Despite the importance of community order and security, individuals often balked at measures to preserve it, even when they concerned public health. Once the settlers passed beyond early garrison conditions when they had no alternative but fatalistically to accept illness and death as God's will, they by no means embraced proposals to cope with general threats to health, despite ample European precedents for such actions. Stubborn evasion and sometimes open resistance greeted the simplest preventive measures.[18]

Communal authority extended only slowly, for instance, to the treatment of contagious disease. Colonial ports were always vulnerable to disorders brought by sailors and passengers; and illness spread easily into the interior. It was tempting to blame outsiders for any malady. Isolation and quarantine were long the only effective means of preventing development of a plague, other than the prayers of a fast day. At news of an epidemic in Barbados, Massachusetts in 1647 placed all incoming vessels under quarantine. Connecticut, learning of pestilence in New Netherland, forbade traffic from the stricken colony in 1663. Virginia required clearance papers of all arrivals certifying the health of the ship's passengers (1722). Neither the ill nor their goods could come ashore without written permission.[19]

But the large numbers of inner harbors and inlets made enforcement difficult, and the potential losses by withholding arriving goods encouraged frequent evasion. Public health was one thing, private welfare another, and rumors of disease, much less an actual threat, seriously damaged business. His neighbors complained when a Salisbury man left home too soon after recovering from smallpox (1679), but the court did no more than admonish him. Captain Gore, whose ship entered Boston harbor carrying smallpox (1720), unbeknownst to the authorities and in clear violation of standing orders, came ashore to be attended by his wife, and died shortly thereafter. A special order from the House of Representatives forbade those around him from coming to town until the threat of the disease had passed, a mild enough punishment. Experience with yellow fever and smallpox induced New York City to order victims buried quickly and to forbid distilling of rum and burning of lime, held responsible for disease. Yet in 1731 the Common Council indignantly denied rumors that frightened business away, only to discover that the epidemic did spread and totally halted trade.[20]

Proven ineffectualness did not staunch the flow of legislation. Connecticut acted by law to prevent peddlers, hawkers, and petty chapmen from spreading smallpox (1722); New York established a quarantine station on Bedloe's Island (1738); and Philadelphia moved against merchants whose ships, overcrowded with immigrants, created a risk of contagion—which did not prevent a typhoid epidemic under precisely those conditions (1754).

The baffled provincial authorities preferred to shift responsibility to the localities. A Massachusetts law (1722) thus empowered judges to oversee public health, with power to set apart separate houses as occasion required and to force the infected to inhabit them during their illness. To avoid abuses and also to involve local communities and reassure the inhabitants, the measure required the previous advice of the town selectmen. Connecticut and New York followed the same course.[21]

The isolation system crumbled when the sick refused to bow to public pressure and insisted on remaining in their own homes. The effort of Hampton, New Hampshire, to remove several people met resistance not only from the patients' families but also from the owners of houses requisitioned to shelter them (1758). The sick remained where they were, spreading the infection, since some of them resided near a major thoroughfare. Ironically, the number of people who used the road declined, to the loss of local merchants. A temporary but calamitous suspension of worship because some of the ill lived near the meetinghouse deprived the townsfolk of communal prayer, their only means of halting the spread of the disease. In desperation, Hampton appealed to the governor and assembly for outside force to remove the infected.[22]

The feasibility of preventive measures had only just dawned. John Tennant's *Every Man His Own Doctor*, published in several editions, enjoyed a minor boom in the spring and summer of 1746 when an epidemic swept through the middle and New England colonies, leaving many dead. However, the book was no more effective in providing cures than were local physicians. Inoculation offered hope but also uncertainty. Unpersuaded by the case for the practice yet powerless to stop those determined to try it, the New York authorities attempted to regulate what they regarded as a dangerous and willful spread of disease. The town of Huntington provided a special house for the physicians and their patients and forbade any inoculation in a public place without the consent of two judges. People nevertheless insisted on taking the treatment in their own homes, or else heedlessly moved around after it.[23]

The rules of personal behavior that in Europe helped preserve order fell into disarray when the absence of guilds and manorial courts deprived communities of sanctions for enforcement. Puritans who accepted the obligation of "holy watching"—of responsibility for the souls of their neighbors—anticipated that every inhabitant, required to attend worship, would inform the church or the government of transgressions. But the new circumstances in time proved incongruous, and almost everywhere bred an attitude of tolerance to actions that did not disturb others.[24]

The colonists at first transferred from across the Atlantic the complex regulations that governed what persons of each social class could wear or eat as well as the title of address accorded each. But already in 1619 a letter from Virginia noted that the Jamestown cowkeeper went accoutred all in fresh flaming silks on Sundays, while the wife of one who in England had been a collier wore a "beuer hat with a faire perle hattband, and a silken suite thereto correspondent."[25]

The Virginia Company (1621) tried to curb excess in apparel and otherwise, as did other colonies later—in vain, even when local authorities lent their support. Watertown, shocked at the enormities of people who disregarded the law, forbade any inhabitant to wear silks, gold or silver, lace or buttons, or ribbons at the knees (1659). Plymouth's code (1685) banned strange apparel worn for lascivious and evil purposes. Perhaps the stern warnings affected only a few residents of agricultural towns. But a matter that touched everyone provided graphic evidence of the slackness of control: year after year, the Watertown selectmen worried about the order of sitting in the meetinghouse, yet many a goodman and goodwife refused to take the places appointed them (1658–1664). An even more persistent problem, lavish funeral expenditures, resisted control despite efforts to set fees and limit the totals and types of costs that might deplete an estate. All these regulations had proven their uselessness by the eighteenth century, although some lingered on the statute books.[26]

Lacking confidence in communal corrective power, people harmed by others sought formal redress in the courts. Crimes defined in the statutes fell within the purview of government, which took the initiative in prosecuting the perpetrators. But satisfaction for damages of another sort required the sufferers to bring suit on their own accounts.

As in England, slander was a frequent cause for litigation, although no specific law prohibited it. The value in a small community of a good name—of a reputation for sobriety, just dealings, and honesty—in the colonies accounted for numerous suits of this sort. The tenacity of the slandered in carrying their cases to trial on the slightest provocation and their willingness to risk the attendant publicity revealed concern about the slender props on which social standing rested. Then too, possible financial losses made it dangerous to leave accusations unanswered. Malicious minds believed any gossip. Sly innuendoes, even open contempt, could inflict serious injuries.[27]

Joan Michel, one of Lord Baltimore's more troubled subjects, thus defended her reputation for honesty in the face of numerous accusations that she used satanic powers. A poor widow, the butt of endless jokes, Goodie Michel tired of dodging stones thrown by servants at the instigation of their masters, even when she went to church. She accused several neighbors of charging her with witchcraft, hoping that vindication would silence the slander. The court did not bother with the witchcraft issue and dismissed her other complaints as lacking substance. Joan Michel continued to suffer accusations that she could make people ill and cast spells on their chickens.[28]

Any case of slander involved the whole community. The plaintiff had to state his grievances before the very group whose judgment he valued and on whose opinion his standing and livelihood depended. The trial thus became a way of recovering a lost position. Men and women repeated the most distasteful details before judges and audiences in the hope of revealing the absurdity of accusations. The reputed cuckold sought to recover his reputation for virility by rebuffing slanders on his marital powers, while a wife wished to regain her good name by disproving the charge that she was seen in the bushes with a man not her husband. Those charged with possessing unnatural powers hoped to prove they had no such powers at all. And tradesmen and craftsmen accused of cheating and malpractice tried to regain the confidence of their customers.[29]

Thomas Baker of Maryland, a troublemaker and slanderer, was known to all as an unstable character whose words carried little weight. Nonetheless several female neighbors felt aggrieved enough to take him into court because his comments exceeded the bounds of even the loosest talk (1662). To be called a common whore was bad enough, but it was too much when Baker charged that a woman who had delivered a girl had yelled to a passerby, "Come to bed to her and get her a boy to her girl," upon which the passerby suggested his dog perform the office. Baker also reported that another woman "had a Cunt enough to make souse for all the dogges in the Countrie." These and other victims dragged him to court, where rehearsal of the charges exposed Baker as "a common defamor of most of all his neighbors." Willem Jeuriaensz, his Dutch counterpart—a rascal, a blasphemer, a public nuisance, a murderer in intention if not in deed, and a disturber of the common peace—announced that he was twenty-one years old when the honorable court knew he was at least seventy.[30]

James Doughtey of New Plymouth feared a threat to his livelihood when Thomas Ingham reported that someone else had heard Doughtey's wife give advice on how to steal yarn by making the cloth seem heavier than it was (sprinkle some water on it). Doughtey correctly assumed that no one would ever bring him any yarn to spin on the suspicion that some of it would not find its way into the cloth (1663). The jury declared the defendant guilty and fined him the large sum of five pounds.[31]

A deacon of Eastham, accused of being a drunken sot, an old knave who taught children to cheat—which made him fitter to be a hangman —saw his whole world collapse. He sued. The jury found the slanderer guilty of defamation, but the court, suspecting that at least some of the charges had a basis in actuality, refused to award damages and ordered each side to pay its own costs.[32]

Most of the slander cases originated in heated quarrels as personal animosities and financial disputes vented themselves in name-calling and charges of dishonesty. Each party felt aggrieved enough to sue in defense of the right to be regarded as an upstanding member of the community. The plaintiff thus often risked winding up with an unfavorable judgment, even more damaging than the original exchange, as well as the high legal expenses that might follow. In 1664 Hugh Standley sued Thomas Pagett for 30,000 pounds of tobacco before the Maryland provincial court. Standley, a supporter of Lord Baltimore and for years justice of the peace and commissioner in Calvert County, felt his prestige slip when Pagett, before a crowd, called him "Knaue Cheating Knaue." Had Standley let it go at that perhaps not everyone in the crowd would have learned of the substance to the accusation. At the trial, Pagett's witnesses testified that Standley would not repay his debt according to contract. The case was dismissed and Standley was charged with the costs of the court, of the witnesses, of the sheriff, of the jurors, of the attorneys, and for the time lost by the defendant.[33]

Trials could thus prove double-edged. They might clear the plaintiff's name, but rehearsal of the details gave the original slander wider currency, so that the suspicion sometimes lingered that only the technicalities of the law or the partiality of the judges accounted for a favorable verdict. No formal judgment could then erase the impression. John Wedge and his wife thus gained apparent vindication in 1672 when the Talbot County Court fined John Wickes 1,000 pounds of tobacco and forced him to ask forgiveness on his knees, as well as pay all the costs, because he had written a "scandalous song" about them. But the song was read in court and by the time the trial ended everyone knew it. On the other hand, a failed suit was disastrous. The Scituate inhabitant who felt slandered by reports of his strictures on government in general and the magistrates in particular not only lost his suit but faced judges who agreed with the verdict, which left his loyalties forever suspect (1674).[34]

Personal behavior that adversely affected a whole community often slipped beyond government control. It was all very well for the Pilgrim leader to observe (1642) that all sins were discoverable "by due search, inquisition and due punishment" by the churches and the magistrates. Almost a century later (1716), a New York Puritan community complained of many moral crimes openly committed because churches and courts were weak and ecclesiastical law had not taken hold in the colonies. Everywhere unclear jurisdictions, minimal penalties, and slack enforcement drained away the effect of statutes, no matter how frequently reenacted. Prosecutions for offenses of no particular immediate harm to the whole community declined.[35]

No one denied the utility, in cities, of ordinances to keep streets free of dirt and ordures, or to limit the places where flax and hemp could be washed; few obeyed or even suffered neighborly criticism for the failure. It was somewhat unusual when, in the interest of decorum, the Accomack County Court, Virginia, in 1634 fined John Davis and Thomas Allen one shilling each for swearing in court. The people in attendance may thereafter have smoothed the rough language; or, more probably, the bench became accustomed to it.[36]

Limited success in some matters did not inhibit legislation in others, even in those touching the most intimate aspects of behavior. New Hampshire in 1648 forbade men to deform themselves by wearing their hair long "after the manner of ruffians and barberous Indians" and contrary to God's word. Rhode Island gave the towns power (1729) to regulate Indian dances, which led to excessive drinking and fighting and wounding each other—and also enticed servants to outstay their time or to run away from their masters.[37]

More determined efforts aimed to control gambling and to ban Sunday labor. The hazards of daily existence, the insecurities of the environment, augmented the propensity to risks the settlers brought with them. Lotteries, raffles, and casting dice were not only amusements but also fund-raising alternatives to taxation and ways of disposing of goods. The ill effects were particularly evident in the south, where horse racing and cockfighting were endemic and where people bet on anything, so long as another party took up the challenge. The frequent violence, the large stakes, the occasional willingness to mortgage whole estates, and the loss of time and wages, encouraged efforts to regulate some side effects.[38]

A 1740 Virginia statute, incorporating earlier legislation, attempted to limit losses in betting on horse races and cockfighting and also outlawed cards and dice in ordinaries, leaving patrons only the consolation of backgammon. The law also impeded collection of large gambling debts in the hope of thus diminishing the attractiveness of betting. Mortgages and securities of more than ten pounds won in a game were to revert to the original heir or grantor; and professional gamblers who lived luxuriously without visible means of support could be called to account by the courts.[39]

In the north the Puritans had always regarded gambling as an unwarranted trespass on God's will. Plymouth flatly outlawed cards, dice, and games of Cros and Pile (1672); and the plea that he was only a beginner and the card party but a means to drive away his wife's melancholy did not spare John Henryson a substantial fine (1662). Nevertheless, lotteries sprouted when traders discovered they could augment the value of their merchandise by selling tickets that entitled the winner to specific goods at a reduced price. Though gambling was illegal, people left their occupations and risked their savings on the chance of success. Tumultuous assemblies and riots occasioned by drawings in private houses in New Haven and elsewhere persuaded the Connecticut governor and council (1728) to issue a proclamation against lotteries. Although New York City had considered the lottery a more equitable way of raising money than a property tax (1746), opinions changed in 1760, when it discovered the inflated prices of goods thus sold and that slaves, servants, and children, eager to take a chance, robbed parents and masters to obtain the price of a ticket.[40]

Sunday labor caused more grief, especially for New Englanders. The Fourth Commandment imposed a categorical obligation on all; whoever disregarded the clear text of Scripture sinned and polluted the whole community. Yet to impose the Puritan concept of rest on converted and unconverted alike required a modification of European habits of recreation and also occasionally economic sacrifices. Many inhabitants of Westerly, Rhode Island, worked on the First Day and otherwise profaned it —a great offense to the observant, bringing "odium upon the whole government." Yet the colony could only ask them to reform, begging them to consider that they must be subject to the ordinance for the Lord's sake, whatever their private beliefs. Elsewhere a firm public posture did not prevent evasions from cropping up again and again; and magistrates slipped into leniency when the offenders were otherwise respectable.[41]

Licensing provided some leverage in the effort to control intoxication. No one in Europe or America questioned the benefits of moderate drinking for medicinal purposes as well as for conviviality. The unpalatable water drove the Old World English to ale and wine. A traveler in 1635 found the Fen people full of unwholesome sack, which they held convenient and necessary to avoid the devilish stinging of their humming gnats. He judged those he met "halfe fish, halfe flesh, for they drinke like fishes and sleep like hogges." Alcohol enabled colonists to bear aches and pains, and to forget themselves and their problems.[42]

The governing authorities however feared the uncontrollable results of the loss of rationality. In times of war, endemic in the colonies, a tippling population endangered security. Legislation aimed to control behavior in accord with the norms of acceptable social intercourse. But in a wilderness society with norms undefined, the constant reenactment of those laws exposed their futility.

The legal definition of drunkenness was simple—"where the same legs which carry a man into the house cannot bring him out again." Plymouth judged intoxicated anyone who lisped or slurred his speech, staggered in his walk, vomited, or was unable to perform his craft (1672). Anyone who reeled to and fro, the Puritans believed, lost self-control and reverted to a savage state on the level of the Indians, whose quickly developed taste for firewater bore grievous results for themselves and for their neighbors.[43]

The amount of legislation on the subject everywhere indicated that some intoxication was the normal state of many colonists much of the time. The water was as bad as in England and the gnats as ferocious. From the highest level of society to the lowest, some people lost themselves in drink, inventing excuses for perpetual intoxication or for displaying the symptoms thereof. Stephen Kellog ascribed his condition on one occasion to the crazy state of his stomach, on another to his talking somewhat briskly (1714). In Virginia common knowledge had it that Mrs. James Blair, wife of the powerful commissary, was usually in the cups, which her family explained as "consolation." Doctor Thomas Spry, hauled before the New Castle court for abusing Captain John Colier (1677), claimed not to remember having done any of the things charged against him because "hee was verry mutch overcome with drinke." The New Castle people accepted this mitigating circumstance, as did justices elsewhere.[44]

Crimes blamed on alcohol frightened authorities with the specter of an uncontrollable population. The grape was God's gift, designed to gladden the heart of man; but sinful people overdid a good thing. The drinking of toasts in 1639 had become an occasion for waste and sins such as "drunkenness, quarreling, bloudshed, uncleannes, mispense of precious time." Refusing to tolerate those "knowne evills," Massachusetts that year forbade the practice. The law remained on the books for nine years, then was repealed, probably because few paid it any heed.[45]

Licensing could limit the pernicious social results of the sale of alcohol, a highly profitable and easy way of making a living. Numerous taverns sprouted along the highways and around the ports, while many householders turned to brewing as a profitable sideline. Already in 1648 Peter Stuyvesant noted the attraction of these pursuits to people who preferred quick returns to the back-breaking labor of tilling the soil. One quarter of the New Amsterdam houses that year, he estimated, became taverns for the sale of brandy, tobacco, and beer; and many inhabitants, at the back doors of their homes, away from watchful eyes, sold cheap adulterated alcohol at exorbitant prices to the Indians for valuable pelts. Fraud, smuggling, and cheating were unwelcome by-products, along with neglect of handicrafts, corrupt servants and laborers, and a debauched younger generation.

The choleric governor may have exaggerated. But he was not alone. A century later, Benjamin Franklin served on a Philadelphia grand jury that protested against the excessive number of tippling houses, little better than nurseries of vice and debauchery. In all the colonies, through the intervening years, complaints about disorderly behavior in inns, and charges that home brewing increased the scarcity of corn and encouraged violence among the Indians drove authorities to use licensing as a means of control, as it had been in England. Regulations in New Amsterdam, in Massachusetts, and elsewhere provided that only upstanding, honest inhabitants, presenting certificates of good behavior, receive licenses to run a limited number of taverns. The law set the hours they were to remain open, as well as the amount of liquor customers could drink, strictly enforced Sunday closings, and prohibited sales to Indians. In a flush of enthusiasm, the ordinances also confined home brewing to home consumption, leaving nothing for trade. Days of public celebration called for particular watchfulness, for the amount of alcohol then consumed frequently left many reeling in the streets.

The statutes on the books notwithstanding, policing the taverns proved impossible, for customers joined the owners in resenting unwarranted intrusion into their affairs and unjustified efforts to limit profits. Quite respectable folk—a tithingman in Massachusetts, two justices of the peace in Pennsylvania—were among those who disregarded the licensing laws. Private houses became happy drinking clubs—only for social purposes, their owners claimed when caught. Dancing, jumping, disorderly entertainments, hair pulling, eye gouging, fights, and bloodshed were the results. Sunday in New Amsterdam, a day particularly favored for drinking, brought the preacher an intoxicated congregation oblivious to the word of God. Traditionally on New Year's and May Day all restraint relaxed, and the beating of drums, firing of guns, carousing, and maypoling accompanied the consumption of alcohol. Efforts to outlaw these and other popular customs, such as Riding the Goose, had little effect, thwarted by people determined to have their own way. Later complications followed upon interference from London, as when the crown disallowed a Pennsylvania act against riotous games because it restrained Her Majesty's subjects from innocent sports and diversions.[46]

Despite its limited utility in regulating behavior, the colonists continued in the recourse to licensing—the only means of assuring controlled services, which had the additional merit of providing exclusive privileges to those the government wished to favor: not only an influential local character like Samuel Marshfield of Springfield, juror, clerk of the train band, and deputy to the General Court, but also Susannah Wood of New York, being an object of charity. Then, too, licensing might prevent cheats from adulterating the beer with mixtures of dirt and filth.[47]

As the number of practitioners in each craft and trade expanded, communities set up guidelines, occasional price tables, and standards of production as protection against fraud and other unscrupulous practices. No guilds performed that task, as in the Old World. Frequent lawsuits occasioned by the "no cure, no pay" maxim for medicine thus forced colonial governments into closer surveillance. In time of war, when the surgeons' business soared, printed lists set the maximum payment for each treatment. When a dispute called for professional evaluation, the court required expert testimony. Jacob Schellinger, although he managed to walk from one village to another, refused to deliver the kettle promised

Aldart Swartout for healing his leg. Swartout sued and the court asked two experienced surgeons to pass upon the case. In 1657 New Amsterdam required all surgeons to report patients wounded in altercations, in effect becoming agents of community surveillance.[48]

A 1716 New York statute prescribed the duties and the oath of midwives—not to charge more than was customary, to be equally helpful to the poor and the rich, to prevent the concealment of bastard children, and to ensure that the father's name was known. To protect inhabitants from environmental hazards, Massachusetts in 1755 appointed a committee to regulate the sale of drugs and poisons by apothecaries and other dealers in dangerous substances. Unable to find better methods of guarding against inferior merchandise, the province turned to the traditional self-policing guilds when complaints about shoddy work spread in Boston. The House of Representatives authorized the formation of shoemakers' and coopers' guilds to ensure that only properly trained people could practice the trade, with the caution not to abuse their monopolies by unreasonable prices.[49]

Bread—the staff of life—was of all commodities most likely to touch popular sensitivities, and particularly in urban centers where people bought it rather than made it at home. Communities gave close attention to bakers, corresponding to their importance in daily life. Thus New Amsterdam and later New York regularly fixed the assize of bread to take account of fluctuations in supplies of raw materials and in demand. Reluctance to rely entirely on market forces led to regulation of content, weight, and price. Compliance was largely voluntary, and—as frequent court cases showed—was not always forthcoming. As early as 1639, Massachusetts admonished John Stone and his wife to bake bigger loaves; and in 1652 the clerks of the markets sent to check weights met the bland excuse that everything they found was for home use and not for sale.[50]

In New Netherland, the problem became more acute when Indians developed a taste for white bread; bakers then sold to them for inflated prices with the result in Fort Orange (1654) that Christian "plain and common people . . . must eat the bran while the savages eat the flour." Rather than alter the practice, the bakers the next year complained that there was too much competition and suggested forming a guild, which the New Amsterdam court refused.[51] It also forbade bakers to sweeten their breads, hoping thus to make them less palatable to the Indians. Vigilant observers nevertheless soon saw tribesmen carrying sweet buns, while local inhabitants were short weighted. Those dependent on bought bread also discovered that bakers varied their practices with the season, turning out little cakes and light white loaves in the summer for Indians and transients, while in the winter, when these customers were elsewhere, baking stopped entirely. In any case, those little cakes used up precious flour not available to the settlers. In response to complaints, the authorities in 1658 refused to license for the summer those who did not accommodate public needs in the winter, and ordered all to bake coarse and white bread twice a week, according to regulation. Repeated ordinances designed to cure the same problems and occasional bread riots revealed how little effect the legislation had.[52]

Available power could not cope with determined defiance; and simple neighborliness ran thin when proximity to the wilderness and uncertainty about status rubbed away conventional manners. Jochem Becker, a Fort Orange baker, was thirty-eight years old when repeated conflicts with his neighbor Jan van Hoesem attracted attention (1653). Ordered to remove a pigsty from opposite Jan's door, Jochem used abusive language, assaulted Magistrate Volckert Jansz, and sued his enemy for trespass. Ordered to remove his lumber from a public road, Jochem complained that the van Hoesem family threw hot ashes against his clapboards. Meanwhile he refused to pay fines or remove the offensive pigpen, insulted the authorities, chased away nesting chickens about to lay, and got into a drunken fight. Somewhat later he testified that Indians got drunk at the van Hoesem home, and was himself accused of selling a barrel of beer to a tribesman. Within the same year he was in court again: in a mass brawl he wound up atop Gerrit Slechtenhorst, tugging at his genitals "in a scandalous way, causing him to yell and scream." Uninhibited, Becker complained about the fire hazard posed by the straw roof of another neighbor, and he faced the problems of others in his valued trade. Then too his wife, Geertruyt, had to pay a fine of six guilders for slander, physical assault, and abusive language. Yet the community could not do without the services of a baker, even Becker.[53]

Edward Colcord of Hampton, New Hampshire, had no such valuable skill, yet for years made his neighbors miserable by vexatious suits, fraud, cheating, and reviling, just within the limits of the law. He created discord, swore falsely, always looked for his own advantage and eluded prosecution by "fair speeches . . . subtile contrivances and underhand practices." After slandering magistrates, he fled and briefly left the town at peace. But no other place would keep him for long. He returned to

Hampton, for a while seemed a reformed character. But "a man habituated to all manner of wickedness" was not so easily reclaimed. He once more reverted to his previous ways and "vilified the chiefest of our magistrates," then spent time in jail. Only his death (1682) brought relief to his battered wife, children, and neighbors.[54]

The temptation to ascribe all problems to outsiders could not stand in the face of experience with Becker and Colcord. Yet hard-pressed officials directed their attention above all to wanderers subject to the discipline of no church or household. Once the wilderness had been tamed and travel eased, people born in America and familiar with its ways, yet responsible to no one, became a threat. The Massachusetts General Court, aware of the increase of profanity and irreligion by reason of the vagrant life of persons who wandered from town to town, apart from families and relations, thereby drawing away children, servants, and others from their lawful callings and hardening the hearts of one another against God's holy word, condemned such persons to corporal punishment or the house of correction. Idle and disorderly persons without visible estates or employments also troubled Virginia (1727). They wandered from one county to another, paying no taxes and leaving their wives and children without support to become burdens to the parish. Moreover divers lewd women being got with bastards refused to reveal the fathers. The ingrained fear of strangers explained the panic caused by the appearance in 1755 of several shiploads of neutral French from Nova Scotia, perhaps to claim residence in New England.[55]

Alas, strangers were not wholly to blame. Misbehavior spread from within, with each successive native generation less restrained than its predecessor. Manners deteriorated with distance from the Old World and more frequent rudeness required correction. The colonists found ample European precedent for the regulation of behavior private and public. Objections in England to making and selling a drink called coffee, which annoyed neighbors by its evil smell and made men unfruitful, never led to a ban. But controls over places of entertainment were otherwise common and provided models for regulations in America. Applied to open spectacles, the rules had some effect. Captain Wing thus learned it was unlawful to let a room fitted with seats to a man to show tricks in at Castle Tavern (1687). Personal behavior, however, slipped out of reach once the settlements moved beyond the forced intimacy of the early days. The tithingmen, designated in each neighborhood of a Massachusetts town to keep watch over the morals of ten families, proved unpopular from the start; few wished to take the unpleasant office, with its potential for quarrels and slander suits; and before long the idea vanished. Eighteenth-century grand juries therefore repeatedly and unavailingly complained about the low state of civil morality.[56] Legislators, ever sensible to the increase of profanity, especially among the younger generation who met together in places of public entertainment and corrupted one another by wanton behavior, rudely singing and making noise, sternly but vainly forbade such disorders (1684).[57]

The maintenance of order was everywhere a problem—even in church. It should not have been necessary, but was, in Puritan Watertown (1640) to fine any person who suffered his dog to come to meeting on the Lord's day. Later, in Virginia bold worshipers took "the liberty to place themselves" in any seat or pew they chose, so that the vestry had to threaten them with punishment as disorderly persons.[58]

The proliferation of regulations produced no corresponding improvement in behavior or resolution of conflicts. Wise—or at least cautious—magistrates, aware of the fragility of their power, sought alternatives to confrontation, ways of attaining social ends without the use of force. The people in control of town, vestry, or county could employ one instrument or another to achieve their goals—so long as they did so with the implied or express consent of the populace.

The constable and the sheriff knew how little they could do as individuals; by raising a hue and cry or posse they could summon aid—if the community wished to respond. The obedience of the train band or militia, the organized local body wielding force, was contingent upon local approval of the purpose of its use. The law required all males aged eighteen to sixty, with certain exceptions, to serve or pay for a substitute; but evasion was common. In any case the officers who gave the orders were men who commanded local respect. For a time, the manner of selecting officers, whether by election or appointment by the governor, was a subject of dispute. In the end, it did not matter. Virginia, on the one hand, recognized "some truly noble spirits" who associated themselves as a company (1756); and, on the other, required that all officers be residents of the county from which they would be commissioned (1757), that is, the people in control, so that the militia tended to become a voluntary association.[59]

Awareness of where power rested lent flexibility to the mode of doing justice. The opinion of the justice or commissioner had almost the same validity when rendered on the bench or off it. Since litigation was in any case heavy, costly, and time consuming, alternatives to the courts were attractive. The people who accepted the Dedham covenant, for instance, undertook to refer all disputes for resolution to "one, two or three of the society." A generation later in New York, the parties to a difference chose their "trusty and well beloved friends and nayghboures" arbitrators to review all the accounts and arrive at a binding decision, with the proviso that the arbitrators, if unable to agree, would choose an umpire with power to render a definitive sentence. Rhode Island and the other colonies formally and informally relied upon similar procedures. It made sense to consult the opinion of community representatives, the same types that would sit upon juries in more regular procedures. Local people the equals of the litigants were best able to decide the issue in dispute. Besides, arbitration offered the possibility of compromise that would avoid the expense and trouble of summoning witnesses. Some such hope moved William Pynchon to suggest arbitration after a quarrel between the Springfield minister George Moxon and John Woodcock— who enjoyed laughing in sermon time—dragged its way through the courts (1639). So too, informal methods replaced more cumbersome formal ones in minor criminal cases, as in reliance upon informers.[60]

Since taxation always evoked resistance, the colonists preferred to achieve worthy social goals through alternatives that drew upon voluntary rather than compulsory financial support. Mrs. Ruth Atwater thus gave New Haven £16, the interest to help defray town expenses. Civil government bore the obligation "carefully to protect the poor laborious and industrious part of Mankind" who composed the body of any people, not only out of compassion and Christian duty, but also to fend off the utopian charge that property was but a conspiracy of the rich (1722). However, British precedent was an uncertain guide for colonial response. The Reformation and the dissolution of the monasteries deprived England of the network of hospitals and refuges that served France; and the marked reluctance to expend government funds created a disposition to depend upon philanthropic endowments, with most of the money coming from the cities.[61]

The settlers wished to follow the mother country's course. But all too often the taxpayers felt demands on the public purse. Gifts spared the localities the difficult choice between paying for relative generosity and the hardened hearts of economy.

The general term *poor* comprehended various categories of persons not members of a self-sustaining household. Those rendered dependent by old age sometimes wished no more than exemption from taxation. In Hampton, New Hampshire, several above the age of seventy, "being past labor and work," thus asked for that token of "tender respect to the decrepit" characteristic of civilized nations (1683). New Haven did remit the town rates of John Brooks (1692), who nevertheless became a charge upon the town by reason of age and impotency, as did Joseph Wooden, whose land had already been sold off (1701). Extraordinary crises also evoked sympathetic responses—veterans injured in war, crops ruined by untimely frost (1726), and a family seized by the smallpox (1732).[62]

Funds expended for these purposes drained away meager public resources and in the end came out of taxes, grudgingly voted. Many a town, like Duxbury (1747), simply preferred to evade the issue without voting upon it. But there was no evading some problems—like custody of Mary Pearson's bastard child, or Sarah Pittman's. The authorities tried to induce some functioning family to take in the orphans and the incompetent, if need be with the inducement of a payment from town or parish funds, driving as hard a bargain as possible.[63]

Dependent persons created annoying problems. It was all very well to protect illiterates and tuck a madman away in a prison; but towns bitterly resisted open-ended obligations to support idiot children, and they used the residence laws to protect themselves against strangers likely to become charges on the public. Many a feud erupted over the attempt of one place to warn out the natives of another.[64]

Ingenious expedients aimed to reduce costs. New York gladly paid the forty shillings' passage to get Mrs. Susannah Rose out of the country —she being old, sick, weak, and an object of charity (1726). Persistently the hope flickered that a well-conducted almshouse or workhouse and house of correction would eliminate cheating and set the ablebodies to earning their keep. Philadelphia (1735), New York (1734), and Virginia (1755) were among the places that made the effort.[65]

Meager financial resources and the feeble sanctions available at any level of government justified the disposition to leave as much as possible to voluntary action. Self-constituted groups could undertake at their own initiative and expense what the state could do only with difficulty and divisive controversy. Religious, educational, and economic institutions formed in this fashion acquired increasing importance in the eighteenth century.

Churches established by law had a claim to support by taxation, but could not count on it. Difficulties in collection left the ministers and buildings alike shabby. Yet these were recognized legal entities with a right to accept and hold property. Generous donors came to the rescue sometimes in bequests, sometimes through gifts and services that earned individuals and families the recognition of prominent pews.[66]

The status of dissenting sects, however, was far from clear. Quakers and Jews had had some European experience in handling their affairs, either through privileges accorded them by the state or through trustees who managed matters for them. In the colonies they gained open, public recognition; and the meeting or congregation acted as a quasi-corporate association. By 1688, wills were leaving land and money to Quaker meetinghouses in Virginia. Other groups also adopted voluntary forms of organization, including some orthodox Congregationalists; Cotton Mather, for instance, encouraged the formation of various religious societies to nourish both piety and good works in the world. Mather's influential *Bonifacius* (1710) suggested that associations to do good could reform manners, correct evils, and relieve the poor and needy, ideas that in time moved many.[67]

Education, like other cultural activities, lay in a shadow territory, supported in Europe sometimes by royal or aristocratic patronage, sometimes by legacies for endowment, sometimes by religious bodies, and sometimes by government funds. The colonies shied away from taxation. Few towns, even in New England, heeded the requirement that each support a school; and although Harvard, Yale, and William and Mary received charters of sorts, they languished for lack of financial aid. At best hard-pressed legislatures handed over tax exemptions and an occasional privilege. Free grammar schools depended on endowments or on bequests —as in the case of that named for Benjamin Symmes. Behind every such institution stood a voluntary association of interested individuals. Nor did aspirations for town libraries come to anything until Benjamin Franklin bustled about and collected some of his friends in the Library Company of Philadelphia (1731), a model thereafter imitated by Newport's Redwood Library.[68]

Once translated into action, the idea spread. Associations of many sorts proliferated in the cities: so much simpler, in a society that depended upon the cumbersome mechanisms of consent, to bring the like-minded voluntarily together, in a commitment specific rather than general and integral. A person who joined for one purpose did not thereby become entangled in multiple obligations, and members could come from various religious and ethnic backgrounds, considerations of some importance in pluralistic communities with heterogeneous populations.

English models stimulated some organizations, as in the case of the Society for Promotion of Useful Knowledge, Philadelphia, modeled on the Royal Society of London. Others bore an American aspect—the Scots Society and the Hungarian Club of New York, founded for good-mannered conviviality. Mutual aid, the relief of members or their widows who suffered misfortune or losses, in Boston drew together the Scots Charitable, the Boston Episcopal, the Charitable Irish, and the Marine Society. Dr. Thomas Bond and Benjamin Franklin joined in creating an asylum for the insane and the poor in Philadelphia, hoping for legislative help (1751) but resolved to proceed in any case.[69]

Association provided a way out of situations in which lack of money and power rendered government helpless. No one liked it when New York's mayor in 1677 simply ordered people on six streets to dig public wells at their own cost. But water was a necessity, as were highways, wharfs, and facilities for transacting business. When the state did not do what needed doing, individuals found other ways of providing service. Norfolk, Virginia, vainly fussed with proposals to build a wharf until thirty-five men put up the money to form a company to erect it. No one questioned the importance of roads in the country, streets in town; and cumbersome arrangements aimed to get them built. But rather than wait for action by the province or county, subscribers enabled John Dalley of Kingston, New Jersey, to survey and mark out the road from Trenton to Perth Amboy (1745) and ultimately to extend his efforts to Philadelphia and New York. Colonial cities, fearful of fire, depended on volunteer companies to deal with the danger.

Associations of the same sort confronted economic problems. Subscribers formed manufacturing societies to encourage industry. Groups of merchants got together informally to insure their ships. The impediments the royal government put in the way of banks and paper money for years led to a search for alternatives. Early proposals in Boston (1687) for a voluntary association to issue bills of credit to circulate as currency came to nothing. But the New London Society for Trade and Commerce (1736), having secured a charter, proceeded to do so until the province, worried about its credit, cut the activity short. Meanwhile various expedients made loans available, as when the South Carolina Vestry of St. Thomas advertised that it had several thousand pounds to let out.[70]

Ways of action that evaded the rigidities of the law and avoided the necessity for taxes were at hand in abundance. Based not on abstract theory, they involved no distinction of spheres between governmental and nongovernmental activity. A public interest imbued them all, and a pragmatic choice fixed on the most appropriate means. Municipalities and counties shifted back and forth between voluntary and paid services, as convenience and opportunity dictated.[71]

It hardly mattered. The people who controlled local government were the same as those who formed the cooperative societies that widened the space within which they could maneuver in dealings with governors and other royal officials in London and the colonies. The idea of an overarching common interest in the commonwealth did not fade; it acquired new means of implementation.

The colonists then were in the position described by a later poet who imagined the confusion of a seventeenth-century character. Lord Chandos had once conceived the whole of existence as one great unit that he could grasp by a single handle, then discovered that everything disintegrated into parts, those parts again into parts, so that a single idea no longer encompassed anything. So the colonists, having come with and never having surrendered the belief in an all-encompassing, integrated community, found it crumble into fragments, each stronger than the whole.

For the poet, the discovery brought a sense of annihilation and despair. But for the Americans it brought a sense of amplitude and opportunity. Having come so far and endured so much, having grasped the opportunities of space, having learned to condition consent on their own decisions and interests, the survivors did not fit comfortably within the cramped confines of integrated communities. The same people who continued to long for a secure and orderly whole also valued the ability to choose and repeatedly kicked away uncomfortable restraints. Meanwhile experience and necessity developed other ways of acting in groups, not as whole bodies, but as voluntary associations of individuals.[72]

V

CHURCH AND CONSCIENCE,

1600–1760

IN SEVENTEENTH-CENTURY EUROPE the church had supplied much of the cement that held communities together. Religion was central to personal life. In every reckoning the balance was clear: a transitory earthly existence had little worth as against the eternal span of heaven or hell. Few incidents of everyday existence lacked an accompanying prayer or ritual; birth, marriage, and death, the sailing of a ship and the sealing of a contract, the acts of sowing and reaping brought thoughts and actions into alignment with revealed faith.

Almost everywhere in that weary old continent, for many decades past, martyrdoms earned on thousands of scaffolds, pyres, and execution blocks, and many more victims of enraged mobs or furious armies, called for remembrance and deepened the beliefs in the name of which rivers of blood had flowed. Disputes over the meaning of God's words were far from over in 1600; but already men and women loaded them with so heavy an explanatory burden that few could risk loosening their hold, lest they lose all means of understanding the legacy of the past, the promise of the future, and the intimate course of their own lives.

Yet early in the seventeenth century religious life in America diverged significantly from that in Europe, and continued to do so thereafter. The process dissolved a vital component of the integrated community.

The people who migrated to the New World brought with them faiths, modes of worship, and understandings of the universe shaped across

113

the Atlantic. Religious concerns pervaded all the colonies, although with particular intensity in Puritan New England; for all the settlers had left societies in which communal life depended on intimate associations with the churches. Religious establishment in Europe was more than legal, more than a product of the relationship to the state. True, governments continued to provide support, through privileges and financial aid and through the definition of correct doctrine and rite; on into the seventeenth century, force remained a recognized means of effecting conversions and ensuring appropriate beliefs and behaviors. But establishment meant more than formal status. It involved also integration with the lives of burdened people whom religion furnished an explanation for life's trials that reached back to the world's creation and looked forward to its redemption; faith to them spoke in the vernacular through folktales and miracles as well as through the holy words of gospel and pulpit.[1]

The total identification of church and community bound individuals together with their neighbors. Since everybody belonged by birth and since every activity had a sacred aspect, any participation in the community required involvement in its religious life. The church defined norms and provided sanctions, supported by tradition, for all personal and social activities. Its counsel of acceptance eased the pain of intolerable but inescapable exactions. When the extortionate prince demanded more tribute than the householder could afford, the English Puritan warned,

> See thou paye it him for Goddes sake,
> Whose officers al princes are.

Similar injunctions helped maintain family discipline and social and political values and preserved group solidarity. Rural villages in which the priest alone had a smattering of learning welcomed his advice or intervention. And threats of eternal damnation invoked against criminals reinforced man-made laws. "If the pulpits teach not obedience," said Charles I, "the King will have but small comfort of the militia."[2]

Conversely, the community supported the church. Lines of religious authority ran off to distant sources—Rome, Westminster, or Amsterdam; and ceremonies of ordination and consecration recognized those ties. But in a practical sense, the church needed and enjoyed local support. It survived from rents for its lands, from tithes, fees, and taxes. Establishment therefore grew out of the relationship with the community and not simply by imposition from without. The medieval church, though universal, was also particular, recognizing saints and saint's days attached to specific places, so that immense variations set apart Ireland and Poland, or southern and northern France; and the Reformation stimulated these tendencies, except where the state attempted to bind a whole realm into a national church.

Heresy introduced a discordant element, not for the ideas from which it sprang but for the acts to which it led. Variations of belief had only marginal importance in village or town life, for churches absorbed intellectual differences without excessive conflict. Nor did diversity in itself create a problem; it mattered little what passed through the minds of Jews or Gypsies or Turks or other foreigners. It mattered scarcely more what thoughts or visions occupied an occasional shepherd or miller, craftsman or peasant. Clerics tolerated the presence of known witches and the persistence of popular beliefs incompatible with Christian doctrine. Agnes Simpson, matronly, dignified, intelligent, did not strain the credulity of her auditors in England when she described the conventicles in which she and other worshipers kissed the buttocks of the Devil. Every word of the followers of Satan excited James I, whose *Daemonologie* (1597) summed up existing wisdom. What was important was the departure not from articles of faith, but from ways of acting. The authorities had extirpated heresy that affected behavior not because it questioned beliefs but because it was disruptive, undermining the unity of the church and community.[3]

The Reformation actively involved the state in these decisions. The subsequent religious and political settlements of the sixteenth and seventeenth centuries left residues of tension in western Europe. In England the Act of Supremacy (1534) proclaimed the king head of the Anglican church, while the Tudor settlement generally expanded the role of government so that it supervised ecclesiastical courts, punished religious offenses, convicted of treason Catholic priests who said Mass, made attendance at worship compulsory, and used the parish as the basic political unit. Supremacy over the national church also gave the monarch the right to designate the upper ecclesiastical officials. The seventeenth-century assertion of parliamentary power still left the church subject to the state.[4]

Disquiet at the outcome accounted for the reformed concept of a church, one of the central features of Puritanism. Rejecting the view that all residents were members, the Puritans who migrated insisted that only the elect, the saints predestined for salvation, had a right to covenant with one another to form a church. The proper organization of society required recognition of the distinction between the sinners and the saints, who would appropriately control the whole community.

Although Calvinism took hold in England and elsewhere in Europe, corruption in religion and government prevented the Puritans from altering established institutions. The lack of political power compelled them to withdraw from the church as it was, to establish the church as it should be. As long as they remained in England, they could not avoid some degree of separatism. Unwilling to continue as a covert minority, many turned to colonization, hoping to resolve by migration the tensions that existed in England. A new society, redefined according to their own ideas, would allow them to manage church and community in accord with God's will.

Migration did not alter the conception of religion's relationship to the state, whether the destination was Virginia or Plymouth. The colonists still assumed an identity of church and community, with the former setting the norms and purposes of social action. "The divine service with its ceremony," wrote Johan Printz, was held in New "just as in Old Sweden, in the good old Swedish language" and with the pastor bedecked in chasuble. Tolerance did not impute parity to truth and error; and few seventeenth-century people relinquished the idea that only threats of hell would assure obedience to the law. William Harris exhausted the patience of Roger Williams, the most permissive of clergymen, with "atheistical denying of heaven and hell," and a willingness to use any means for his own ends (1679).[5]

In the New World unexpected conflicts modified the practices if not the concept of establishment. The temptations of space and the need for labor brought together different types of people, of diverse religious persuasions. In the effort to develop trade and to stimulate growth, Virginia early on tried to import settlers with useful skills or at least muscles, of whatever origin, holding whatever beliefs. So too, the local authorities in New Netherland protested that efforts from back home to limit migration to communicants of the Reformed Church would damage the colony's economic future. A little later, the Dutch West India Company in Amsterdam reversed Governor Peter Stuyvesant's attempt to prevent Jews from entering.[6]

The important business of settlement and expansion encouraged a welcome for everyone willing to work. Variations of belief and practice diminished in importance as long as the new arrivals contributed to growth. Establishment persisted, but people could choose where to worship and how; they set up churches without hindrance from the authorities; and that subtly subverted the identification of any particular one with the community.

Then, too, the simple forces of negligence and self-interest intruded in the wilderness. In rural Virginia, the churchwardens reluctantly tried to obey an order to distrain upon the goods and chattels of inhabitants who failed to support the minister, in accord with an act of the General Grand Assembly (1632). A year later the minister still complained of laxity in collections; and the wardens pleaded helplessness because recalcitrants simply tore up the warrants executed upon them. Two years later the complaint dealt with the building of a parsonage the assembly ordered, referred first to the county court and then to the vestry, which however had yet to be appointed. Even in the absence of conflict, the New World raised troubling questions. The fees and duties of the parish clerk and minister who buried the dead at a distance from the church thus required adjustment, lest the bereaved managed to do without their services.[7]

The passage of time and the advance in civility only altered, but did not end, the difficulties. Certainly Williamsburg's Bruton Parish Church (1715) flaunted, for the place, a kind of splendor, with an elevated canopied pew for the governor, his name inscribed in gilt letters; and St. Paul's in frontier Hanover County built a new gallery for the gentlemen justices and their families (1745), as well as ledges and kneeling boards. Still, untoward incidents erupted even in Bruton Parish, as when Colonel Daniel Parke dragged Mrs. James Blair out of a pew—perhaps because he did not know she was there by invitation, perhaps because her husband had preached a tough sermon on adultery, staring all through it at the colonel. It made less of a stir, indeed seemed quite usual, when a stranger in Westmoreland County (1715) found every one of the men in church smoking a pipe of tobacco.[8]

More serious difficulties arose with regard to control and finance. Queen Anne's attorney general (1703) ruled that English law governed the right of presentation to church benefices, so that the governor as representative of the sovereign had the right to induct and remove clergy; and a committee of Virginia ministers in 1714 thanked His Excellency Alexander Spotswood for having prevented local authorities from ousting them at pleasure as they had in the past. But when the parish dug in its heels and refused its consent and approbation, it also did not feel obliged to pay a salary until mollified. Nor did court orders help Amilius De Ringh when people simply refused to contribute to his maintenance as reader in the New Castle church (1675). Establishment everywhere created difficulties, for its underlying premise was support by a coherent, unified community wielding power.[9]

Peculiar ambiguities in Maryland and New York compounded the difficulties of establishment. Once Lord Baltimore perceived the impracticality of creating a Catholic refuge on the Chesapeake, he deemed it prudent to assent to an Act Concerning Religion that assured freedom of conscience to all Trinitarians as long as they did not conspire against the established civil government. The measure rested on no high principle, but rather on the ground that "the inforceing of the conscience in matters of Religion hath frequently fallen out to be of dangerous Consequence in those commonwealthes where it hath been practiced." Furthermore, the law punished blasphemy with death and forfeiture of all property, prohibited reproachful speeches concerning the Virgin Mary and the Holy Apostles, and proscribed epithets reviling the holders of any of seventeen named religious viewpoints. The Toleration Act also provided for fines or whippings for profanation of the Sabbath. Maryland was thus no haven for religious freedom; yet neither did it have a properly established church. No taxes supported the ministry and no obligation bound anyone to come to public worship. The number of churches was small and few residents attended regularly, not many even intermittently.[10]

In New York, settlement by the Netherlands and conquest by the English complicated old problems. Governor Kieft had accused the Reverend Evardus Bogardus of preaching while intoxicated and berating the chief magistrate as a child of the Devil (1645); the retort—cannons fired in front of the windows while the minister spoke—left hard feelings which did not subside with the change in sovereignty. After 1664, the Dutch classis, the governing body of the Reformed Church in Amsterdam, continued to provide guidance and to appoint ministers, who remained subject to its jurisdiction. The English inhabitants for a considerable period used the same building after the conclusion of the Dutch services. In addition, by 1682 Lutherans, Quakers, Jews, and Labadists (a quietist sect) met in organized groups, Dominie Henricus Selyns noted. These circumstances dulled the significance of establishment and continued to do so in the eighteenth century.[11]

New York law (1689) required public compensation of £100 for "a good and sufficient Protestant minister," which in England meant Anglican, but in the colony could mean a dissenter as well, a condition the governors could not alter. Some supporters of the Church of England indeed believed that it would have been better off without establishment, as in Pennsylvania and New Jersey. As it was, disputes over the appointment of clergy, location of meetinghouses, and the arrangement of pews required complicated negotiations. In addition, on Long Island ancient settlers transplanted from New England remained Puritans. In Jamaica they rioted, seized control of the church and parsonage for thirty years (1701–1731), and refused to pay taxes. The authorities could do nothing because the local magistrates and vestrymen were all dissenters. Discouraged after having buried two wives and several children in the course of the arduous struggle, the Episcopal minister finally resigned. The government also became entangled in the difficulties of other sects, as in the falling out between the consistory of the French church and the Reverend Louis Rou. It was hardly surprising that two justices of Queens County should have said (1702) that "sinfull men of the like passions as we" wrote the Scriptures and that religion was only an invention for the profit of the cunning. Sadly Samuel Seabury observed (1759) the progress of open infidelity, the hatred of the clergy, and the contempt for the sacraments in the province. Only an external disaster, as in the desecration of Trinity Church (1714), united New Yorkers in religion.[12]

Virginia and the Carolinas also lacked a central disciplinary element. The Church of England established there was episcopal. Yet there was no American bishop, hence no rite of confirmation, no diocese, hence no organization to regulate relations of ministers and parishioners. The remote bishop of London, nominally in charge, provided little guidance; and the Commissary James Blair was not an adequate substitute. The skimpy support provided by law was less important than the benefices, with the larger and richer parishes more likely than the poorer to increase income by marriages and funerals. Many clergymen never inducted into office served at the pleasure of the vestry; turned out from one parish, they could always move to another, so short was the supply. And often the colonists asked no questions about orthodoxy. John Lyford, who came to Plymouth a Puritan but couldn't keep his hands off the local maidens, left in haste for a post as Anglican minister in Virginia. With no sense of reverence for the house of God, people were as likely as not (1724) to conduct marriages, burials, baptism, and the churching of women from their homes.[13]

As a result, the missionaries sent by the Society for the Propagation of the Gospel encountered endless difficulties. Lacking a replacement for the Reverend Henry Gerrard, the church kept him at his post in North Carolina despite the scandal of his debauched practices (1706). James Adams complained to the SPG: drunks in the church brought the holy sacrament into contempt; masters refused instruction to their slaves; and a pillar of the church found guilty of fornication discredited the persuasion. Two years later the disheartened John Urmstone wrote of a miserable year plagued by illness and starvation, living on dry crust and salt water. He could not preach to people who preferred drunken orgies; nor could he deal with a vestry that met in the inn where rum was their chief business. Since the key was usually lost, the chapel door remained open so that it provided shade in summer and warmth in winter for pigs and cattle, who left dung and nastiness as evidence of their occupancy.[14]

The realities of life in Carolina or even Virginia did not match the expectations of men trained for an English vicarage. William Byrd observed in the 1720s that North Carolinians, the least troubled with religious fumes of any people living, knew not Sunday from any other day, although they kept so many Sabbaths every week it made no difference. The priests sent by the SPG were either too lewd for them, or—what oftener happened—they too lewd for the priests. When poor Reverend Urmstone had to work hard with ax, hoe, and spade to dig his own garden with the help only of a sorry wench his wife brought from England, his neighbors shrugged; they expected no one to do well without first "having undergone the slavish part and learned to live independent of others." He could not understand why they should "think there is no difference between a Gentleman and a labourer."[15]

Urmstone was clearly not one for this country; he could get by in the summer like Indians and pigs by eating fruit from the trees, but then was afflicted with the flux for three months before his departure. An unfortunate temper, the SPG learned, was unsuitable to "the humors of the natural born people of America" who could only be won "by gentle methods." Yet Commissary Gideon Johnston feared (1712) that the ridiculous concessions of popular elections would always prevent the church from prospering. Nevertheless there as elsewhere, for want of an alternative, the vestries kept on the likes of Richard Marsden, willing to serve without pay (1732), or even ministers guilty of debauched practices.[16]

The ever advancing frontier decade after decade created the old problem anew. Some Anglican ministers gladly served, like Anthony Gavin, a Spaniard by birth who arrived in Virginia in 1736. The scattered mountain people in his care had never seen a clergyman before, and he officiated in three churches and "seven places of service," doggedly traveling the more than twenty miles among them. And sometimes the commissary conceded a great improvement in himself from coming to America (1710). "I scarce knew what it was to be a minister before; but the strangeness and singularity" of the people "awakened my care and diligence to an uncommon degree."[17]

Such devotion was not common; and that left the field open to sects unsupported by the establishment. Into the space thus left there spread a variety of dissidents—"anythingarians," a dismayed Anglican called them. The "hotch potch made up of bankrupts, pirates," and sectaries of all sorts, possessed of strange notions and whims, had fallen into a comprehensive and latitudinarian way, not to be reasoned with. "That which gains most upon them is the appearance of a good life joyned with an obliging and condescending temper."[18] Quakers, denying the need for ordination, affirming that the inner light could strike any man or woman, were among the first in the field. Henry Phillips and his wife wept when William Edmundson stopped at their house on the Albemarle River in North Carolina (1672). They had not seen a Friend for seven years and hastily summoned a meeting from among people in the vicinity. Those who attended had little or no religion, for they sat smoking their pipes. But the Lord's testimony reached their hearts and several received the truth with gladness. Baptists, Presbyterians, and Methodists, eschewing establishment, also preached in the wilderness and won converts by reaching toward hearts.[19]

The Puritan colonies strongly resisted this tendency. Indiscriminate appeals to the heart were not the way to conversion. That migration had included an unusually large percentage of university graduates; and the ideal of a learned ministry always remained attractive. True, for a time plausible scamps also appeared. The court of Saco, Maine (1640), fined George Burdet, minister of Agamenticus "of ill name and fame, infamous for incontinency, a publisher and broacher of diverse dangerous speeches, the better to seduce the weaker sex," £10 for entertaining a certain Mary, £20 for a certain Ruth, both married matrons. A year later, Stephen Bachiler arrived in the neighborhood after having preached briefly in

Lynn, Ipswich, Newbury, and Hampton. Well into his seventies but vigorous, he abandoned his third wife in Saco and returned to England, where he took a fourth. Time and improved communications sifted the scoundrels out, although Hezekiah Usher (1689) still guarded his suspicions of ministers who sought out the favor and company of "the affectionate good Madams." Enthusiasm and appeals to the heart remained suspect, the credentials of learning more reliable in the absence of a hierarchy or even a synod to sift out error.[20]

Not the state but a covenant established the Puritan churches; and the minister as a party to the covenant entered upon a permanent relation with his flock. David Stearns thus served the town of Lunenberg for almost thirty years until his death, having taken the place vacated by Andrew Gardner, who resigned because there was not the affection "that there should be from a people to their gospell minister." The covenant created an all but autonomous congregation, free, John Cotton's "Moses His Judicials" explained, to celebrate days of fasting, prayer, and thanksgiving according to God's word and subject to no restraint in point of doctrine, worship, or discipline. But of course the civil authority could in its own way see that people observed the ordinances of Christ.[21]

The distinctions were not easily drawn. Plymouth in 1645 grew more slowly than other colonies and its relative influence consequently diminished. The radical proposal in court that year to allow and maintain toleration to all men who would abide by the law revealed the desire even in that staunch community to attract population in the interest of expansion. The governor considered the suggestion intolerable and refused to allow it to come to a vote, for diverse influences in the community would weaken the sense of common purpose and endanger control by the church. Take heed of variety in religion, John Davenport warned in 1661. "If Christians will break one from another, and churches break one from another," explained Thomas Shepard, Jr. (1668), "have we not cause to fear that God will suffer some wild boar or beast of the forest to enter in at the breaches and lay waste this vineyard, and turn it into a wilderness again." Thomas Gorges, who trumpeted the merits of liberty of conscience (1641), was one such wild boar. Yet the Puritan colonies could not permanently resist the appearance of strangers in order to preserve homogeneity. In vain Massachusetts explained that it was a corporation, the place of its cohabitation private property, so that "no man hath right to come in to us without our consent." In vain the General Court in 1654 ordered the notorious heretical and blasphemous books of Lodowicke

Mugleton and John Reeves burnt after the next lecture. In vain John Norton's *Heart of New England Rent* (1660) deplored the peril to the standing order from the assaults of Quakers, Baptists, and others. The threat persisted. Plymouth could not induce the Baptist Charles Chauncy to compromise on the issue of dipping, despite the inconvenience in a cold country; requested to leave, the Quakers refused to engage themselves to any certain time of departure, only that they would go "in the will of God ere long."[22]

The ultimate hazard, however, lay within. In stable communities intellectual differences were dangerous only when they led to deviant action. But congregational organization, lacking centralized control, exposed the Puritan churches to disruptive novelties. Each, subject to its own discipline, lacked defenses against internal division. The Dover, New Hampshire, people "soon fell into factions and strange confusions, one part taking upon them to excommunicate and punish the other" (1638). Strange ideas filtered in, the ordinary effect of pragmatic spirits under any popular government. The claim of each individual to hear God's voice personally and act upon his or her own conviction divided society and weakened the church as an instrument of discipline. Intolerance of dissent was consistent with the basic premises of the Puritan magistrates.[23]

Massachusetts confronted the issue in the mild form raised by Roger Williams, a sweet man who retained the friendship even of intellectual opponents. Since Puritans regarded universal attendance as their ultimate safeguard, Williams, a seeker, imperiled both church and commonwealth by insisting that genuine religion could flourish only with complete liberty. He ran into trouble in 1633 when he attacked the charter at just the time when royal officials threatened to invalidate it; and moreover did so by challenging the prevailing belief that land titles derived from the crown, arguing that they could come only by purchase from the Indians. The crisis passed when the General Court withheld a censure after Williams pledged his loyalty to the colony.

A more serious conflict erupted the next year when a Massachusetts statute required all freemen to swear to be true to the commonwealth and refrain from plots against it, in addition to a resident oath to submit to existing or subsequent laws and constitutions. Williams objected that the oaths put the godly in communion with the wicked and again attacked the charter. He also clashed with the ministers and magistrates over a law requiring everyone to worship publicly on the Lord's Day, which would, he feared, mix unredeemed natural men with the godly. The power of civil magistrates, Williams contended, extended only to breaches of the civil peace and to the individuals' relations to their fellows—obedience to constituted authority, covetousness, slander, theft, sexual wrongs, and murder. But duties to the Creator were beyond the power of the state to judge. One pungent declaration in his book, *The Bloudy Tenent of Persecution for Cause of Conscience,* expressed his entire attitude: "Forced worship stinks in God's nostrils." Massachusetts officials and ministers judged Williams' opinions erroneous and dangerous. But he stood firm. Unintimidated by the charge that he pitted his judgment against the elders and magistrates, he set a higher value on "one Scripture in the mouth of one simple Mechannick" than on the whole council. He thus threatened the colony's intellectual foundations. In October 1635 Massachusetts banished him.

Williams moved to Providence, where he defended his position in an exchange with John Cotton. Williams' *The Bloudy Tenent,* Cotton's *The Bloudy Tenent Washed in the White of the Lamb* (1647), and Williams' *The Bloudy Tenent Yet More Bloody* (1652), revolved about the question of whether the true Church of Christ could identify itself with any nation. Williams denounced Constantine as worse than Nero, for Christ finally fell asleep when the state recognized Christianity. Williams loathed all national ecclesiastical establishments, including the Roman and Anglican churches and also that of Massachusetts. He rejected both the Anglican view that the national church embraced everyone at birth, and the Congregational view that the covenant of visible saints constituted a church. Rather, he argued that individuals formed churches out of personal godliness after totally repenting false worship and separating from all pollutions. Having found no satisfaction in existing churches, he ceased to frequent any and worshiped in purity according to the light given him.

But he distinguished between voluntary withdrawal and involuntary civil banishment. Williams charged the Puritans with persecuting all consciences but their own. He opposed compulsory prayer because it combined church and state. God gave the ordinance of magistracy to preserve civil harmony; and temporal good required correction of "seducing teachers" and "scandalous livers." But while he insisted upon punishing those whose acts disturbed social order, he also wished to safeguard soul liberty against external restraint. The government that enforced public worship could also "enforce people to bee of no Religion at all." Religious truth, the gift of God, resulted from a hard search that civil authorities could not hasten without damaging consequences. Forced worship left the impression that religion was untrue and cruel and the state at fault when resistance to its violations of free conscience led to breaches of peace.[24]

The theologically touchy belief in the adequacy of faith alone for salvation erupted in the antinomian controversy of 1636. Anne Hutchinson, the central figure, was not the learned minister Williams was; disputes with her did not take the form convention dictated, and the special meetings in her home, outside the accepted structure of authority, threatened the church and the community.

Anne Hutchinson had arrived in Boston in 1634 expressly to live under the ministry of John Cotton. A compassionate nature and knowledge of roots and herbs and the healing art gave this magnetic woman nursing skills and rewarded her with gratitude and respect. A passion for religion and a bold spirit drew other men and women to her in sessions that expounded Scripture and sought to resolve doctrinal differences between Cotton and Pastor John Wilson. Cotton they believed preached a strict covenant of faith, by which the saints, elected by God's grace, could do nothing to alter their state, while sinners, by striving, could at most moderate their unhappy predestined fate. The circle feared that Wilson, by contrast, taught a covenant of works; careful observance of religious duties, he implied, could earn the individual election, thus limiting God's grace and making worldly condition evidence of future salvation.

The contest for control of the Boston church in 1636 coincided with the political ferment that followed from the demand for a written law. The dismayed magistrates confronted dissent even more dangerous than that of Roger Williams. Anne's arguments rested not on books or theories but on feelings derived from direct communication with the divine spirit. And if one person could thus receive God's word, so could others; and all order would rot away in the state as in religion. Insistence on the individual conscience as an adequate guide to truth weakened the church as an instrument of discipline and endangered society. The need to cast out divisive members lay behind the decision to banish Anne Hutchinson.[25]

The exclusion of one woman did not end the matter. Others promptly affirmed the claim to private, personal judgment—whatever the views of established authority. Up in Salem, Lady Deborah Moody,

rich and well connected, held firm dissenting views and read and pur-
veyed unorthodox books. When she tired of the nagging about her, she
departed for Long Island, taking her sizable fortune with her. The little
New Haven Colony shook with the effects of an even more disruptive
dissident, wife of the governor, personally wealthy and endowed with
a temperament not easily bent to the will of others. Mrs. Anne Eaton
shrugged off censure and publicly flaunted the neglect of marital obligations with which she punished her husband. Her example encouraged
other women, and some men also, to seek their own answers and to
disregard community disapproval.[26]

The lack of respect for authority spread to all levels of society. After
1637, appeals to private judgment in matters large and small justified
disregard of properly executed rules in Rhode Island. The quirky Samuel
Gorton tumbled from one doctrine to another; sober Baptists began to
explore the implications of separation of church and state; and the
thoughtful John Clarke persuaded his neighbors "that none bee accounted
a Delinquent for Doctrine." Even in Massachusetts Ambrose Marten
called the church government "a stinking carryon" and wondered at
God's patience in withholding punishment from it. John Smyth rallied
opposition to the Weymouth church. And Thomas Starr and Richard
Silvester spoke against an ordinance about hogs, saying "the law was
against Gods Law and . . . [they] would not obey it." Small fines—
sometimes paid, sometimes not—did not put an end to the rumblings.[27]

The Quakers at first seemed no greater threat to the New England
way than did other dissenters. In England George Fox, a weaver's son
(1624), apprenticed to a shoemaker, at the age of nineteen deserted his
last to attend meetings and study the Scriptures. Asking provocative
questions of the ministers, he entered tortuous disputes with learned men.
He rejected the unreformed Church of England, but could not accept the
stern Calvinist God who left men utterly helpless in their quest for
salvation. In 1647 he found the answer. Through repentance and personal
striving the individual could attain a saving relationship with his maker.
A complete victory over sin was thus possible and salvation was within
the reach of all. Fox preached this message, attracting a widening circle
of followers.

The Friends recognized no priesthood, no authority between God and
man. Even Scripture did not have the binding force for them it had for
other Protestants. Fox insisted that every individual commune directly
with the divine spirit. Within each regenerate soul, an inner light brought

direct revelations and inspirations to those who sought it. The appropriate mode of worship was not in churches served by ministers or priests, but in meetings where each person could bear witness to the truth within his own heart. Despite bitter persecution by the government, the sect continued to gain proselytes.

The lax atmosphere of English society after the Restoration in 1660 brought Fox's group new strength. Its simplicity and righteousness attracted men and women disgusted with the luxury and worldliness about them. The Quakers made respectable and even wealthy converts. A conviction that their message ought to be heard everywhere inspired them with missionary fervor, expressed in part in the foundation of Pennsylvania with its promise of religious freedom to all comers, with results so irenic that the Reverend Daniel Pastorius counted among his domestic staff a Roman Catholic, a Lutheran, a Calvinist, an Anabaptist, a Quaker, and an Anglican.[28]

Conflicts arose, however, when the Friends carried their doctrines to other colonies. Those who lived peacefully among their neighbors attracted attention only when they questioned taxes to support the minister or the obligation to serve in the militia. Responses to their doctrinal challenges rehearsed the familiar Puritan arguments; and even Roger Williams entered the lists against them. But the situation changed when some fervent Friends moved beyond discussion to direct action. So annoying were the nuisances they committed that the New Amsterdam magistrates took them as "signs of God's just punishment" (1658). Boston bore the brunt of their zeal. Mary Dyer was no Anne Eaton or Lady Moody; once a follower of Anne Hutchinson, a termagant, and perhaps slightly mad, she insisted not only in following her own correct way but also in preventing others from following theirs. Banishment, the usual response, proved ineffective; when she continued to return, she went to the gallows on Boston Common—not for her views but for her acts. The General Court explained (1678) that the Quakers, like the Jesuits under Elizabeth, suffered death justly not for their beliefs but for contempt of the laws. And indeed the appearance of a female Quaker in the South meetinghouse at sermontime, in a canvas frock, her hair disheveled, her face black as ink, occasioned the most amazing uproar the normally placid Samuel Sewell ever saw.[29]

Down in Rhode Island the followers of Roger Williams and of Anne Hutchinson, along with settlers of other affiliations and none, traced another path. This quarrelsome batch of sects regarded government as a purely secular institution and drifted toward acceptance of any company of people gathered together as a church—including Baptists and Quakers. All could rant and rave as they pleased. Yet the Rhode Island authorities found "that in those places where these people . . . are most of all suffered to declare themselves freely, and are only opposed by arguments in discourse, there they least of all desire to come, and . . . begin to loathe this place for that they are not opposed by the civil" powers.[30]

Attitudes in the other New England colonies eased. After 1690 the New England situation changed. The Puritans moved toward the pattern to the south of them. Theological controversy moderated; earlier passions subsided, new ones did not erupt until the intrusion of pietism in the second quarter of the eighteenth century. The Reverend Timothy Walker, Harvard 1725, came to Concord, New Hampshire, in 1730 and remained as minister the rest of a long life. His diaries recorded close concern with the business of his farm, no anxieties about faith. Heterogeneous elements infused the population—not only Scottish Presbyterians and French Huguenots, but an occasional Jew. Walking to an ordination, Samuel Sewell discovered that his companion was a Hungarian and an Arminian. Moreover the Restoration left the New Englanders in the anomalous position of denying parity to the established Church of England, of which the king and many royal officials were communicants.

Boston could not indefinitely forbid the Anglicans to build a church, and thus deny a place of worship to the governor appointed by the crown under the new charter. The irony could not have escaped Increase Mather and other petitioners for a new college charter, who promised to admit persons of all religious persuasions. The old Puritans evaded the governor's request for use of the meetinghouse (1687); but there was no denying the Anglicans the right to build their own chapel in Boston. To the distress of the orthodox, Massachusetts had thus recognized the Church of England. Connecticut also yielded; and Rhode Island and New Hampshire presented no problems. In 1685, despite the refusal of the governor to permit it, the Quakers fenced off the spot on Boston Common where their martyrs had gone to the gallows a few years earlier, another sign of change. Not long thereafter, Cotton Mather wrote in praise of William Phipps, "He was very zealous for all Men to enjoy such a *Liberty of Conscience,* as he judged a *Native Right of Mankind.*" Prejudice against Anglicans and Catholics lingered in New England, where toleration was a grudging acknowledgement of political necessity, a de facto willingness to accept a variety of types of individuals in the community.[31]

Tolerance exposed the issue of religious equality. As long as a church took in the whole community, it was plausible to lend it civil support and to tax everyone to maintain the building and the minister. But the fragmentation of the populace among several sects raised demands for a change. The New Hampshire Council thus left the people of the several towns "at the liberty whether they would pay their ministers or no" (1683). The Reverend Seaborn Cotton of Hampton, abandoned without resources, complained in vain. Connecticut and Massachusetts also allowed taxpayers some degree of choice. But town by town, the issue stretched out for decades, as the colonists explored the implications of pluralism. Any group could, in effect, split away and hire a preacher to its own taste, thus diminishing the resources available to the old church, a situation that often left the minister without bargaining power compelled to accept whatever the congregation offered.[32]

Vestiges of establishment remained, as in sermons and prayers that marked ceremonial occasions. But increasingly piety became personal, marked by private fasting and solitary prayer, a transaction between the individual and his God. Left to the independent reflection of each person, religion became a matter for voluntary choice. Good Puritan churches ceased to require public confession for membership. "Let it be our ultimate Ambition, to read the Scriptures with our own Eyes and practise their Meaning without being Hood wink'd by Jugglers and Visionaries," wrote William Livingston (1753). "Let us never desert the Law and the Testimony, for the airy Figments of Dreamers of Dreams, Venders of Jargon, gloomy impostors, devout System Mongers and spiritual Conjurers."[33]

Many colonists discovered that light from the Scriptures flickered uncertainly on the inescapable problems of life. The traditional ways of worship involved not only ritual but also the understanding of the world and the place of humans in it, revealed in sermons or theological tracts but also in tenaciously held strands of popular culture. Profound changes followed upon the altered status of the churches and the shift away from communal habits of thought to personal efforts to know.

Seventeenth-century people had lived in a half-known, dimly perceived universe, of which the visible material world was not a whole, but only a part. The devout learned from sermons of an invisible world of angels and spirits ruled by God's inscrutable will, with direct effects on every human. Disasters, small and great, were evidence of his loving wrath, which people could fend off only by humble prayer and fasting and by life in accord with his commandments. It pleased God that Mrs. William Peirce lost valuable linens in a fire (1641), both in taking off her heart from worldly comfort and in preparing her for a far greater affliction by the untimely death of her husband. John Baker of Boston grew wealthy, fell into drunkenness and lying, until warned by a neighbor's suicide, whereupon Baker humbled himself before the church and confessed his wickedness; pardoned, he alas fell into gross errors again. The sovereign ruler of the world never needed to seek a ground to bring a scourge upon people—to humble and test those who took peace and prosperity as a sign that they were less sinners than others, to prevent evil from growing among them or corruptions from budding forth, as pride, luxury, and inordinate love of the world.[34]

Often the settlers wondered why they had left the safety of the civilized Old World and exposed themselves in the wilderness to the attacks of the greatest antagonist of all, Satan. It was helpful then to learn that there was a special purpose to their coming. The usual lives of ordinary men and women ran according to rule and ended when their time came. But events far out of the ordinary reflected some particular divine intention. With John Smith the colonists saw themselves at the climax of a process of colonization that had begun with Adam and Eve. With the Puritans, they bowed in awe at the awareness that God had particularly chosen them to come to the New World to build a city upon a hill toward which men everywhere would look to understand righteous living. Everywhere they quivered in pride at their role in the divine scheme for the redemption of mankind.

In Jamestown in 1612, daily prayers consoled worshipers with the assurance that they were building up the walls of a New Jerusalem; and that figure of speech became common in many parts of America in the decades that followed. So Nicasius de Sille, son of a good Dutch family, happy father of five children, suddenly encountered disaster. His wife died and serious financial difficulties drove him to New Netherland in 1650. His luck did not improve. A second marriage turned out badly; in 1659 he asked for a divorce on the grounds of his wife's drunkenness. His children learned the language of the Indians and acquired their loose habits. He saw disorderly living, drunkenness, and excessive smoking everywhere and retreated to a farm in New Utrecht on Long Island, where he lived until his death in 1669. As he pondered the matter in his *History* of New Utrecht, he became convinced that God must have brought the Dutch to the New World with some special intention of the highest importance.

Three years later in North Andover, Massachusetts, Anne Bradstreet died, mother of eight children. She had

> nursed them up with pain and care,
> nor cost nor labor did I spare,
> till at the last they felt their wing,
> mounted the trees, and burned to sing.

At her first arrival in America, she had fallen into a lingering sickness. Her heart sank in the face of the difficulties about her and she admitted to troubling doubts. But she submitted to the ways of the traditional God, and her poems testified to the strength of her faith in the land to which he had brought her. The dying Ezekiel Cheever explained (1708): "The afflictions of God's people, God by them did as a Goldsmith, knock, knock, knock, knock, knock, to finish the plate, it was to perfect them not to punish them."[35]

Faith accounted for death, the frequent visitor to every household, otherwise inexplicable. For six weeks the plague swept through Charleston (1698), left corpses heaped up in carts one upon another, and nothing to do but dig graves. Robert Carter later accepted the loss of fifteen working slaves with resignation. "Afflictions are very proper for us in our way to heaven. Its a rugged path yet it is the road that all the blessed above had trod before us" (1721). Samuel Sewall and others carefully noted deaths and funerals in their diaries. His son Sam cried at the burial of an older brother but had to be reminded a year later really to pray when he said the Lord's Prayer, then burst into a bitter cry, saying he was afraid he should die. Sewall phlegmatically noted the passing of other of his children, but once dreamt they were all dead. Much affected when his wife died in May 1720, he nevertheless courted another in September, whose turn came five years later. After that funeral he repaired to a marriage party for the daughter of an acquaintance and wrote down a full account of the refreshments—all in good cheer, knowing how to locate death in a larger scheme of life. Acceptance was not evidence of a want of feeling; two years after his wife died, the suggestion that he put off mourning moved Ebenezer Parkman so much that his passions flowed almost beyond control.[36]

Other unexplained forces also made their presence felt in that invisible world. Many New Englanders took the appearance of the northern lights (1719) as a sign of the last judgment. Ghosts appeared in the night; strange forces out of nature made themselves felt if not known; and everywhere the apes of God—witches and devils, creatures of the enemy of man, Satan—manifested themselves. A substratum of beliefs not entirely extirpated by Christianity flourished in the American wilderness, often more frightening than anything experienced in the old country. Satan was peculiarly powerful in the scarcely settled New World, where barriers to his evildoing were weak. The frequency of transgressions and the violence of life were signs of the Devil's malign influence. Crime waves and unexplained disasters created suspicions of pernicious influences that left local magistrates helpless. Furthermore, many remained unpersuaded by the Christian dogmas that assigned the Devil a significant but subsidiary role in the cosmic scheme. To those neither able nor willing to follow the theological intricacies, Satan appeared an almost equally powerful force in daily life, most likely to yield to folk remedies, charms, cunning, and incantations. Even those who tried prayers and fasting, the approved methods, sometimes gave way to the temptation of unapproved supplements, so that the church had to condemn the impious resort to conjurors.[37]

These beliefs endured on into the eighteenth century. Commissary Gideon Johnston in 1708 commented that the ineradicable strange whims and notions of the Carolinians differed fundamentally from the doctrinal delusions of Quakers, Anabaptists, Antinomians, and others which he could combat with weapons forged in decade-long debates, revolving around a common set of assumptions and of basic texts. It was quite another matter to deal with unarticulated credulities and beliefs that Christianity should have buried long ago.[38]

Massachusetts, still Puritan in 1687, did not know what to do about Boston youths who observed Shrove Tuesday (the day before Lent) with rites more appropriate to Catholic countries and England than to a saintly commonwealth. Travelers in New York encountered a mundane, carnal, covetous, and artful woman, the follower of a man who declared himself Jesus, while other persons passed themselves off as Mary Magdalene, Martha, and John. Was it simply irreligion or something more serious when celebrations in honor of coronation day profaned the day of rest? "Down sabbath, up St. George," one Bostonian commented (1704).[39]

Transgressions, however minor, threatened all with judgment. Failure to attend worship, muttered threats, swearing, and curses were primeval rejections of the church in favor of earlier beliefs not entirely superseded.

The attractions of taverns during sermon time, the insistence on celebrating old rituals of pagan origins, and abuses of the Sabbath expressed hidden beliefs. Coming drunk to services slighted the minister and disregarded the word of God. Dances in the wood at night revived fears of satanic rituals during which men reverted to their beastly Adamic form. Nature, the Devil's domain after the Fall, where Indians and animals reigned, also sheltered faeries and demonic forces, whose influence offerings and incantations could win over, or which Robert Roman claimed to decipher by divining with a stick (1696). Half-understood Indian tales about good and evil spirits cast a lurid light upon tribal ceremonies that may have conjured up the Devil. Officials vainly forbade servants and others to celebrate pagan and popish feasts; and now and again victims of evil influences claimed that they could not work, but in doing so might well draw suspicion of collusion upon themselves.[40]

Overwhelmed by the unpredictable strange new environment, many a settler saw the universe as a vast battleground between good and evil, with the outcome wholly undetermined, a world lacking order or fixed rules, with accident and chance merely words for the unaccountable. Where evil flourished and the just suffered, not everyone believed that God alone ruled creation and for man's eternal benefit. Young Theunis Idenson led a godless and dissolute life in the wilds of New York. He had been in the clutches of the Devil for more than six years, he knew. The more he tried to get away, the closer the grip became, the more he tried to reform, the more Satan assaulted him. His nasty and mean wife complained that he did not earn enough; his children swore and cursed, his cows died, he quarreled with the neighbors, his badly wounded daughter was never expected to marry; his land was unproductive, a storm destroyed his canoe, a tree fell on him crushing his hand, and a black slave whom he loved died suddenly. In despair, with the Devil about to devour him, Theunis tried to hang himself and only then felt that God's help might enable him to triumph. Joseph Hawley cut his own throat (1735) in response to a sermon; his wife, busy making cheese when the news came, did not leave the buttery until she had finished.[41]

Thunder, earthquakes, disease, shipwreck, or drought were not—or, not only—manifestations of divine wrath, but—or, but also—reminders of the existence of independent evil forces, to be propitiated by age-old means. Many a settler mixed the socially approved methods of prayer with older techniques of supplications such as charms, incantations, cunning words, and folk practices that paid homage to the power of evil.

These issues, far from theoretical, arose repeatedly in the day-to-day life of the people. A hostile neighbor with a reputation for supernatural cunning defied communal norms and threatened property and health. The customary legal weapons might fail against powers beyond human control. Those endangered could submit and try to propitiate the Devil's emissaries, purchasing security at the risk of eternal damnation. Or they could cry witchcraft and appeal to ecclesiastical and civil authority, in the belief that a good Christian could always triumph over the forces of darkness.

The problem was peculiarly difficult for Protestants unwilling to set up counterrites to deal with such dilemmas. The devout believer could only rely on prayer and faith, good enough for the strong, but leaving the weak yearning for their own black magic. Both the clergy and the government failed them. The former could only preach and hope that the enthusiasm generated by faith would offset inner doubts. As for the civil authorities, their legalism and respect for the law, while protecting the innocent, also sapped the ability to fight the forces of Satan, clever enough to find loopholes and get the accused off scot-free.

Witchcraft was commonplace in the seventeenth century. It surprised no one when Suzanna Man accused John Thomas of theft and then confessed that she had slandered him because "God had given her over to the Devil to make her lie" (1641). A fine punished her. Massachusetts courts (1648) used the same methods as those in England for the discovery of witches, and on that basis found Hugh Parsons not legally guilty. A few years later the evidence was also inadequate to convict him and his wife, Mary, again accused of having made a pact with the Devil (1651, 1652).[42]

Everywhere judges examined the proofs proffered with the utmost seriousness, usually to dismiss the charges, leaving neighbors to solve their own problems. The overzealous constable and overseers of the town of Seatallcoot on Long Island in 1665 accused Ralph Hall and his wife, Mary, of causing the death of several persons by cunning means. Unable to find witnesses to the acts, the local court dismissed the charge. When widow Katherine Harrison removed with her children from Connecticut to Westchester, neighbors suspected that the house of Captain Richard Panton, where she lodged, harbored a witches' conclave. After learning that Wethersfield had driven the unfortunate woman out in 1670 on the same suspicion, the Yorkers too sought to warn her out. The court however found nothing in the testimony to prove her guilt and allowed her to remain. As late as 1701, a Pennsylvania court dismissed the case against Robert Guard and his wife, charged by the local butcher with bewitching another woman, because the complaints were "trifling."[43]

In the seventeenth century, no judge or jury failed to convict out of skepticism about the actuality of witchcraft. On the contrary—as in the case of Margaret Mattson, acquitted in Pennsylvania in 1683 for a flaw in the indictment, although the jury found her "guilty of haveing the common fame of a witch." In small communities where all believed in it, common fame was enough to make the phenomenon real. Occasional guilty verdicts and even the death penalty were not surprising, as when Massachusetts tried and executed Anne Hibbens, a longtime troublemaker, in 1656.[44]

The Salem witchcraft trials attracted attention for their revelation of a new spirit. The settlers of the first generation had brought with them memories they could not easily efface. Precepts handed down over many generations and supported by unquestioned authorities formed the body of wisdom on which they relied and which they attempted to pass on to their American children. Yet the surroundings frequently challenged that heritage, created uncertainty, compelling people to reexamine age-old habits of thought, to venture upon new lines of speculation.

The Salem cases followed the usual course—accusations made, evidence proffered and scrutinized with care, witnesses, verdict, execution, all commonplace. The unusual feature was the learned divine brought up from Boston, a sign of the care given the test of the evidence, in view of the number and the respectability of the accused. Neither the accusations nor the outcome put this case out of the ordinary, but questions about the results despite the punctilious regard for procedure. And neither in Salem Village nor in New England nor in any of the colonies did these specters reappear. The discussion that reversed opinion did not turn about proof, nor did it seek support in scriptural authority or theological doctrine. The controversy turned rather on assumptions about the character of the universe as revealed by the light of reason. Witches had no place —could not exist—in an orderly world.[45]

The judgments about nature that banished witches from eighteenth-century thought permeated many aspects of behavior, including those related to illness and death. In the 1680s, belief that the royal touch could cure the disease known as the king's illness persuaded William Honchins to petition New Hampshire for help to pay his passage to England. In 1727 sermons in the vicinity of Boston interpreted an earthquake as a sign of divine anger at degeneracy. But already by then a change had occurred. The Reverend Increase Mather and others explained comets as among the natural movements of the heavenly bodies. When smallpox struck in 1721, his son Cotton Mather, who had read widely in the literature, advocated inoculation to control the disease. A few years later he published a handbook of practical remedies for physical ailments, well seasoned with pious reflections. In the 1740s, Virginia, after considering alternative safe, easy, and speedy cures for cancer, awarded Mary Johnson £100 for communicating her remedy to the public. Natural evils had natural causes and responded to natural treatment. Even earthquakes, John Winthrop, Jr., argued, followed orderly rules. Persuaded that the telescope was an aid to piety, Americans turned their attention to science; and a respectable number won election to the Royal Society.[46]

Ever more often, reasonableness entered into religious judgments. In the winter of 1712 Thomas Banister, one of the founders of the Brattle Square church in Boston, performed a journey on the sabbath that exposed him to the castigations of the Reverend Timothy Woodbridge. Banister's rejoinder cited Scripture as Woodbridge had, but went on to argue the journey's necessity for his health. Banister denied that "a mercifull God who takes so much care of the souls and bodys of the rational world will ever impute it as a sin . . . , agreeably to that charity which begins at home," to take prudent, natural, and Christian care of one's own welfare. God made his will known in two ways—"either by the light of nature or that Revelation which he has made of it in the Scriptures"; and "The light of nature strongly obliges to self preservation." "Who can doubt," Banister asked triumphantly, "but the Lord of the Sabbath knew that the Sabbath was made for man and not man for the sabbath"? The essence of religion was simple: "give God and Caesar their due, learning to love our neighbours as ourselves."[47]

The proposition that ethical behavior was the essence of religion diminished the importance of creeds; all who obeyed the laws and conducted themselves well in regard to others met their obligations no matter what doctrines they believed or what rites they performed. Robert Carter (1720) saw no reason for great stress on ceremonies, which were but the shell. Practical godliness was the substance.

And let each one who dwelleth on
our country's outmost border
who can't enjoy a ministry
nor ecclesiastic order . . .
let them . . .
. . . do their best endeavor
each sabbath day to sing and pray
and read god's word together.

The same proposition justified the sectarianism circumstances had thrust upon the colonies. The experience of living in relative harmony with neighbors of many faiths had taught the residents of Newport or Philadelphia that there were worthy and unworthy individuals among all of them. Disclaiming partiality to any religious faction, the Massachusetts House declared (1717) that the churches of the province rested on "the indisputable points of the Solid Piety wherein all good men are united." Salvation depended not upon whether one was a Friend or an Anglican but upon whether one led a good and virtuous life; and indeed, New York Quakers were "as redy to obey orders as ye rest of" the company.[48]

These practical adjustments in the eighteenth century subtly modified religious ideas. The minority of educated colonists who then read the latitudinarian sermons of Archbishop Tillotson or the essays of rationalist philosophers recognized abstract Enlightenment propositions which conformed to the lessons of their own society. The early visionaries, sticklers for pure doctrine, refused to compromise the beliefs for the sake of which they hazarded removal to the New World. Others, searching for an ever truer faith, had split apart in separate denominations. The desire to attract more settlers also increased diversity, and novel conditions fostered toleration. Churches, initially powerful but unable to restrain their own members, faced unwelcome divisions and quarrels that weakened their hold on recalcitrant parishioners and undermined the standing order.

Contemporaries differed in their explanations. To Cotton Mather, himself troubled by fiery darts of doubt from Hell, the seeds of religious pluralism were "political and vexatious"; he could not comprehend why anyone would honestly wish to diverge from the path his forefathers had marked out for the faithful. He still expected "the true American pietism," real and vital, to shine as the notable dawn of the kingdom of God among the children of men (1713). But every village, however pious, he assumed, had at least "a dozen litigous families"—"odd people who know nothing of the matter," but who provided a convenient excuse for others to move in and disrupt religious unity (1717). Mather singled out the Society for the Propagation of the Gospel, which used such families as an excuse for unneeded missionary activity, not only in that woeful country Carolina, not only in Pennsylvania and the Jerseys, but even among the well-ordered churches of God in New England. Mather also blamed human nature, knowing, as his ancestors did, that there was nothing too low or mean to which man would not stoop in sinfulness and stupidity. His own neighbors, mainly to vex him, he thought, built the most magnificent new church structure in Boston, instituted what he called "the religion of the Pues," and raided his own congregation for members (1721). He could not admit that his own inability to give satisfactory answers to parishioners who no longer shared either his certainties or his doubts, but asked novel questions, contributed to Boston's religious diversity.[49]

Further to the south, Hugh Jones in 1724 argued that diversity was really a cloak for no religion at all, as in North Carolina, where nominal Christians no better than heathens could not cope with the social problems created by the absence of official beliefs. In Virginia, Robert Beverly noted a vicious cycle connecting poor tobacco crops and Presbyterianism: the poorer the crop, the less ability to pay for a decent minister; and the less decent the minister, the more likely the slide into irreligion. Mather, Jones, and Beverly found nothing good in the diversity they bewailed but were powerless to halt.[50]

Popular satisfaction with matters as they were infuriated some magistrates, particularly when it came to finances. Large landholders did not mind who served as minister as long as costs stayed down; but officials who expected the church to sustain the government resented niggardly attitudes toward salaries. Governor Alexander Spotswood of Virginia could not get the assembly to provide proper support. To the argument that the "gentlemen of the clergy" were well paid, he replied that none of the representatives were willing to raise their children to holy orders, while at the same time they enacted laws that allowed "the meanest blacksmith for his mechanic work" more than "the learnedst pastor for his divine labors." Virginians found nothing incongruous in this situation. Good or bad preachers, of whatever denomination, were a dime a dozen, and their effects long range at best, while good blacksmiths were hard to find and harder to keep, and their contribution to social welfare immediate and concrete.[51]

Irreverence and multiplying sects weakened established, organized worship. The arrival of the Moravians, said Gilbert Tennent in 1742, was not only evil in itself—for he considered them rank Antinomians and Quakers—but also created factions, divided communities, and weakened the power of ministers. Elsewhere religious divisions led to violence and disrespect. When John O'Hara's Anglican congregation in Providence, displeased by him to such an extent that they refused to hear his preaching, locked the meetinghouse doors in 1727, the offended minister broke his way in, only to be hauled from the pulpit and sent to prison. Such incidents convinced Hugh Jones of the damaging effects of local control. "This Liberty without restraint may prove of bad consequence" when any heterodox, libertine, or fantastical persons may plead prescription for their bad tenets and resist eradication.[52]

Any turn to the secular authorities in time of trouble undermined autonomy. The inability of the French church in New York in 1724 to rid itself of the unwelcome minister Louis Rou embroiled Governor Burnett and the council, for motives none too pure, as everyone knew. When representatives of the Society for the Propagation of the Gospel tried to penetrate Connecticut they drew occasionally curious listeners resentful of magistrates who threatened to jail anyone attending Anglican services. In Georgia fiery preachers reminded hearers that Christian Liberty meant giving to Caesar only what was his due and opposing those who exceeded their authority. In 1703 the New Jersey Assembly chastised the governor for disgracing his office by involvement in religious squabbles. "It is not our business to enter into religious controversies we leave them to devines." The governor's task was to protect everyone, not to take one side against another.[53]

Without external authority to resolve them, disputes sputtered on. The Londonderry, New Hampshire, Presbyterians squabbled for years over a problem Congregationalists had frequently faced—the division of the parish and the consequent necessity of supporting two meetinghouses and two ministers. A peace agreement ended the dispute in 1737 after both sides requested the Congregationalists, once their enemies, to arbitrate. Nearby Chester reversed the situation. Here a Presbyterian church flourished without undue excitement under the pastorate of John Willson, while Congregationalists were at loggerheads over efforts to dispose of their minister Moses Hale, who, "bereaved of his reason and understanding," cost them money while failing to provide the customary services. The problem baffled two ecclesiastical councils, while for three years the town's Congregationalists went without a spiritual guide. Disputes not settled voluntarily remained unsettled.[54]

Congregational autonomy was hard on the minister who did not hold the devotion of his flock and tried to maintain his own dignity. Bound to a covenant from which he could not depart without consent, he had no means of defense, particularly in small towns. Hugh Adams, after taking a degree at Harvard, served in South Carolina, where he cured himself of sundry diseases but could not shake off "the hypocondriack melancholy" that drove him into such despair that he envied the happiness of a toad hopping upon the ground. Hard luck clung to him when he came to Durham, New Hampshire, in 1718, hopefully aiming at scholarship as well as pastoral service. After seven years he presented a manuscript entitled "A Theosophical Thesis" for approval to the General Assembly, which gingerly passed it on to an ecclesiastical council. The ministers did not like it at all; they condemned it as full of enthusiasm and impertinence, wretchedly perverting the sacred Scriptures to support extravagant notions. Thereafter Adams attended to his duties. After twenty-one years of service, however, his patience ran out. He complained that in all that time, the townspeople had never once paid him in full and on time, so that he frequently had to borrow at usurious rates to stay alive. The courts ruled in his favor, but the sheriff did not serve the order. When the town meeting did vote to levy funds to meet the judgment, the Quakers protested that the province laws did not oblige anyone to pay for the support of any worship but that which they attended. Subsequent appeals were fruitless; and the accusation that he had offered a bribe to the governor and the secretary exposed Adams to censure from an ecclesiastical council. Personal eccentricities contributed to, but did not account for, his difficulties. Between 1736 and 1754 the town of Duxbury called five ministers to its pulpit, plunged into salary conflicts, appointed negotiating committees, then refused to vote the agreed-on sums. Niggardly Yankee farmers, hard pressed for cash, never were certain that ministers delivered their due. It was all very well to proclaim (1738) the absolute duty of the people "to receive instruction and to hearken to the counsels of God." But who could blame the Mattapoisett people that year when they had difficulty verifying Elisha Tupper's credentials to dispense the gospel.[55]

By contrast, the widening distance between church and state enabled rambunctious individuals to take on what remained of the ecclesiastical establishment. The Essex County Court sentenced Thomas Maule, prosperous Salem shopkeeper and town official, to ten stripes for suggesting that the Reverend John Higginson was in league with the devil (1669); and the Massachusetts Council banned his publication denouncing Puritan persecution of Indians and Quakers. But when a later book, recounting his battles with the authorities, also brought him before a court, an effective plea on his own behalf induced the jury to find him innocent. Massachusetts in 1718 suppressed a tract by John Checkley, an Episcopalian, who argued that dissenters were no better than deists and thus threatened "to disturb the peace and good agreement among the churches in this province of all denominations." But by 1724 Checkley was back with his book (although also once more before a court). Maule's snickering at the hireling ministry who preached for money and James Franklin's jibes in the *New England Courant* made Cotton Mather yearn for the good old days when the government could still clamp down on scoundrels who libeled upstanding ministers. All these opinions were now the province of personal judgment.[56]

The men and women expected to render those judgments sometimes found the burden too heavy; not at the set, formal occasions when the clustered group supplied the responses appropriate to the occasion—as at a deathbed or funeral where sermon, ritual, and ceremony smothered emotion into edifying forms; but in the loneliness when questions loomed about the meaning of life and about the person's place in the universe. The seventeenth-century Puritans had not only supplied the questioner firm answers, but had outlined the proper course for response in the conversion experience. The hovering minister had urged the potential saint on, and the engulfing community had validated the authenticity of the conversion, both in open public examination of its nature and in surveillance of daily life. Now whoever read and observed could understand the orderly natural universe and the rules by which it functioned. But beyond nature lay a realm unexplored and uncharted, within which people had to seek the answers alone when unexplained occurrences or simple loneliness raised troublesome questions. A Massachusetts youth upon firing a gun—it broke into pieces, wounding him, and made him cry out, "O Lord if thou hadst not upheld me, I had sunk into the depth of wo" (1725). That year, terror struck seven-year-old David Brainerd in Connecticut when he thought of death, and secret prayer did not erase the worry, which remained with him until a wave of illness carried off his mother and destroyed all carnal security. He thereupon set forth on a spiritual quest recorded in his journal.[57]

Many therefore listened responsively to the voices that sounded fresh calls to conversion, using a new style—not argumentative appeals to theory, but emotional appeals to conscience. In both Europe and America, independently, pietist preachers called the people to redemption in the new way.

John Wesley, dissatisfied with the rigidity and aloofness of the Church of England, preached in the fields to the poor, urging a new dedication to a personal religious life. In Georgia he bid open defiance to the officials and urged the people to insist upon their rights, as well as to seek salvation (1737). In the Raritan Valley of New Jersey, Theodore Frelinghuysen, a German immigrant, aroused his Dutch Reformed congregation to an emotional revival in 1719. In 1734 Jonathan Edwards, in Northampton, Massachusetts, called for a religious rebirth, while in Pennsylvania William Tennent, a Scotsman, trained young men to bring the gospel to the frontier. They prepared the ground for the arrival of George Whitefield, sent to the colonies by the Georgia Trustees in 1739. He carried his pleas for regeneration throughout the continent. In Boston (1740) perhaps twenty thousand people came to hear him on the Common. Laymen too went about exhorting large assemblies, and many listeners cried out and were so struck that they lost their senses and reason for a time.[58]

The message of the Great Awakening was timely and especially appropriate to the New World in the eighteenth century. The revivalists in effect asked men and women to redeem themselves, and implied that salvation was not an inscrutable decision predetermined by God, but rather a prize earned by the exercise of will. Those who earnestly wished to be saved would indeed find divine grace extended to them. The ultimate decision rested not so much on the particular doctrines to which believers adhered, but on their ethical behavior. The revivalist thus appealed to individual conscience, that umpire the Deity placed within each heart as source of inward knowledge. Let the listeners but repent and be reborn, let them but will to lead an ethical life, and redemption would be theirs. The line between sinner and saint was not permanent or fixed; anyone who responded to the summons could pass over it.

The Old Light stalwarts had long before identified these New Light heresies as Arminianism, latitudinarianism, and Antinomianism. In church after church, the itinerants left divided congregations, conflicts over the minister, censures of admonition and separations. The antirevivalists wanted, above all, order and conformity, which government lacked the power to provide. Eighteenth-century Americans found the New Light message attractive, for it matched experience and confirmed social expectations. Men and women dissatisfied with the dry formality of the church hungered for a more personal, more direct, and more confident faith.[59]

The Great Awakening ideas accorded with the conceptions of humanity and the universe at which the colonists had already arrived. The assurance that an exercise of the will could gain salvation followed consistently upon the assumption of a reasonable, orderly, and beneficent universe. In their condemnation of the formalism of existing churches and in their objection to an unconverted ministry, the revivalists challenged established institutions and appealed to common sense. Their auditors, ignoring rigorous theology, found emotional reassurance in sermons that condemned the dry doctrines handed down from conventional pulpits. Stress upon proper behavior and acts of benevolence offered satisfactory resolution to practical issues and linked the piety of George Whitefield to the rationalism of Benjamin Franklin. The well-born, the learned, and the poor could share the experience.

Revivalist ministers and their adherents justified the excesses of the movement by the good accomplished, which even detractors could not deny. In Londonderry, New Hampshire, the son of the original Presbyterian minister, caught up in the movement, provided eloquent testimony to his own and his parishioners' accomplishments. David MacGregor had learned on his father's knees the problems occasioned by deviant sects, but vigorously defended his own actions as different. He had seen very little or no "growth of Antinomian errors or anything visionary or enthusiastic" in his own congregation or in the neighborhood. His emphasis on "the eternal obligation of the law as a rule of life . . . maintained in practise as well as profession" had none of the evil side effects of the sectarianism his father had once fought. Indeed the benefits were such that MacGregor only wished "they overspread the whole land." What opponents of revivalism regarded as "most damnable errors and confusion," at once "enthusiastical, proud and schismatical," to MacGregor's supporters appeared only an affirmation of beliefs incorporated in their daily lives.[60]

Sympathetic observers acknowledged the achievement. James Blake, no supporter of the revivalists, noted how Dorchester listeners riveted their attention on the preachers' words, unlike the restless and bored audiences of conventional ministers. Religion once again became a serious topic of discourse; and the good in the land impressed even those who resented the believers' temporary loss of sense and reason. Occasionally self-defined old Calvinists and new revivalists made common cause against a mutual enemy. When William Shurtleff came to preach there in 1732, he found Portsmouth rife with Pelagianism and Socinianism. To his wealthy congregation, nothing more mattered than "to smoke and eat together, to tell a pleasant story and to talk of the common and ordinary affairs of life." They expected from their new pastor "a nice and philosophical account of the nature, influence and motions of the stars," in accord with current trends in science and philosophy. Shurtleff's response was reversion to old-style Calvinism, which aligned him with the revivalists.[61]

But the excesses and deceptive slogans of the Great Awakening outraged others, who counterattacked. Enthusiasm was a delusion in which the believer screamed himself into a false conversion, Charles Chauncy charged. He reassured those temporarily swayed by guilt about their wealth by arguing that the revivalist ministers sought "to destroy all property, to make all things common, wives as well as goods." During the decade of turmoil in the 1740s, bitter controversies between the Old Lights, or defenders of the orthodox position, and the New Lights, or revivalists, split community after community, usually with the minority going its separate way.[62]

The law everywhere changed to deal with the problems occasioned by the revival. Often the result further increased the power of congregations at the expense of the clergy, along with the general drift toward greater separation of church and state, more tolerance of sectarianism and pluralism. Churches faced with loss in membership relaxed their standards. The requirement of a public confession dropped away; and people expelled or dismissed, even in Connecticut, could gain readmission after a suitable acknowledgment of error. Local considerations became more important than doctrinal tenets in the distinctions between those who could or could not join existing congregations.[63]

Significant implications followed from the practices and assumptions of the Great Awakening. Experience validated the assertion that all humans were potentially saints, all equally capable of earning salvation.

The thriving society that had replaced the empty wilderness showed that men and women in an orderly universe could improve themselves, for they were creatures of limitless capacities. Rank, wealth, and breeding were not measures of saintliness, for all were equal in the eyes of God. The poor and even slaves and other people of color were all potentially precious in God's eyes—propositions that in time raised troublesome questions about the propriety of existing inequalities. Every person bore an obligation to deserve the salvation within reach of those who willed it. The believers had to destroy external impediments in the way of the desired goals through moral improvement—through temperance, relief from poverty and illness, and emancipation from slavery. Skeptics scoffed (1755) at the unnatural sight of "a parson with a florid countenance and double chin" preaching up abstinence during Lent. Still, the way to improvement was clear:

> Let men renounce the tippling house
> Let frolicking be loathed,
> Women lay aside the fruits of pride
> And decently be cloathed.[64]

Revivalism affected politics, with far-reaching results. The erasure of the line between elect and damned raised doubts about the legitimacy of control over the whole society by an elite group and forced reconsideration of old social and economic arrangements. Connecticut thus had to decide whether the New Lights or the Old Lights should control the church in each town, an issue particularly grave in Kent in the 1740s. The province law exempted sectarians, mainly Baptists and Quakers, from taxes to support the Congregationalist minister, provided they maintained their own orderly worship. That did not answer the question of their status in town meetings, a problem ultimately resolved by a compromise (1746) that allowed them to vote on all issues except church affairs. The town, reputed a stronghold of orthodoxy, before then had excluded three New Lights from the congregation. When a law (1742) allowed a majority to decide whether itinerant ministers could preach, there were enough New Lights in town to make it worth the congregation's while to invite the return of those barred.

Abel Wright, an original settler, holder of three shares, active land speculator and by some reputed the richest man in the vicinity, refused to avail himself of the privilege. He had frequently held office and was an original church covenanter. But in 1743 he was suspended because of his New Light views and quarrels with the pastor, for whom he had little respect. Convinced that he was right, Wright defied the secular authorities and the church. He found some Moravians (in the area preaching to the Indians) much more attractive because they preached "a practical, good religion" and resolved to bring its benefits to others. In spite of a multitude of other obligations, Wright went from house to house arguing with all. Powerless to halt him, the town eventually requested the General Assembly to deprive him of his captain's commission. But before the assembly acted, Wright moved to Fairfield.[65]

Wright no longer responded to civil, religious, or communal pressure. He listened to an interior voice that informed him of his obligations. The preaching of Old Lights, New Lights, or even Moravians provided the stimulus; but he himself decided with the guidance of reason. Salvation of his soul rested in his own hands. Such people as he bore a weighty responsibility. They inhabited a world that, while it valued order, in its spaciousness encouraged disorder. That world, visible and invisible, housed forces that pushed people away from inherited modes of thought and action, and compelled them to devise new ones to test against experience.

The fragmentation of communities had drained established rituals and beliefs of sanctions. Faith, like all else by the eighteenth century, sprang from the voluntary decisions of individuals. But the human condition denied that bold proposition. Victors though they were in the contest for survival, the colonists shrank from the necessity for frequent consultations of conscience in questions of right and wrong, illness and health, success and failure. With heaven and hell in the balance, to be free they had to believe, even if only in the power of their reason.

V I

THE GOVERNMENT

OF FAMILIES,

1600–1760

THEY WERE ADAMS ALL, at the start, not through innocence but through the lack of Eves.

Colonization began as a masculine enterprise, for it partook of maritime and military qualities. Companies of men set to sea for months on end, in a business not shared by women; and the armies on land also consisted entirely of males, although camp followers bustled about in the train. For that matter, too, Europeans recalled cloistered and secular communities of religious composed of a single sex. The idea was therefore not in itself strange. Females were conspicuously absent from the first plantations.

Still, the American situation was not quite the same as that of Europe. Only a few colonists made a temporary or permanent choice of celibacy out of vocation, as seamen, soldiers, and monks did. Most hoped that the temporary deprivations of migration would in time open into a period of release that would find them heads of households, husbands of wives, and fathers of children. The great migration to New England in the 1630s was exceptional in the extent to which it brought whole families together to the New World. Other settlers, not having come in such units, had to reconstitute those they had known at home.

The easy gratification offered by compliant Indian maidens satisfied errant passions but left the emptiness of want of a permanent relationship. Sexuality was a means and not an end in itself. The Puritans clearly articulated the attitude toward carnal pleasures that their contemporaries

147

shared. Every experience, a gift of God as an instrument for his glory, had some reason behind it. It was therefore sinful to satisfy human appetites with passions properly meant for divine purposes. In their relationships with one another men and women, however loving they might be, had always to consider the broader context—offspring, servants, the community, and the salvation of the eternal soul. Those considerations quickened the urgency to reconstruct the family so that no one would have to live alone and all could serve the Lord in accordance with their natures.[1]

The spread of settlement away from the original centers increased the need. In the first plantations, the men had close neighbors and might at least hope for assistance in illness and accident. Once dispersed and alone, many departed "the World in their own dung" for want of such help in their sickness as only a dutiful wife could provide.[2]

Moreover, the family became the overarching metaphor for the whole social order. "By Father and Mother," declaimed Cotton Mather in 1699, "ALL SORTS OF PARENTS are intended. . . . There are *Parents* in the *Common-Wealth,* as well as in the *Family;* there are *Parents* in the *Church,* and *Parents* in the *School,* as well as in the *Common-Wealth.*"[3]

The family to which Cotton Mather's thoughts turned was a household, encompassing all who lived and worked together, all who accepted responsibility for one another: a community in microcosm. In an orderly society, each person belonged to such a group held together by relationships of kinship, labor, and faith. Hence the suspicion of strays who lived alone and the mistrust of those who presumed to get by as isolated individuals.

Early on, therefore, colonial policy aimed to bring whole families across despite the hardships of the crossing and of wilderness life. Any disposition of bachelors to live alone earned communal disapproval and sometimes consequential penalties. New Haven in 1640 ordered all single persons to betake themselves forthwith to some family; and Massachusetts later restricted freedom of movement on the grounds that the "loose and sinful custome of going or riding from toune to toune," was really an excuse "to drinke and reuell in ordinaries and taverns," a hazard to chastity and "a notable meanes to debauch our youth." As late as 1703 Nathaniell Turner, a single person, needed town permission to keep house alone in Connecticut.[4]

The Massachusetts Bay governor and company regarded as a threat the people already settled in Dorchester. Suspicions of witchery at Merry Mount aroused by strange rites, and ceremonies and animosity stirred up by the suggestion of sexual license there convinced the Puritans that it endangered social order by undermining all family relations. Families, "the First Combinations of mankind," Cotton Mather later explained, were the nurseries of societies; ill-disciplined, they infected the whole community with error. The welfare of all demanded correction or extirpation of the source of evil.[5]

However determined the effort, the new circumstances compelled the family to change. Even Plymouth, a small, closely knit settlement, had its share of men whipped for adulterous practices and of women who yielded without making such resistance as they ought (1655). In the absence of oversight by a powerful community, temptations, irritations, and eccentricities of behavior erupted among people unaccustomed to the new scale of existence. Those either crowded in upon one another in small houses and palisaded settlements or lost from one another in the wilderness slipped into misbehavior or appeared to do so. Cross-accusations of adultery and of who called whom whore dotted the court records. The New England town, homes one close upon the other, inquisitive neighbors on the alert, more diligently searched out misbehavior than scattered farms and plantations or cities. The balance between legal and extralegal mechanisms for dealing with offenders varied according to place and time, but everywhere reflected similar pressures. Separations took their toll in divided experience; and communal discipline failed when space offered individuals who desired it the opportunity to escape. The resulting tension long endured and reshaped the character of the American family in an experience later generations of newcomers would repeat.[6]

Toward the middle of the eighteenth century, colonists, aware that the system had broken down, vainly sought an appropriate replacement. Once upon a time, a preacher, Samuel Dexter, wailed in 1734, fathers ruled, family government had force, with good order, peace, and regular conduct the results. He urged his congregation to recover "the spirit of family government," when men held "their households in good subjections, children and servants knew their places and kept their distance." In the degenerate days of 1734 dependents displayed little reverence toward superiors, and having abandoned the notions of stewardship, everyone behaved without suitable decorum toward others.[7]

The New World family had narrowed down. Kinship ties in practice lost the primary importance they had enjoyed in the Old World where traditions of fostering and gossipred (spiritual affinity) or compaternity reinforced them. The Scottish and Irish clan or band was the focus of people's loyalty; and marriage was a means of quieting feuds. Elsewhere, too, the compelling ties of blood derived from community, place, and faith informed all group members of the degrees of their relationships. Those linkages tended to dissolve in America. Clan lines that held firm in Scotland carried over to North Carolina as long as the newcomers clustered in the same neighborhood, but grew weaker with migration and mobility. Although in ways not quite articulated the ties of blood bound cousins after several generations by sentimental and emotional power, kinship in practice faded to inconsequence. The act of migration tore cousins, indeed brothers and sisters, apart. Those out of sight soon also faded out of mind. And the experience repeated itself decade after decade. Furthermore the possession of land, a unifying factor in the old home where it represented the site of generations of life, became divisive here, a prize for which rival heirs contended.

His relations, Hezekiah Usher sourly wrote (1689), only waited to learn what his will left them. A gap opened between experience and sentiment, between the reality of detachment and isolation and the abstract insistence on the high value of kinship.[8]

Seventeenth-century people agreed upon the lineaments of the well-regulated family and of the reciprocal duties and rights of its members, with superiors and inferiors, as much in reason and in justice as by God's command, obliged to discharge what they owed one another. The boundaries were those of the household, so that often the same language served both, as when Cotton Mather expressed the hope that "every one that is the Owner of a *Family*, would faithfully *Command* and manage those that belong unto him."[9]

The ability to command and manage depended upon the relationship of the conjugal pair one to the other. Like every other distinction in nature, the difference between male and female signified some meaning intended by the Creator. To ancient connotations, implanted through family lore, religious precept, and communal custom, the New World added reactions emanating from imbalance of sex ratios, from life under hard conditions, and from the disruption of familiar modes of action.

On one side of the ocean as on the other, the husband provided the household's sustenance, guiding its affairs, performing much of the physical labor. The wife's more complex role depended upon location and social position—humility, prudence, affability, piety, and charity, Robert Carter specified from the vantage point of a Virginia planter; good fiscal management, according to Samuel Sewall, not the only colonist to hand over custody of the family's estate to his wife.[10]

These were eighteenth-century judgments. In the beginning, however, everything was provisional and would repeatedly become so again at each advance of the frontier. Necessity then forced a recasting of roles. Dowries in the wilderness seemed irrelevant, so scarce were females. "The first planters were so far from expecting money with a woman that twas a common thing for them to buy a deserving wife, at the price of 100 pounds, and make themselves believe they had a hopeful bargain." What had to be done had to be done, no matter who did it. No one could survive in this country without a wife, one settler complained in 1644; for unlike the easier old country life, here many a man found it difficult to cook and bake and "himself do all the things that women do." When Mrs. Skelton of Salem, wife of the minister, died in 1631, an observer noted the effect on her family. "She was a godly and helpfull woman," he wrote, "and indeed the maine pillar of her family, haueing left behind her an husband and four children, weake and helpless who canne scarce tell how to liue without her."[11]

The colonists and promoters made every effort to induce women to migrate in order to offset the sexual imbalance. The Virginia Company, convinced that it would never flourish till wives and children fixed the people on the soil, shipped over a widow and eleven maids (1621) to be sold for marriage to freemen or tenants who had means of maintenance, not to servants. The women were free to marry "according to the law of nature," and of their own will, in the hope that dramatic improvement in their condition would allure multitudes of others to come. The multitudes never followed. And the poor, unable to pay the price, grumbled, while those who carried off mates complained that the women refused to labor hard and consumed precious food without benefit to the colony, company, or country. Such efforts rarely made a difference; later in the century, Massachusetts, Virginia, and Maryland declined the English government's offer to send over female prisoners.[12]

As soon as possible, some breathing spell allowed people to get back to familiar divisions of labor and responsibility. In time, too, household duties fell along lines of gender, with the husband defender of the hearth and good provider, the wife mother and molder of youth. Heirs of the Lutheran strictures against monasticism, the settlers rejected the older view of woman as a biologically misshapen man and looked back upon the end of nunneries as the liberation of women from unnatural bondage, the freeing of their instincts and bodies for what God had intended them to be. Those not content to do such things as belonged to their sex and meddled in affairs proper to men risked loss of their reason and understanding, the fate of the deranged wife of Connecticut's governor, a goodly young lady of special parts who had given herself wholly to reading and writing. A century later (1737), Abigail Colman's father ascribed her disastrous marriage to early sins of reading novels and idle poems. Those who confined themselves to their own sphere avoided the danger.[13]

Marriage, the cement that bound the family together, marked out conjugal rights and duties. It ceased to be a sacrament and, according to the laudable custom of the Low Countries, became "a civil thing, upon which many questions about inheritances" depended. That contractual relationship, signifying the consent of the two parties, was subject to the rules that governed other contracts. Puritan colonies accepted civil marriage and the same result followed elsewhere from the absence of ecclesiastical courts administering their own law. Legislation defined permitted degrees of marriage, as it attempted to regulate other aspects of family life. Indeed, marriage in Virginia became a source of income for officials—twenty shillings to the governor and five to the clerk for each license issued, only five to the minister if by banns.[14]

Everywhere the government insisted upon parental consent for the marriage of minors and took oral promises seriously, particularly when they involved property or sexual irregularity. Verification of consent and undertakings was difficult, when people agreed for what they could get rather than for romance and when no family maintained effective oversight. Pieter Kock, bachelor, burgher, and inhabitant of New Amsterdam, brought suit against Anna van Vorst, spinster (1654), respecting an oral engagement as a result of which he had given her various gifts. She had changed her mind. Though two witnesses testified that Kock had released her from the promise, the court declared the agreement valid. She could retain the presents until the marriage or until the magistrates approved their separation.

More often, women were the aggrieved parties, for the consequences might well burden the whole community. All too often a swain, smoothly promising, wiggled his way into a maiden's graces and left her a token of affection no one wished to support. Women whipped for begetting a bastard child dotted the records of English local government and of the colonies also. It was vital therefore to knot such promises into matrimonial actuality. Geertruyt Wyngaart dragged Geleyn Verplanck before the New Amsterdam magistrates for agreeing to marry her and then leaving her helplessly pregnant (1661). The court ordered him to pay one guilder a week for the child's maintenance. Baudewyn van Nieuwlandt, also reluctant to carry through on his vows, had the support of influential creditors who did not wish his assets tied up in romantic obligations. But the court sympathized with Maria Besems and attached all van Nieuwlandt's goods to the expenses of the pregnancy and child support. Poor Elizabeth Soule, however, got little satisfaction from her complaint that Nathaniel Church had committed the act of fornication upon her (1663). Carnal copulation before marriage was not unusual even in Plymouth, and if caught out was subject to a five-pound fine. But Nathaniel's refusal to go on to marry Elizabeth only doubled the amount of his fine, did nothing for her.[15]

Unsettling passions did not fade away. New Amsterdam in 1658 reaffirmed the custom and law of the fatherland, which forbade cohabitation and required marriage after banns were published three times. Reality flew in the face of legislation. To add to the confusion local regulations varied, so that young people, in disobedience to parents and guardians, secretly eloped to villages with loose standards. Those with parents elsewhere so that consent was difficult to come by presented special problems. In a particularly involved case (1654), New Amsterdam, taking account of the ages of the couple, the distance to Holland, the state of war with England, the danger that delay would disgrace all, and the fact that the pair had been living together for some time, declared the marriage legal, although contracted without the knowledge of the parents. On into the eighteenth century, angry fathers continued to pull down the banns published by stubborn youths; but passion continued to find or create loopholes.[16]

In well-ordered marriages, premarital contracts stipulated mutual obligations. Thus Roger Baxter, planter of Kent County, Maryland (1655), "being truly affected in loue" to Mary Croutch, widow, gave her full control of her deceased husband's estate for her children's use. When Jan Sieriks married Wybregh Jansen, widow, in 1676, he declared her four children to be as his own, each to inherit a portion equal to that of future offspring, with the rights of all protected in the event of the death of one partner and the remarriage of the other.[17]

Conditions often discouraged well-ordered marriages, however. Gils Thomkinson denied that she was illegitimately pregnant because, as her husband declared in court, their marriage was as good as it possibly could be, since with no appropriate minister available, all that was required was publication of their agreement "for the worlds Satisfaction." Samuel Hoskins and Elizabeth Cleverley did not get off as lightly. Unable to prove the parental consent they claimed to have, they entered into a private contract and "sinfully and wickedly defiled each other with filthy dalliance and uncleane passage," which, as the Connecticut court recognized, made them unfit for marriage to anyone else. The result was public correction, and then liberty to marry (1642). The town of Oyster Bay, having made the mistake of implying that a man of twenty-one and a woman of eighteen were of a fit age and needed no parental consent, quickly reversed itself by explaining that fitness did in no "wise take off the naturall bonds of duty and obligation which children owe to their parents," whose concurrence was still necessary.[18]

No doubt the wait for parental permission provided reluctant suitors with the excuse for procrastination. Claes Ripsz of Fort Orange, having entered into carnal conversation with the sister-in-law of Teunis Jacopsz upon a promise of marriage, found himself blessed with a child, but delayed the wedding while waiting to hear from his father in Holland. The court judged these excuses subterfuges, because the couple continued to live together. A month in irons persuaded the hesitant bridegroom to yield to his fate, prompt marriage.[19]

Passions not contained in legitimate forms overflowed dangerously. Love, while as good a reason as any for marriage, was suspect when contracted too quickly at first sight. John Leverett worried about his fifteen-year-old stepson who fell in love with the daughter of the Reverend Timothy Woodbridge. The boy was in a "passion," which Leverett hoped to cure by sending Mary away to her parents, so that distance and absence would bring him back to his senses.[20]

Illicit passion yielded the fruit of illegitimate offspring and, even worse, led to infanticide. Such crimes, "committed through ignorance of the law," occurred at too frequent a rate; Massachusetts ordered a printed copy of the statute transmitted to every minister in the colony, to be read on Sundays twice a year. Jane Crips of Talbot County, Maryland, disposed of her unwanted child by leaving it in the woods where the hogs ate it. Those willing to take less drastic steps to escape the punishment for having such children in the first place moved away from their homes. New Castle became one of their havens; there the case of Margret Lee, who came from Maryland, led the authorities to order that "no such persons may bee here harboured and this place may not serve and be counted as shelter for whoores" (1679). The penalty usually was death by hanging, as Elizabeth Greene found out when witnesses proved that she had burned her newborn baby. The one extenuating circumstance— that she had given birth prematurely to something that resembled the head of a dog—was not sufficient to get her off (1663). So suspicious were the authorities that the mere implication of having only spoken about the possibility of disposing of newborns was enough to lead to investigations.[21]

The nuptial pair, the focal point of family life, the permanent core where all else was temporary, knew that their union was subject to interruption, as when death removed one of the partners. Society intervened when the household lost its head, particularly if he left no will. In Rhode Island, when the widow would not settle her husband's estate, the town meeting did so (1658). Rapacious relatives circled about, small children needed indentures, and resources needed conservation to prevent future calls on community support. Widow Hanson with five little ones (1655), Widow Croker with a tiny plot (1661), Widow Shorter, illiterate but suspicious of the paper her son-in-law wished her to sign (1687), Mrs. James Arden, her husband *non compos mentis* and a boy to provide for (1731), and Widow Howland, who wished to send her son to Harvard (1738), were among those who turned to the courts for aid.[22]

But legal arrangements did not fill the emotional and practical vacuum left by the departure of a spouse. Remarriage was the expected response, and not through lack of feeling or want of foresight about the drawbacks. Ten years after his second wife's death, Robert Carter still felt a mourner and proposed to remain single; while a rhymer asked,

> To wed a widow, is it not to marry trouble,
> And *woe with woe* to double?

Still, the compelling claims of loneliness and the day-to-day needs of the household pulled men and women to the altar. Captain Timothy Dwight, one of the first children brought to Dedham, Massachusetts (1635), died in 1717, the same day as the sixth of his wives, evidence of his persistent needs.[23]

Samuel Sewall, in search of a new wife, surveyed the widows' pews and saw five sitting there. Cotton Mather also worried about the large number, among which he would dip. Sewall took care—"they that had been at sea should be careful how they put to sea again." Katherine Winthrop and Widow Denison rejected his suit. He often consulted his children and relatives—a large household would have to welcome a new mistress. He also set cooling financial preconditions. "My bowels yearn toward Mrs. Denison," he told his diary, "But I think God directs me in his Providence to desist." He finally married the suitable Mrs. Tilley (1718), who fell ill on their marriage night and died a year later.[24]

Sewall's next effort (1722) enlisted the aid of sympathetic children, concerned for their parent's welfare. In his businesslike courtship of Mary Gibbs, widow, her son Henry served as go-between, in part to collaborate on the financial arrangements. "What his mother would have done the children would agree to it," Henry told Sewall. On the other hand, where space and funds were scarce, some children resented their parents' remarriages. He "was as hot as a Skunk and the woman as hot as a Bitch," Abigail Bush commented on the nuptials of her father, in his sixties, to the Widow Pomery of Northampton (1697). Ashley Bowen and his sister Elizabeth in later years recalled with bitterness how after their mother died, leaving nine children, their father went a suiting a rich widow, Mistress Hannah Harris, willing "to separate his own family or anything else" to obtain her consent. Elizabeth was sure that the father, like "most men . . . [was] too much taken with the things of this world to the neglect of their children and familys." The thirteen-year-old Ashley and the son of the Widow Harris were promptly sent to sea as apprentices aboard ship on the ground that it "would lessen their family much if they were both bound out."[25]

In Massachusetts (1650) and elsewhere, the law forbade husband and wife to come to blows. But generally, whatever happened between them, the state preferred to stand apart— even when Jacob Hap of Fort Orange, having beaten his spouse, threw firebrands at her, thus endangering surrounding residences. The court vainly suggested that Nicholas Boot and his wife patch matters up when he complained of her drunkenness and household incompetence and when she rejoined that he was a poor provider who beat her and failed to meet his marital obligations (1658). Diane Foster White's husband, having gained control of her property, sold off some of her goods and ejected her from her home (1692), a fate that also befell Ann Steward, left a destitute cripple by her spouse. In neither case did the law provide an adequate remedy.[26]

Wives also went on the offensive, forgetting the obedience owed their husbands—and not only that tough Grietjen, wife of Anthony Jansen who measured the penises of visitors with a broomstick and cried out, "I have long enough been the whore of the nobility, now I want to be the rabble's whore" (1639). With what provocation the record does not state Joane Miller of Taunton beat and reviled her husband, bidding her children "knock him on the head and wishing his victuals might choke him." A move to another town did not ease relations, she still called him fool, toad, and vermin and scratched his face and hands (1656). At another pole, Joshua Verin suffered from his helpmate's insistence on going to hear Roger Williams preach as often as she wished. Women without means turned to the state to force errant husbands to support them. Women of means simply decamped as did Lady Hatton in England, who left Edward Coke to the mercy of a slovenly cook while she feasted in splendor (1617). Hezekiah Usher's genteel wife, covetous and cunning, slipped off to England but got her deserts in a will that reduced her portion and also lectured her on her duties.[27]

When no other course availed, there remained the alternative of divorce, within proper procedures. William Tubbs could publicly state that he refused to pay any debts incurred by Mercye, his wife (1664); but it would not do that he should get some friends to make a writing, effecting their separation. On the other hand, Thomas Holland, whose wife Elizabeth returned to New Hampshire after a two-year stay in England and three weeks later gave birth to a daughter, gained not only a divorce but also custody of the children (1704). Sarah Pearce earned a sympathetic response to her petition to the New Hampshire Council for the annulment of her marriage (1681). Her husband, a notorious fornicator, had left her seven years earlier, had squandered her estate, and threatened to kill her by poison or "knocking of the head." The "unerring rule of God and the laws of our nation," she protested, freed her from the bond of matrimony. To clinch the point, she added, "THE LAWS OF NATURE BEING THE FOUNDATION, ETC., OF HUMAN LAWS, AND NO WAY CONTRARY TO THE DIVINE, TEACHETH ME TO SEEK MY OWN PRESERVATION." Meanwhile she was living with, and wished to marry, the son of Thomas Seavy, who supported her petition.[28]

In all the colonies legislation to regularize marital relations reflected the uneasy feeling that orderly society was impossible without a framework for these basic forms. Neither the biblical commandments nor European laws applied at all comfortably under New World conditions. Yet colonial regulations, shaped by local circumstances and varying in detail, revealed how weak was the power to contravene individual choices. A residue of legal prescriptions not always enforceable cluttered the statute books.

In 1679 one of the church wardens of New Castle presented Evert Hendricks of Crainhoek to the local court for having two wives. Hendricks turned up at the next meeting with documents from a former Dutch commander and from English authorities proving that his two marriages were both valid; and when the wives expressed their consent to the arrangement, the court dismissed the case. In other instances, too, community pressure was strong enough to override authority, as when Edward Coppedge was found guilty of living in sin with Elizabeth Risby in Kent County, Maryland (1652), on the ground that she was unable to prove the death of her husband. But their neighbors considered the fine of six hundred pounds of tobacco for him and the sentence of fifteen lashes for her a gross violation of justice. Whatever the court ruled, they held the couple innocent of any crime, regarding them as lawfully married, except "only for ceremony."[29]

Ceremony counted for ever less. The law could not box in people who glimpsed unexpected possibilities of gratification in defiance of habit and custom. Men able to move from place to place weighed the advantages of desertion; and obstreperous women asserted their own wills. The thirty stripes Dorothy Steele received for leaving her husband (1697) did not stop her from running away with a lover, from trading with local blacks, and from fighting the North Carolina Indians. Spirited wives learned to punish their husbands through the withdrawal of favors, as did Governor Theophilus Eaton's Anne and as did Cotton Mather's beloved Lydia. Even in the staid New Haven Colony, respectable women asserted their own views in defiance of authority. Insofar as its government rested on paternal authority, the family had arrived at a parlous state by the eighteenth century.[30]

Now and again husband and wife pondered the bond that held them together. John Winthrop noted a story in his journal. William Hudson, away in England for two years, left his wife in the care of a young man "of good esteem for piety and sincerity," whose wife had not yet come across. Man and woman worked together, in effect lived together, until one night—it happened—he crept into bed with her. But she dissuaded him "so as he lay still and did not touch her." She did not cry out, she later explained, because he had been very faithful and helpful in her husband's absence and she did not want him disgraced. Snoopy servants having spread the story, she came to trial not for adultery but for adulterous behavior. A jury declared her innocent; but the magistrates ruled her guilty and condemned her to stand on a ladder with a halter for one hour and be whipped or pay a £20 fine. Hudson chose to pay. "But their estate being but mean, she chose rather to submit" to punishment "than that her husband should suffer so much for her folly. So he received her again, and they lived loving together." To live lovingly was to apprehend the unity of affections, of shared interests and prospects. All else changed about them. Others passed in and out of the household. But these two clung together in immediate tasks and future hopes.[31]

Relations between the conjugal pair were pivotal to the household, procreation being the ultimate purpose of marriage and custody of children the family's primary function. Few women matched the twenty-six offspring produced by William Phips's prolific mother, but six to eight births was not unusual, and left parents weighty responsibilities.[32]

The natural ties of parental affection gained force from the occasions for mourning the high rate of infant mortality created and from awareness that the surviving progeny would be sole memorials of the long migration. Children were therefore invaluable blessings of God, and in addition their labor contributed to the household's welfare. In return for spiritual and material nurture, they owed their parents obedience and support. Hence the greater potential value of boys over girls; Norwalk, Connecticut, expressly excluded females from the benefits granted males born in the town (1721). Small wonder that Timothy Edwards lamented his sixty feet of daughters—ten of them. However, not only sons but also daughters had to read, write, and cipher, and beyond all that had to prepare for some agreeable calling. Children of both sexes also needed instruction in divine matters. For in the end, mothers like fathers would be obligated to further the salvation of their children.

Seeds of corruption implanted in nature and nurtured by the environment threatened fulfillment of generational obligations. Sons negligent of filial responsibilities troubled the whole community. In 1680, the New Hampshire Court indicted John Waldron, already found guilty of vicious living, alcoholism, and neglect of his calling, for physically abusing his aged father. The terrified old man gladly saw his offspring imprisoned for the relief it gave the entire family.[33]

The young, occupied with their own affairs, lost patience with the old, who took up places they should have vacated and postponed the time of inheritance. Tempers flared. John Stebbins called his father an old fool (1655), Joseph Porter, Jr., called his "theife, lyar, and simple ape, shitta-bed"—in each term of invective perhaps a grain of truth (1660). James Barker did not meet the conditions of the contract with the aged father whose house he occupied (1690). James Doake gave his father the lie and perhaps beat him also (1723). Repeatedly litigation exposed family quarrels, greed, and private arrangements without basis in law. Rapacious children or their spouses persuaded the old folk to transfer estates in return for maintenance and support with the siblings sharing duties and costs. When unforeseen circumstances—like the death of one brother—intervened, agreements made in good faith broke down, as they did for John Clifford (1718). The problem gained in complexity when it involved several sets of children, as with the offspring of Walter Lee's three wives (1712). The elderly had their faults, and the young their virtues. Samuel Sewall did not like it when Martha Oakes publicly struck her daughter-in-law in the face; and he did like it when Joseph Prout's young son every day dressed and tended the ten fistulous wounds on his father's thigh. Young and old recognized, though they did not always adhere to, the obligations of a code that expected honor to the father and mother.[34]

The obligations ran in both directions. Society held the guardians responsible when the immature got into or caused trouble. It was a clear case, even at home, that rigid discipline was essential. An English servant at the end of the sixteenth century noted that "overmuch cherishing" gave occasion to great and incurable vices in children, who ought to be "holden down by fear" if not otherwise, and particularly during adolescence. When childish stone-throwing in Old World lanes endangered innocent lives, the Edinburgh authorities as a matter of course held fathers and masters answerable for their charges (and ordered vagabonds caught in the act scourged and banished from the town). The colonies also held parents to blame for the transgressions of offspring. Of course, the American setting was uncongenial—witness the laxity of the upbringing of Indian children that earned the disapproval even of the mild-mannered Roger Williams.[35]

Therefore no task was more urgent than to maintain parental authority. Only thus could the boy or girl learn self-control and mastery of the will. Lightness and weakness were folly. A strict inspection upon how the young spent their time, upon their conversation, and upon the company they kept would prevent costly errors. A prompt and stern rebuke must follow every misbehavior. Proper education would tame the animal impulses through which Satan did his work. "Don't you Know," thundered Cotton Mather, "That your *Children,* are the *Children* of Death, and the *Children of Hell,* and the *Children of Wrath by Nature;* and that from *you,* this *Nature* is derived and conveyed unto them!" That reason alone made it necessary to instruct youths in the great matters of salvation.[36]

The improvement of his sons in learning and manners was one of the greatest blessings Robert Carter expected in this world (1720). Cadwallader Colden stated the goals of good parents (1742). He aimed to put his children "in a way to provide for themselves by their own industry," which was more advantageous than leaving them estates from which they could live without thought or care. His son was a merchant, his younger children were growing up to industry and virtue, and his daughter made the ideal catch by marrying a DeLancey, the scion of "one of the most noted merchants in America," which, Colden could not restrain himself from noting, made her a fortune beyond his expectations.[37]

Not all fathers and mothers were so dutiful. Parental affection, indulgence, and pity, human failings not easily suppressed under any circumstances, erupted particularly when all else had changed. To maintain discipline called for uncommon fortitude and determination. His mother hesitated to say no to Josiah Willard out of fear that a positive command would only incite him to disobedience. In cases of excessive leniency, the authorities stepped in, as New Amsterdam did in 1657 when it decided to punish parents who allowed a child to steal timber, and thus "grow up in wickedness," as if they themselves had committed the deed. Inquisitive relatives intervened as did Goodwife Cumming, who complained that her son-in-law did not take care of his children, to give "them due edducation and to bring them up in sum honnest imployment" (1678). Indeed parents sometimes turned to the courts to reassert authority over wayward offspring, as Edward Jones did in complaining that his son was living "in unlawful lust" with Sary Minkings; in response the reprobate spread the rumor that his father was a cattle thief. Runaway marriages usually evoked first protests, then reconciliations. Massachusetts also made itself guardian of children sent over from England in the hope that the pure country manners of New England would divert them from "extravagant and riotous courses." Alas, the authorities noted in 1647, unscrupulous dealers extended credit to such children "to ye great greife of yir friends, dishonor of God and reproach of country." Anyone giving credit to youths under the age of twenty-one would forfeit the debt. The state also intervened in cases of parental mistreatment, as it did when it stripped Alexander Ray of custody of his daughters-in-law and of their estates.[38]

Parents sought to extend their authority, some even beyond their lifetimes. The will of John Boswell of St. George's Parish, Virginia (1740), divided 980 acres among his children equally, with the injunction that the court bind his sons, when they reached the age of fifteen, one to a joyner, one to a carpenter, and one to a blacksmith. But in death as in life, parental sanctions lost force as a means of control. Contests in New Amsterdam (1658) and Massachusetts (1715) challenged the rights of parents to disinherit some of their children. In any case, the effectiveness of the threat of disinheritance in the Old World had depended upon scarcity of land and continuity of ownership that raised the value of holdings. The gravity of the penalty diminished to the vanishing point in a setting abundant in space and opportunity. Furthermore those children born to the place, without recollections of any other, older world, were often more at home in the wilderness, better able to fend for themselves than their parents were.[39]

Many a father and mother, after diligent endeavors at proper upbringing, regarded the results with dismay. Samuel Sewall had to whip his pride and joy, Joseph, for hitting his sister with a brass knob and for playing at prayertime (1693); little Sarah suffered from convulsions (1695); Betty fell into depression at the thought that she was a reprobate; and nephew Sam, not yet twenty, got his mistress's maid pregnant (1696). No one understood the correct course of family life better than Cotton Mather, who knew how to accept the death of his beloved daughter Jerusha—he "would endeavor exceedingly to glorify God by making a sacrifice of the lovely child." But he was at a loss over the agonizing problems with his son Increase, which culminated in 1721 when the wretch and some other rakes caused a riot in Boston. Mather was beside himself and vented his sorrow in reflecting how to glorify God "on this deplorable occasion and what is my duty in relation to the incorrigible prodigal." There seemed no alternative but to cast Creasy out until he repented. So too, fearful of being overindulgent, Landon Carter concealed his affection for his namesake—his greatest happiness. But from early on Landon Carter, Jr., was a source of trouble, which his parsimonious, hardworking, and diligent father could not understand. Even before he was of age, the boy enjoyed fast living and good company and took up with a woman Landon Carter, Sr., was not prepared to accept as a daughter-in-law. Threatened, "If you do not henceforward leave her you must leave me," the youth answered, "I will leave you," upon which his father threw him out of the house. (1757).[40]

Departures and separations were, in any case, normal incidents of family life, though rarely accompanied by the bruised feelings of the Carters. Sons entering their teens usually left the parental household, either to embark upon an occupation through apprenticeship or to live under supervision with discipline untainted by the sentimental weakness of father and mother. Well-to-do youngsters in a minister's home could acquire a smattering of letters and habits of sobriety and good behavior. Lads in the cities trudged off to schools which instilled fear by the shadow of the rod. Israel Pemberton never forgot the schoolmaster's beating with a thick stick about the head and arms until the blood came and the flesh turned black and yellow and green (1698). Nevertheless people bemoaned leniency, not harshness. What an abuse it was of precious time, what a profanation, to tolerate April Fool's Day pranks! Late in life, Joseph Green complained that he had not learned what he should have because his aged and feeble instructor let the boys have their own way. Some young men even went off to the academies at Cambridge, New Haven, and Williamsburg, although concerned parents worried about the sins to which students were prone—"youthful lusts, speculative wantonness, and secret filthiness, which God sees in the dark."[41]

Much better, young Sam Sewall told his uncle, to go as apprentice to a good master who would keep him occupied and prevent the idleness on which he blamed his romantic difficulties. Most boys made the same choice. The children of craftsmen and merchants prepared for life under the oversight of someone not related to them. Only one heir could take over the enterprise; the brothers had to leave town to practice the same trade or else learn some other. And those unwilling to follow their father's calling preferred to move off, to become men by asserting their strength, testing and proving themselves. The wish to quit the parental roof united the motives of doing better in life and of displaying individuality. The fathers generally approved. Departure would advance the son's welfare, subject him to stricter discipline and more rigid training than at home, and remove the source of running tension when those still young in years but growing in power competed with their elders.[42]

Apprenticeship in Europe had acquired a regular pattern. Transplanted to the New World, it remained vital, although altered. Apprenticeship in Europe meant life in a family of contract rather than of birth; ideally it remained so in America. The master took the place of the blood father; the apprentice became a son for the duration of the agreement. The older man undertook to house, feed, and clothe the youth, to train him for the chosen vocation, to supervise his behavior and guard his moral welfare, and to teach him to read and write. The youngster became subject to family discipline and to the requirement to labor faithfully and obey all commands. The contract, consented to by the boy and signed by the natural and adoptive fathers, set out the terms in detail.

In Europe, the system operated within communities powerful enough to regulate and enforce such agreements. The municipal authorities registered the documents and passed judgment on grievances. The guilds established standards about the length of service, quality of instruction, and other obligations, and treated those who did not conform as outsiders, forbidden to practice the crafts or engage in trade. Communal controls did not endure in America. With town and parish oversight lax, masters and boys fumbled through trial-and-error adjustments to take account of differences in tools, materials, and business methods. Contracts lost uniformity, and certainty of enforcement faded. Each arrangement became the product of individual negotiation, resulting less in a coherent system than in a loose bundle of practices.[43]

Ben Franklin (b. 1706) had the choice among many crafts in the Boston of the 1720s. The tenth son of a tallow chandler, he early decided not to follow his father's calling. For a time the family believed he might aspire to the ministry—his bookish tastes pointed in that direction. But he was restless, already twelve years old, and eager to be off like his brother Josiah, who had gone to sea. His father took him on walks to see joiners, bricklayers, turners, and braziers at work, knowing the youngster would not stay home, hoping to settle him in a desirable vocation rather than lose him forever. When another brother, James, acquired a press and set up as a printer, Ben entered his service as apprentice. He learned to clean up the place and handle accounts, to distribute type and set it to make up a page, and also, when space required, to write a column. Nevertheless a brother's control was almost as irksome as a father's. One way or another Ben, at seventeen, found an excuse to be off to Philadelphia, seeking an opportunity to be on his own.

Farm boys also broke away. The first generation or two waited for the patrimony, as in Europe; but by the third, and sometimes sooner, impatience set in. Fathers lived longer and sons faced the prospect of postponing independence and marriage for decades. The calculation became clear—the inheritance was not worth the wait, when youthful labor applied to abundant land not too far away would yield greater immediate rewards. Even in New England, communities could not hold on to young people. And elsewhere the move out and away was swifter still.[44]

Communities that retained power, as in New England, could bring sanctions to bear upon deviants. In extreme cases, they executed those who committed sodomy or bestiality, and hedged the behavior of youths about with vigilant defenses. Noting the spread of "ignorance, ill manners and irreligion," because families failed in their educational obligations, New Hampshire recommended that selectmen examine all children above ten years old, and bind the illiterate out to reading and writing masters. The measure implied that the state had rights over the young, regardless of parental wishes. The court disposed of Jedidiah Lumbert of Barnstable in some honest family in response to his father's complaint (1660). But the authorities also acted spontaneously against abusive or negligent parents. For their own good, "and bringeing up soe as they may be usefull in the common weal or them selves to liue comfortable and use fuly in the time to come," the town put out and apprenticed the children of the poor "with the consent of their parents if it may be hade and if the parents shall oppose them" with the help of the magistrate (1671). By the same token, Massachusetts granted some poor parents the money with which to redeem children from Indian captivity while others received help to support "distracted" offspring.[45]

North Carolina also sought to bind children out to trades. But weak community controls there, in New York, and in Virginia left the young headstrong, disobedient, making their own way—"as wild, uncultivated, and unimproved as the soil was when their forefathers first had it."[46]

Everywhere parental ambiguity increased. As time went on, more often than not, experience proved that the very attributes they knew they should condemn—curiosity, willfulness, determination, and the hunger for novelty—led to success and improvement, novel concepts in a world theretofore accustomed to thinking of fixed status. Hence while mothers and fathers wished to hold on, they knew that they had to push their children out; and separations became normal incidents of life.

By the eighteenth century, people had learned to accept the wrench of departures, and the transient relationships of one generation to another produced a subtle change in personalities. The father, having himself once gone off to make his way, could not object—indeed, learned to approve —when his sons packed up. He retained authority at home while the children were there, but his rule was temporary and the dawning awareness that the proper rearing for boys prepared them to go, not to stay, qualified his power. As for himself, the father understood that life's satisfactions were not patriarchal, not the pleasure of knowing that an endless tribe would extend through time his own labors on the earth. Whatever joy life held in store was individual, the product of his own achievement.

Sons, too, acquired values that conformed to the situation. The emotional ties to mother or father, to brother or sister, did not affect the certainty of separation. A boy learned to act independently and to get along on his own resources. Self-sufficiency was the immediate goal, and the sooner achieved the better, in earning a livelihood, in gaining affection, in gratifying the needs of the spirit. The early assumption of responsibility was not only an unavoidable hazard where mortality was high; the experience of shifting for himself forced the child to be a man in order to survive. The lad in his teens left without a father, who took on the charge of a whole family, matured in a day. Parents did well to hasten the moment at which the youth completed his education through the practical encounter with life. The necessity for standing alone became a preference. Boys eagerly awaited the test, and if it took too long in coming, precipitously hastened forth to meet it.

The family relationship was clearest where the property issue was unambiguous. No such claims of affection as influenced children, spouse, or kin complicated the situation of servants. For the duration of their terms, they belonged clearly and without qualification to the head of the household, enjoined to remember that the master was their father and the mistress their mother; and they, correspondingly, were in some sort children. If they lacked the privileges of offspring, they were also quit of some of their obligations. An Englishman (1705) accorded them one obligation only: "to do the work that lies before them." Few actually believed that theirs was a favored status, that in spite of all the discomforts to which they were exposed, they were insulated from the world to an extent which actually favored them. "They have their Masters only to please," an Englishman wrote, while others took care of them. Whatever calamity befell a family, they were not responsible. However mean or low the appearance of their circumstances, yet servants were often better off "for ease and happiness of mind," than their masters.[47]

Young people in stable settings entered service through a contract or indenture, a written agreement formally executed and signed on their behalf by a parent or guardian, that specified the duration of service, the dues awarded at freedom, and the amount and quality of instruction, clothing, and food provided. Apprenticeship made them temporary members of the family. An expanding and mobile society suffering from a consistent shortage of skills did not exclude outsiders or examine plausible credentials. Masters, pressed for help, took on anyone willing to do a job and treated apprentices simply as extra hands, trying to get as much work as possible out of everyone, not to waste precious time on instruction.

The apprentice mingled in the family with other kinds of dependent laborers. At a public auction, the head of the household could buy orphans or the children of the poor or incompetent, to be held until the age of twenty-one, or he could buy indentured servants for a term of years, or he could buy African or Irish slaves. The confusion of rights and responsibilities deepened when these purchases jumbled together under the same crowded roof: colonial, English, Welsh, Scottish, German, Irish, and Africans, lads and maidens, men and women.

Servants, like children, lacked the freedom to act on their own behalf; the head of the household supervised their morals and exercised the power of attorney for them. Samuel Terry, caught standing with his face to the meetinghouse wall, chafing his yard to provoke lust, got six lashes from his master, who then sold away the remainder of his time (1650). They could not marry without leave lest that affect the length of their terms. They owed their masters obedience and labor, in return for which they were due their nurture, a term that comprehended not only food, shelter, and clothing, but also instruction in the Way of the Lord as well as in the skills necessary to strike out on their own account some day. Their servitude and therefore their position in the household was temporary and provisional, extending for a fixed period that ended with the majority of mature persons capable of making their own way in the world as master or mistress of their own household.[48]

The ambitious apprentice could appeal to the law to secure the proper training and he could refuse to work, or worse, slack at his trade, or worst of all, spoil costly materials, damaging tactics that limited the master's negligence. But no lively boy protested when the old man for want of time skipped family prayers or the study of the Bible or the oversight of the morals of his charges or even the requirement that they be taught to read and write. The familial aspects receded to the background and the relationship became a kind of employment, not education preparatory to a vocation.

The townspeople could not impose order. A master's discipline was not enough to assure good behavior. The lads and wenches met when they wished, they drank rum at the taverns, they danced together till late in the night. Reproved, they threatened to burn the town down. From time to time disorderly gatherings and riots showed the limits of control. Apprentices were often among the active elements in the eighteenth-century mobs.

Nevertheless apprenticeship remained an important means of transmitting skills from one generation to another. Learning was a matter of demonstration, imitation, and experience. The novice watched how the task was done, tried his own hand at it, and then by repeated practice acquired the ability to do the same.

In the absence of guilds capable of setting standards for apprentices, journeymen, and others, each negotiation took its own course. There was always danger in these relationships, for servants, like children, were usually helpless except to flee, unless the community was strong enough to intervene, as in other family matters, to enforce the terms of the agreement. Women were particularly at risk, for promises of marriage and freedom softened sexual inhibitions and plunged Mary Hews (1662) and Anne Mardin (1661) into trouble. Female servants, rarely protected by contracts, suffered severe punishment for yielding to temptation. Servants' sex lives concerned masters not only on grounds of morality but also for the loss of time in pregnancy. The father, when known, had to pay for the child's maintenance and also for the mother's inability to work. But collecting the amount due was difficult. John Griffith did not pay the 1300 pounds of tobacco as the court ordered and in time married the girl, which did not help the master (1667).

Margerie Goold accused John Lumbrozo, her master, of trying to rape her (while offering her scriptural proof that it was the right thing to do) (1663). Lumbrozo had more success with another maid, Elizabeth Wild, but gave her medicine that induced an abortion. True, John Pecke of Rehoboth never got "to satisfy his fleshly beastly lust" for his father's maid. A good girl could resist. But what did it profit Philip Taylor's servant when her master sued John Little for going to bed with her? Little confessed, blaming intoxication, and paid a fine of five shillings; but this hardly took the sting out of the whipping she got for her part in the affair.[49]

Where the contract was clear, courts sustained the rights of bondsmen and women, ordering additional clothing and freeing servants who could not read and write, one of the conditions of their indenture. Indeed, public assurance of fair judicial treatment aimed to induce servants not to run away. But the law generally favored the master in disputes over length of service or that arrayed his word against theirs. Despite evidence that Captain William Powell was a drunkard, he persuaded Virginia to have his man whipped with ears nailed to the pillory for slander (1619). Servants like James Crayford who complained of hard usage (1677) often had in response only warnings that they improve their behavior. And even when a Maryland court found Mistress Ward guilty of "unreasonable and unChristian like punishment" in the treatment of her servants, one of whom died in a runaway effort, the fine amounted to but 300 pounds of tobacco. Pope Alvey, Maryland hangman, whose abuse killed his girl Alice, got only a branding. Nor was there a desire to investigate whether Captain Thomas Bradnox's servant James Wilson had died from fever and dropsy or from the stripes his master administered.[50]

But Bradnox and his wife went too far. When Sarah Tailer, their servant, was found, a runaway in the woods, starved by eating trash by reason of their brutal treatment, she was spared the lash; the evidence of her wounds persuaded the magistrates that she had been beaten enough. But she had to beg forgiveness on her knees and promise to do better (1659). Two years later, at last, the court discharged her from her obligations on the ground that she was in "eminent Danger" from "the invetterate Mallice of hur Master and Mistress."[51]

The vestry or town took a direct interest in arrangements for the young servant, for they were responsible for placing in homes parentless or illegitimate children, according to their condition; Elizabeth and William Fewson were thus to have two years' schooling and each of them £5 and a cow and calf at the end of their terms (1733), while two bastards the next year received no such assurance.[52]

In principle, contracts signed in England or on the continent of Europe had the same effect as those signed in America. The prospective emigrant agreed to serve for a stated number of years in return for passage while the middleman recouped the costs by a sale to a willing master. For the duration, the foreign servant enjoyed the same status as the native-born. In the absence of precise knowledge of conditions, indentures signed abroad were less specific than those negotiated on the spot, and much depended on the honesty of the ship captain or contractor and on the level of skill of the newcomer. Yet the interest in sustaining the movement kept conditions good.[53]

Occasionally, as in Europe, men and women in the New World served from year to year without a contract. They lacked any protection against the greater power of the master, other than the ability to run away. But in the Old World the abundance of labor and close distances increased the chances of recapture when cruelty provoked the effort to escape. In any case the runaway rarely had any place to go in an over-stocked labor market. The legendary Dick Whittington of the story was wise to turn back before it was too late; such as he might well run afoul of stringent laws against vagabonds.

American statutes also sought to prevent servants from wandering away from their families, a practice at the root of much disorder. Yet the Massachusetts authorities ruefully conceded an increase in the sin of idleness despite numerous wholesome laws against it (1675). In the colo-nies space limited the absolute power of the strong over the weak, of masters over servants. Beyond the plantation or the clearing or the town lay the wilderness, and those impatient with restraint or resentful of lowly status could escape if they chose to take the risk, substantial but ever less intimidating as the interior filled up, as the wild beasts receded and the native inhabitants grew less strange. The prudent householder knew that hands pushed too hard would vanish, whatever the law said of the obligation to stay. Over the borders lay North Carolina and Pennsylvania and opportunity. Hence some masters, out of fear lest their servants run away, tried to ease court-imposed sentences. Richard Crabb of Stamford, Connecticut, thus protested (1643) against the whipping of his Indian with the excuse that family correction had already punished the offense. The court ordered the sentence executed and in addition fined Crabb for putting concern with his property above public order.[54]

Crabb and in time other masters feared that extreme penalties would damage their own welfare and that of the province, defeating their own purpose by making the disgruntled desperate and lowering the colony's reputation. The Virginia statute of 1705 forbade immoderate correction, regularized the status of servants without indentures and guaranteed the right of complaint. In the wings were notorious characters like Thomas Norris, ready to help bondsmen escape to New England for a fee (1671).[55]

In the final analysis, surly types damaged a master's economic interest. Suicide, the ultimate protest, and even debilitating illness, were pure loss to those in need of labor. "Servants eat a man up if he is not constantly over their heads," one colonist complained. Even when supervised, they left much to be desired. An absentee New Jersey master learned that one of his hands was so slovenly and sickly, drunk half the time, that it would be more profitable to sell him the rest of his time than continue the employment. Another was a great rascal and liar "and would steal the teeth out of a man's head"; no one would buy his time, so well were his misdemeanors known. Two others were really naughty boys. Richard Preston's people refused to work when a shortage eliminated meat from their diet, leaving them, they said, too weak for physical labor. Preston sympathized with them, offered to let them go off for a week to look for meat elsewhere, and added sugar, fish oil, and vinegar to their provender. But the servants remained "peruerse . . . [and] in their obstinate condicion" refused all compromises. The court made a show of ordering them lashed, then remitted the penalty.[56]

Out of concern for the colony's reputation if not for humanitarian reasons, authorities in the New World showed more solicitude for the rights of dependents—servants, apprentices, orphans—than did European governments. If he were in Holland and did not take better care, he should get a flogging, explained the New Amsterdam cooper of a boy habitually late who did his work poorly. But the effort at discipline only landed the master in court. The state also intervened in cases of neglect or failure to live up to contractual terms. A Maryland court, shocked at his disheveled emaciated appearance, released an orphan from all obligations to a delinquent master—"the voice of the People Crieth shame thearat."[57]

Then, too, the relationship was transient. The servant bound himself or herself to work for the number of years specified and then earned freedom, along with agreed-upon dues. In this respect, too, circumstances altered cases. Freedom was but a poor prize unaccompanied by opportunity. During Virginia's hard times (1623), Richard Frethorn could not even keep all his servants, for want of bread to feed them. In many districts of England, France, Ireland, and Germany more eager hands crowded around the landlord or craftsman than there were jobs to do, so that often the expiration of a term brought with it no hope other than to be taken on for another. In the colonies, however, hands were at a premium and whoever gained freedom could marry or earn an independent livelihood, become master or mistress of a household.

The expectation of a rise in status was realistic. To become at once a freeholder required money for fees, tools, seed, and livestock and for provisions on which to live while clearing the land. But freedmen who hired themselves out or took plots on shares or as tenants expected to rise and did. The availability of land practically for the taking opened up the prospect of advancement; and high wages and the crying need for skilled workers in town created chances for all. The shortage of women widened chances, as for Robert Carter's Margaret Upton, who "married very well after she was free" (1721). The number or percentage of those who actually rose, and how soon and how far, had less consequence for people in service than the glimmer of hope presented by an occasional example of improvement unthinkable in the Old World.[58]

The origins of the bondsmen at first made little difference. People preferred to take into their families servants most like themselves. In the cramped quarters, every difference was a potential source of conflict. Still, that preference was not decisive to begin with, not even in the case of Africans, those most distinctive in color and in culture. The laws, at first, protected all. When James Knott misused her son "Pharaoh," an apprentice, his mother Jane Winlee sued and forced the master to remedy what was amiss.[59]

But the involuntary character of African servitude in time set those people apart. Others, with the choice of whether to come or not, could negotiate the length of their terms; the blacks could influence neither conditions nor destination. After 1660 a gulf steadily widened between Africans and others, between the involuntary and the voluntary. The effort to recruit ever more servants led to steady improvement in the lot of those closest in culture to the masters, and especially of the English. Complaints of cruelty and of failure to live up to promises, communicated in letters to friends and relatives, reduced the flow, while good treatment attracted additional hands. The interests of masters and of the colonial governments therefore coincided in making the terms of service tolerable. By contrast the Africans, seized by force, lacked choice; even had they been able to communicate with family or friends, they would not have influenced the numbers exported. In the eighteenth century the flow increased steadily. Although as many as half the slaves died in transit, from disease, suicide, or beatings, the survivors added significantly to the colonial population. At 1760 blacks formed about 10 percent of the total.

In the absence of incentives to improve their conditions, their status remained fixed and indeed deteriorated. Complaints about the quality of their work became justifications for less favorable treatment, and lack of contracts led to extension of terms. The law forbade intermarriage to prevent that "abominable mixture," with offspring of indeterminate status. White women in Virginia rarely worked in the fields and were exempt from taxes unless so employed, unlike blacks expected to labor out of doors. The Africans served in perpetuity, themselves and their offspring, and gradually sank into an impersonal status as slaves.[60]

Marked regional and local differences emerged in the course of the changes in African servitude, depending upon the percentage of blacks in the population, upon whether they lived concentrated in cities or dispersed in the countryside, and upon whether the plantation or the yeoman farm predominated. In rural New York, trades and sales took slaves from one household to another without fuss (1754–1766). Massachusetts tended to resolve doubtful cases in favor of liberation of bondsmen (1716, 1738), although most colonies regarded manumission suspiciously as a device of masters to shift to the public the burden of supporting the aged and infirm.[61]

Whether on isolated estates or among the urban crowds, fear of an uprising deepened as the black population increased. Governor Spotswood in 1710 warned the Virginians not to count on "that Babel of Languages" to divide the blacks. "Freedom wears a cap which can without a tongue, call together all those who long to shake the fetters of slavery" in an insurrection with dreadful consequences. A restrictive law in response did not quiet the fears. Nor did indignant expostulations about the great indulgence of slavery in the colonies that left the blacks better treated than the poor of most Christian countries. Grown wanton with excess of liberty, ruined by idleness, the bondsmen ungratefully conspired to burn down the town. Nor did it help to limit the number of slaves at funerals where they could plot and confederate together (1731); or to forbid them from going in the streets after night without a lighted lantern. It did help to emancipate Will as a reward for fidelity and as encouragement to others after he uncovered a conspiracy of other slaves in Virginia (1710).[62]

Crime created complex problems. It was all very well to hang Exeter for killing his own master—that was an act of revenge and a warning to others. But slaves were not altogether free moral agents and sometimes punishment damaged their masters, who sought compensation from the government. Other irritations reminded people of the anomalies of considering people property, like the practice of Guinea men anchored in the York River of throwing dead blacks overboard to the annoyance of planters along the shore, or the issue of whether slaves were to count as chattels or real estate in cases of inheritance. Then, too, burdensome regulations aimed to discourage runaways, like laws requiring a pass or certificate for those who traveled.[63]

Free blacks, outside the confines of any master's family, heightened the insecurity, for the model of independence unsettled people still in bondage and created troubling issues about status, as when Pennsylvania finally released a mulatto who claimed that he had been born free of free parents and could not be made a slave. Laws limited the rights of blacks (or Jews, Moors, or Moslems) to hold slaves or even to entertain servants. The disquietude grew when Quakers and others raised the issue, whether descent or color made it right to steal or buy men's bodies, denying them the liberty other people enjoyed.[64]

The widening disparity between the status of Africans and that of other servants by the eighteenth century caused concern. In Massachusetts Judge Samuel Sewall, puzzling over the issue, saw a contradiction between the new form of bondage and Christianity. He sadly concluded in a tract, *The Selling of Joseph* (1700), that there would be no progress in the spread of the gospel until the abolition of slavery. He objected to dehumanizing discriminatory laws, "an oppression provoking to God," and considered it offensive when legislation rated Indians and blacks with horses and hogs. "These ethiopians as black as they are, seeing they are the sons and daughters of the first Adam, the Brethren and sisters of the last Adam and the offspring of God, they ought to be treated with a respect agreeable." Later some Friends also sensed a religious imperative against bondage.[65]

The gradual improvement in the condition of other servants left the Africans and their descendants debased and apart. Still members of their masters' families, but linked by no ties of affection and destitute of rights, they differed fundamentally from others, who all enjoyed some degree of freedom. By contrast blacks were totally unfree; marked, a sharp line separated them, lacking liberty, from others who possessed it, in however small a measure.

Indians fell into quite another category. Members of their own tribes, their social organization intact, they drew upon an alternative culture that enabled them at first to ease the adjustment of the Europeans to the new continent. Curiosity and mutual interests sometimes united red men and Europeans, as in pursuit of the fur trade. Competition for land and different perceptions of property rights divided them. Hopes of imminent conversion proved unrealistic. The Puritan conception of the covenant as the basis of the church was inappropriate to the missionary task; and elsewhere clergymen were too few in number to move into the wilderness. Moreover contacts at the frontier rarely persuaded the tribesmen of the depth of Christian virtue. Nevertheless Governor Dinwiddie of Virginia, among others, continued to believe that acts of kindness would propagate love and amity along the frontier.[66]

The colonists were dubious of the propriety of allowing Indians (or mulattoes) to keep Christian servants; but they also forbade the seizure of tribesmen for servitude except as punishment for crimes deserving the death penalty. When Tom the Indian in Massachusetts (1675) petitioned for remission of the sentence passed on him for rape on the grounds of his ignorance of the law, the court spared his life, but ordered him sold as a slave for ten years. Rhode Island, a year later, outlawed Indian slavery except under narrowly defined conditions. In 1715 a rash of "conspiracies, insurrections, rapes, thefts and other execrable crimes" persuaded that colony to prohibit the further importation of Indian slaves or servants, which in any case had discouraged the flow of white servants from England. Virginia, a decade earlier, had bound some out for service "beyond the seas." The provinces also showed some solicitude for the rights of free Indians, accepting their unsworn evidence in some cases and admonishing settlers who used excessive force against them.[67]

By the 1760s the Indians seemed children requiring guardians because unable to take care of themselves. Without community protection they would sink even lower than they already were. The Mashpee Indians, Massachusetts concluded, were "of an indolent slothful disposition and averse to any kind of labour for their support." Out of "meer compassion," the General Court prevented them from selling land to the English "without the consent of guardians appointed by the Court." The desire for "as full Liberty of disposing of their real estate as his majesty's English subjects enjoy," was the kind of "Liberty the most sensible part of the Indians themselves are averse to," knowing it would lead to their speedy ruin and destruction. The community felt empowered to restrict the liberty of inhabitants for their own benefit.[68]

What *racial* meant was ambiguous. William Byrd in spite of all the miscegenation laws believed it a pity that the settlers did not intermarry with the Indians, which would have produced a healthier breed of people while civilizing the aborigines more swiftly. By contrast, the debased status of the Africans unsettled attitudes toward them. Dominie Selyns (1664) "refused to baptize their children . . . partly on account of their want of knowledge and belief, and partly on account of the material and perverted object which they had in view—nothing else than liberating their children from bodily slavery, without striving after godliness and Christian virtue."[69]

Although for different reasons, neither black nor red people fitted comfortably within the colonial conception of the family, derived as it was from European antecedents. Occasional individuals found places within the households that took form in the New World, but only after surmounting substantial cultural and social hurdles. And changes within the settlers' families raised the difficulty of the effort.

Outsiders rarely sensed the transformation effected by the American environment in husbands, wives, parents, children, masters, servants. None were quite the same on the western shore of the Atlantic as on the eastern. The burdens of decision and challenges to exercise of the will shaped personality types prepared for encounters as individuals with whatever else life might bring. No longer contained within an encompassing community, the family lost cohesive power and set its members loose to fly or to fall. The household persisted as a productive unit that provided a provisional home for children during the age of dependency. But boys sooner, girls later moved out into independence, leaving husband and wife with each other. Parents and children then explored the novel relationship among individuals united not by need or habit but by ties of feeling outsiders did not share.

VII

ENTERPRISE AND

MOBILITY, 1600–1760

THE TRANSFORMATION of religious and family life proceeded within the context of drastic economic changes that altered transplanted institutions and rules of behavior, thereby broadening individual opportunity.

The original plan of the settlements rested on firm assumptions about the communal nature of the productive system. The first plantations, modeled on the successful Dutch and British East India trading companies, held joint stocks and common property and operated for the benefit of the corporate entity. Promoters expected individuals to gain as investors insofar as they would share in the prosperity of the enterprise. The New World experience, however, modified the attitudes of participants, even of those who originally subscribed in good faith.

A migrant people, at the start and later, carried with it layer upon layer of expectations. Superimposed upon the motives for departure, themselves complex, were intentions discovered only in the course of the journey; and arrival opened glimpses of possibilities beyond past imaginings. The one certainty: habits and customs would not remain intact.

Survival was the first concern of passengers aboard ship, as at each advance into the wilderness. Whatever other calculations filtered through the thoughts of the tempest-tossed, of the becalmed who measured the declining stores against the passing days, of the timid who caught sight of strange sails on the horizon, the salient concern was safe arrival in a sheltering port. So too, in every clearing the residents awoke from dreams of ease and plenty to confront the reality of lurking beasts and savage foes, of illness and of dearth by reason of natural disaster. They too wished first of all to endure. Impatiently Governor Printz responded to suggestions from Sweden that he catch whales, find minerals, and cultivate silkworms: he had all he could do to provide people something to eat. But once the anchor dropped, the home arose, and the crop came in, other prospects crowded to the fore.[1]

From the Old World the colonists brought ideas, most clearly articulated by the Puritans, that explained why people did what they did. Though not as explicitly stated by others, all seventeenth-century colonists shared the same views. Each person had a calling, a state in life only in part the product of individual choice, indeed partly ordained and imposed by God's will. Each occupied his or her position not simply to earn a livelihood but to supply a need, and therefore bore responsibilities altogether apart from the desire for gain. The community had a right and an obligation to pass upon the extent to which each actually fulfilled an appropriate function in society. These traditional concepts, phrased in corporate terms, made comprehensible the hierarchy of callings within which individuals occupied a place and which determined status. Sir Thomas Smith listed the main classes in the English commonwealth: the monarch, aristocrats, knights, squires, and gentry; the yeomen; and what he described as the sort of men who do not rule—day laborers, poor husbandmen, merchants or retailers, copyholders, and all craftsmen. A comparable list for France displayed more numerous and more precise gradations.[2]

Early on, however, fixed, inherited places no longer satisfied the colonists. Survival ceased to dominate their concerns. Inner discontents and ambitions that had moved them to migrate rose to the surface, and as strength drained away from the community, personal motives moved to the foreground of their attention. The Puritans had always condemned the sins of sloth, idleness, and sensuality, advocated prudence and autonomy. But the shift of focus away from common to individual concerns in religion and family relations also altered the emphasis in economic life.[3]

Well before the transformation of companies into colonies dissolved the legal basis for a joint stock held in common, people showed a preference for working on their own accounts. The New Amsterdam gristmill proved so unprofitable that the authorities engaged a miller to run it. Once set free, planters, owning their own land, prepared to labor, to build houses, and to clear the ground, which gave them the greatest hope to make the colony flourish that ever yet happened to them (1620). A century later, "the desire of being independent and of leaving a certain estate to their children" remained the salient motive of people in America. They therefore insisted on working for themselves even when it endangered survival. Regulations to force the settlers to grow some basic foodstuffs, and thus prevent a return to the starving times, ran afoul of the greed of Deliverance Louly and other Kent Islanders (1659), who did not bother to fulfill the corn-growing quota.[4]

The conception of a common fund or a common magazine disappeared. Common fields, familiar features of European village life, survived as long as space remained abundant and there was no harm to allowing anyone to graze cattle. Through the seventeenth century New England towns apportioned fence and thatch and located parcels. But after 1670, competition for acreage developed, rights to the common acquired value, and newcomers no longer received shares. Billerica, Massachusetts, at first drew no distinction between proprietors and nonproprietors; later the two groups met separately; and by 1760 all common land was gone. Towns encroached on each other's borders; boundary disputes erupted and land became a tradable commodity rather than a patrimony fixed in the family.[5]

The Virginia Company settlers and officials had suspected the speculative worth of land; hence their own concern about the authority to grant it. But for a century sparse population and abundant acres kept that presumed value on the far horizon. Then the distance shortened, not for lack of space—with a continent still available—but from competition. Massachusetts worried (1732) that many subjects inclined to industry who could not obtain land removed to neighboring colonies. Veterans put up for sale warrants received for service; a land market developed and the increase in holdings by nonresidents raised the question of whether to subject them to taxation. Pennsylvania and other newer colonies formed dispersed farms which they treated as speculative commodities for sale rather than inheritance.[6]

Some fisheries fell within similar constraints. Oysters, for a time so plentiful that they furnished the poor with food while the shells, ground into lime, made fertilizer, threatened to run out. In 1721 Norwalk therefore prohibited anyone not an inhabitant to approach the beds, and a year later even forbade the sale to outsiders. When prices rose, Lynn rented out its Nahant beaches for the digging of clams and shells, reserving access to local inhabitants for family food (1730). On the other hand, New York Governor Robert Hunter's abortive attempt to seize the whale fishery to the crown elicited a storm of complaints as oppression, destructive of community good (1716); and an exclusive right to take fish from the Skatucket River, "obtained in a sort of sly manner," evoked outrage from others who claimed the same natural right to the privilege (1757).[7]

The absence of coercive central power wore away communal discipline in economic relationships, permitting each household to pursue its own goals as its master wished. Plymouth could not maintain its common stock, despite its cohesion and discipline. The transformation of the trading companies into agricultural societies everywhere proceeded as the settlements took form.

Even separate, self-seeking households expected communal standards and values to guide their conduct. From Europe, the settlers could remember both inducements and penalties to shape correct behavior; and they used methods of both sorts. They disapproved of unauthorized monopolies and of usury: it was not appropriate for one person to take advantage of another either in creating an artificial shortage of goods or in a loan, ideally an act of neighborly kindness. Centuries of Englishmen had considered engrossers "wycked people in condicions more lyke to wolves or cormorants than to naturall men, that doe most covetously seeke" to raise the "pryces of corn and all other victualls by ingrossing the same into their private hands." Deeming excessive interest on loans a "great discouragement of ingenuity and industry in husbandry, trade and commerce," Virginia in 1730 set the rate at 6 percent but in 1748 lowered it to 5. A code that transcended the immediate interests of individuals governed dealings among community members. To monopolize supplies or extort as much as possible ran counter to the belief that social relationships were not purely economic.[8]

Though the words, transferred from the Old World, remained important, the meaning grew vague. The community had the right and obligation to establish answers to difficult questions. What was a just price? Or a proper rate of interest? Was it fair dealing when Jacob Vander Veer slipped a stone in among the feathers he sold to Thomas Harwood to increase their weight (1678); or was it up to the buyer to beware? At what stage in the control of supplies did the reward for foresight end and extortion begin? Europeans could give the appropriate responses; the colonists could not. Captain Robert Keayne of Boston complained (1639) of the difficulty of establishing a true price. His will recalled the admonishment for not adhering to the price current, a practice common in every shop. Contractual transactions involved not only the parties to them but everyone around them. True, but their regulation depended on a failing authority. Boston spent almost two decades (1734–1753) in debate on strategy for avoiding forestalling until Peter Faneuil's gift provided it a market. New York City long before (1731) had ordered all grain sold and slaves hired at the lower end of Wall Street.[9]

Economic activity involved more than individual choices. But the requirement of consent complicated efforts to concert action for the common good. Dispersal and governmental weakness nullified traditional controls and opened attractive possibilities for pursuing personal advantage. As late as 1667 the selectmen ordered the inhabitants of Springfield not to deal with James Osborne, who prejudiced himself and his family by disadvantageous bargains. But disputes once resolved by neighborly injunction or by informal discussion with the elders or local gentry ever more often fell to the courts, themselves not powerful enough to deal with all the matters before them. The ability to give orders slipped away from the vigilant unified church that had once called Captain Keayne to account; and the state, in economic matters, rarely had the means to command. Virginia from 1622 onward repeatedly tried to regulate the quality and price of its mainstay, tobacco, never succeeding in doing so. So too, laws governing usury and monopoly lingered on the statute books, and Governor Belcher of Massachusetts in 1730, in response to numerous complaints against extortion, suggested renewed enforcement. No action followed.[10]

Efforts to turn the economy toward communal ends foundered on the lack of means of compulsion. Everyone knew, as the *New American Magazine* put it (1759), that an idle man was "a drawback on the publick wealth," while industry was "the mistress of convenience and source of plenty," which in turn meant strength. It remained as true then as it had been in 1623 that "where the business of the commonwealth" was left to many, everyone put it off so that nothing was done. Even vital matters suffered neglect when dependent on arguments for the common welfare. Covetousness was the root of all evil in every age of the world, William Hubbard sadly observed (1677). Corporal Baren Enessen van Noorden deserved heavy punishment for selling company armaments to traders who passed them on to the Indians; but New Netherland needed his services and let him off lightly (1648). Down in Carolina, Thomas

Archcraft, gunsmith, preferred to make Indian hatchets for gain rather than repair colonial arms promptly (1672). A little lucre induced civil and Christian folk to instruct the savages before ever they were reduced to good order in the use of weapons and likewise to furnish them ammunition. Nor did heavy fines and the threat of losing both ears stop William Clift from profitable trade with the enemy during the French war (1755). Talk about the good of the whole fell on deaf ears even when it came to vital matters. Concerned with the food supply, the South Carolina Council (1672) had to order settlers who dissipated their energy in pursuit of "imaginary profits" to plant two acres with corn or peas for every family member.[11]

The conception that the commonwealth had a stake in the economy remained intact through the eighteenth century. But only persuasion elicited consent, and government could most readily induce people to act by grants of privilege. No province commanded the array of favors available in Britain, much less in France; but all had some to dispense. Monopolies and licenses, which prevented competition from consuming the value of a sizable investment, thus rewarded the promise to supply a badly needed service or product, as in encouragement of a ferry or mill. To further their interests, enterprising men appealed for subsidies and other favors familiar from the European past. The Boston merchants who proposed to discover the great northwest lake from which the beaver came sought and secured an exclusive right to that trade for twenty-one years (1644). The Massachusetts General Court in 1679 granted the copartners in the dry dock at Charlestown tax exemption and a monopoly for thirty years. Thus too, Sybella and Thomas Masters received a patent for fourteen years to refine Indian corn in a way more suitable for shipping and transportation than earlier (1717). To prevent the great fraud and deceit in the sale of foreign linens under the pretense that they were made in Londonderry, despite the act against hawking and peddling New Hampshire authorized the town to seal all genuine cloth. New York and other cities set the weight and price of bread.[12]

But the monopoly provided the Boston merchants little protection when hostile fire sank their ship in the Delaware; passengers on the Charlestown ferry found excuses to evade the toll (1649); and enforcement difficulties drained other privileges of value. Saco, Maine, granted Roger Spencer the right to build a sawmill but demanded favored treatment for the townsfolk. Protesters objected that such grants raised prices, caused smuggling, and hindered immigration. Indeed in 1727, the

Virginia burgesses resolved that no legislation against trade monopolies was necessary since there were none such in the colony. Not even more general restrictions were effective; the futility of efforts to limit the amount of tobacco each planter could raise did not head off petitions for such controls. Nor did ineffectiveness forestall laws (1738, 1749) restricting hunters "to preserve the breeding of deer," and confining the keeping of horses to persons who possessed substantial acreage and income, to relieve pressure on the land and improve the breed.[13]

Regulation, though for the common good, evoked controversy when it hampered trade, with the outcome usually a collapse of controls. Dealings with Indians, potentially profitable, always presented problems and posed potential dangers, for quarrels and misunderstandings antagonized the tribesmen while the rum and munitions exchanged for furs inflamed hostility. It was plausible to expect that a monopoly or at least strictly regulated conditions would eliminate the sources of trouble. So it seemed to Massachusetts, which wished to limit the trade in beaver and wampum to authorized dealers. The province, like the Dutch, Virginians, and other English authorities, discovered that it never worked that way.[14]

At the opening of the trading season the dealers of Fort Orange drifted away into the woods, out from under watchful eyes, all because "of no other motive than greed." For a time the province allowed everyone to employ Indian brokers, which lessened the need to wander about. But a 1654 ordinance, yearly renewed, outlawed the middlemen, allowed Indians to come and trade their beavers where they pleased, and forbade local inhabitants from going beyond a fixed line to meet them. By 1660, the magistrates confronted violators like Jan Harmsen, who claimed he went into the woods to catch an Indian who had robbed him, and not to attract those with beavers. The list of those charged grew so long that a new ordinance, "at the request of the community," granted everyone the right to employ Indian but not Dutch intermediaries, and forbade presents sent into the woods. But the "rabble," motivated "by excessive greed and jealousy," protested against such unwarranted attempts to restrict the trade to a few hands. Some proposed to appeal to the authorities in the fatherland; others threatened to go into the woods in defiance of the law. Indian counterpetitions, complaining of Dutch violence and threatening to shift the beaver trade elsewhere, complicated matters. Thereupon, the government barred the Dutch from roaming the woods to attract Indians. One week later violators faced the court. Not so, claimed Poulis Jansen, who admitted to being in the woods, but only to gather blueberries. Another conceded that he had sent his servant there, but not to commune with the Indians. Willem Brouwer claimed he did not understand the regulations, and thought all were free to enter the forests. Another servant was looking for hogs, and yet another searching for servants sent by someone else. Still another inhabitant explained that he only did what everyone else did.[15]

Repeated efforts to regulate trades and professions stemmed from attitudes transposed from Europe. "The Liberty of our commonwealth," urged a seventeenth-century Englishman, was "most infringed by three sorts of men, Priests, Physitians, Lawyers," who deceived people in matters belonging to their souls, their bodies, and their estates. All three professions lost esteem in America. The colonists took a dim view of attorneys who depended upon strength of lungs and mechanical tricks of pleading to worry poor men out of their rights (1720). New Jersey sought by licensing to keep the unqualified from dragging out cases for their own benefit (1738). In the eighteenth century slackened limitations on who could preach in effect lowered the status of ministers, even in New England. Virginia statutes, noting the excessive fees, the overdosing, and the other abuses in the medical profession, set the payments for physicians, depending upon the number of visits, the distance traveled, and the ferries used. The law also forbade the use of drugs unless patients learned in advance what they were and how much they would cost.

To the extent that any controls appeared, it was not through government action, but through measures adopted by local, voluntary associations. Americans of 1760, living in a more stable and more complex society than their grandparents, ceased to be content with unpredictable rule-of-thumb judgments, particularly in the city. The protection of persons and property, the enforcement of contracts, and the collection of debts involved heavy stakes. Judges needed a knowledge of the acts of parliament and of earlier precedents, and losers could appeal to superior courts, even to London. Training gained value—how to draw up a binding document, for what writs to petition, the technical language in which to argue—and apprenticeship with an established advocate brought those skills. Those already admitted to the bar thus influenced the entry of others. Comparable tendencies operated in medicine and the ministry, creating some sense of professional solidarity. In none of these occupations, however, did the new trends altogether prevent the unlicensed from practicing.[16]

Efforts to control other crafts gradually petered out. Early shortages, as well as English practice, created the temptation to legislate. The very first Massachusetts court fixed the wages of bricklayers, joiners, carpenters, sawyers, and thatchers; but within the year the regulations lapsed and subsequent town efforts at control led to endless difficulties, as did later attempts to set rates for porters. New Haven's table of wages distinguished among occupations according to skill and strength, season of work, number of hours and, of course, between work done by masters and that of apprentices. But the small fine, when levied, hardly discouraged demands for higher pay. The Dutch early recognized the futility of excessive wage regulation and, except during serious emergencies, disallowed occasional local efforts to set up such scales as injurious to economic growth. Attempts to put a value upon commodities, Virginia discovered, simply "sett out in print fancies and imaginations in stead of reall truth" (1623). "The merchant knew what to give and the planter, loving his liberty, esteemed a set price a bondage." Nor did Governor Stuyvesant succeed in fixing the prices even of goods traded with the Indians.[17]

Schemes to dull competition by limiting the numbers entitled to practice or trade invariably failed in the absence of guilds and even of incorporated municipalities. New Amsterdam excluded all foreign traders without a burgher right (1660); and New York's carters got exclusive recognition conditioned upon services to the public (1667), then lost and regained their privileged position. That city also set the fees for "inviters" to funerals (1715). Uncertainties clouded the security of other licensed occupations. Virginia optimistically authorized the creation (1705) of fifteen towns, guilds and all; but royal officials called into question charters given to aspiring cities by all provinces and proprietors, thus undermining the favored position of freemen. Belligerent artisans thundered into court in disputes over craft boundaries; what tasks butchers, tanners, curriers, shoemakers, and cordwainers could do—such decisions taxed the ingenuity of local authorities. As late as 1731 the New York Common Council tried to restrict the number of merchants and artisans in the city, by granting the freedom of the corporation—including the right to trade or to practice a craft—only to those who paid a substantial sum. Abundant loopholes however permitted anyone to deal, so that only those who valued participation in municipal and provincial politics bothered to receive the freemanship. By the 1740s, the little citadels of protected occupations seemed hardly worth defending.[18]

Inherited concepts lingered. But communal controls, out of accord with realities, withered. The process of settlement demanded uninterrupted expansion incompatible with traditional constraints upon the economy. The companies and colonies depended on the outside world for imports to hold back the wilderness and had to generate exports to pay for them. The incentive of individual enterprise they learned would attract labor and increase the population. Moravians, unconcerned with such considerations, maintained their stability through self-supporting agriculture. Others felt unremitting pressure to lure newcomers by the prospect of making their own way unshackled, at once or in the near future. Despite warnings that error and contention would creep in, colonists eager to fill their purses with coin encouraged immigration and did what they could to hold the arrivals. Many of the best farmers in New Netherland threatened to leave for a place where they would have their own land, unless relieved of burdensome obligations. They observed the English thrive and scoff at the Dutch, who would doubtless flourish as well or better if invested with the same free privileges.[19]

The drive to produce exports sprang in part from initial dependence on Europe, the source of capital for settlement. Debts long remained, investors clamored for some return, and supply ships brought the very food and drink to sustain the colonists. And when the pressure for survival eased, the desire to expand persisted and challenged communal controls. The personality types prominent in colonization found little contentment in what God sent or in sharing His bounty with strangers or even friends. Wealth was the magnet that drew on most of those who migrated out of their own wills—officials and merchants, adventurers avid for riches, yeomen seeking to improve a status threatened at home, and servants aspiring to freedom. Devout though some were, their calling demanded that they improve themselves. Greed was a sin; but so too was idleness. William Bradford noted that as the herds increased and found a market there was no longer any holding the Plymouth people together. None thought they could live without increasing the number of their cattle and expanding the acreage on which to keep them. Whatever the injunctions of government, whatever the preachings against avarice, few restraints inhibited the head of each family from making his own decision about what to plant or make or sell, about where to live or when to work, about what to buy and what to save. Perhaps Governor Winthrop took some consolation in the thought (1645) that John Pratt, upon departing, died in a shipwreck; still the Puritan founder failed to understand why an experienced surgeon, having lived in New England many years and lacking nothing, should have gone off, aggrieved that his practice was not as profitable as he wished it to be.[20]

Merchants, planters, yeomen, and artisans, well enough off where they were, also itched for the rosy glow of some unfound elsewhere at sea or in the west. The Virginia and the Dutch West India Companies voiced the same complaints: people abandoned their occupations, invested their all, for the sake of trade. Always the lands to the west seemed better than those already occupied, and not only out of preference for shifting to virgin plots rather than investing effort in preserving hastily cleared and carelessly cultivated old ones. Confidence in the superiority of what lay to the west also reflected a faith all too often doomed to disappointment—the faith of men on the edge of a continent who believed that the deficiencies of the present would vanish in the further future; the disappointment of those who, having reached the future, found it the same present and therefore could only continue to look ahead. The west, wherever it was, was best because the east never satisfied the quest initiated at the first departure. Unpredictable and therefore uncontrollable, such people bubbled about, kept the economy constantly expanding, and frustrated efforts at constraint.[21]

Commerce involved everyone. The early settlers had planted corn for their own sustenance and had rejoiced when domestic cattle and hogs proliferated. Fine for a while! But prosperity and growth depended on production of a staple with immediate worth in international trade. Undaunted by experience, promoters dreamed of crops of coffee, tea, figs, raisins, currants, almonds, olives, silk, sassafras, wine, and oranges in Carolina and Georgia—provinces on the same line of latitude as the Mediterranean.

More readily at hand, the sea and the woods both yielded valuable products—at first simply extracted and sent off, later worked up, as skill permitted, for export. Off the Grand Bank, for years before the appearance of permanent settlements, Europeans had scooped up, dried, and salted huge schools of fish for ready markets in the Mediterranean regions and in the West Indies. Thousands of colonists joined the fleet and their towns became centers for outfitting the craft, for packing the catch, and for selling it overseas. Rivers teemed with herring, salmon, and shad awaiting the fisher. Springfield and other towns, for a fee, allowed several inhabitants to barrel up and sell the catch (1677).[22]

The woods were more difficult to exploit, for settlers long dreaded the unfamiliar forests. With the aid of Indians, European traders had carried off the furs much in demand in the Old World. The colonists zestfully plunged into that commerce also. Within a few years the Dutch and English were sending home beaver skins worth thousands of pounds. In both hunting and fishing, chance played a large part, and success attracted rivals who tended to deplete the game. The lack of political controls to ration the take made it ever necessary to seek out new grounds.[23]

Tobacco, highly prized throughout Europe and therefore profitable, quickly exhausted the soil. Planters knew that this precious export was "neither for necessity nor for ornament to the life of man," but rested only on a humor which might soon vanish into smoke and come to nothing. Competition with cheap Spanish tobacco raised by black labor in the West Indies kept prices low. Yet persistent efforts to restrict acreage and limit supply failed, as they had in the case of another promising crop, sassafras. And pleas to the crown to allow a free search for markets without the shackling requirement that everything pass first through English ports proved vain. The only alternative, cultivation of plants of the highest quality, made it necessary to put ever new acreage to the plow. A knowledgeable English visitor to Virginia in 1688 found good yields, but total ignorance of drainage and a disposition to clear new ground every four years.[24]

Within the first generation, with abundant space still there for the taking, the value of land soared in all the colonies. Roger Williams, ever the idealist, discovered reality in the acquisition of Rhode Island. Believing that the Indians had made the land over to him not for money but for love and not in fee simple but for use, he sought to assign portions to settlers on the same terms, but finally had to yield to the desire for ownership. It did not help. By 1669, "disagreement and dissatisfaction about divisions and dispositions of lands" rendered Providence incapable of transacting its own affairs "in any measure of satisfactory order with peace and quietness." The Rhode Island General Assembly complained in vain that the town failed to select deputies or jurymen, to the injury of the whole colony. The abandonment of older property patterns everywhere divided original settlers from newcomers, as in the recurrent debates over allocations of the commons. In this respect, too, orientation toward the market weakened the corporate quality of rural life, emphasizing expansive individual as against static communal motives.[25]

The colonies between Maryland and Georgia most closely matched imperial expectations. Their soil yielded the staples—tobacco, rice, cotton, and indigo—that crossed the Atlantic in return for manufactured goods, in a trade handled by British merchants whose liberal credit terms generated an ever increasing debt.

As the seventeenth century drew to a close, agriculture in Virginia, Maryland, and the Carolinas outgrew its earlier small scale. Until then, with plenty of room available and labor scarce, settlers had cleared a few acres and then, having exhausted the carelessly tilled soil, shifted to other parts of their holdings. The situation changed when English commercial policy encouraged large-scale production, when colonial laws defined slavery, and when trade with Africa increased the supply of blacks. The Carolinians and others then learned from the West Indies how to operate extensive holdings, which became the characteristic unit of production and to which the term *plantation* now applied. Small farms survived in many places, but the new plantation gained economic and social importance, raising indigo and rice as well as tobacco on great tracts, using hundreds of slaves who toiled under rigid discipline supervised by overseers. In time, too, the internal slave trade gave Virginia and Maryland an interest in the sale of surplus hands to the deeper south.

Yet the mainland planters differed significantly from their counterparts on the islands. The West Indians were Englishmen, absentees or on the way to becoming so; once they could rely on income from fortunes, they withdrew to live in the mother country. Rarely did that happen on the mainland. Even the wealthiest Carter, Byrd, or Washington considered Virginia his homeland. Their future lay in the continent's interior. The lure of empty western lands gripped the imaginations of the wealthy, who could have lived in ease where they were but preferred to strike out toward the remote Ohio Valley, toward outposts in the wilderness, whether to wipe away debts or for affluence beyond present reach.

The western spaces attracted southerners who harbored doubts about the permanence or even desirability of the slave plantation as a mode of production. They accepted the riches and status the labor of others brought them; and Georgians in 1750 actually repealed the original exclusion of slavery from that colony. But many owners questioned the justice of the institution and expected it to disappear some day. Moreover the plantation was not quite the same as on the islands. Rather than mobilizing their bondsmen in gangs or treating them as a disciplined mass labor force, masters in Virginia and Carolina tolerated family life among the blacks and allowed some to advance toward emancipation, inconsistencies that revealed ambiguous attitudes. There remained something incongruous about the plantation as an institution; it did not conform to the social norm that assumed that the household was the appropriate unit of work. The effort of some slaveholders to act as if the estate was a kind of family invariably broke down at the same stubborn fact: the blacks were chattels, not children, and labored for the master's advantage, not their own. The pretense of a great, enlarged family did not hold.

The attractions of overseas and domestic markets also transformed agriculture where climate and social structure inhibited the cultivation of tropical crops. The desire to produce a staple drew colonists beyond extraction to fabricating products from the sea, the forests, and the soil. The yield from the fisheries never slackened; and demand from across the Atlantic encouraged the production of naval stores. The trade in timber helped supply masts to the royal navy; shipbuilding used the ample resources of the forests close to the ocean; and expanding commerce produced a demand for casks and staves supplied by coopers in towns and by whittling farmers in the country.

Agriculture also felt the impact of urban growth and the expansion of West Indian markets. The bread trade sent biscuits made of flour from native grains to supply the needs of the islands, French and Dutch as well as English. Once the frontier receded, specialized crops aimed for the market—vegetables, horses, and tallow for the West Indies, clams dug from the shore and dried in the sun for sale to the Indians, and lumber for England, flax seed for Ireland.

Almost every yeoman learned to do a variety of things and had a plot on which to cultivate something other than the family's subsistence. The diary of Manasseh Minor of Stonington, Connecticut, recorded his weaving as well as when he plowed, hilled corn, and carted dung. Such people acquired skills different from those of the Old World. The wilderness produced its own subsistence for those able to hunt and fish. Observing the Indians, they learned to hasten the clearing of the soil by girdling the trees; they planted corn instead of wheat and allowed cattle and pigs to forage for themselves. Knowing little of fertilizers, they depended upon meadow grass to feed their stock; they sowed by hand, having laboriously turned up the soil with wooden plows; and they improvised almost everything they used. They developed abilities: carpentry to build houses, barns, fences, and furnishings; ironwork to shoe horses or repair utensils; and cobbling for footwear. The influential or wealthy built mills to utilize power from the streams—grinding corn, sawing lumber, or crushing the oak bark used in tanning leather worked up from the neighborhood's hides. Swapping led some into trade; others experimented with iron, glass, and brickmaking. The women learned to smoke meat; they baked shortbread on the griddles, washed clothes by the brook, milked the cows, churned the butter, spun, wove and sewed, dipped the candles, and boiled the soap. The more industrious these husbandmen and their families, the less likely to remain content with a subsistence drawn from the soil and the more likely to accept the challenge of nearby and foreign markets. And once they considered the sale of a surplus, the intrusion of a range of commercial considerations transformed their way of life.[26]

The cities through which the streams of commerce passed grew substantially—seaports on the coast, transfer points inland. Towns of the second rank—Gloucester, Salem, Providence, New Haven, and New Castle—competed vigorously with their larger rivals. Urban places now appeared natural features of civilization, attracting population and stimulating the economy as well as advancing learning and religion—the appropriate setting for the labor of numerous artisans. Schemes for glassmaking and silk weaving came to little. But hatters, cordwainers, ropemakers, coopers, and carpenters turned out hats, shoes, and barrels, and met the calls for new housing, their services in great demand. Printers provided important channels of information and began to rival ministers as molders of opinion. Persons of substance, their own bosses, the craftsmen increased in number and influence, many of them eroding the market for British manufactures. Restrictive laws enacted in London failed to halt the rising output of colonial shops.[27]

Large, powerful, and dynamic groups of indigenous merchants also operated in Boston, Newport, New York, Philadelphia, and Charleston. A surprising share of North American commerce fell to colonists whose operations England could not control and whose interests sometimes ran counter to those of the empire. Business forms, simple: the individual or occasionally the partners who owned a ship loaded whatever cargo was available and dispatched it when the hold was full. The captain chose the ports of call, and at each stop made the best deals he could—selling what he had, buying what he might dispose of elsewhere, paying or accepting gold or drafts on known correspondents. Chance played an important part in every outcome. The successful calculated shrewdly, faced up to risks and, ever on guard, seized opportunity when and where it presented itself. They therefore urgently desired liberty of trade, impatiently disregarding boundary lines and paying as few taxes as possible.[28]

Personal connections helped. Relatives, coreligionists, or friends in foreign ports provided information, credit, and assistance and acted as trustworthy correspondents for transactions at a distance. Family ties brought access to capital and links to worldwide networks of buyers and sellers. Insiders got their sons taken on as apprentices in good counting-houses, knew what discounts to demand, received preferential treatment, and sent small consignments on the vessels of friends and relatives. Ties of marriage and kinship linked the DeLancey, Van Cortlandt, Heathcote, and Philipse families in New York with lines across the Atlantic to Walpole's political manager, a rear admiral, a well-established trading house, and the archbishop of Canterbury. Such people enjoyed enormous advantages in operations on both sides of the ocean. But determined outsiders also established themselves since neither guilds nor restrictive laws set limits on who could buy and sell.[29]

Trade with the British Isles was basic. Correspondents in London or Bristol received and disposed of cargoes from American ports, either retaining the gross receipts as credits or exchanging them for goods salable across the Atlantic. The colonists, at a disadvantage in exchanges that always seemed to benefit the mother country, were ever on the lookout for alternatives. Times of war in the century after 1660 created opportunities for the venturesome. Favorites of the governors got contracts to supply the British forces in America; yet they and other merchants found an unfamiliar welcome in the French, Spanish, and Dutch West Indies, usually closed to them but now open to anyone who could get by English blockaders. At the same time Americans, commissioned by their governments, profited from privateering raids on enemy shipping; and during peacetime, some continued under the black flag of piracy the seizures no longer permissible under the royal standard. Always, smugglers got around the restrictions of their own and other governments. Colonials thus had some advantages over their British counterparts. John Winthrop had early perceived the advantages of trade with the West Indies, which concentrated on sugar and purchased from the mainland the barrel staves, timber, corn, fish, horses, and biscuits they did not produce themselves. Such exchanges, profitable enough when legal among British possessions, returned even greater rewards when illegal in deals with Spaniards and Dutch.[30]

Shipwreck, piracy, unpredictable changes in supply and demand and in the whims of government officers compounded the risks of commerce under these terms. Therefore the most successful merchants longed for means to stabilize their wealth. They envied the dependable established trade, the monopolies, the access to public office, and the fees that gave their counterparts in settled countries some security. Persistently they sought somehow to develop a flow of exports to support their business in good times and bad. To assure the reputation of the products they shipped, they wanted casks properly packed and inspected. They willingly made loans to farmers and to one another, speculated in land, and ventured upon industrial enterprises, applying for privileges to build mills and to further mining and the manufacture of pig iron and linseed oil.[31]

Ironically, the actors in an economy devoted to expansion and subject to unceasing risk could not muster the political strength to supply themselves with an adequate currency. The colonists disagreed on the problem, and imperial vetoes frustrated attempts to find an appropriate solution. Fluctuations in the amount of money available unsettled commerce and affected the general price structure. Buying and selling, as important in agriculture and the handicrafts as in trade, required a reliable medium of exchange. Yet poor communications kept the circulation of money sluggish; and the unfavorable balance of trade drained specie to England. Now and again shortages precipitated crises; at other times excesses triggered inflationary price rises.

Although some colonies for a time minted coins—when they laid hands on gold or silver, which was but rarely—most depended upon barter and commodities, tobacco, beaverskins, or wampum, none reliable. In 1641, New Netherland could not cope with the tendency of dirty unpolished stuff used at a 50 percent discount to displace good wampum. By 1658 the surplus caused a price hike of 300 percent, especially of beaver skins. Workers and merchants then refused to accept shells as currency. The New Amsterdam magistrates revealed their weakness when they admitted that they had "no better means or expedient than to declare once more as they have already done several times, to wit, that wampum is only merchandize, bought sold or bartered" as the parties agreed. Since no other ready money was available, they fixed the prices of bread, beer, wine, and other products "according to three measures—silver, wampum or beaver."[32]

In an expanding market economy cumbersome country commodities did not compensate for the lack of an adequate currency. Traders relied on Spanish dollars and pieces of eight and Portuguese Joes and Moidores, the available gold and silver coins, though hard to translate into pence, shillings, and pounds and in short supply. The scarcity lowered prices. Penn's agent wrote in 1704, "neither rents nor other pay can be had in money, and wheat for two years past has been worth but little."

Paper, the most attractive solution, added to the amount in circulation and also avoided disagreeable taxes, although it created problems of its own—as when rats and mice got at the bills Jacob Royal left in his coat pocket (1736). In 1690 Massachusetts, preparing an expedition against Canada, paid its suppliers in transferable bills of credit or bonds issued in small denominations that soon circulated as money, a practice other colonies imitated with beneficial economic effects, despite the nagging of royal officials who wanted the debt retired as soon as possible. Indeed some provinces issued to individuals, on the security of land or other property, notes that also passed as currency; and enterprising groups formed land or silver banks to do the same. The crown in 1741 and the Currency Act ten years later forbade all these subterfuges. Though some merchants complained that the paper issued with abandon in New Hampshire and Rhode Island was "a cheat and a fraud," the inflationary effects further stimulated the economy. As a result the population thickened. The 200,000 colonists of 1660 had become about 2,000,000 a century later and had spread from the ocean's edge to the Alleghenies.[33]

A consistent pattern emerged in the system of production as in family life and religion. Settlement had started with a conception of the community as an integrated cohesive whole, within which interlocking institutional arrangements, among them government, church, and family, used compulsion to maintain discipline. The disturbing effects of space and the constraints consent put upon power required deep adjustments in the social order.

People habituated to instability and expansion treated risk as an unbidden guest. Few sought it out, but neither did many shoot the bolt shut. The frequency varied as the rate of population growth and of economic expansion waxed and waned. But the unexpected knock always stirred interest. It might be danger at the door. Or it might be opportunity. The colonists learned to respond with a prudent welcome, club within reach.[34]

Population growth revealed shortages of skilled hands to reckon the sums or write the letters, to caulk the ships or clapboard the houses, to make boats, boots, coats, bread, and candles, to fashion silver bowls and mahogany chests. In addition, the willingness to chance the unexpected paid off often enough to affect individual status and to permit ascent in society. Luck turned now one way, now another. A ship went forth and months later either came back or not. The seasons favored the crops or ruined them; and commodities sent overseas brought high prices or low. But the proper education and capital enabled the ingenious to make the most of good fortune, mitigate the effects of bad. Not all who strove succeeded and some did better than others; but opportunity and the inability of privileged families or groups to shut out competitors gave almost everyone a chance.

Hence the difficulty of applying old conceptions of rank to American conditions. Sermons and abstract discussions assumed, as did contemporary Europeans, that each person had a place in a hierarchical society stratified in distinct layers from top to bottom. Actuality increasingly deviated from that assumption. The owners of vast landed estates were as far above the yeomen, tenants, servants, and slaves who made up the bulk of the population as were the great merchants of Newport and Boston from the petty traders, craftsmen, apprentices, and laborers who moved through the city streets. Yet though differences deepened in the eighteenth century, the distances between ranks did not diminish the incentive to move up. Since neither legal nor informal barriers blocked the way, all who wished remained free to scramble for the best places.

The recognized gradations of rank originated in feudal Europe but in the Old World of the seventeenth century had become far more complex than earlier, reflecting as they did occupation, wealth, family, lineage, political power, and different degrees of privilege and rights. Rank depended less on personal qualities than on position in a household and relationship to a community. In England, and even more so on the continent of Europe, the lines were meticulously precise. The marble monument for the Duke of Somerset, his effigy "in garment and ruff all in coullours," made room also for his lady, but she occupied a position "one step above him because she was daughter to the Dowager of France and sister to Henry the 7th of England by her second husband Charles Brandon Duke of Suffolk." What "a Gentleman is, 'tis hard for us to define," said John Selden, for it was necessary to distinguish those ennobled by blood from those created by the king. True, the turbulent world of the sixteenth century made room for rises in status; Thomas Cromwell was the son of a blacksmith and Cardinal Wolsey of a butcher. But power did not obliterate the memory of their lowly origins. An extensive institutional apparatus—crown, government, church—reinforced social ranks; and each had its own expected ways of living, acting, believing.[35]

Moralists defended those distinctions as appropriate.

> The heavens themselves . . .
> Observe degree, priority, and place . . .
> . . . O, when degree is shaked, . . .
> The enterprise is sick! How could communities,
> Degrees in schools and brotherhoods in cities,
> Peaceful commerce from dividable shores, . . .
> But by degree, stand in authentic place?
> Take but degree away, untune that string,
> And, hark, what discord follows! . . .
>
> (Shakespeare, *Troilus and Cressida* [1603], I, iii)

Wealth carried with it the obligations of stewardship in God's household, for all the descendants of Adam had an equal right to riches. A sixteenth-century Puritan criticized the merchant who no sooner enjoyed a surplus than he sought to purchase land and to edge in among the gentry. He would do better to marry his daughter to one of his trade than to strive to make her a lady; and let his sons at nine or ten be bound a prentice to learn some art to live upon, for why should they be gentlemen? Who desired to play the lord showed himself no Christian. Wicked ambition destroyed many fortunes. Much better to

> walk in thy vocation
> And do not seke thy lotte to chaunge.

And indeed while some individuals surmounted the lines between ranks, throughout the society the fences continued to interpose barriers, supported at every level by organized community power.[36]

The colonists did not challenge hierarchical social arrangements. They knew that great men fared better than the poor. But the terms *great* and *poor* lacked the precision of the Old World. Benjamin Franklin's fledgling try at humor poked fun at persons of small fortune who, under the dominion of pride, struggled to imitate their superiors in estate or equals in folly. Sumptuary laws prescribed the life-style, clothing, and jewelry appropriate to every condition, but an observer noted many in garments too good for their circumstances (1724). Titles of address also reflected the importance of rank; and in the meetinghouse or church where the whole community assembled, the geography of the seats corresponded to the layout of the social order. Concern with the issue, explicable in great places where officialdom required recognition, also permeated little towns; the assignment of pews—whether next to the pulpit or in additional rows or in the gallery—turned on fine distinctions of dignity. Hackles rose when Harvard placed a Winthrop below a Bradstreet in defiance of rank, "a Sacred Thing" (1696). Each position determined privileges or rights, for freedom was not an abstract whole but existed in degrees, and the colonists had had no other thought but to carry that order to the communities they wished to build across the Atlantic.[37]

It was difficult, however, to transfer European patterns to the New World. The conception of rank persisted but was significantly modified by accelerated movement from one level to another. Ultimate social alignments therefore differed significantly from those in the Old World.

The gangs of rogues and vagabonds who thronged the roads of England and France, the professional beggars and thieves who besieged helpless passersby in London and Paris had no counterparts in the New World. Even persons from among those dangerous classes transported as convicts or arrived voluntarily as servants found places in households from which some could achieve independence. The poor and dependent in the colonies were mostly people incapacitated by accident or illness, by the death of parents or husbands, or by old age. Rarely did anyone make a vocation of crime or mendicancy.[38]

The social order measured degrees of freedom. At the lowest level stood people in absolute bondage. Considered chattels in law, subject to purchase, sale, and transportation, ruled by masters and overseers who wielded the lash with few restraints, slaves enjoyed little present protection and no prospect of improvement. The courts took some cognizance of abusive treatment, but not enough to provide personal security. The number of free blacks in the cities grew; hemmed in by burdensome restraints, they enjoyed only limited access to opportunity and their relative well-being scarcely encouraged those who remained enslaved. Occasional blacks did well, but had to be prepared for the rebuff that greeted Robert Jacklin's effort to buy land in New London (1717). The town meeting utterly opposed and protested against an action that would give him the rights of an inhabitant.[39]

By contrast, for servants for a term the goal of foreseeable freedom did promise access to opportunity; for them this was "the best poor man's country in the world" (1705). How many achieved in actuality the status to which they aspired counted for little; the visions did not flicker of a craft mastered, a holding acquired, a husband married—prospects real enough to lend hope substance, for every community housed examples of those who had advanced by some degree, as did Rawlins Lowndes, a parish orphan boy who became a South Carolina planter, magistrate, and judge.[40]

The urban places, comparatively small but growing, valued the services of artisans who felt no need of such protection as guilds and privileges offered their European counterparts. Owning their own tools, the craftsmen benefited from the shortages of labor and wished orderly markets undisturbed by drastic currency fluctuations such as government caused by inflating the money supply. The artisans also worried about places for their offspring. Although growth made some room, second or third or fourth sons had either to stay on as journeymen, move elsewhere, or find apprenticeships in trades other than those of their fathers. Skilled cabinetmakers and silversmiths, printers and carriage makers now joined the carpenters and bakers who had formerly supplied the simple needs of urban residents. Expansion opened places for all willing workers so long as no artificial restraints limited opportunities for advancing upward in the hierarchy of trades.

Artisans, as a matter of course, dabbled in trade—printers bought and sold books, cordwainers leather, and carpenters lumber. The very fortunate became merchants or planters, although it took a store of capital and new talents to do so. Pierre Manigault started as a victualler in Charleston and grew rich in trade; his son became the wealthiest man in the province. Transition to the ranks of the yeomen called for a less drastic break, for no city was sharply cut off from the countryside, land—available for speculative purposes and for cultivation—kept opening opportunities, and some skills were transferable. With labor scarce and business booming, an observer noted, "this makes tradesmen turn planters and these become tradesmen" (1711).[41]

Artisans or their sons occasionally gained entry into an occupation acquiring professional status. A printer with ingenuity and enterprise, like Benjamin Franklin, became a journalist. A little learning and a brief apprenticeship opened the way into the practice of law and physick and opportunities abounded in the city to pick up the smattering of Latin and the manners to comply with the custom of the country, so long as no capricious licensing requirements posed obstacles to the ambitious.[42]

The independent farmers, the most numerous element in the colonial population and often referred to as yeomen, differed markedly from those of the Old World. The Atlantic crossing unfastened the complex varieties of tenure that law and custom had riveted to the land in England and elsewhere in Europe. In the New World all ownership was of freeholds —unencumbered. Once the colonists spread away from the palisaded enclosures and from the village centers, they consolidated scattered plots and moved off to their own tracts, often out of sight, sometimes quite remote from their neighbors. Some held larger parcels, more servants, and greater power than others, but the forces for dispersal played upon them all. There was no European equivalent for this manner of life—where each person lived as a detached individual in his or her household on land set off from everyone else.

Differences in soil, climate, and the persistence of communal institutions affected the quality of agriculture and also the yeomen's style of work and life, but so too did personal attributes—the intensity of religious zeal, the strength of the family, and the desire for improvement. Some husbandmen, content to subsist on what the country offered, minimized toil and drifted from season to season. Already in 1705, observers who praised the Indian closeness to nature and "enjoyment of plenty without the curse of labor" bitterly criticized settlers who sponged upon the blessings of a warm sun and fruitful soil without art or industry. Neglect of cattle in the winter, reliance upon pone for bread because it required little effort, and the import of bowls and brooms from England despite the abundance of wood were all evidence of indolence.

A caustic traveler explained why some Carolinians loitered their lives away with their arms across and at the winding up of the years scarcely had bread to eat. They lie and snore, until the sun has run one-third his course, and dispersed all the unwholesome damp. "Then, after stretching and yawning for half an hour, they light their pipes, and, under the protection of a cloud of smoke, venture out into the open air; though if it happens to be ever so little cold, they quickly return shivering into the chimney corner." In mild weather, "they stand leaning with both their arms upon the cornfield fence and gravely consider whether they had best go take a small heat at the hoe; but generally find reasons to put it off until another time" (1728).[43]

Other husbandmen, driven by ambition, tempted by the marketplace, refused to subsist on what they had and labored to produce the salable surplus. Some rented as tenants while they waited to inherit from long-lived fathers or while they accumulated funds to buy their own holdings. But the overwhelming majority of all cultivators owned their own land and tilled it with their own labor, and that of their immediate families. Their households, cut away from the village community, set apart by broad acres from their neighbors, operated with few communal controls, for expansive opportunities in empty space encouraged people to strive for gain rather than for stability, to move about rather than to strike roots, to produce by calculation for the market rather than by habit for subsistence. They put a premium on skills different from those of the Old World. Outside the plantation south, numerous family farms generated almost the whole flow of colonial exports.

Thrifty, industrious farmers did not idle away the long intervals when they had finished the chores of plowing, reaping, and caring for the animals. They turned their hands to tasks that brought in cash. With wood abundant, they whittled shingles and barrel staves; everywhere they spun and wove, or else their wives did. Others combined fishing with agriculture. Slack seasons saw Yankees off to sea and the catch, salted and dried, added to the cargoes for the Caribbean, as did whale oil from Nantucket.

The sea, link to the outer world, challenged farmers' and artisans' sons for the wealth it brought to successful merchants. With luck, it provided the means of accumulating capital, of founding a great fortune. Governor Samuel Cranston of Rhode Island noted (1708) that the children of husbandmen and tradesmen in that crowded colony betook themselves to navigation; the industrious and thrifty built up a small stock and improved it by getting a share of a vessel, thus opening the way into overseas commerce.[44]

Colonial governments imposed no restraints upon the number or quality of persons who could do business as merchants, and family connections, while useful, did not raise barriers to the operations of outsiders. Foreigners were everywhere familiar figures in the marketplaces of the big cities, even in Europe; among the prominent merchants of Bordeaux were a native of Hamburg who had spent his youth in Stockholm and an immigrant from Waterford in Ireland. It was not therefore surprising that the Huguenot Benjamin Faneuil, whose grandfather had come to LaRochelle in 1640, a half century later moved to New York City to escape persecution. His brother André settled in Boston, thrived, and left the foundations of a fortune to his son, Peter.[45]

The big mercantile families of the eighteenth century (Bowdoin, Manigault, Hutchinson) were not the descendants of those already prominent in the seventeenth. John Hull, a blacksmith's son, hoed corn for seven years, then served an apprenticeship to a goldsmith before becoming mintmaster and Boston's wealthiest merchant. His widow married William Phipps, a poor Maine boy apprenticed to a ship carpenter who multiplied the riches and, knighted, played a prominent role in politics and trade. "He was of an Enterprizing *Genius,*" wrote Cotton Mather, "and naturally disdained *Littleness.*" Outsiders who could not relax comfortably in established trades had to take risks, which often enough paid off in high returns. Thomas Hancock (1703–1764), one of those new men, turned a profit on difficulties. Son of a poor schoolmaster and minister, Thomas served a seven years' apprenticeship to a bookseller in Boston, then began to trade on his own account. The scarcity of currency forced him to take commodities in payment and in turn to deal in the goods he received. Soon he was buying and selling pork, cheese, cloth, paper, and tea. The inability to remit sterling for books and other imports from England forced him to seek out exports that would earn specie—dried fish, whale oil, and rum. He thus drifted into trade with the West Indies, Newfoundland, and Spain, became part owner of a vessel, then of a small fleet. When the royal authorities changed the duties in a fashion he believed unfair, he took to smuggling and in wartime (1739–1744) to privateering, but also profited from contracts to supply government troops. By then he had built a grand house on Beacon Hill, embellishing his garden with plants from Britain.[46]

However well they did, security remained out of reach of such merchants. They carried no insurance against losses at sea, from nature, enemy craft, or pirates. Gluts and scarcities, unexpected price rises and declines might as well lose as make fortunes. And even when all went well and the cash came in, the absence of banks left no alternative to reinvestment, thus renewing the risk. Hancock put some money into manufacturing, some into land speculation—no certainties there.

Social recognition therefore remained tentative. The owner of the big house on the hill was a person of consequence, but still a merchant, not a gentleman. No title marked him off, no special privilege or access to office or power, no clubs free of jostling by the masses, no certainty about the inheritance that would pass to his children. All he owned might vanish as unpredictably as it had come.

Only possession of a great landed estate provided the conditions for establishment of a fixed social rank. At the start, suspicion fell on overly great estates, lest one become "stronger than any of his order." An early Virginia reformer thus hoped that the daughters of the rich would marry the sons of the poor, so that "all degrees may be bound thereby togather in the bonds of love that none may be scorned but the scorner" (1623).[47]

But by the eighteenth century the southern plantations and the great estates of the Narragansett country of Rhode Island and of the river valleys of New York and New England housed an authentic provincial aristocracy. These were still far from the baronial establishments of England, the Grande Monde of France or the Dutch Groote Wereld, far even from the million-hectare estate of the Jugo-Urquidi family or the six million hectares of the Marquis de Aguayo in eighteenth-century Mexico.[48] A lavish style of life, power, and association with people of wealth and influence did set good colonial families off from others. William Penn, an aristocrat despite Quaker convictions, built a great country seat near Philadelphia, imported race horses, and enjoyed his wine and good food. The Wentworth mansion in New Hampshire boasted fifty-two rooms; and Westover, the stately home of the Byrds in Virginia, was a visible symbol of the great plantation it ruled. Anyone with money could buy gold buttons for his coat, but not the presumption of authority, the recognition by the established church, and the links to officialdom—the true marks of aristocracy.[49]

Friends of the proprietors; favorites granted land or privileges by the crown or governor, familiar with London fashions and lavish with hospitality; the great landowners—all these hunted, raced, gambled, and danced and also bought books and sat on the council. They achieved some recognition from the rest of society but could not develop the institutions to set themselves decisively apart. Every place had its own leading men, by no means all elegant if spelling and orthography were any indications; and the governor's circle was hardly equivalent to the royal court. The planters had to devote time to management of their estates; and their domestic life-style depended upon poorly trained slaves. It took years of correspondence and exorbitant outlays to import carvings, clocks, and hangings, so that some people of wealth had no curtains to their windows and sat on stools instead of cane chairs.

Above all, claims to preeminence rested on unstable foundations. Debt troubled even William Byrd of Westover. Few families had been long where they were; and swift changes in fortunes enabled new people to challenge the superiority of the old. Any plausible character with a well-cut coat and a show of manners could pass himself off as a gentleman, even as a nephew of the famous Chief Justice Hale. That rascal Tom Bell made a career of it, moving from one colony to another in the 1730s and 1740s under a variety of pseudonyms, defrauding his hosts and seducing their daughters, all because there was no way of recognizing who was who in this society in the absence of institutions that in Europe marked one rank off from another. There was no hereditary nobility. Nor did the law in the colonies emphasize difference in status to the degree that it did at home; even the principles of primogeniture and entail designed to transmit family fortunes intact from one generation to another did not in America effectively hold large landed estates together. At the common inns and taverns, the only meeting places, anyone could crowd in and destroy the pretense at gentility. The gentry could not assert superiority or maintain adequate distance from others insistently pushing upward.[50]

The colonies moved beyond the midpoint of the eighteenth century with a truncated class system unlike that of Europe. Distinctions among servants, yeomen, artisans, and merchants bore a surface similarity to those of the Old World except that space, opportunity, and expansion kept the lines among those groupings porous. All the people within them therefore associated liberty less with a specific privilege or status than with a generalized condition that permitted them to pursue individual goals. At the apex of this fluid society stood a few aristocratic families who still defined *liberty*—specifically—as privilege, and who expected to command, if not always obedience, then at least deference, and even that subject to uncertainty.[51]

Usually the would-be aristocrats received the recognition they believed their due. No one objected; most people scrambling upward saw the step just above them, not the peak of the social pyramid; and everyone who possessed anything had a stake in maintaining order. Reflexively people accorded deference to those who claimed it.

An incident of slight importance in Massachusetts, 1760: A gentleman standing on the stairs going to the council chamber did not recognize

Governor Pownall coming down and therefore did not pull off his hat, whereat the outraged chief magistrate "gave him a good box on the ear which struck off his hat." A lesson in deference.[52]

Much earlier, another incident revealed the limits of deference; and this occurred not in some remote quarter among perennial troublemakers, but in Roxbury, Massachusetts, and involved sober, law-abiding subjects. In 1705 Governor Joseph Dudley, riding on horseback with his entourage, saw carts approaching and instructed his son to get them to give way. The younger Dudley rode ahead and told the carters to move aside. To which one carter responded, "I am as good flesh and blood as you, I will not give way, you may goe out of the way." Dudley drew his sword and gave the same command, whereupon a carter took the sword away and broke it. At which point a justice of the peace appeared and sent the carters to prison, the governor complaining meanwhile that they did not take off their hats in his presence. Ultimately the carters went free, after explaining that it would have been easier for the governor to move his horses a little sideways than to maneuver the wagons. It seemed hard that true subjects should be so run upon. The affair intrigued Samuel Sewall, who described it in detail and for months reverted to it in discussion with the governor.[53]

No one questioned the privileges, the authority, or the claim to deference of a governor, a king's favorite, once a member of the English parliament. But carters also had rights, although of what nature was by no means clear in 1705, or even in 1760. Experience had taught them all to look out for themselves, the boys in leaving home and making their own way, the girls in preparing for marriage and for widowhood. Moving forth, they observed about them an expanding productive system that used the resources of a virgin continent and the strategic position in an imperial system to open unbounded opportunities. Whoever grabbed might succeed—or fail. Both possibilities kept class lines fluid, permitting some to rise, others to fall. Scrambling about, the individual found it less useful to clutch at privileges attached to a particular status than to reach toward generalized rights useful wherever he or she might be.

VIII

RIGHTS,

1600–1760

A FEW YEARS BEFORE THE EPISODE of the carters in Roxbury, John Locke used the term *right* to refer to a quality inherent in men; he wrote, for instance, of people's "Right of Defence" against enslavement by any of their own or by foreigners.

A hundred years earlier the word had quite another meaning, derived from its usage as *correct, just, equitable,* but more akin to *power* or *posses- sion,* that is, to the ability to act or dispose of, as in the right to one's own coat or land. In that sense, which prevailed in Europe and America at the start of settlement, *right* was not far different from *liberty* or *privilege,* words also associated with order and status.[1]

The transformed meaning of *right* between the beginning and the end of the seventeenth century bore some relationship to the social changes that altered the terms of colonial politics. New ways of gaining and exercising control forced the colonists to reconsider the structure of authority by which government operated; and in the process rulers and ruled discovered limits beyond which power would not intrude.

Seventeenth-century people had linked power with status, so that the appropriate holder of every position, self-evident by birth and rank, depended on no choice among alternatives. Rarely would a question rise, who should serve as justice of the peace or county commissioner, much less who go to the assembly. In effect, officeholders enjoyed life tenure, periodically confirmed. The magistrates of Gravesend (1651) indignantly rejected the very idea of elections. Were that to become the practice, they warned, communities already riven by factions and impatient with restraints, however mild, would despise, scorn, or disobey authority. By means of elections or choosing, "everyone would desire to do what would please and gratify himself," so that "the strongest would swallow up the weakest." A magistrate who depended upon popular approval could hardly act, as John Cotton wished, as a partition, dividing right from wrong and giving every man his civil dues (1655). Making "treats" to procure an election was ground for questioning the qualifications of a Virginia burgess well into the eighteenth century.[2]

But toward 1700, with ranks not as clear as before and new claimants pushing themselves forward, elevation to office and control of government ceased to be a matter of course. Rival candidates actually presented the electorate with choices, and elections became more than ritual occasions. The vote acquired significance in the location of power; and when that happened, people discovered the new meaning of *right* and its relevance to liberty.

In some places, contests arose from challenges to the self-perpetuating group of magistrates through the injection of discordant elements from outside the community. In stable situations, local magnates and their heirs went on from year to year much as before, while the community inculcated obedience and it occurred to no one to object—except that each parish and town was part of a county and province and therefore exposed to raids from across the borders. Certainly, social position and the disposal of privileges gave the royal governor the weapons with which effectively to rival entrenched local groups as a center of influence. The governors, knowing the need for collaboration with legislatures, moved cautiously if they were wise. But prudence also reminded them of the need to forge alliances, sometimes effected by judicious dabbling in local politics in support of favorites who contested positions. Few were as adept at these maneuverings as Robert Hunter, who became New York's governor in 1710 and whose political skill, responsiveness to colonial wishes, and even-handed distribution of offices broke up the older factions.[3]

Divisions also appeared in the operations of the assemblies. On important issues members voted in terms of dependable factions and connections, as on paper money, free trade, the silver and land banks, and religious issues.[4] Conflicts over these matters generally remained enclosed within the legislative chamber, but sometimes spilled over among the electorate and produced challenges within the constituencies of rivals.

Benjamin Franklin's association with the Norris people among the Pennsylvania Quakers in 1755 thus depended on their desire to build centers of support that would cooperate with them against the proprietary group in the General Assembly.[5]

Splits in the ruling element also produced contests. In New York, Virginia, and South Carolina no one could gain office without the cooperation of important landowners; where they united, no contest was likely. Where the gentry divided, effective electoral appeals appeared, as in the Dutchess County rivalry between Henry Beekman and Adolphe Philipse. Beekman stirred up the small farmers on his own behalf, but once aroused they did not readily subside. In Virginia, family rivalries and the scramble for offices sometimes had the same effect.[6]

Urban places presented the most fertile field for electoral divisions. In Boston, New York, and Philadelphia a diversified population, not rigidly stratified, by the 1750s contained sizable groups susceptible to appeals for political support. In New York, with land grants and offices up for grabs and taxes, currency, and commercial policy subject to manipulation, merchants, landlords, yeomen, artisans, fur traders, seamen, Anglicans, Yankees, Presbyterians, Quakers, Dutch, and Huguenots formed pockets of interest that occasionally coalesced to fight an election. Artisans in 1734 thus turned out to defeat seven merchants up for reelection to the Common Council. Rival candidates in Philadelphia could appeal to economic, social, religious, and ethnic differences among the Welsh, Germans, Jews, Irish, and Quakers, all with leaders and views of their own. Generally, the contests amounted to no more than rough stuff at the polling places, as when the Quakers brought in Germans to fight the sailors who came off ship to help William Allen's side in 1742.[7]

In the south, the plantation system gave the aristocracy some coherence and diminished the likelihood of contested elections. Long-term continuity of officeholding broke down only when occasional feuds among rival great families edged over into politics, or when new people made themselves felt, as in Charleston, South Carolina, or when competition heated up the tobacco market.[8]

More significant divisions appeared in the interior, where large constituencies set up in the seventeenth century suffered from the failure to adjust boundaries to the shifts in population, a situation that evoked resentment and the potential for conflict, so that elections there meant more than tenure of office by gentry as a matter of right.

In New England there was little leverage for divisions outside the larger cities. Electoral procedures often revealed their purpose—to force reluctant nominees to take up the burden of service. While communities held together and towns and churches remained undivided, the prospect of meaningful political contests was slim, except in such matters as location of the county courts. Campaigning for office had the same baleful effects as corruption and bribery, "the subversion of Liberty and the Destruction of good government in Free States." Even Connecticut and Rhode Island, which elected not only the legislature but the governor, rarely faced choices. Samuel Cranston (born 1659), the son of one governor, the grandson of another, and the nephew of still a third, held various posts in Rhode Island until he himself became governor, to be reelected thirty years in succession. Disputes about paper money and the manner of designating militia officers did lead to the ouster of twenty-three of the twenty-eight members of the Rhode Island assembly in 1715; a requirement that year that voters affix their names to their ballots in order to prevent fractious freemen from putting two or three or more into the hat produced such outrage that it vanished the next year. But Cranston remained firmly in place; and a prolonged conflict beat back a "caballing crew" of new people who attempted to gain control of the Falmouth government in 1728. Town meetings heard plenty of hot words and saw evidences of bitter feelings among neighbors but generally chose officials as in the year past.[9]

Meaningful elections appeared in New England when politics felt the effects of the Great Awakening. That religious disturbance tore apart formerly homogeneous communities—the New Lights accepting the techniques and ideology of revival and the Old Lights insisting on traditional ways. These divisions emboldened Baptists and Quakers in forming churches of their own and in protesting against state financial support of the orthodox. When the town ceased to be a community that gathered in one meetinghouse to attend one minister, pluralism shattered the ability to mobilize religious discipline on behalf of the existing order. The clergy, still active in politics, now spoke in various, dissonant voices.

The Connecticut effort to stamp out revivalism by a law licensing ministers failed in its purpose, indeed had the opposite effect (1744). Royal officials threatened to seize the opportunity to move against the charter, and the imprisoned revivalists, glorying in their suffering, preached daily, moving the compassion of their listeners. The issue intruded into elections to the assembly, affected the choice of council members, and hung on through the 1750s, so that none could take tenure of office for granted as voters aligned themselves on one side or the other. The Great Awakening also posed a more general challenge. Emphasis upon individual judgment, the injunction that people think for themselves and consult their own convictions, undermined the power of all governing groups.[10]

The Canterbury dissidents who refused to pay rates to support the established church acknowledged that God had ordained civil authority to punish evildoers but rejected the proposition that anybody could take any person's worldly goods upon pretense of religion. Elisha Paine, jailed for unauthorized preaching, denied that he was "triable by any court or law" but that of God and the King (1744). Independent action spilled over from religious to other questions. People who questioned the stand of the established church had already (1733) dared to proclaim the governor a fool and the councillor a knave. Now they could turn out the knave and the fool. The breach in authority never healed. New England towns, once homogeneous in politics, fragmented just as cities already had.[11]

With the weight of authority lightened, other groups associating for ethnic, social, and business purposes perceived the utility of politics—not of the older sort involving approaches to influential individuals, but of a newer sort involving accumulations of votes. In 1760, no formal institution as yet recognized the fact that elections could involve an actual choice between rivals. The popular noise made by a party little moved Connecticut Governor Jonathan Law (died 1750), who took pride in keeping a happy medium between responsiveness to every breath of opinion on the one hand and tenacity in his own judgment on the other. He deemed divisions exceptional and not quite proper. Such people still preferred to arrive at decisions not by counting heads but by reason and justice—as they understood it. Nevertheless, ever more often the shadow of reelection hung over officials who, like the New York aldermen, stood "in more Awe of a Band of Carmen [teamsters] than of an armed Host" (1752).[12]

Everywhere political contests acquired increasing intensity. Not that every district every year had a genuine election; and some leaders still held office by virtue of their local authority. But with growing frequency they confronted rivals and voters who expected to decide who their rulers should be.

The style changed drastically. Discussion once had turned about such questions as whether to vote by voice, by raised hands, or by paper, whether secretly or with ballots identified. And no doubt some who had participated in the polling were not qualified according to the letter of the law. It mattered little until rival candidates soliciting support made the choice real. Then campaigns heated up. Printed handbills appeared (1744). On occasion, as in 1737 in New York, the polls remained open for twelve hours; there was so much shouting half the men in town were hoarse, soldiers were paid or bribed, the prisons and the poor houses emptied for the event, and "the sick, the lame and the blind were carried to vote." Passions rose, along with calls for recounts. New Jerseyites angered by an election pamphlet sentenced it to be nailed to the common whipping post, gave it the customary thirty-nine lashes, and then burned it.[13]

The nascent press and the well-entrenched pulpit entered the fray, bombarding the voter with advice and warnings. *The New York Gazette* (1751) appealed to common sense, duty, and interest in urging the people to elect only those free of entangling loyalties who would balance support for the crown with tenacious defense of liberty. The voters were to be on guard against placeholders, the well-off, and the ambitious who put their own interests before the common good; and they were to reject the timorous who, having good principles, dared not own or act upon them. Many talked high and made a great noise about conscience and love of country, yet private interests were their dominant concerns. The intrigues and largesse of candidates for office had ended the liberties of Rome. "To ask a man's vote is a tacit Declaration that he acts from Caprice, and abandons his Reason," said the *Independent Reflector* (1753). To wheedle him into a choice by treats and frolics was downright bribery and corruption. The best candidate, able to distinguish "between the powers and rights of government and the liberties and privileges of the people," was likely to be a poor speaker, while "the rising twittle twattler" swayed assemblies in the wrong direction when they weighed words more than reason.[14]

The reckoning of results depended upon point of view. In the jaundiced opinion of Governor George Burrington of North Carolina, electioneering deterred good men from becoming candidates and encouraged lies, disturbances, and disregard of the injunction that only freemen vote. The atmosphere of heat and partiality, he complained, made the assembly "the greatest grievance and oppression to the country." In all the colonies, taverns "very liberal of their drams of brandy and lumps of sugar and their punch" became the nurseries of legislators. Voters who found refreshment there were more likely, when they drifted to the meetinghouse, to choose a retailer of rum and small beer than a gentleman (1760). On the other hand, some contests, as in Burlington County, New Jersey (1738), had no ill effects. Electioneering lasted for three days and "the leading men" arranged everything without defaming characters or using canes in a hostile manner. With no actions "inconsistent with the freedom which ought to subsist in our elections," two proper gentlemen won. A meeting in Boston (1740), so crowded that it had to move to a larger hall, managed without disorder to count 367 yeas and 360 nays with no fraudulent voting.[15]

However, even when orderly, contests altered the meaning of representation. Landon Carter noted (1755), in the midst of a heated debate on a tobacco law, that the burgesses, bent on pleasing their constituents, argued one way privately and another publicly on the floor of the chamber, feeling themselves obliged to follow the will of the majority that had put them in office. He himself, an admirer of reason and liberty, was willing to heed the wishes of the electorate in small measures but not in such as affected the common good.[16]

Since they occupied office by the choice of their constituents, assembly members believed themselves guardians of the liberties, rights, and privileges of the people. The Massachusetts House thus explained (1729) that election left it "free from all prejudices and prepossessions" and gave it greater sensitivity to public safety than the other branches of the government. Indeed, Benjamin Franklin claimed for the Pennsylvania assembly "additional Liberties and Privileges not used in England" but earned by the initial sacrifices of settlement.[17]

The inference followed that all offices should be assigned not as patronage or by purchase but by ability to serve. Merit, a Massachusetts clergyman declared in 1758, ought to be the only true avenue of appointment and promotion, unaffected by bribes, flattery, or the insinuations of courtiers. Certainly, the sermon argued, wealth did not qualify anyone for governing; God often bestowed the greatest rewards on the most worthless mortals to show the slight esteem of riches in his sight. Besides, the well-to-do, more self-centered than others, pursued only their own narrow view of the common good. The best officeholders therefore originated from among the middling sort, who acquired their competency honestly, valued liberty and, having little wealth behind which to hide, remained responsive to public pressure. Mental integrity, public spirit, and knowledge of how men and women behaved counted for more than rank. The colonies produced few practitioners of the arts, an observer conceded, but greater insight into people (1684). In the absence of higher education everyone studied to be half physician, half lawyer, but with a natural acuteness because "for want of bookes they read men the more."[18]

Magistrates received the deference accorded their positions in 1760 as in 1600. But those who puffed themselves up in pride did not escape derision, as when a New Amsterdam inhabitant expressed contempt for the West India Company directors who wished to be addressed as lords, though they were but merchants. Such mockery called forth only feeble punishment or was forgiven.[19]

The gradual changes in the manner of choosing officials did not drastically alter the kinds of men who exercised political control. Much the same types of persons held office in 1760 as earlier, only now more responsive than formerly to those by whose mandate they ruled. Nor did connections with the mother country suffer. The authority of the crown remained intact, particularly after the Glorious Revolution resolved anxieties about the Protestant succession. Indeed, the importance of the crown in thinking about government grew as the provincials bestowed on the king a role as guarantor of political liberty. His representatives, the governors, the colonists thought conveyed to them "assurances with reference to our Religious and Civil Rights, Liberties and Privileges" (1717). An address by the House of Representatives to the governor of Massachusetts (1719) began with the usual protestations of loyalty to the glorious prince "who ever since his Happy Accession . . . has manifested a tender regard to the liberties of his subjects," but then expressed the hope "that our happy constitution will be preserved to us and our posterity." To that end the House wished "to inform our selves of our rights, because our prosperity or infelicity intirely depends upon the enjoyment or deprivation of Liberty."[20] Almost a half century later (1756), James Alexander's obituary in *The New York Mercury* referred to the rights of the crown as the "Bulwark of the Liberties of the People," whose liberties were "the safety and honour of the Crown," so that "a just temperament of both in the administration of government" constituted the "health of the political body."[21]

These unexceptionable sentiments, expressed in familiar words, concealed ambiguities created by shifting meanings. Since the early settlements, the colonists had appealed frequently to their liberties, that is, to the privileges connected with whatever status they occupied, and which they believed they had brought with them in migration. But they also used the term *liberty* to refer by extension to the personal and property rights embraced in charters and traceable back to Magna Carta. Back in 1637, Roger Williams had thus warned John Winthrop of golden knives to cut your own throat. Under the cloak of an enlargement of authority "lies hid the hook to catch your invaluable liberties. Better an honorable death than a slave's life." Since personal and property rights depended upon status, the two meanings were really one, or at least were closely related. Praying for Margaret Rule, Cotton Mather (1693) had "a sort of *right* to demand" for her "such a *liberty*" as would enable her to glorify the Lord.[22]

In the eighteenth century the term acquired fresh meaning in the course of political discussion and experience in government, for the requirement of consent called for continual reinterpretation of the charters and constitutions to which rulers and ruled alike appealed. The understanding of rights that emerged in the process found expression not in formal political theory but in some aspects of an evolving American law.

The determined but blundering steps to establish legality in the first decades of settlement stumbled over simple ignorance about what law was and how to proclaim it. Legislatures met but irregularly and sometimes acted without awareness of statutes already enacted. Courts passed judgment with no recollection of precedents. Insofar as the law of the mother country applied to the colonies, that meant the common law—murky terrain within which few knew the way. Even within England, skilled pleaders had to penetrate thickets of peculiar local customs, distinctive regional practices, and complex, overlapping jurisdictions; and the century after 1600 in all European states witnessed dramatic changes in legal conceptions. The colonists could not cope. To cast doubt on the titles of many New Jersey landholders because a grant had said "or" when it should have said "and" (1676) baffled people who simply disregarded such distinctions, whatever the law. Similar uneasiness lay behind the controversy in Massachusetts (1641) about whether to fix punishments by law or leave them to the discretion of magistrates.[23]

Repeatedly people demanded written laws so that they not be unwittingly drawn into slavery (1642), and officials of the courts begged the governors for books for their own guidance. We "humbly desier that the sending of the Lawe Booke may not be forgott; there being great occasion for the same," New Castle plaintively reminded Governor Edmund Andros (1677).[24]

Yet to write the law down was difficult. Massachusetts discovered that the Bible was not a sufficient source, when John Cotton attempted to compose a code based upon it. Nor did the body of liberties prove adequate. Fourteen years after Boston's settlement there was still no particular fixed punishment for burglary. Precedents just did not hold. John Winthrop objected to Nathaniel Ward's political discourse grounded much "upon the old Roman and Grecian governments" (1641). Religion and the word of God after all had made men wiser, and besides modern times had the advantage in experience and observation of all that went before. "We may better frame rules of government for ourselves than to receive others upon the bare authority of those heathen commonwealths."[25]

Forgetfulness and ignorance of precedents required frequent codifications. Springfield, Massachusetts, and Germantown, Pennsylvania, were among the places that periodically read all the laws out to the inhabitants, holding it unjust to punish offenders for violating ordinances of which they were ignorant. Plymouth, the smallest and most intimate of the colonies, published such codes in 1636, 1658, 1672, and 1685, the last also including tables of fees and standard forms. Rhode Island (1647), New Hampshire (1679), and other colonies went through the same exercise, sometimes only to have the crown set their efforts aside.[26] Royal officials in the effort to rationalize the imperial system insisted that English law applied to the colonies—pure and simple; and at least in the larger cities, courts began to issue appropriate writs, follow appropriate forms.

But although the trend was genuine, the law that applied in the lives of Americans was far from anglicized, even in 1760. Eccentricities persisted, as in the Court of Common Right established by the proprietors of East New Jersey (1683), or in the need to adapt to the German traditions of some Pennsylvanians. A few provinces had no attorney generals and some which did depended on men "wholly ignorant of the Laws and practices in the Courts of England" (1696). Above all, the colonists, whatever their professions of loyalty, never wavered from the insistence "that the lawes of England are bounded within the fower seas and doe not reach America. The subjects of his majesty here being not represented in Parliament" (1678). Rhode Island in 1749 quite suddenly plunged into doubt about the validity in the province of "the statutes of that part of Great Britain, formerly called England," so that scarcely any legal proceeding could commence or be brought to issue; and within the year reenacted a long list of measures "so far as they are applicable in this colony and where we have no law of the colony."[27]

In time printed statutes and the practice of keeping notes on judicial decisions formed a basis of consistency. By the 1730s and 1740s, also, facilities for training lawyers by apprenticeship produced skilled practitioners, ready to play parts in both politics and litigation. The Boston town meeting (1735) voted for large judicial units to render justice more uniform and steady and to permit judges to apply themselves not only to the ordinary business of the courts but also "to the Books of the Law, to Instruct their minds and form their Judgments, that their Administration of Justice may be the more conformable to the Universal Reason of all Mankind." Nevertheless for a long time the law was indeterminate, varying from county to county and therefore unpredictable in administration.[28]

"Yet common right we are bound to doe him," wrote the deputy governor of Maine about an enemy (1641). What he had vaguely in mind, Francis Daniel Pastorius, who had studied jurisprudence in Germany, put more explicitly: the law rested on "the firm foundation of reason and daily experience." That proposition conformed to what the colonists knew of the common law which, the most widely used handbook informed them, sprang principally from "the laws of God and nature, which Law of Nature, as it pertaineth to man, is also called, the Law of Reason." That law, not being plainly written, called for interpretation and meant what people wished it to, so there was no need ever to challenge it head on. Winthrop had insisted therefore that the magistrates retain a veto over the acts of the assembly lest the government become "a mere democracy" (1642). But in the end, more important than the statutes on the books produced by the legislative bargaining process was the ability to put them into practice, and that often revolved about the administration of the law.[29]

In doing justice, traditional methods of proof did not suffice; wounds that began to bleed condemned John Dandy to death (1657), but Thomas Mertine went free because nothing happened when he touched the corpse (1660). Those procedures hardly squared with the rules of nature or of reason. And the difficulties increased as the colonial courts absorbed the autonomous jurisdictions that in England handled equity as well as ecclesiastical, family, and business matters.[30]

The appearance of skilled attorneys created dangers of its own, for while laws were made that men oppressed might in them find remedies and lead their lives in quiet rest, the lawyers were so passing greedy that God's fear was out of their sight. Their arguments, often beyond popular comprehension, had "as much Logick as the Boy, that would have lain with his Grand Mother, us'd to his Father, you lay with my Mother, why should not I lie with yours?" Besides in some places the conduct of trials commanded little confidence.

> Now here the judges try the suit,
> And lawyers twice a year dispute.
> As oft the Bench most gravely meet,
> Some to get drunk, and some to eat
> A swinging share of country treat.
> But as for justice right or wrong,
> Not one amongst the numerous throng,
> Knows what they mean, or has the heart,
> To give his verdict on a stranger's part.
>
> (1708)

It hardly helped when the North Carolina court barred two controversial characters from pleading, and then went on to require licenses to practice in order to prevent inconveniences that hindered and perplexed cases (1695).[31]

It came down to this: who would determine guilty or innocent, liable or not?

The charters assured settlers that they possessed the rights of Englishmen, which meant dependence upon the common law. But the history, recent and past, of how judges interpreted that law taught both Englishmen and colonists wariness of that bulwark of their liberty. Winthrop's preference (1644) for a threefold division of power—legislative, judicial, and administrative—dropped out of sight. In the last analysis, people defended their liberties locally in the towns and courts which interpreted the law in the light reason threw on recollected customs and habits. In response to a court order, the Boston selectmen paid "all due deference to your Honours and that Authority the Law has Vested this court with, but your Honours will permit us to pay the greatest deference to the Laws and Constitutions of our Country and the discharge of the Trust reposed in us by those laws"; and refused to obey. The judges acquiesced.[32]

People like the selectmen, tough, rude, and self-reliant, gave their own readings to the law when they served on juries. Since 1606 when the instructions for Jamestown had called for a jury of twelve in all criminal cases, those panels had gained steadily in importance, embodying as they did neighborhood opinion and local power. By the eighteenth century, enthusiastic colonists described juries as "arbitrators and umpires between our prince and his subjects," pillars of liberty and ramparts in the defense against tyranny and slavery. Ever more often, authority in practice shifted into their hands.[33]

Caprice, leniency, and erratic judgments in time transformed criminal law. The juries who shared the power of decision with the judges reflected the views of the populace and inclined to softness, particularly where— as in New Hampshire—the defendant had a right to disallow prospective members. The reluctance to administer the death penalty in effect reduced the number of capital offenses and of corporal punishments. While the fifty crimes punishable by death in seventeenth-century England continued to increase, Connecticut listed only fourteen (1650), and Pennsylvania only eleven (1676). Maryland explained (1681) that the severity of English law suited a thickly settled country but not a thinly populated province. Besides, penalties involving loss of limbs, maiming, burning, or death required so many expenditures for witnesses that many offenders went altogether unpunished. Juries deliberately undervalued goods stolen in order to avoid the execution of thieves, like John and Mary Williams (1658). It was not unusual that Rodger Measure, sentenced to be whipped, got off with a £5 fine (1680) or that Thomas Gibbons got off in the hope he would become "a new man" (1661) or that the conviction of Anne Huson for burglary, a felony punishable by death, sent the Pennsylvania government into turmoil. Death by mutilation persisted for slaves who murdered their masters to "be something of a terror to others from perpetrating of the like barbarity for the future" (1707). But largely without legislation, the eighteenth century saw a sharp diminution of burnings, hangings, beatings, and other brutal tortures or punishments. The change contributed to a new, more favorable view of the courts and of litigation as methods of replacing faded communal controls in defense of rights.[34]

The jury played a part in defining rights, just as it did in reshaping criminal law. Some important rights became established without legislation, indeed contrary to the express letter of the law. In England, Elizabethan statutes against wandering strangers strictly hedged about the freedom to move. The colonies tried to replicate those sensible provisions; New England in particular was dubious about the propriety of either admitting newcomers or allowing local people to depart. Church members, having subscribed to a covenant, needed permission to go elsewhere. John Winthrop, for one, condemned the demand for "Liberty of removing for outward advantages" (1642). People who had come together and confederated in a wilderness where there were only wild beasts and beastlike men implicitly bound themselves to support one another and could not therefore conscientiously break away without the society's consent. If one went, another would, leaving church and commonwealth destitute and all for the ease and pleasure of the deserters. Even fugitives from Indian attacks did not legally become inhabitants of the towns in which they took refuge, although they deserved public support; and the General Court forbade men with military obligations to leave exposed settlements. Other colonies enacted similar measures, as Maryland did (1661) when it required anyone planning to move to give three months' notice and secure a pass. Yet Boston and other places complained that people drifted freely in and out. Space, restlessness, and greed set individuals and whole families in motion and entrenched in practice if not in law the right to establish residence wherever people wished, subject only to assurances they would not become public charges.[35]

Other changes took hold in the same informal fashion. The law continued to recognize the principle of primogeniture, by which estates passed intact to the oldest son. But the Connecticut courts and legislature wished John Waitstill Winthrop to divide his inheritance with his sister despite the principle. A tantrum and an appeal to England, arguing that the local government was "wholly vested in the hands of levelling spirits and anti-monarchical principles" allowed him to have his own way (1726). But Governor Jonathan Law continued to argue that "ye common law was never received here as ye Rule of Descents of Inheritances" (1742); and since few colonists had Winthrop's prestige, wealth, or arrogance, the practice gradually changed in subsequent decades. So too,

English efforts to outlaw colonial paper money evoked the argument that emission of bills of credit was "a Natural and Civil Right" (1746).[36]

Abstractly considered, no right was more important than personal security, the assurance that people proceeding peaceably about their affairs would suffer no molestation in bodies or property. The English Statute of Apprentices (1563) had condemned to servitude persons without households of their own. But few colonists dissented from the need "to prevent the atrocious crime of man stealing" and the similar villainy of blackmail, "a new sort of robbery by wicked persons writing anonymous menacing letters to extort money from their neighbours" (1737,1749).[37]

Yet redress against the government's seizure of persons presented problems. True, the English had resisted royal suggestions for limited detention; "At this little gap every man's liberty may in time go out," John Selden commented. An act of 1679, effective in England, Guernsey, and Jersey made the Writ of habeas corpus, in existence since the Magna Carta, a complete instrument for protecting personal liberty, prescribing the exact manner of its use, and penalizing officials who failed to act according to law. A party imprisoned without sufficient warrant could recover damages against those responsible. In 1710 Queen Anne extended the statute to the colonies.[38]

However, the statute in itself had little consequence. Those who suffered did not easily find relief, as Adam Cogswell of Ipswich discovered when he complained unheeded of fourteen months' unjust confinement to prison (1719). Incarceration was particularly onerous when due to procedural charges, as in the case of Isaac Green, Jr., of Barnstable (1737), the original judgment against him but £3 and the court costs more than £30. Philip Power, arrested in November 1746, languished in jail more than a year without trial, under suspicion of having deserted, although he said he had served out his time as a volunteer. Power waited while the Massachusetts House and Council debated the form of redress. Appeals like his did not invariably invoke a favorable response, for a statute on the books assured no one a right in the absence of communal support.[39]

Impressment raised more complex questions about personal security. The church and the state categorically upheld the obligation to serve in war. Even the God of peace proclaimed the call to arms. "Then the sword is, as it were, consecrated to God, and the art of war becomes a part of our religion." "Cursed is he," a Virginia minister thundered, "that keepeth back his sword from blood." The governments sympathized: New Hampshire awarded a premium of £75 to a Brentwood laborer who served in Canada, fell into the hands of Indians who handed him over to the French, and suffered grievously during his captivity (1759). The Moravians who would not bear arms found their welcome in Georgia terminated; and the Pennsylvania Quakers suffered through convolutions of conscience while voting funds to support war without appearing to do so. Most colonists had no doubt about the appropriateness of manpower drafts for defense. Yet disobedience was common. Exasperated, Governor Joseph Dudley complained in 1709 that of the hundred men he needed, only sixty had turned up and eight of those had run away; and the reason was the legislature's unwillingness to provide funds to pay them. Although the assemblies of New Hampshire (1707) and Connecticut (1724) forbade residents to leave their towns in time of danger, the persistent impulse for self-preservation drew many away. Characteristic outcome: Rhode Island (1745) empowered its governor to impress as many troops as needed—provided that he took only "transient sea faring men and persons who have no certain place of abode."[40]

Whatever the situation in wartime, personal security, in the absence of immediate foreign threats, outweighed the obligation to serve. Impressment then excited indignant protests and indeed direct action. William Partridge having been grossly abused by being taken on board a British vessel, the New Hampshire Council ordered the justices and high sheriffs of the province, agreeable to law, to take care that none of Her Majesty's subjects be carried away (1712). The Massachusetts House of Representatives ordered the release of Thomas Picket's servant seized on the Long Wharf in Boston and forcibly carried aboard His Majesty's ship *The Shark*, in "a great breach on the rights of his majesties subjects of this province," and refused to allow the vessel to sail out of the harbor until it be done (1720). The crew out of Marblehead hid three men liable to seizure in lockers and foiled the searchers; almost strangled to death, the seamen reflected afterwards that they had rather stood on deck and opposed the press gang (1741). In 1745 and 1746, Boston appealed against the horrid abuse of impressment—illegal, oppressive, a breach of both Magna Carta and the charter, diminishing the liberties of the people and costly because of its interference with the fisheries. The Massachusetts House asked the governor to stop the practice of enlisting children under sixteen years of age which brought great distress and difficulty on parents and masters. *The Independent Advertiser* of Boston (1748) attacked the government for inadequate protests against unlawful press gangs "permitted to rob us of our people." That criticism evoked an effort in the council to condemn the newspaper; but the House refused to concur. In 1758, the Boston selectmen voiced the same complaints. By then personal security was a right the colonists defended with any means at hand.[41]

Taxes, unless local and for clearly visible uses, evoked the sternest assertion of principle. The reluctance to part with hard-earned money had a long history in all the colonies. The brewers who evaded the New Netherland exaction explained that they would otherwise have the community about their ears; and the Rhode Island assembly pointed out that having escaped the iron yoke of wolfish bishops, its members had almost forgotten what taxes were—to church or to commonwealth.[42]

Boston's repeated complaints (1752, 1753, 1754, 1759) about the excise and excessive taxation—tending to destroy dear liberties—surprised few; in 1745 the selectmen had refused to contribute small arms for an expedition against Cape Breton. But so strong was the tradition of public miserliness that a petty charge disrupted even the irenic atmosphere of mutual congratulation between the crown and Virginia. Gone, declared the governor in 1736, were the horrid days of rule by "an arbitrary despotic power," under legislation enacted in England without the consent of the people. In response the Speaker of the House expressed "the universal satisfaction of the people" with the "faithful trustee for the public good." In 1742 and again in 1755 the governor promised to preserve the "invaluable priviledges" of the people's religious and civil rights. Harmony vanished when a small fee in connection with grants of royal lands seemed to the Virginians a veritable "subverting of the laws and constitution of this government," contravening the charter and previous instructions to the governors, an infringement of the rights of the people, "so secured by law that they cannot be deprived of the least part of their property but by their own consent." The law guaranteed the rights of subjects, argued lawyer Richard Bland (1751). "The liberty and property of every person who has the felicity to live under a British government" rested on the certainty that none could be deprived of the least part of their property without their own consent. The question was not the smallness of the demand but the lawfulness of it. Outraged, the House of Burgesses declared anyone who willingly paid the fee "a betrayer of the rights and priviledges of the people."[43]

Whence came those rights and privileges—by whose authority granted—it was not necessary to say; nor did eighteenth-century Americans ever compile a reasoned statement of them. Force provided the ultimate argument, in 1760 as in 1690. The readiness to disobey an intolerable or inconvenient law easily erupted into violence. In 1704 a riot in Hampton, New Hampshire, under pretense of an order by the selectmen, shocked the governor and the province enacted a new law to prevent tumultuous assemblies. In 1728 the legislature repealed that act, having discovered that there was not as much as one disaffected person within the province. Alas, in 1734 a gathering in Exeter beat up the surveyor general of His Majesty's wood and his men in a conflict over rights to the forest. The House of Representatives condemned this vile piece of disobedience and feebly ordered an investigation and punishment of those responsible.[44]

Meanwhile perennial hot spots heated up from time to time. Fluctuations in the prices they received kept tobacco growers on the verge of desperation. That they did well in most years did not ease their anger when times turned bad. In 1682, down there in Virginia, the Gloucester County inhabitants decided to produce no tobacco, cut their own plants, and moved from plantation to plantation telling the owners to do the same "or they would create willingness in them by force." A 1729 inspection law led to disorders in the Northern Neck—not too serious in the outcome, especially when the governor treated the rioters with mercy.[45]

Over there in Dutchess County, New York, the problem sprang from tenantry, compounded by the greed of aristocratic landowners and of aspiring speculators, by an uncertain boundary with Massachusetts, by Indian alliances, and by social conflicts between Yankees and Yorkers. Opposition to quitrents in New Jersey and the difficulties of the Palatine German settlers in Schoharie had earlier erupted in violence. But little guerrilla skirmishes flared along New York's eastern frontier in 1753 and the raids of armed bands continued until the French and Indian War temporarily diverted energies elsewhere.[46]

Force remained the ultimate recourse. But the rioters never intended to subvert the law—only to assert their own understanding of it; as the eighteenth century advanced, appeals to the judiciary became more common and to some extent, although not entirely, replaced riots and political action. The trend owed something to the character of colonial lawyers, still poorly educated by English standards; many, lacking even the books and collections of cases to cite authority, fell back upon what seemed reasonable. Depending on common sense as they did, they framed original arguments that persuaded juries and won popular support. They cited statutes when convenient, but the principles they deduced they identified not with obscure man-made laws but with self-evident propositions comprehensible without recourse to ancient texts.[47]

Therein lay the significance of the Zenger case (1735). John Peter Zenger, born in 1697, had escaped lifelong misery by migration from Germany at the age of thirteen. After an eight-year apprenticeship to William Bradford, New York City's only printer, Zenger set up his own business, but with little success, until he became involved in a bitter political quarrel. For years, the DeLancey family had controlled the assembly. Their rivals, the Morris family, established their own newspaper, edited by James Alexander and printed by Zenger, as a medium for criticizing the government. *The New York Weekly Journal* attacked the governor and the DeLanceys for destroying the liberties of their country and imposing slavery upon their posterity. "A Governor turns rogue, does a thousand things for which a small rogue would have deserved a halter; and because it is difficult if not impracticable to obtain relief against him, therefore it is prudent to keep in with him and join in the roguery." He does "all he can to chain you, and it being difficult to prevent him," it is prudent "to help him put them on and to rivet them fast." The printer's arrest and indictment followed and exorbitant bail kept him in prison for nearly twelve months. His acquittal was a decisive victory for the Morris faction from which Zenger also profited. In 1737 he became public printer and thrived until his death in 1746.[48]

Yet with the facts at issue clear, a well-ordered English court would have found no problem in interpretation or decision. Certainly the *Journal*'s sentences sinned in not displaying appropriate deference; and not in a careless manner—failure to uncover in the governor's presence—but in calculated insult set in type. Print on both sides of the ocean directed dangerous political barbs at the established order and more so in newspapers than in tracts or pamphlets. English law was explicit: evil words spoken against any public person or officer were breaches of the peace, of which any justice could take cognizance. The colonists, it was true, had in the past heard the cry, "No Lords, No Masters," from outcasts who styled the government "thieves, robbers, hypocrites, satyrs, owls, courts of owls, dragons and devils and soldiers, legions of devils" (1667). But there was no shrugging off accusations embedded in type by a respectable artisan. English law made Zenger guilty of a libel, a published statement damaging to a person's reputation. It remained only to prove that he had printed the defamatory article.[49]

Abundant precedents for censorship reflected official fears about the potential power of a new means of exerting public influence. Virginia's Governor Berkeley had complained (1671) that learning brought disobedience into the world and that printing spread libels against the government. The Duke of York's Laws (1676) had punished publication of news that disturbed the people or injured reputations. Newspapers made matters worse. The Massachusetts governor in 1720, noting the scandalous papers that disquieted the minds of His Majesty's good subjects, suggested that lovers of peace and good order might prevent this pernicious practice by a law requiring a license before printing any book or paper. A year later Andrew Bradford was in trouble, and in 1729 found himself before the Provincial Council of Pennsylvania for wicked sedition "tending to introduce confusion under the notion of Liberty and to lessen the just regard due to persons in authority." Two years later James Franklin's *New England Courant* stirred up concern. Zenger's indictment therefore rested on solid precedent as well as on the letter of the law. But his lawyer, Andrew Hamilton, injected a novel argument by maintaining that the critical question was not whether Zenger's statements attacked the governor, but whether they were true or false. His reasoning convinced the jury, which returned an acquittal.[50]

What a victory that was!

Or was it?

Well, in fact, not really.

But, in truth, yes indeed.

One case by no means settled the issue of press freedom, which lingered in the colonies and would linger on in the republic. In 1743, at the urging of a revivalist that they burn their idols, New Londoners tossed offensive books into the flames. In the 1750s Massachusetts still tried to hunt out printers who circulated seditious expressions and jailed Daniel Fowle of Boston for contemptuous expressions that constituted a breach of the privileges of the House of Representatives. His pamphlet *Monster of Monsters* having been burned on King Street, he moved in disgust to New Hampshire.[51]

Nevertheless popular support spread for the principle that a newspaper had the right to print what it wished, with truth the sole limit upon its freedom; and in that sense Hamilton's argument prevailed. In 1751 *The New York Gazette* defiantly explained that even if the council "thought they had a right, as being within the pale of the old doctrine, vis. that a libel is never the less a libel for being true, to call it so" required the assurance to go to desperate lengths. An unshackled press, *The Boston Gazette* argued (1755), guarded the subjects' liberty. *Poor Richard* intoned (1757):

> While free from Force the press remains
> Virtue and Freedom cheer our plains.

Any effort to silence it, "treason against sense," was itself a sign of guilt. Only those tainted by pride, those who sought by carnal ease the flesh to please, would wish to use the gag first to rob and then to stop complaint. Fowle rehearsed his tribulations in a pamphlet entitled *A Total Eclipse of Liberty* (1755), and a suit ultimately brought him a small award. Officials backed away from suggestions of censorship, which became presumptive evidence of wrongdoing, politically awkward in gaining consent.[52]

Zenger's case did not establish a right. No single incident did. Rights developed over time. But Zenger's case did illuminate the issue and thus furthered that development.

It would have been difficult to explain where belief in the right to freedom of the press originated. It could not be found in either the common law or in the line of documents that reached from Magna Carta to the Bill of Rights, that usually enshrined the rights of Englishmen to which the colonists insistently laid claim. In their view, rights of this sort did not depend upon royal favor or acts of Parliament. They were not granted; people possessed them as necessary conditions of existence.

Zenger won acquittal because his lawyer convinced the court that truth was a permissible defense, and that the jury, not the judge, had the power to decide—both propositions alien to English law, by which truth was irrelevant and the jury dealt only with facts, not law. To support his position, the attorney appealed not to the charter or to precedent or to statutes. His defense rested on the claim that Zenger's rights were anterior to, independent of, legal formulation; they were his simply by nature. *"Truth* ought to govern the whole affair of libels." Fallible men once burned as heretical dissenters, those who owned such "opinions in matters of religion as are publicly written and printed at this day" without prosecution by the government. "From which I think it is pretty clear, that in New York, a man may make very free with his God, but he must take special care what he says of his governor." Were people, within the bounds of truth, forbidden to speak and write their sentiments of the conduct of the administration, "then the next step may make them slaves," suffering oppression without the liberty of complaining. Zenger's attorney pleaded for acquittal to preserve the liberty of opposing arbitrary power by the truth. Power, a great river, both beautiful and useful while kept within due bounds, brought destruction and desolation when it overflowed its banks. Hence the duty to support liberty, the only bulwark against lawless power, against which every honest man (while paying all due obedience to authority) ought to be upon guard.[53]

The defense, which persuaded the jury as well as many other people, appealed to rights that natural rights philosophers would later explain. The colonists who accepted the defense were not philosophers reasoning about the nature of man or political society, although some learned of the theories and in time cited them in arguments. Experiences, not books, were their teachers. And the judges, legislators, governors, and other royal officials who acquiesced also knew from experience that the alternative was forfeiture of the consent to govern and possible violence.

Hence neither the rulers nor ruled made any effort to prepare systematic lists of rights, or to sort out intellectual inconsistencies and ambiguities. The ruled knew that they had rights—like those of expression in print, or of movement or of personal security. The rulers, without conceding them in principle, refrained from overt infringement upon them.

Whence came those rights? If the law asserted them, did they become rights when enacted by an assembly or enunciated by judges? Or were they there all along and simply recognized when magistrates put them into words? And if there was no statute or judicial decision, what gave life to a right?

The colonists did not confront those questions. They knew the answers. They had reserved those rights to themselves in consenting to be governed, that is, in refraining from violence on their own behalf. The charters to which they now often referred as constitutions derived not from ancient precedents or from grants from the crown but from agreement between king and subjects. Charter rights were the same in substance as inherent rights in their protection of individual freedom. The king thereby became the defender of popular liberties in a formulation based on practice, similar to John Locke's based on theory, similar too to Bolingbroke's vision of the patriot king.[54]

The conception of rights protected by the charter/constitution and guaranteed by the crown, attractive as it was, did not fit the facts. The crown did not always play the protector of liberties and the texts of the charters did not support the interpretive burdens placed on them. But the claim to rights, in the final analysis, did not depend upon the old documents or the citations dredged up by lawyers. Rights antedated those fading papers which created nothing new, but only recognized what already existed as essential aspects of human character. People who had grasped a share of power, who knew the ability to act, believed that they had been born with inherent rights which they had the means to defend, if necessary.

The conception of king as defender of liberties raised the question of the relationship of the individual to the crown. Legally, all the people who lived in his realm were subjects of the king, although there were differences among them. A black slave in Jamaica or Carolina differed in status from a merchant in Boston or New York. Loyalty, allegiance, and obedience applied to all cases, but the meaning varied from place to place and from one social group to another. Residents of England and Scotland were not only royal subjects but also Englishmen and Scotsmen. Ireland was subject to the crown but not to England, for it had its own parliament.

It was not so simple in the American colonies. Seventeenth-century settlers referred to themselves as English, and some continued to do so in the eighteenth century—three or four generations away from England. Newcomers not English by birth presented no problem; whatever the legalities, the settlers proceeded to take them in. In the case of John Martin, a Persian stranger (1622), the Virginia Company decided that the charter gave it the privilege "to enfranchise strangers and make them capable thereby of the like immunities that themselves enjoy." Despite persistent objections from London, the practice continued; and the company also helped Ursula the French widow. Parliament controlled naturalization and denization, issues remote from the concerns of most settlers. The status of inhabitant, resident, or freeman (terms variously used) depended upon the localities, which set their own qualifications of property, religion, and character.[55]

Most places also learned to live with the issue of identity. People who down to 1664 were Hollanders in New Netherland, then became subjects of the king of England, yet still remained Dutch. The transfer of sovereignty did not change their social character. German immigrants landing in Philadelphia took an oath of fealty to the king, but did not become Englishmen. Their position was analogous to, though not the same as, that of the Welsh or Cornish in Britain. Nicole Godin, though a Frenchman, was an English subject (1707); and references to Jews were more general than religious.

Injection of the concept of rights created a problem of terminology, for there was no European equivalent of a generalized political condition, independent of status, to which rights adhered. What was a person with reference to government who held the rights colonists claimed? In respect of their liberty, they were all Englishmen, "free born brave," their rights secured by good and wholesome laws, whereby each might have his property. Such liberty, which Englishmen in England did not enjoy, a Philadelphia almanac of 1753 explained, was the chief cause for the city's rapid growth.[56]

The difficulty arose from the lack until 1776 of the word or even the concept adequately to describe the status—*citizenship*. Within the broad affirmation of loyalty to the crown, another set of relationships had developed—the key to which involved novel obligations. Central to the new association was the assumption of novel ties by people united through participation in the society and in the polity. In form, the oath of loyalty to the king required obedience to lawful orders, defense against enemies, and the cheerful payment of taxes, all far from actual. The colonists did not automatically obey the laws; did not always fight the crown's enemies; and handed over taxes quite grudgingly, if at all. The takers of the oath, not hypocrites, built into the affirmations enough qualifications to escape its burdens. The obligations they honored were not to the crown but to one another.

By the definition of Daniel Defoe (1701), the colonists had more claim to the designation *True-born Englishman* than did many a native of the home islands.

> The meanest English plowman studies law,
> And keeps thereby the magistrates in awe,
> Will boldly tell them what they ought to do,
> And sometimes punish their omissions too.

Though by English law, only the crown and Parliament could turn foreigners into British subjects, colonial governments proceeded to bestow status as they wished, together with the privileges of land ownership and trade, partly out of the urgencies of settlement and partly because they were redefining affiliation.[57]

The important obligations on which people did follow through were those connected with local society and with their neighbors. They obeyed not the laws royally sanctioned but those promulgated by authority derived from consent. They provided defense and taxes for the benefit of the community in which they lived. The valid requirements were those of active participation in the political order, formally connected with the crown but operating in its own way. Imperceptibly, new ways of using power had transformed the subjects (although still referred to as such) into something as yet unnamed: citizens. The ties among them were not feudal or national but political, based upon the willingness of individuals to recognize each other's rights and to limit power by consent.

Many issues remained unclear because people had not yet perceived the implications of a process that had just begun. The question of who was eligible to play a political role was not answered or recognized. The matter had not been important when the community was an aggregation of households, with the head of the household the only participant in political decisions. Widows and other females alone often acquired all the rights connected with the household. In England such a woman could name the member of Parliament; in the colonies she could sometimes vote and hold property. When the integrated community disintegrated, the unanswered questions arose whether women could be citizens and play a role in political and other communal processes.

So long as the community rested on the household, landless servants or laborers were not an issue either. Property qualifications for suffrage became important only in the case of people qualified in some ways but without the attributes of total participation.

Citizenship was no issue only with reference to slaves. Their status was absolutely clear, bound as they were within households of others. On the other hand, blacks once qualified by virtue of freedom were eligible to participate in the life of the community, although to what degree was unclear, for the issue was only being explored, with resolutions varying from place to place. The fact that the problem was raised and debated was an indication of a new concept in the life of the colonies. Later still the implications of citizenship would emerge from the redefinition of nationality and from new connotations attached to rights.

In more than a century and a half of experience much had persisted in the European heritage, but much also had changed under the impact of American conditions. To describe the process as modernization is to oversimplify it.[58]

The effort to carry across the Atlantic familiar communal institutions included political, religious, and economic patterns of behavior and belief in the expectation that all would cohere in a unified fashion and would control the whole life of the people. But that kind of integrated community was already losing strength in Europe; and transplantation would weaken it further. Instead, unnoticed often, unintentional often, newer communal forms appeared within the colonies. Not everyone took part in all of them. Nor did the settlers attempt to integrate each into a unified whole.

Within the fragmented sectors of that community, individuals found some areas of choice in which they could, to some extent, shape their own ideas, behavior, and affiliations. Associated with an intricate pattern of separate institutions, they ceased to identify themselves with the crown even as symbol of a whole community, and defined their relationship to the state in purely political terms, involving a share in the power to govern, whatever their family, religion, or economic or social status. Just as Zenger's attorney argued that his position was reasonable and natural, so the colonists expanded their claims to rights beyond the texts of charters or acts of Parliament, to claim also those common sense showed were their due.

Therefore they would find attractive the line of political theory that stemmed from the writings of Hugo Grotius, Samuel Puffendorf, and John Locke. In the works of these thinkers Americans would discover the argument that described their own situation. People were, by their very character, endowed with a natural right to life, liberty, and property, in defense of which they created governments by joining in a social contract, agreeing to obey a ruler who undertook to preserve and further their rights.

Only a few learned colonists read the philosopher's books. But the ideas derived from those works conformed to the beliefs many already held or toward which they were groping. To New World people these were not simply abstract speculations but general confirmations of attitudes shaped by the practical experience of developing a polity. The state to them was not merely an inherited institution that had grown up since a time long out of mind. It had originated in their own lifetimes and had changed before their very eyes. The difficulties they encountered as they interpreted and reinterpreted their charters, while bickering with the governor, the proprietor, and London, forced them to think about the meaning of rights.

Government they understood as a necessity, but a product of human intentions. The settlers had reached the wildnerness in a state of nature, and the frontier, even in 1760, had nowhere receded so far as to leave any illusions about the ability of humans to survive in peace without order and mutual assistance. To provide security through law, the colonists had associated themselves in social compacts which they identified with such actual documents as the company and province charters, and the covenants that established new towns and churches. When Americans thought of rights or the consent of the governed, therefore, they had in mind the actualities of their own experience.

In 1760, the Massachusetts House and governor outdid themselves in self-congratulation. The legislators viewed the times with inexpressible joy. The British constitution, excelling all others, now exceeded itself. "It raises new ideas for which no language had provided words because never known before, contradictions are become almost consistent," while the clamor of factions had fallen silent. Whereupon Governor Francis Bernard reminded them of the blessings derived from subjection to Great Britain, "without which you could not now have been a free people."[59]

A free people had frequent occasion to consider the meaning of liberty. Back in 1645 John Winthrop had described two kinds of liberty. The first, natural, allowed man to do what he wished, evil as well as good, without the least restraint of the most just authority. So in a day of celebration, children and servants had their liberty. This Winthrop judged "the great enemy of truth and peace." By contrast, civil or moral liberty was a liberty to do only what was good, honest, and just, exercised by subjection to authority. Therein he echoed a common English distinction.[60]

A century later (1753) an influential essay denied the distinction and instead described liberty as self-rule, in the nature of things inseparable from human existence. "For by admitting the Rationality of Man, you necessarily suppose him a free Agent. And as no political Institutions can deprive him of his Reason, they cannot by any Means, destroy his native Privilege of acting freely."[61]

Experience had taught the colonists the meaning of freedom and restraint. A writer in *The New York Weekly Journal* in 1740 explained that liberty was "a latitude of practice within the compass of law and religion." It released man from the arbitrariness and ill humor of others, and encouraged "the improvement of reason . . . leisure for reading and contemplation." Absolute liberty was "a jest, tis a visionary and roman-tick priviledge and utterly inconsistent with the present state of the world." Mankind had neither enough understanding nor honesty to be left entirely to its own resources. Factions and seditious individuals fired up the populace by telling them that "they are fit to be at their own disposal": in effect, that "they are free to be out of their wits and to be undone." With this specious cant, "state gipsies pick the pockets of the ignorant." "Liberty against virtue and laws is only a privilege to be unhappy and a licence for a man to murder himself."[62]

Liberty did not consist of indifference in "choice or will to either side of the question, to assent or to deny, to act in one way or in the contrary." Cadwallader Colden of New York explained in 1746, "After I under-stand a proposition in Euclid I cannot refuse my assent and yet I give my assent with full liberty." Every intelligent being was truly free while acting only from principles within itself, without compulsion from any efficient cause without it. And intelligent beings, he believed, were those conscious of their own actions who altered and determined those actions according to their perception of other beings around them and did so to some purpose or end, and therefore were of themselves properly moved or determined only by final causes.[63]

History taught the colonists that lesson. In 1730, during the usual squabble between governor and assembly about salaries, *The New York Gazette* took to poetry in defense of liberty.

> Oh no, we are strong and we will stand our defence
> altho you are pleased to call it Insolence
> this for our Freedom is good pretence.

Then proceeded to explain,

> And having crost the wide Atlantick sea,
> and purchased dear a perfect Liberty
> we wil keep it still and what is that to thee?[64]

The discovery of liberty, in its own way as unexpected as the discovery of America, was about to unfold its momentous consequences.

Latter-day Columbians, they had hit upon a continent they had not known existed. In the confused effort to reorder their lives they had learned novel ways of behaving and thinking; out of the effort to grapple with a new reality, they had stumbled upon a new meaning of liberty, one not attached as a privilege to a particular status but general to all humans. The discovery would cause the generations that followed much pain, but also reveal vast potentialities for further exploration.

The train of events that produced Independence extended on into the middle of the nineteenth century. In the quarter century after 1760, new political patterns took form—or seemed to do so. The events that led to the separation from Britain created a heady sense of novelty, an impression of the birth of an entirely new type of people, dedicated to liberty in a unique way. Coming as they did at the start of a period of great expansion, these events opened out into an era of experimentation that Americans defined as progress, tremendously significant for the future, within the country and throughout the world. Down almost to the midpoint of the nineteenth century, explorations of liberty penetrated economics, religion, culture, and ideas as well as politics.

The shocking awareness of insoluble problems and of civil war dominated popular consciousness in the 1850s and 1860s; yet as important in the long run were the economic innovations and changes in population that endured down till 1920. Despite the battlefield losses after 1861 and 1917, the seventy years after 1850 were a time of expansion. The country reached its territorial limits; and more significant criteria measured the continued upward thrust in population, in wealth, in industrial and agricultural output. An immense reshuffling of population followed the arrival of great numbers of immigrants and the drift of rural population into the cities, as well as the movement of all sorts of people from east to west. These dramatic social changes forced men and women to consider new thoughts, to reexamine inherited patterns of faith, to reorder the means of expression, and to forge new cultural forms. The altered context put pressure on the inherited American conception of the Republic's place in the world, and—even more drastically—forced citizens to consider their polity and in the process to change the terms of liberty.

After 1920, the New World no longer seemed new. Economic development created a massive industrial plant, situated in a great urban complex, within which people moved in an impersonal network of relationships that yet again recast conceptions of liberty. Furthermore, the successes created stakes that many wished to preserve; they became more cautious, averse to risks. Now too the United States no longer stood in the forefront of the world's historical development. Other societies, moving in newer directions, unhinged certainty in the nation and that for which it stood. The effort to lend reality to the promises of American life ignited group conflict and challenged inherited patterns of morality and belief. Whether the values of individuality and daring would persist or whether loss of nerve would induce paralysis at critical moments raised questions about the meaning of liberty, never more challenging than in the 1980s.

NOTES

The notes that follow do not constitute a systematic or complete bibliography. They provide references to the illustrative material used as evidence in the text.

Abbreviations Used in the Notes

Conn. Hist. Soc. Colls.	Connecticut Historical Society, *Collections,* 31 vols. (Hartford, 1860–1967)
Conn. Pub. Recs.	James H. Trumbull and Charles J. Hoadly, eds., *Public Records of the Colony of Connecticut, 1636–1776,* 15 vols. (Hartford, Conn., 1850–1890)
Hening Statutes	William Waller Hening, ed., *The Statutes at Large, Being a Collection of All the Laws of Virginia,* 13 vols. (New York, 1819–1823)
Mass. Bay Co. Recs.	Nathaniel B. Shurtleff, ed., *Records of the Governor and Company of the Massachusetts Bay,* 5 vols. (Boston, 1853–1854)
Mass. Hist. Soc. Colls.	Massachusetts Historical Society, *Collections,* 70 vols. (Boston, 1792–1942)
Mass. House Jour.	*Journals of the House of Representatives of Massachusetts, 1715–1760,* 36 vols. (Boston, 1919–1964)
Md. Archives	William H. Browne et al., eds., *Archives of Maryland,* 70 vols. (Baltimore, 1883–1982)
New Castle Recs.	Colonial Society of Pennsylvania, *Records of the Court of New Castle on Delaware, 1676–1681,* 2 vols. (Lancaster, Pa., 1904)
New Plym. Recs.	Nathaniel B. Shurtleff et al., eds., *Records of the Colony of New Plymouth,* 12 vols. (Boston, 1855–1861)

235

N.H. Hist. Soc. Colls.	New Hampshire Historical Society, *Collections*, 15 vols. (Concord, N.H., 1824–1939)
N.H. Prov. Papers	Nathaniel Bouton et al., eds., *Documents and Records Relating to the Province of New Hampshire, from the Earliest Period of Its Settlement,* 39 vols. (Concord, N.H., 1867–1949)
N.H. Towns	Isaac Hammond, ed., *Documents Relating to Towns in New Hampshire,* 3 vols. (Concord, N.H., 1883)
No. Car. Col. Recs.	William L. Saunders, ed., *The Colonial Records of North Carolina, 1662–1776,* 10 vols. (Raleigh, N.C., 1886–1890)
N.Y.C. Comm. Coun. Mins.	*Minutes of the Common Council of the City of New York, 1675–1776,* 8 vols. (New York, 1905)
N.Y.C. Mayor's Ct., Select Cases	Richard B. Morris, ed., *Select Cases of the Mayor's Court of New York City* (Washington, D.C., 1935)
Pa. Archives	Samuel Hazard, ed., *Archives of Pennsylvania,* 1st series, 12 vols. (Philadelphia, 1852–1856)
Pa. Prov. Coun. Mins.	Samuel Hazard, ed., *Pennsylvania Colonial Records: Minutes of the Provincial Council of Pennsylvania,* 10 vols. (Philadelphia, 1851–1852)
R.I. Hist. Soc. Colls.	Rhode Island Historical Society, *Collections,* 34 vols. (Providence, R.I., 1827–1941)
Va. Burgesses Jour.	Henry R. McIlwaine et al., eds., *Journals of the House of Burgesses of Virginia, 1702–1776,* 13 vols. (Richmond, Va., 1905–1915)
Va. Co. Recs.	Susan M. Kingsbury, ed., *Records of the Virginia Company of London,* 4 vols. (Washington, D.C., 1906–1935)

I. POWER, 1600

1. Peter H. Brown, ed., *Scotland before 1700* (Edinburgh, 1893), p. 162; William Croft Dickinson, *Scotland from the Earliest Times to 1603* (New York, 1961), pp. 228 ff.; Richard Bagwell, *Ireland under the Tudors,* 3 vols. (London, 1885–1890), 1: 165, 3: 7; Alfred L. Rowse, *Tudor Cornwall* (London, 1941), pp. 106 ff.; Peter H. Brown, ed., *Early Travellers in Scotland* (Edinburgh, 1891), p. 259.
2. Hugh R. Trevor-Roper, "George Buchanan and the Ancient Scottish Constitution," *English Historical Review,* Supplement 3 (1966): 47, 48; John Bowle, *Charles I* (London, 1975), p. 101.
3. Daniel P. Walker, *The Decline of Hell: Seventeenth Century Discussions of Eternal Torment* (London, 1964).
4. Constantia Maxwell, *Irish History from Contemporary Sources, 1509–1610* (London, 1932), p. 199; Bagwell, *Ireland under the Tudors,* 2: 113, 3: 102, 435.
5. William E. H. Lecky, *History of the Rise and Influence of the Spirit of Rationalism in Europe,* 2 vols. (New York, 1890), 1: 122 ff.; John Lothrop Motley, *The Rise of the Dutch Republic: A History,* 3 vols. (Philadelphia, n.d.), 1: 605, 2: 443, 455.

6. Dickinson, *Scotland,* p. 249; James Wilson, ed., *The Victoria History of the County of Cumberland,* 2 vols. (Westminster, 1901–1905), 2: 273 ff.; Maxwell, *Irish History from Contemporary Sources,* p. 23; Bagwell, *Ireland under the Tudors,* 2: 91, 335, 3: 74 ff.

7. Dickinson, *Scotland,* p. 374; Henry Stephenson, *The Elizabethan People* (New York, 1910).

8. David Masson, ed., *The Register of the Privy Council of Scotland,* 14 vols. (Edinburgh, 1877–1898), 4: 424, 428, 591.

9. Montague Summers, *The History of Witchcraft and Demonology* (New York, 1926); Robert Chambers, *Domestic Annals of Scotland,* 2 vols. (Edinburgh, 1858–1861), 1: 207 ff., 211 ff.; Thomas I. Rae, *The Administration of the Scottish Frontier, 1513–1603* (Edinburgh, 1966), p. 213; George P. Akrigg, *Jacobean Pageant* (Cambridge, Mass., 1963), pp. 13, 14.

10. William S. Holdsworth, *A History of English Law,* 14 vols. (London, 1966), 5: 187; Henry C. Lea, *Superstition and Force: Essays on the Wager of Law—the Wager of Battle —the Ordeal—Torture* (New York, 1968), pp. 323 ff.

11. Sir Thomas Smith, *De Republica Anglorum,* ed. Mary Dewar (Cambridge, 1982), p. 117; Holdsworth, *History of English Law,* 4: 501.

12. Bowle, *Charles I,* p. 15.

13. Holdsworth, *History of English Law,* 6: 298; Vivian C. Fox and Martin H. Quitt, *Loving, Parenting and Dying* (New York, 1980), pp. 166–170, 294.

14. Ruth Pike, *Enterprise and Adventure: The Genoese in Seville and the Opening of the New World* (Ithaca, N. Y., 1966), p. 35; William Croft Dickinson and Gordon Donaldson, *A Source Book of Scottish History,* 3 vols. (London, 1958–1961), 3: 353; Robert Crowley, *Select Works,* ed. Joseph M. Cowper (London, 1872), pp. 133–134.

15. Michael Dalton, *Country Justice* (London, 1697), pp. 297–298, 306; Holdsworth, *History of English Law,* 5: 199; Joyce Youings, *Sixteenth Century England* (London, 1984), pp. 228, 229.

16. Elizabeth Hamilton, *Henrietta Maria* (New York, 1976), p. 172.

17. John Ponet, *A Shorte Treatise of Politike Pouuer* (Amsterdam, 1972), n.p.

18. Ponet, *Politike Pouuer,* n.p.; Holdsworth, *History of English Law,* 4: 86–87, 6: 37–38; Crowley, *Select Works,* pp. 95, 99.

19. Bagwell, *Ireland under the Tudors,* 1: 116; Quentin Skinner, *The Foundations of Modern Political Thought,* 2 vols. (Cambridge, 1978), 1: 6 ff., 77 ff., 157; Rachel R. Reid, *The King's Council in the North* (London, 1921), pp. 9 ff., 31 ff., 59 ff., 101 ff., 147 ff.; Holdsworth, *History of English Law,* 4: 110–111, 6: 560; also John Mackrell, "Criticism of Seigneurial Justice in Eighteenth-Century France," in *French Government and Society, 1500–1850,* ed. John F. Bosher (London, 1975), p. 124.

20. Dickinson and Donaldson, *Source Book,* 3: 386–389.

21. Crowley, *Select Works,* p. 12; Brown, *Scotland before 1700,* p. 199; Holdsworth, *History of English Law,* 4: 521, 6: 296.

22. Conyers Read, *William Lambarde and Local Government* (Ithaca, N.Y., 1962), pp. 59, 63, 70.

23. Dickinson, *Scotland*, pp. 240 ff., 373; Peter Laslett, *The World We Have Lost* (London, 1965), pp. 60–62, 147; Georges Duby and Armand Wallon, eds., *Histoire de la France rurale*, 4 vols. (Paris, 1975–1977), 2: 282 ff.; Philip J. Greven, *Four Generations: Population, Land and Family in Colonial Andover* (Ithaca, N.Y., 1970), p. 44; Sumner C. Powell, *Puritan Village: The Formation of a New England Town* (Middletown, Conn., 1963); Emile Benveniste, *La Vocabulaire des institutions indo-européennes*, 2 vols. (Paris, 1969), 1: 70 ff.

24. Youings, *Sixteenth Century England*, p. 336.

25. Dalton, *Country Justice*, p. 1; Dickinson, *Scotland*, p. 332; Holdsworth, *History of English Law*, 6: 277; Wallace MacCaffrey, *The Shaping of the Elizabethan Regime* (Princeton, N.J., 1968), p. 9; Richard L. Bushman, *King and People in Provincial Massachusetts* (Chapel Hill, N.C., 1985), pp. 17 ff.

26. *Md. Archives*, 54: 634.

27. John H. Gleason, *The Justices of the Peace in England, 1558 to 1640* (Oxford, 1969), pp. 25, 46; Rae, *Administration of the Scottish Frontier*, pp. 166 ff., 170.

28. Joel Hurstfield, *Freedom, Corruption and Government in Elizabethan England* (Cambridge, Mass., 1973), pp. 14, 60, 61; William McElwee, *The Wisest Fool in Christendom: The Reign of King James I and VI* (London, 1958), p. 99; also Hans W. Rosenberg, *Bureaucracy, Aristocracy and Autocracy: The Prussian Experience 1660–1815* (Cambridge, Mass., 1958).

29. For the Continent, see especially Koenraad W. Swart, *The Sale of Office in the Seventeenth Century* (The Hague, 1949); Franklin L. Ford, *The Robe and Sword: The Regrouping of the French Aristocracy* (Cambridge, Mass., 1953); Richard Gascon, *Grand Commerce et vie urbaine au XVIe siècle Lyon et ses marchands: Environs de 1520–Environs de 1580*, 2 vols. (Paris, 1971), 2: 811 ff.; John F. Bosher, "Chambres de Justice," Julian Dent, "The Role of Clienteles," and Nora Temple, "Municipal Elections," in *French Government and Society, 1500–1850*, ed. John F. Bosher, pp. 19ff., 41 ff., 86 ff.

30. Skinner, *Foundations of Modern Political Thought*, 1: 173 ff.

31. Crowley, *Select Works*, p. 68; John Selden, *Table Talk* (London, 1798), p. 54; Perez Zagorin, *The Court and the Country: The Beginning of the English Revolution* (London, 1969), p. 311; James H. Kettner, *The Development of American Citizenship, 1608–1870* (Chapel Hill, N.C., 1978), pp. 13–28.

32. *Md. Archives*, 54: 7–8.

33. James I, *Political Works*, ed. Charles H. McIlwain (Cambridge, Mass., 1918), pp. xvii ff., 53, 307; David Mathew, *James I* (London, 1967), pp. 220, 221; Joseph R. Tanner, *Constitutional Documents of the Reign of James I, A.D. 1603–1625* (Cambridge, 1930), p. 15; Skinner, *Foundations of Modern Political Thought*, 2: 342 ff.

34. Akrigg, *Jacobean Pageant*, pp. 227 ff.; McElwee, *Wisest Fool in Christendom*, pp. 109 ff.

35. Read, *William Lambarde*, p. 21; Dalton, *Country Justice*, p. 65; Duby and Wallon, *Histoire de la France rurale*, 2: 300 ff.

36. Holdsworth, *History of English Law*, 4: 23.

37. André Corvisier, *Armies and Societies in Europe, 1494–1789*, trans. Abigail T. Siddall (Bloomington, Ind., 1979).

38. Dalton, *Country Justice*, pp. 119 ff.; Alexander Brown, *The Genesis of the United*

States, 2 vols. (New York, 1964), 1: 288; Crowley, *Select Works,* pp. 133–134; John L. McMullan, *The Canting Crew* (New Brunswick, N.J., 1984), pp. 34 ff.; Duby and Wallon, *Histoire de la France rurale,* 2: 179 ff.

39. Basil Sollers, "Transported Convict Laborers in Maryland during the Colonial Period," *Maryland Historical Magazine* 2 (1907): 17ff. See also Joan Thirsk, *English Peasant Farming* (London, 1957), pp. 167 ff.; David E. Vassberg, *La Venta de tierras baldias* (Madrid, 1983); Maureen F. Mazzaoui, *The Italian Cotton Industry in the Later Middle Ages* (Cambridge, 1981), pp. 129 ff.

40. William Page, *The Victoria County History of the County of Durham* (London, 1907), p. 162; Dickinson and Donaldson, *Source Book,* pp. 274 ff.; Maxwell, *Irish History from Contemporary Sources,* p. 177.

41. David Masson, ed., *The Register of the Privy Council of Scotland,* 14 vols. (Edinburgh, 1880–1898), 3: 448; Chambers, *Domestic Annals of Scotland,* 1: 202 ff.; Dickinson and Donaldson, *Source Book,* pp. 278–281.

42. Penry Williams, *The Council in the Marches of Wales under Elizabeth I* (Cardiff, 1958), pp. 31, 63, 101; Rae, *Administration of the Scottish Frontier,* pp. 7 ff.

43. M. E. Bratchel, "Regulation and Group-Consciousness in the Later History of London's Merchant Colonies," *Journal of European Economic History* 9 (1980): 585 ff.; Pike, *Enterprise and Adventure,* pp. 7 ff.; Jan Albert Goris, *Études sur les colonies marchandes méridionales (portugais, espagnols, italiens) à Anvers de 1488 à 1567* (Louvain, 1925), pp. 37 ff.; Gascon, *Grand Commerce et vie urbaine,* 1: 357 ff.

II. SPACE, 1600–1690

1. *R.I. Hist. Soc. Colls.* 2 (1835): 193; William Hubbard, *The History of the Indian Wars in New England,* 2 vols., ed. Samuel G. Drake (Roxbury, Mass., 1865), 2: 287.

2. Richard Gascon, *Grand Commerce et vie urbaine au XVIe siècle Lyon et ses marchands: Environs de 1520–Environs de 1580,* 2 vols. (Paris, 1971), 2: 538 ff., 597, 625 ff., 735 ff.; Michel Morineau, *Les Faux-semblants d'un démarrage économique: agriculture et demographie en France au XVIIIe siècle* (Paris, 1971).

3. Samuel Gorton, "Innocency's Defense," *R.I. Hist. Soc. Colls.* 2 (1835): 146; Robert Crowley, *Select Works,* ed. Joseph M. Cowper (London, 1872), pp. 86.

4. John Mandeville, *Travels: The Version of the Cotton Manuscript* (London, 1915), pp. 126, 178 ff., 198.

5. Charles Verlinden, *Précédents médiévaux de la colonie en Amérique* (Mexico, 1954); Charles Verlinden, "From the Mediterranean to the Atlantic Aspects of an Economic Shift," *Journal of European Economic History* 12 (1983): 625 ff.

6. Amandus Johnson, *The Instruction for Johan Printz* (Philadelphia, 1930), pp. 3 ff., 47.

7. George Chapman, Ben Jonson, and John Marston, *Eastward Hoe* (London, 1605); Philip L. Barbour, *The Three Worlds of Captain John Smith* (Boston, 1964); Alden T. Vaughan, *American Genesis: Captain John Smith and the Founding of Virginia* (Boston, 1975).

8. *Pa. Archives,* 1st Ser., 1: 49–50.

9. *Va. Co. Recs.* 1: 229, 409–410, 4: 77, 78, 160, 232–233; [Robert Cushman,]

"Reasons and Considerations Touching the Lawfulness of Removing Out of England into . . . America," *Mass. Hist. Soc. Colls.*, 2nd Ser. 9 (1832): 69; David Cressy, "The Vast and Furious Ocean," *New England Quarterly* 57 (1984): 520.

10. *New Castle Recs.* 1: 94; Joan Thirsk, *English Peasant Farming* (London, 1957), pp. 41, 43; [Cushman,] "Reasons and Considerations," loc. cit., 9: 69, 70.

11. William Bradford, *Of Plymouth Plantation, 1620–1647,* ed. Samuel E. Morison (New York, 1952), p. 61.

12. *Va. Co. Recs.* 3: 222; Roger Williams, "A Key Into the Language of America" (1647), *R. I. Hist. Soc. Colls.* 1 (1827): 73, 97; William R. Staples, ed., *The Proceedings of the First General Assembly 1647* (Providence, 1847), pp. 15, 16, 17, 21, 47.

13. Lyon G. Tyler, ed., *Narratives of Early Virginia* (New York, 1907), pp. 363, 364.

14. *Pa. Prov. Coun. Mins.* 1: 499–500; Tyler, *Narratives of Early Virginia,* pp. 239, 240; Philip A. Bruce, *Institutional History of Virginia in the Seventeenth Century,* 2 vols. (New York, 1910), 1: 4 ff.; "Richard Treat's Memorial," *Conn. Hist. Soc. Colls.* 5 (1896): 478 ff.; Roger Williams, *Complete Writings,* 7 vols., ed. John Russell Bartlett et al. (New York, 1963), 6: 34; Bradford, *Of Plymouth Plantation,* pp. 299 ff.; John Winthrop, *The History of New England from 1630 to 1649,* 2 vols., ed. James Savage (Boston, 1825), 2: 83, 84; *Md. Archives* 53: 415, 54: 375; Berthold Fernow, ed., *The Records of New Amsterdam 1653–1655* (New York, 1897), p. 11; *Mass. Bay Co. Recs.* 4, pt. 1: 245.

15. David Mathew, *James I* (London, 1967), pp. 78, 79; Bradford, *Of Plymouth Plantation,* pp. 316 ff., 320; *Md. Archives* 54: 222–223, 382, 390–391; James Blair, ed., *Charter to William Penn and Laws of the Province of Pennsylvania* (Harrisburg, Pa., 1879), p. 14.

16. Williams, "Key Into the Language of America," loc. cit., 65.

17. Fernow, ed., *Records of New Amsterdam 1653–1655,* p. 11; Mattie Parker, ed., *North Carolina Higher Court Records 1670–1696* (Raleigh, N.C., 1968), pp. 270, 309, 319; Blair, ed., *Charter to William Penn,* p. 176; Bradford, *Of Plymouth Plantation,* p. 247; John L. Sibley et al., eds., *Harvard Graduates,* 17 vols. (Boston, 1873–1975), 9: 375 ff.; New York Historical Society, *Collections for the Year 1918* (1919), pp. 266, 269 ff.

18. *Va. Co. Recs.* 2: 96, 3: 171, 4: 70; Blair, ed., *Charter to William Penn,* p. 72.

19. Fernow, ed., *Records of New Amsterdam 1653–1655,* pp. 19–20; *Conn. Hist. Soc. Colls.* 21 (1924): 442.

20. Johnson, *Instruction for Johan Printz,* p. 157; *Pa. Archives,* 1st ser., 1: 108–109.

21. Winthrop, *History of New England,* 2: 84; Alexander Young, ed., *Chronicles of the First Planters of the Colony of Massachusetts Bay* (Boston, 1846), pp. 83–84, 187–188; *Pa. Prov. Coun. Mins.* 1: 26–27; Bradford, *Of Plymouth Plantation,* p. 33; Michael Zuckerman, "Pilgrims in the Wilderness," *New England Quarterly* 50 (1977): 255.

22. Charles M. Taintor, ed., *Extracts from the Records of Colchester* (Hartford, Conn., 1864), p. 156; Thomas Morton, *New English Canaan,* ed. Charles F. Adams, Jr., *Prince Society Publications* 14 (Boston, 1883): 306.

23. Bradford, *Of Plymouth Plantation,* p. 334.

24. *Va. Co. Recs.* 2: 165–166.
25. Richard Bagwell, *Ireland under the Tudors,* 3 vols. (London, 1885–1890), 1: 254; Marian Tumler, *Der Deutsche Orden* (Bonn-Godesberg, 1974).
26. Rachel R. Reid, *The King's Council in the North* (London, 1921), pp. 6 ff.; Thomas I. Rae, *The Administration of the Scottish Frontier 1513–1603* (Edinburgh, 1966), pp. 116 ff.
27. William Croft Dickinson and Gordon Donaldson, *A Source Book of Scottish History,* 3 vols. (London, 1958–1961), 3: 261; Constantia Maxwell, *Irish History from Contemporary Sources, 1509–1610* (London, 1932), pp. 229 ff., 242 ff.; Joyce Youings, *Sixteenth Century England* (London, 1984), p. 246; David B. Quinn, *The Elizabethans and the Irish* (Ithaca, N.Y., 1966), pp. 106 ff.; Nicholas P. Canny, "The Ideology of English Colonization from Ireland to America," *William and Mary Quarterly* 30 (1973): 575 ff.; Williams, "Key Into the Language of America," loc. cit., 74.
28. Quinn, *Elizabethans and the Irish,* pp. 109 ff, 111 ff.
29. Dickinson and Donaldson, *Source Book,* 3: 262.
30. Anthony N. B. Garvan, *Architecture and Town Planning in Colonial Connecticut* (New Haven, 1951).
31. *Va. Co. Recs.* 1: 436, 3: 268, 269.
32. "Circular Letter" (1610), in Alexander Brown, *The Genesis of the United States,* 2 vols. (New York, 1964), 1: 463–465; E. de Golyer, ed., *Across Aboriginal America: The Journey of Three Englishmen Across Texas in 1568* (El Paso, Tex., 1947).
33. Thomas Dudley to the Countess of Lincoln, March 12, 1631, *N.H. Hist. Soc. Colls.* 4 (1834): 238.
34. Roger Clap, *Memoirs* (Boston, 1844), p. 42; *Va. Co. Recs.* 4: 94; *Va. Burgesses Jour.* 1: 21–22; "Observations by Master George Percy," Tyler, ed., *Narratives of Early Virginia,* pp. 20 ff.; [William Simmonds,] "Proceedings of the English Colonies [1612]," ibid., p. 127; also Johnson, *Instruction for Johan Printz,* p. 40; Edmund S. Morgan, *American Slavery, American Freedom* (New York, 1975), pp. 133, 134.
35. *Va. Co. Recs.* 4: 74.
36. Williams, "Key Into the Language of America," loc. cit., 106.
37. William S. Maltby, *The Black Legend in England: The Development of Anti-Spanish Sentiment 1558–1660* (Durham, N.C., 1971).
38. *Va. Co. Recs.* 1: 267–271, 3: 160–161, 236–238; Tyler, ed., *Narratives of Early Virginia,* p. 336; Morgan, *American Slavery, American Freedom,* pp. 159, 160, 163.
39. *Va. Co. Recs.* 1: 446–447, 454, 483, 3: 310; Samuel G. Nissenson, *The Patroon's Domain* (New York, 1937).
40. *Va. Co. Recs.* 2: 42, 3: 163; Wesley Frank Craven, *Dissolution of the Virginia Company* (New York, 1932), p. 213.
41. *Va. Co. Recs.* 1: 399–404, 411–412, 457, 488, 2: 293–295, 373, 375–376, 3: 277, 278, 4: 469.
42. *Va. Co. Recs.* 1: 333, 394–395, 3:269, 4: 223–224, 413, 414; *R.I. Hist. Soc. Colls.* 5 (1843): 36; John Cox, Jr., ed., *Oyster Bay Town Records,* 6 vols. (New York, 1916–1931), 1: 217.

43. *Va. Co. Recs.* 1: 251–252, 335, 456; Morgan, *American Slavery, American Freedom,* pp. 153–154.

44. *Va. Co. Recs.* 3: 259; [Cushman,] "Reasons and Considerations," loc. cit., p. 71; Michael Dalton, *Country Justice* (London, 1697), p. 146; Reid, *King's Council,* pp. 125 ff.; Edwin E. Rich, "The Population of Elizabethan England," *Economic History Review* 2 (1950): 263–264.

45. *Va. Co. Recs.* 4: 416, 417; Robert Beverly, *History and Present State of Virginia,* ed. Louis B. Wright (Chapel Hill, N.C., 1947), pp. 277, 278; Maxwell, *Irish History,* p. 166; Basil Sollers, "Transported Convict Laborers in Maryland during the Colonial Period," *Maryland Historical Magazine* 2 (1907): 18.

46. *No. Car. Col. Recs.* 1: 394; Sollers, "Transported Convict Laborers," loc. cit., p. 20; Johnson, *Instruction for Johan Printz,* pp. 129–130.

47. Arnold J. F. Van Laer, ed., *Minutes of the Court of Rensselaerswyck, 1648–1652* (Albany, 1922), pp. 142, 143; Mattie Parker, ed., *North Carolina Higher Court Records, 1697–1701* (Raleigh, N.C., 1971), pp. 81, 241.

48. *N.H. Hist. Soc. Colls.* 4 (1834): 245; *Mass. Bay Co. Recs.* 4, pt. 1: 344.

49. *Va. Co. Recs.* 2: 129–131, 3: 165.

50. Joseph H. Smith, *Colonial Justice in Western Massachusetts, 1639–1702* (Cambridge, Mass., 1961), p. 228; *Va. Co. Recs.* 3: 15, 28, 310, 311; Raphael Semmes, *Crime and Punishment in Early Maryland* (Baltimore, 1938), pp. 3–4; Allen D. Candler, et. al., eds., *The Colonial Records of the State of Georgia,* 30 vols. (Atlanta, 1904–1985) 4: 32.

51. *New Plym. Recs.* 3: 44; Johnson, *Instruction for Johan Printz,* pp. 23, 24, 41, 93–94, 120; Edmund B. O'Callaghan, ed., *Documents Relative to the Colonial History of the State of New York,* 15 vols. (Albany, 1858–1887), 2: 155, 156; Michael Kammen, *Colonial New York: A History* (New York, 1975), pp. 51–52; Carroll T. Bond, *The Court of Appeals of Maryland* (Baltimore, 1928), pp. 14, 15.

52. Johnson, *Instruction for Johan Printz,* pp. 121–122, 190; *Va. Co. Recs.* 3: 28, 170, 4: 180–182; Blair, ed., *Charter to William Penn,* p. 46; Boston Record Commissioners, *Report,* Document 9 (1880): 289; *Mass. Bay Co. Recs.* 5: 90; *New Castle Recs.* 1: 194–195, 2: 495–497, 514–516; Berthold Fernow, ed., *Records of New Amsterdam 1658–1661* (New York, 1897), pp. 263–265; *R.I. Hist. Soc. Colls.* 5 (1843): 118–119; William Whitehead et al., eds., *Documents Relating to the Colonial History of the State of New Jersey,* 30 vols. (Newark, N.J., 1880–1906), 2: 315–317.

53. William S. Holdsworth, *A History of English Law,* 14 vols. (London, 1966), 4: 79; *N.H. Hist. Soc. Colls.* 8 (1886): 134–135, 177; Parker, ed., *North Carolina Higher Court Records 1670–1696,* p. 421; Whitehead et al., eds., *Documents Relating to the Colonial History of New Jersey,* 2: 314; *Md. Archives* 54: xvi, xvii, 197; Arnold J. F. Van Laer, ed., *Minutes of Fort Orange and Beverwyck, 1657–1669,* 2 vols. (Albany, 1923), 2: 201, 221, 222; *New Plym. Recs.* 7: 189.

54. *N. H. Prov. Papers* 1: 267–269; Edmund B. O'Callaghan, *History of New Netherland,* 2 vols. (New York, 1846–1848), 2: 21–22; Johnson, *Instruction for Johan Printz,* pp. 216–217, 238, 239; *Mass. Bay Co. Recs.* 3: 97; *New Castle Recs.* 1: 100; *Pa. Prov. Coun. Mins.* 1: 527.

55. Arnold J. F. Van Laer, ed., *New York Historical Manuscripts—Dutch,* 4 vols. (Baltimore, 1974), 4: 224–225; *Va. Co. Recs.* 3: 74, 175; Arnold J. F. Van Laer, ed., *Minutes*

of the Court of Rensselaerswyck, 1646–1652 (Albany, 1922), pp. 50–52, 59–60; Fernow, ed., *Records of New Amsterdam, 1658–1661,* pp. 263–265, 213–214; Berthold Fernow, ed., *The Records of New Amsterdam, 1662–1663* (New York, 1897), p. 230; *Mass. Bay Co. Recs.* 4, part 2: 11; *New Castle Recs.* 2: 322–328; Parker, ed., *North Carolina Higher Court Records, 1670–1696,* p. 208; *N.H. Prov. Papers* 1: 140, 143.

56. Van Laer, ed., *New York Historical Manuscripts* 4: 100, 528–529; David Thomas Konig, *Law and Society in Puritan Massachusetts* (Chapel Hill, N.C., 1977), p. 176.

57. *R. I. Hist. Soc. Colls.* 1 (1843): 73–74; *Pa. Prov. Coun. Mins.* 1: 76, 129.

58. *Mass. Bay Co. Recs.* 2: 213; Blair, ed., *Charter to William Penn,* p. 51; *Pa. Prov. Coun. Mins.* 1: 35–37, 138, 142, 151, 457.

59. William Nelson et al., eds., *Documents Relating to the Colonial History of the State of New Jersey,* 40 vols. (Paterson, N.J., 1880–1949), 12: 138; Adelaide L. Fries, *The Moravians in Georgia, 1735–1740* (Raleigh, N.C., 1905); Gillian L. Gollin, *The Moravians in Two Worlds* (New York, 1967).

III. CONSENT AND CONTENTION, 1600–1760

1. Edmund S. Morgan, *American Slavery, American Freedom* (New York, 1975), pp. 143, 150.

2. Dietrich Gerhard, ed., *Ständische Vertretungen in Europa im 17. und 18. Jahrhundert* (Göttingen, 1969), pp. 398 ff., 435.

3. Joyce Youings, *Sixteenth Century England* (London, 1984), p. 125; Arnold J. F. Van Laer, ed., *New York Historical Manuscripts—Dutch,* 4 vols. (Baltimore, 1974), 4: 168, 218; Alfred L. Rowse, *Tudor Cornwall* (London, 1941), pp. 441 ff.

4. Roland Mousnier, *La Famille, l'enfant et l'éducation en France et en Grande-Bretagne du XVᵉ au XVIIIᵉ siècle* (Paris, n.d.), p. 331; Radegunde Amtmann, *Die Bussbruderschaften in Frankreich* (Wiesbaden, 1977), pp. 225 ff., 234 ff.; Giancarlo Angelozzi, *Le confraternite laicali: un'esperienza cristiana tra Medioevo e età moderna* (Brescia, 1978), pp. 13 ff., 126 ff.

5. James I, *Political Works,* ed. Charles H. McIlwain (Cambridge, Mass., 1918), p. xlix; *N.Y.C. Comm. Coun. Mins.* 3: 392.

6. Perez Zagorin, *The Court and the Country: The Beginning of the English Revolution* (London, 1969).

7. *Va. Co. Recs.* 2: 240.

8. *Va. Co. Recs.* 3: 100, 103, 104.

9. *Va. Co. Recs.* 2: 325–326, 3: 130, 133, 199–201; *Hening Statutes* 1: 125, 224; Cyrus H. Karraker, *The Seventeenth Century Sheriff* (Philadelphia, 1930), p. 154; Joel Hurstfield, *Freedom, Corruption and Government in Elizabethan England* (Cambridge, Mass., 1973), pp. 236 ff.

10. William Bradford, *Of Plymouth Plantation, 1620–1647,* ed. Samuel E. Morison (New York, 1952), pp. 75, 76.

11. Constantia Maxwell, *Irish History from Contemporary Sources, 1509–1610* (London, 1932), pp. 384–387.

12. Wesley F. Craven, *The Southern Colonies in the Seventeenth Century* (Baton Rouge, La., 1949), p. 160.

13. *Va. Co. Recs.* 3: 158, 159, 177, 484, 4: 581.
14. *Va. Co. Recs.* 4: 418–419.
15. *Va. Co. Recs.* 2: 350, 358–360.
16. John Winthrop, *The History of New England from 1630 to 1649,* 2 vols., ed. James Savage (Boston, 1825), 1: 132, 164, 301, 302; George H. Haynes, *Representation and Suffrage in Massachusetts, 1620–1691* (Baltimore, 1894), pp. 41 ff.; *Mass. Bay Co. Recs.* 2: 95–96.
17. *N.H. Prov. Papers* 1: 126, 134; Roger Williams, *Complete Writings,* 7 vols., ed. John Russell Bartlett et al. (New York, 1963), 6: 4–6; Horatio Rogers et al., eds., *The Early Records of Providence,* 20 vols. (Providence, R.I., 1892–1915), 1: 1; Henry M. Burt, *The First Century of the History of Springfield: The Official Records from 1636 to 1736,* 2 vols. (Springfield, Mass., 1899), 1: 156.
18. *Mass. Bay Co. Recs.* 3: 106, 207, 217, 228, 302, 348, 4, pt. 1: 9; *R.I. Hist. Soc. Colls.* 5 (1843): 73–74.
19. *N.H. Hist. Soc. Colls.* 8 (1866): 1, 6–7; *N.H. Prov. Papers* 1: 272, 274–277, 281, 322–326, 332–333.
20. *Md. Archives* 53: 633–634; Craven, *Southern Colonies,* p. 207.
21. *N.Y.C. Comm. Coun. Mins.* 4: 19 ff.; *Hening Statutes* 3: 427, 4: 541.
22. *R.I. Hist. Soc. Colls.* 5: 123, 127.
23. *N.H. Prov. Papers* 4: 400, 419; *Mass. House Jour. 1732–1734,* p. 29.
24. Winthrop, *History of New England,* 1: 152; *Mass. Bay Co. Recs.* 3: 404, 4, pt. 1: 263; *Mass. House. Jour. 1715–1717,* p. 10.
25. Bernard Bailyn, "Politics and Social Structure in Virginia," in *Seventeenth Century America: Essays in Colonial History,* ed. James M. Smith (Chapel Hill, N.C., 1959).
26. *Mass. Bay Co. Recs.* 1: 79, 75; *Hening Statutes* 1: 403, 530; *Va. Burgesses Jour. 1702–1712,* pp. 108, 116, 147; *No. Car. Col. Recs.* 3: 451–456.
27. *Mass. Bay Co. Recs.* 3: 436; *Pa. Prov. Coun. Mins.* 1: 494.
28. *Mass. House Jour. 1715–1717,* pp. 171, 221; *Mass. House Jour. 1729–1731,* pp. 16, 53, 141; *Mass. House Jour. 1731–1732,* p. 213.
29. *Va. Burgesses Jour. 1712–1726,* pp. xli, 230, 243.
30. William Whitehead et al., eds., *Documents Relating to the Colonial History of the State of New Jersey,* 30 vols. (Newark, N.J., 1880–1906), 2: 102, 270–271, 273–274; *Va. Burgesses Jour. 1712–1726,* pp. 107–110; *Va. Burgesses Jour. 1702–1712,* pp. 346–347; William R. Smith, *South Carolina as a Royal Province* (New York, 1903), p. 8.
31. *Va. Burgesses Jour. 1702–1712,* pp. 354–355; *Va. Burgesses Jour. 1712–1726,* p. 122; also Penry Williams, *The Council in the Marches of Wales under Elizabeth I* (Cardiff, 1958), p. 152.
32. *R.I. Hist. Soc. Colls.* 5 (1843): 132–133.
33. *Va. Co. Recs.* 4: 415–416.
34. *New Plym. Recs.* 9: 223; *N.H. Prov. Papers* 1: 161; *Mass. Bay Col. Recs.* 2: 29, 3: 109–110, 279, 294; *Va. Burgesses Jour. 1712–1726,* p. xvii; *Hening Statutes* 4: 475–476; Ernest S. Griffith, *History of American City Government* (New York, 1938), p. 205.

35. "Certificate of John Wilson and Hezekiah Usher" (1665), *Proceedings of the Massachusetts Historical Society* 12 (1871): 105; *Mass. Bay Co. Recs.* 3: 90.

36. *N.Y.C. Comm. Coun. Mins.* 3: 48; *Va. Burgesses Jour. 1702–1712*, p. 277; Joseph Dow, *History of the Town of Hampton*, 2 vols. (Hampton, N.H., 1977), 1: 109; H. D. Biddle, "Colonial Mayors of Philadelphia," *Pennsylvania Magazine of History and Biography* 19 (1895–1896), 65; Burt, *First Century of Springfield*, 1: 69; Griffith, *History of American City Government*, p. 187.

37. John Russell Bartlett, ed., *Records of the Colony of Rhode Island and Providence Plantations*, 10 vols. (Providence, R.I., 1856–1865), 4: 425; Burt, *First Century of Springfield*, 1: 187, 2: 214; *Hening Statutes* 1: 333, 334, 411, 412, 475, 2: 280; Wilcomb E. Washburn, *The Governor and the Rebel* (Chapel Hill, N.C., 1957), p. 55; Philip A. Bruce, *Institutional History of Virginia*, 2 vols. (New York, 1910), 2: 409 ff.; Louis B. Wright, *South Carolina* (New York, 1976), p. 102; *No. Car. Col. Recs.* 3: 560.

38. Michael Zuckerman, *Peaceable Kingdoms: New England Towns in the Eighteenth Century* (New York, 1970), pp. 94–95; Quentin Skinner, *The Foundations of Modern Political Thought*, 2 vols. (Cambridge, 1978), 1: 125; Sir Thomas Smith, *De Republica Anglorum*, ed. Mary Dewar (Cambridge, 1982), pp. 78, 79; Hurstfield, *Freedom, Corruption and Government in Elizabethan England*, pp. 54 ff.; Gordon J. Schochet, *Patriarchalism in Political Thought* (New York, 1975), pp. 82, 83.

39. Brent Tarter, ed., *The Order Book and Related Papers of the Common Hall of the Borough of Norfolk, Virginia, 1736–1798* (Richmond, Va., 1979), pp. 101–102.

40. James Blair, ed., *Charter to William Penn and Laws of the Province of Pennsylvania* (Harrisburg, Pa., 1879), pp. 92–93; John C. Rainbolt, "The Alteration in the Relationship between Leadership and Constituents in Virginia, 1660 to 1720," *William and Mary Quarterly* 27 (1970): 411–434.

41. Milton M. Klein, "Democracy and Politics in Colonial New York," *New York History* 40 (July 1959): 221–246; Richard Bushman, *From Puritan to Yankee* (Cambridge, Mass., 1967), pp. 7, 259.

42. *Mass. Bay Co. Recs.* 4, pt. 2: 131–132, 136–137; *N.H. Prov. Papers* 1: 259, 260–263; David S. Lovejoy, *The Glorious Revolution in America* (New York, 1972), pp. 290, 292–293.

43. Williams, *Complete Works*, 6: 401–402; *Mass. Bay Co. Recs.* 3: 90, 91, 97; *N.H. Prov. Papers* 1: 455–456; Michael Dalton, *Country Justice* (London, 1697), pp. 320, 324–325.

44. Lovejoy, *Glorious Revolution in America*, p. 82.

45. *N.H. Hist. Soc. Colls.* 8: 168–173, 179–181, 188–191.

46. *N.H. Prov. Papers* 2: 43–46, 58, 64, 65.

47. "Mrs. Bacon's Letter, June 29, 1676," *William and Mary College Quarterly* 9 (1900–1901): 1–11.

48. Oscar Handlin, "The Eastern Frontier of New York," *New York History* 35 (1937): 50–75; Whitehead et al., eds., *Documents Relating to the Colonial History of the State of New Jersey* 2: 108–109, 320, 323, 328–331, 346–347; *Memoirs of the Historical Society of Pennsylvania* 2, pt. 2 (1830): 188.

49. James H. Hutson, *Pennsylvania Politics, 1746–1770* (Princeton, N.J., 1972), p. 20.

50. Samuel Sewall, *Diary,* 2 vols., ed. M. Halsey Thomas (New York, 1972), 2: 637–638, 715.

51. Whitehead et al., eds., *Documents Relating to the Colonial History of New Jersey* 2: 333–334, 338; *Pa. Prov. Coun. Mins.* 3: 260; Dalton, *Country Justice,* p. 204.

52. William S. Powell, ed., *The Regulators in North Carolina: A Documentary History* (Raleigh, N.C., 1971), pp. 4, 5, 7, 10, 11.

53. *Mass. Bay Co. Recs.* 4, pt. 2: 3, 24, 25, 33.

54. *Md. Archives* 2: 168–169, 174–184.

55. Richard R. Johnson, *Adjustment to Empire: The New England Colonies, 1675–1715* (New Brunswick, N.J., 1981); Lovejoy, *Glorious Revolution in America,* p. 125; Richard L. Bushman, *King and People in Provincial Massachusetts* (Chapel Hill, N.C., 1985), pp. 79 ff.

56. *Va. Burgesses Jour., 1712–1726,* pp. 143, 144, 147–149, 152, 153, 159, 166–170.

57. Carroll T. Bond, *The Court of Appeals of Maryland* (Baltimore, 1928), p. 19; *No. Car. Col. Recs.* 3: 511.

58. Whitehead et al., eds., *Documents Relating to the Colonial History of New Jersey* 2: 127–128; Matt Bushnell Jones, "Thomas Maule, Salem Quaker," Essex Institute, *Historical Collections* 72 (1936): 21, 24.

59. Carl J. Vipperman, *The Rise of Rawlins Lowndes, 1721–1800* (Columbia, S.C., 1978), pp. 62–63; *Md. Archives* 49: 199, 203; *Mass. Bay Co. Recs.* 3: 242.

60. *Memoirs of the Historical Society of Pennsylvania* 2, pt. 2 (1830): 188.

IV. COMMONWEALTHS, 1600–1760

1. Robert Crowley, *Select Works,* ed. Joseph M. Cowper (London, 1871), pp. 168–169; Alan Heimert and Andrew Delbanco, *The Puritans in America* (Cambridge, Mass., 1985), p. 166; Sir Thomas Smith, *De Republica Anglorum,* ed. Mary Dewar (Cambridge, 1982), pp. 58 ff.

2. Smith, *De Republica Anglorum,* p. 57.

3. John Cotton, "God's Promise to His Plantation," in Heimert and Delbanco, *Puritans,* p. 80.

4. Roger Williams, "A Key Into the Language of America," *R.I. Hist. Soc. Colls.* 1 (1827): 100; Charles H. Lincoln, ed., *Narratives of the Indian Wars* (New York, 1913), pp. 112–167.

5. Carl N. Everstine, *The General Assembly of Maryland 1634–1776* (Charlottesville, Va., 1980), pp. 81, 82; Edwin B. Bronner, *William Penn's "Holy Experiment"* (Westport, Conn., 1978), p. 40; Joseph J. Kelley, Jr., *Pennsylvania: The Colonial Years, 1681–1776* (Garden City, N.Y., 1980), pp. 50, 87–88.

6. Cotton, "God's Promise," in Heimert and Delbanco, *Puritans,* pp. 78, 80.

7. *New Plym. Recs.* 1: 6–7, 102; Watertown Historical Society, *Watertown Records,* 8 vols. (Watertown, Mass., 1894–1939), 1: 113.

8. William Bradford, *Of Plymouth Plantation 1620–1647,* ed. Samuel E. Morison (New York, 1952), pp. 186, 187; Heimert and Delbanco, *Puritans,* pp. 164, 186; Richard Bushman, *From Puritan to Yankee* (Cambridge, Mass., 1967).

9. Heimert and Delbanco, *Puritans,* p. 192.

10. Kelley, *Pennsylvania,* p. 128.
11. Bradford, *Of Plymouth Plantation,* pp. 120, 121, 253.
12. Watertown Historical Society, *Watertown Records* 1: 1, 2, 4, 6.
13. George Sheldon, *History of Deerfield,* 2 vols. (Deerfield, Mass., 1895), 1: 9–10, 39–40.
14. *Mass. Bay Co. Recs.* 5: 21, 23; Charles M. Taintor, ed., *Extracts from the Records of Colchester* (Hartford, Conn., 1864), p. 13.
15. John Cox, ed., *Oyster Bay Town Records,* 6 vols. (New York, 1916–1931), 1: 220; Watertown Historical Society, *Watertown Records* 1: 1; Henry Burt, *The First Century of the History of Springfield: The Official Records from 1636 to 1736,* 2 vols. (Springfield, Mass., 1899), 1: 244–246, 272, 278, 283, 285.
16. Crowley, *Select Works,* p. 21; Bradford, *Of Plymouth Plantation,* pp. 316, 318; William Staples, ed., *Proceedings of the First General Assembly, 1647* (Providence, R.I., 1847), p. 24; Heimert and Delbanco, *Puritans,* pp. 254, 256; John Cotton, *The Bloudy Tenent* (London, 1647), p. 50; also James Willard Hurst, *Law and the Conditions of Freedom in the Nineteenth-Century United States* (Madison, Wis., 1956), p. 37.
17. Carl J. Vipperman, *The Rise of Rawlins Lowndes, 1721–1800* (Columbia, S.C., 1978), p. 51; *Mass. House Jour. 1736–1737,* p. 244.
18. Peter H. Brown, ed., *Scotland Before 1700* (Edinburgh, 1893), pp. 199 ff.
19. *Hening Statutes* 4: 99–103.
20. David T. Konig, *Law and Society in Puritan Massachusetts* (Chapel Hill, N.C., 1979), p. 129; *Mass. House Jour. 1718–1720,* p. 275.
21. *Mass. House Jour. 1722–1723,* pp. 59–60; Julius Goebel and T. Raymond Naughton, *Law Enforcement in Colonial New York* (Montclair, N.J., 1970), pp. 37–38.
22. *N.H. Towns* 2: 123–124.
23. Charles Street, ed., *Huntington Town Records,* 3 vols. (Huntington, N.Y., 1887–1889), 2: 445–446, 454–455.
24. John Winthrop, *History of New England, from 1630 to 1649,* 2 vols., ed. James Savage (Boston, 1825), 1: 279; also George L. Haskins, *Law and Authority in Early Massachusetts* (New York, 1960), p. 89; Lawrence Stone, *The Family, Sex and Marriage in England, 1500–1800* (New York, 1977), pp. 142–149.
25. Joyce Youings, *Sixteenth Century England* (London, 1984), pp. 110–111; *Va. Co. Recs.* 3: 221.
26. *Va. Co. Recs.* 3: 469; John D. Cushing, ed., *The Laws of the Pilgrims* (Wilmington, Del., 1977), p. 25; Watertown Historical Society, *Watertown Records* 1: 62; Herman Mann, *Historical Annals of Dedham* (Dedham, Mass., 1847), p. 18; Henry A. Hazen, *History of Billerica* (Boston, 1883), pp. 169–170; Sheldon, *History of Deerfield,* 1: 205; *N.Y.C. Comm. Coun. Mins.* 3: 97.
27. Philip A. Bruce, *Institutional History of Virginia in the Seventeenth Century,* 2 vols. (New York, 1910), 1: 50 ff., 278 ff.; Joseph H. Smith, *Colonial Justice in Western Massachusetts, 1639–1702* (Cambridge, Mass., 1961), pp. 116–117.
28. *Md. Archives* 53: 54–55, 142–145.
29. *Md. Archives* 54: 26; Berthold Fernow, ed., *The Records of New Amsterdam 1653–1655* (New York, 1897), pp. 51, 62–63; Berthold Fernow, ed., *The Records of New Amsterdam 1656–1658* (New York, 1897), p. 265; Berthold Fernow, ed., *The*

Records of New Amsterdam, 1661–1663 (New York, 1897), p. 248; Arnold J. F. Van Laer, ed., *Minutes of the Court of Fort Orange and Beverwyck, 1625–1656,* 2 vols. (Albany, 1920), 1: 198–201; *New Castle Recs.* 2: 434, 435, 438; Smith, *Colonial Justice,* pp. 207, 236, 237, 247.

30. *Md. Archives* 53: 13, 231–235; Arnold J. F. Van Laer, ed., *Minutes of the Court of Rensselaerswyck, 1648–1652* (Albany, 1922), pp. 121, 123; also Fernow, ed., *Records of New Amsterdam, 1658–1661,* pp. 213, 214.

31. *New Plym. Recs.* 7: 111.

32. *New Plym. Recs.* 7: 159.

33. *Md. Archives* 49: 208–209, 243, 270.

34. *New Plym. Recs.* 7: 189; *Md. Archives* 53: 229, 54: 558.

35. Bradford, *Of Plymouth Plantation,* p. 317; Goebel and Naughton, *Law Enforcement in Colonial New York,* p. 105; David Flaherty, "Law and Enforcement of Morals in Early America," in Donald Fleming and Bernard Bailyn, eds., *Law in American History* (Boston, 1971).

36. *N.Y.C. Comm. Coun. Mins.* 4: 103; Burt, *The First Century of Springfield,* 1: 190; Susie M. Ames, ed., *County Court Records of Accomack-Northampton, Virginia 1632–1640* (Washington, D.C., 1954), pp. 15, 24.

37. *N.H. Prov. Papers* 1: 191–192; John Russell Bartlett, ed., *Records of the Colony of Rhode Island and Providence Plantations,* 10 vols. (Providence, R.I., 1856–1865), 4: 425–426.

38. For one colony, see William Nelson et al., eds., *Documents Relating to the Colonial History of the State of New Jersey,* 42 vols. (Paterson, N.J., 1880–1949), 12: 476, 516; see also 20: 284, 301, 324–325, 351.

39. *Hening Statutes* 4: 214–218, 6: 102–103.

40. Cushing, ed., *Laws of the Pilgrims,* p. 9; Smith, *Colonial Justice in Western Massachusetts,* p. 258; *Conn. Pub. Recs.* 7: 161–162, 175; *N.Y.C. Comm. Coun. Mins.* 6: 204; Michael Kammen, *Colonial New York: A History* (New York, 1975), p. 288.

41. Bartlett, ed., *Records of the Colony of Rhode Island,* 4: 362; Bruce, *Institutional History of Virginia,* 1: 28 ff.; Smith, *Colonial Justice in Western Massachusetts,* p. 310; Winton U. Solberg, *Redeem the Time: The Puritan Sabbath in Early America* (Cambridge, Mass., 1977).

42. Christopher Morris, ed., *The Journeys of Celia Fiennes* (London, 1947), p. 156.

43. Michael Dalton, *Country Justice* (London, 1697), p. 29; Cushing, ed., *Laws of the Pilgrims,* p. 10.

44. Thomas M. and Virginia L. Davis, *Edward Taylor's Church Records and Related Sermons,* 2 vols. (Boston, 1981), 1: 236–237; Parke Rouse, Jr., *James Blair of Virginia* (Chapel Hill, N.C., 1971), p. 37; *New Castle Recs.* 1: 103.

45. *Mass. Bay Co. Recs.* 1: 112, 271–272; William Whitehead et al., eds., *Documents Relating to the Colonial History of the State of New Jersey,* 30 vols. (Newark, N.J., 1800–1906), 2: 206–207.

46. Fernow, ed., *Records of New Amsterdam 1653–1655,* pp. 6, 255–256, 286, 420; *Pa. Archives* 1: 155, 160; Brent Tarter, ed., *The Order Book and Related Papers of the Common Hall of the Borough of Norfolk, 1736–1798* (Richmond, Va., 1979), p. 71; Smith, *Colonial Justice in Western Massachusetts,* pp. 121, 122, 250; Richard D. Younger, *The People's Panel: The Grand Jury in the United States, 1634–1941*

(Providence, R.I., 1963), p. 15; Kelley, *Pennsylvania,* pp. 51, 95, 107, 117, 237, 238, 266, 289–290, 363. For England, Conyers Read, ed., *William Lambarde and Local Government* (Ithaca, N.Y., 1962), pp. 37, 46.

47. Smith, *Colonial Justice in Western Massachusetts,* pp. 350, 381, 386; *N.Y.C. Comm. Coun. Mins.* 3: 125; Kelley, *Pennsylvania,* p. 156.

48. Fernow, ed., *Records of New Amsterdam 1656–1658,* p. 213; Fernow, ed., *Records of New Amsterdam 1653–1655,* p. 34.

49. *N.Y.C. Comm. Coun. Mins.* 3: 121–124; *Mass. House Jour. 1755,* p. 179; *Mass. Bay Co. Recs.* 3: 132–133.

50. *Mass. Bay Co., Recs.* 1: 278, 4, pt. 1: 79.

51. Van Laer, ed., *Minutes of the Court of Fort Orange* 1: 62–63, 66, 128, 218–219.

52. Ibid., 1: 280, 2: 166–167; Samuel Sewall, *Diary,* 2 vols., ed. M. Halsey Thomas (New York, 1972), 2: 384.

53. Van Laer, ed., *Minutes of the Court of Fort Orange,* 1: 17, 23, 47, 52, 62–63, 66, 103–105, 117–118, 130, 164–165, 226–229.

54. *N.H. Prov. Papers* 1: 236, 237, 367.

55. *Mass. Bay Co. Recs.* 4, pt. 2: 43; *Hening Statutes* 4: 208–214; *Mass. House Jour. 1755,* pp. 179, 218, 235, 266; *Mass. House Jour. 1756,* p. 118.

56. Frederick W. Hackwood, *Inns, Ales and Drinking Customs of Old England* (London, 1909), pp. 267, 359, 366; Sewall, *Diary,* 1: 154; Younger, *People's Panel,* p. 18.

57. *Mass. Bay Co. Recs.* 4, pt. 2: 101.

58. Watertown Historical Society, *Watertown Records* 1: 6; George C. Mason, ed., *Colonial Vestry Book* (Newport News, Va., 1949), p. 23.

59. *Hening Statutes* 7: 57–58, 93; John E. Pomfret, *Colonial New Jersey* (New York, 1973), p. 83.

60. Erastus Worthington, *History of Dedham* (Boston, 1827), p. 32; Cox, ed., *Oyster Bay Town Records,* 1: 137–138; Ames, ed., *County Court Records of Accomack-Northampton,* pp. lvi–lix; Smith, *Colonial Justice in Western Massachusetts,* pp. 204–205, 208.

61. Zara Jones Powers, ed., *Ancient Town Records* (New Haven, Conn., 1962), p. 571; Kelley, *Pennsylvania,* p. 157; Camille Bloch, *L'Assistance et l'état en France à la veille de la Révolution* (Paris, 1908): W. K. Jordan, *The Charities of Rural England, 1480–1660: The Aspirations and the Achievements of the Rural Society* (London, 1961).

62. *N.H. Prov. Papers* 1: 457–458; Powers, ed., *Ancient Town Records,* pp. 92, 177, 181, 593; *Conn. Pub. Recs.* 7: 36–37; *Mass. House Jour. 1718–1720,* p. 242; *Mass. House Jour. 1734–1735,* p. 183; *N.Y.C. Mayor's Ct., Select Cases,* p. 68.

63. *Copy of the Old Records, Town of Duxbury, Massachusetts* (Plymouth, Mass., 1893), p. 277; Gibson C. Chamberlayne, ed., *The Vestry Book of St. Paul's Parish, Hanover County* (Richmond, Va., 1940), pp. 17, 139, 142; *Records of ye Town Meetings of Lyn, 1730–1742* (Lynn, Mass., 1964), p. 36; Robert Beverly, *History and Present State of Virginia,* ed. Louis B. Wright (Chapel Hill, N.C., 1947), p. 275.

64. *Records of ye Town Meetings of Lyn, 1730–1742,* pp. 26, 33, 45; *Records of ye Town Meetings of Lyn, 1759–1771* (Lynn, Mass., 1970), pp. 3, 4; Bartlett, ed., *Records of the Colony of Rhode Island* 4: 229; *New Castle Recs.* 2: 405–406; *Mass. Bay Co. Recs.* 3: 377; Berthold Fernow, ed., *The Records of New Amsterdam, 1658–1661* (New

York, 1896), p. 431; *N.Y.C. Comm. Coun. Mins.* 4: 52; *N.Y.C. Mayor's Ct., Select Cases,* pp. 68, 69; Street, ed., *Huntington Town Records,* 2: 396; *Conn. Pub. Recs.* 7: 51, 71; *N.H. Hist. Soc. Colls.* 8: 71, 103.

65. *N.Y.C. Comm. Coun. Mins.* 3: 225, 4: 240–241, 306–311; *N.Y.C. Mayor's Ct., Select Cases,* pp. 69, 70; *Pa. Prov. Coun. Mins.* 3: 589; *Hening Statutes* 6: 477–478.

66. Mason, ed., *Colonial Vestry Book,* pp. 21, 69; Bruce, *Institutional History of Virginia,* 1: 102 ff.; Mann, *Historical Annals of Dedham,* p. 29.

67. Bruce, *Institutional History of Virginia,* 1: 245; Cotton Mather, *Bonifacius: An Essay Upon the Good,* ed. David Levin (Cambridge, Mass., 1966); Kenneth Silverman, *The Life and Times of Cotton Mather* (New York, 1984), pp. 232. ff.

68. Bruce, *Institutional History of Virginia,* 1: 331, 347, 350, 387; Louis B. Wright, *The Cultural Life of the American Colonies, 1607–1763* (New York, 1957), pp. 145–146; Susan J. Ellis and Katherine H. Noyes, *By the People: A History of Americans as Volunteers* (Philadelphia, 1978).

69. Carl Bridenbaugh, *Cities in the Wilderness* (New York, 1938), pp. 394, 396; Kammen, *Colonial New York,* p. 271; Kelley, *Pennsylvania,* pp. 282 ff.; William A. Baker, *A History of the Boston Marine Society, 1742–1967* (Boston, 1968), pp. 5, 9, 11.

70. John Duffy, *History of Public Health in New York City, 1625–1866* (New York, 1968); J. Keith Horsefield, "The Origins of Blackwell's *Model* of a Bank," *William and Mary Quarterly,* 23 (1966): 121 ff.; *Conn. Pub. Recs.* 7: VII, 423; Carl Bridenbaugh, *Cities in Revolt* (New York, 1955), pp. 56, 93, 95, 100, 124; Tarter, ed., *Order Book,* pp. 115–116; James Blair, ed., *Charter to William Penn and Laws of the Province of Pennsylvania* (Harrisburg, Pa., 1879), pp. 276–277; *Pa. Prov. Coun. Mins.* 1: 26; Chamberlayne, ed., *Vestry Book of St. Paul's Parish,* pp. 17, 18, 25.

71. Ernest S. Griffith, *The History of American City Government* (New York, 1938), pp. 264, 267, 268, 273.

72. Hugo von Hofmannsthal, "The Letter of Lord Chandos," *Selected Prose,* trans. Mary Hottinger and Tania and James Stern (New York, 1952), pp. 132 ff.

V. CHURCH AND CONSCIENCE, 1600–1760

1. Alfred L. Rowse, *Tudor Cornwall* (London, 1941), pp. 24 ff.

2. Robert Crowley, *Select Works,* ed. Joseph M. Cowper (London, 1871), p. 67; William Haller, *Liberty and Reformation in the Puritan Revolution* (New York, 1955), p. 66.

3. David Mathew, *James I* (London, 1967), pp. 75 ff.; William E. H. Lecky, *History of the Rise and Influence of the Spirit of Rationalism in Europe,* 2 vols. (New York, 1890), 1: 98 ff.

4. Joel Hurstfield, *Freedom, Corruption and Government in Elizabethan England* (Cambridge, Mass., 1973), pp. 214 ff.

5. Amandus Johnson, *The Instruction for Johan Printz* (Philadelphia, 1930), pp. 163–164; Roger Williams, *Complete Works,* 7 vols., ed. John Russell Bartlett et al. (New

York, 1963), 6: 397–398; also John Winthrop, *The History of New England from 1630 to 1649,* 2 vols., ed. James Savage (Boston, 1825), 1: 122, 123.

6. Edmund Morgan, *American Slavery, American Freedom* (New York, 1975), pp. 153–154; Michael Kammen, *Colonial New York* (New York, 1975), pp. 61–62.

7. Susie M. Ames, ed., *County Court Records of Accomack-Northampton, Virginia, 1632–1640* (Washington, D.C., 1954), pp. 1, 10, 39, 43, 54, 64.

8. Mary Frances Goodwin, ed., *The Records of Bruton Parish Church* (Richmond, Va., 1941), p. 13; Gibson C. Chamberlayne, *The Vestry Book of St. Paul's Parish, Hanover County* (Richmond, Va., 1940), pp. 187, 195; Alden Hatch, *The Byrds of Virginia* (New York, 1969), p. 73; Edward Porter Alexander, ed., *The Journal of John Fontaine, 1710–1719* (Charlottesville, Va., 1972), p. 81.

9. Henry R. McIlwaine, *Executive Journals of the Council of Colonial Virginia,* 4 vols. (Richmond, Va., 1925–1930), 3: 388; Goodwin, ed., *Bruton Parish Church,* pp. 19–20, 22, 27, 28; *New Castle Recs.* 1: 78.

10. Anson P. Stokes, *Church and State in the United States,* 3 vols. (New York, 1950), 1: 189 ff.

11. Henry C. Murphy, *Anthology of New Netherland* (New York, 1865), pp. 94, 100; Arnold J. F. Van Laer, ed., *New York Historical Manuscripts—Dutch,* 4 vols. (Baltimore, 1974), 4: 291, 293.

12. Dixon Ryan Fox, *Caleb Heathcote* (New York, 1926), pp. 200, 201, 206, 207; Charles Street, ed., *Huntington Town Records,* 2 vols. (Huntington, N.Y., 1888), 2: 321–325, 327, 335; Edmund B. O'Callaghan, ed., *The Documentary History of the State of New York,* 4 vols. (Albany, N.Y., 1850), 3: 118, 122, 199, 201, 202, 206–212, 218–224, 230, 278, 279, 311, 321, 445, 451, 452, 465–466, 473, 475, 477, 478.

13. Robert Beverly, *History and Present State of Virginia,* ed. Louis B. Wright (Chapel Hill, N.C., 1947), pp. 262–264; William Bradford, *Of Plymouth Plantation, 1620–1647,* ed. Samuel E. Morison (New York, 1952), p. 169; Hugh Jones, *The Present State of Virginia* (New York, 1865), pp. 67–69.

14. *No. Car. Col. Recs.* 1: 720, 721, 763, 768, 769, 770.

15. *No. Car. Col. Recs.* 1: 764, 771; Frank J. Klingberg, ed., *Carolina Chronicle: The Papers of Commissary Gideon Johnston, 1707–1716* (Berkeley, Calif., 1946), pp. 112–113; Hugh Talmadge Lefler, *North Carolina History as Told by Contemporaries* (Chapel Hill, N.C., 1965), p. 57.

16. *No. Car. Col. Recs.* 1: 572, 630, 690, 849–851, 887, 3: 392.

17. Helene Barret Agee, *Facets of Goochland County's History* (Richmond, Va., 1962), pp. 116–117; Klingberg, ed., *Carolina Chronicle,* p. 53.

18. Klingberg, ed., *Carolina Chronicle,* pp. 22, 39, 53–54, 73.

19. *No. Car. Col. Recs.* 1: 215, 216, 572, 602–603, 690, 769, 885.

20. *N. H. Prov. Papers* 1: 121–122, 146; *Historical Magazine* 4 (1868): 120–122.

21. Walter A. Davis, ed., *The Early Records of the Town of Lunenberg* (Fitchburg, Mass., 1896), pp. 75–77, 82, 192; Erastus Worthington, *History of Dedham* (Boston, 1827), p. 32.

22. *Mass. Bay Co. Recs.* 1: 76, 4, Pt. 1: 204; *New Plym. Recs.* 3: 184; Alan Heimert and Andrew Delbanco, *The Puritans in America* (Cambridge, Mass., 1985), pp. 220, 257,

260; Bradford, *Of Plymouth Plantation*, p. 313; Robert E. Moody, ed., *The Letters of Thomas Gorges, Deputy Governor of the Province of Maine, 1640–1643* (Portland, Me., 1978), pp. 57–58.

23. *N.H. Prov. Papers* 1: 121.

24. Winthrop, *History of New England* 1: 151, 158, 162 ff., 170, 171, 175, 176; Sydney V. James, "Ecclesiastical Authority in the Land of Roger Williams," *New England Quarterly,* 54 (1984): 323 ff.; Winton U. Solberg, *Redeem the Time: The Puritan Sabbath in Early America* (Cambridge, Mass., 1977), pp. 138 ff.

25. David D. Hall, ed., *The Antinomian Controversy, 1636–1638* (Middletown, Conn., 1968).

26. Lilian Handlin, "Dissent in a Small Community," *New England Quarterly* 57 (1985); Philip F. Gura, *A Glimpse of Sion's Glory* (Middletown, Conn., 1984).

27. Stokes, *Church and State in the United States,* 1: 203; *Mass. Bay Co. Recs.* 1: 213, 220, 252, 265.

28. Berthold Fernow, ed., *The Records of New Amsterdam, 1656–1658* (New York, 1897), pp. 346–347; Stephanie G. Wolf, *Urban Village* (Princeton, N.J., 1976), p. 129. See also William G. McLoughlin, *New England Dissent, 1630–1833: The Baptists and the Separation of Church and State,* 2 vols. (Cambridge, Mass., 1971).

29. *Mass. Bay Co. Recs.* 5: 199; Samuel Sewall, *Diary,* 2 vols., ed. M. Halsey Thomas (New York, 1973), 1: 44; Carla G. Pestana, "The City upon a Hill under Siege: The Puritan Perception of the Quaker Threat," *New England Quarterly* 56 (1983): 323 ff.

30. James, "Ecclesiastical Authority," loc. cit. 54: 332 ff.; Thomas Hutchinson, *The History of the Colony and Province of Massachusetts Bay,* 3 vols., ed. Lawrence S. Mayo (Cambridge, Mass., 1936), 1: 426–427.

31. Joseph B. Walker, ed., *Diaries of Rev. Timothy Walker* (Concord, N.H., 1889), pp. 6–19; John Russell Bartlett, ed., *Records of the Colony of Rhode Island and Providence Plantations,* 10 vols. (Providence, R.I., 1856–1865), 4: 206–207; *Records of ye Town Meetings of Lyn, 1717–1730* (Lynn, Mass., 1960), p. 16; *Records of ye Town Meetings of Lyn, 1730–1742* (Lynn, Mass., 1964), p. 58; *N.H. Prov. Papers* 1: 260; Sewall, *Diary,* 1: 54, 67, 73, 116, 119–135, 2: 681; *Mass. Hist. Soc. Colls.* 12 (1871): 112, 374 ff.; Cotton Mather, *Magnalia Christi Americana,* ed. Kenneth B. Murdock (Cambridge, Mass., 1977), p. 344; Edwin Hall, ed., *The Ancient Historical Records of Norwalk, Connecticut* (Norwalk, Conn., 1847), pp. 122, 124; Gertrude S. Kimball, *Providence in Colonial Times* (New York, 1972), pp. 161, 163; Mary H. Mitchell, *History of the United Church of New Haven* (New Haven, Conn., 1942), pp. 3, 5; Fox, *Caleb Heathcote,* pp. 255–256; Clyde A. Duniway, *The Development of Freedom of the Press in Massachusetts* (New York, 1906), p. 106.

32. *Mass. House Jour. 1734–1735,* pp. 52, 65, 251; *Mass. House Jour. 1737–1738,* pp. 78, 218; Hall, ed., *Norwalk,* pp. 156, 157; Sewall, *Diary,* 2: 717, 735; *N.H. Towns* 2: 119–121, 275–277; *Records of the Town of Weston, 1746–1803* (Boston, 1893), pp. 8–10, 12–14, 18–19; *N.H. Prov. Papers* 1: 587.

33. Sewall, *Diary,* 2: 851; William Livingston et al., *The Independent Reflector,* ed. Milton M. Klein (Cambridge, Mass., 1963), p. 276.

34. Winthrop, *History of New England,* 2: 29, 30, 31, 61, 85, 95; William Hubbard, *The History of the Indian Wars in New England,* 2 vols., ed. Samuel G. Drake

(Roxbury, Mass., 1865), 2: 253–254; David D. Hall, "A World of Wonders: The Mentality of the Supernatural in Seventeenth-Century New England," in David D. Hall and David G. Allen, eds., *Seventeenth-Century New England* (Boston, 1984), pp. 239 ff.; on good angels, see also Cotton Mather, *Paterna,* Ronald A. Bosco, ed. (New York, 1976), pp. 111–113, 120–126.

35. Sewall, *Diary,* 1: 599.

36. John L. Sibley et al., eds., *Harvard Graduates,* 17 vols. (1873–1975), 4: 322; Louis B. Wright, ed., *The Letters of Robert Carter, 1720–1727* (San Marino, Calif., 1940), p. 87; Sewall, *Diary,* 1: 145, 249, 328, 343, 360, 367, 2: 707, 812, 874, 945, 951, 1037; Harriet M. Forbes, ed., *The Diary of Rev. Ebenezer Parkman* (Worcester, Mass., 1899), p. 18; Frank D. Miner, ed., *The Diary of Manasseh Minor, Stonington, Conn.* (n.p., 1915), pp. 43, 46, 75, 76, 96.

37. Joseph Dow, *History of the Town of Hampton* (Hampton, N.H., 1977), p. 180; Ellen D. Larned, *History of Windham County, Connecticut,* 2 vols. (Worcester, Mass., 1874), 1: 258–259.

38. Lefler, *North Carolina History as Told by Contemporaries,* p. 57; Klingberg, ed., *Carolina Chronicle,* pp. 22, 39.

39. Sewall, *Diary,* 1: 133, 502; Jasper Dankers and Peter Sluyter, *Journal of a Voyage to New York, 1679–1680,* ed. Henry C. Murphy (Brooklyn, N.Y., 1867), p. 184.

40. Joseph J. Kelley, Jr., *Pennsylvania: The Colonial Years, 1681–1776* (Garden City, N.Y., 1980), p. 86; Dankers and Sluyter, *Journal,* p. 275; Berthold Fernow, ed., *The Records of New Amsterdam 1653–1655* (New York, 1897), p. 173.

41. Dankers and Sluyter, *Journal,* pp. 288–293; Perry Miller, *Jonathan Edwards* (New York, 1949), p. 103.

42. Charles Hoadly, *Records of the Colony and Plantation* (Hartford, Conn., 1857), p. 51; *Mass. Bay Co. Recs.* 3: 126, 273, 4, pt. 1: 47, 96.

43. O'Callaghan, ed., *Documentary History of the State of New York,* 4: 132–135, 137–139; *Pa. Prov. Coun. Mins.* 2: 20; Charles Hoadly, *Some Early Post Mortem Examinations in New England* (Hartford, Conn., 1892).

44. *Pa. Prov. Coun. Mins.* 1: 93, 95, 96; *Mass. Bay Co. Recs.* 4, pt. 1: 269.

45. Chadwick Hansen, *Witchcraft at Salem* (New York, 1969); Paul Boyer and Stephen Nissenbaum, *Salem Possessed: A Study in the Origins of Radical Politics* (Cambridge, Mass., 1974); Samuel E. Morison, ed., "The Common Place Book of Joseph Green," Colonial Society of Massachusetts, *Publications* 34 (1943), p. 195.

46. *N.H. Hist. Soc. Colls.* 8: 454; *Va. Burgesses Jour. 1742–1748,* pp. 12, 314; Miller, *Jonathan Edwards,* pp. 18–19; Cotton Mather, *The Angel of Bethesda,* ed. Gordon W. Jones (Barre, Mass., 1972), pp. 93 ff.; Kenneth Silverman, *The Life and Times of Cotton Mather* (New York, 1984), pp. 338, 406; O'Callaghan, ed., *Documentary History of the State of New York,* 3: 882; David Levin, *Cotton Mather: The Young Life of the Lord's Remembrancer* (Cambridge, Mass., 1978), pp. 91–92.

47. *Conn. Hist. Soc. Colls.* 21: 372–377.

48. Louis B. Wright, ed., *The Letters of Robert Carter, 1720–1727* (San Marino, Calif., 1940), p. 25; *New England's Misery: The Procuring Cure and a Remedy Proposed* (Boston, 1758), p. 14; *Mass. House Jour., 1715–1717,* p. 176; *N.H. Towns* 1: 150.

49. Cotton Mather, *Diary,* 2 vols., ed. Worthington C. Ford (New York, 1974), 2: 3, 23, 151, 184, 193, 239, 395, 412, 447, 516, 616, 663, 717.

50. Jones, *Present State of Virginia*, pp. 67, 78–79; Beverly, *History and Present State of Virginia*, pp. 261–262.

51. Jeremias Van Rensselaer, *Correspondence 1651–1674*, ed. and trans. Arnold J. F. Van Laer (Albany, 1932), p. 91; *Va. Burgesses Jour., 1702–1712*, p. 352; *Va. Burgesses Jour., 1712–1726*, p. 34.

52. Jones, *Present State of Virginia*, p. 70; William Nelson et al., eds., *Documents Relating to the Colonial History of the State of New Jersey*, 40 vols. (Paterson, N.J., 1880–1949), 12: 128–129; Kimball, *Providence in Colonial Times*, p. 166.

53. O'Callaghan, ed., *Documentary History of New York*, 3: 456–466; Allen D. Candler et. al, eds., *The Colonial Records of the State of Georgia*, 30 vols. (Atlanta, 1904–1985), 4: 24; *Journal and Votes of the House of Representatives of the Province of Nova Cesarea or New Jersey in their First Sessions of Assembly, 1703* (Jersey City, N.J., 1872), pp. 134, 135.

54. *N.H. Towns* 1: 305–328; 2: 438–440; Edward L. Parker, *The History of Londonderry* (Boston, 1851), p. 148; also Roger Welles, *Early Annals of Newington* (Hartford, Conn., 1874), pp. 5, 9, 23, 55, 57.

55. *N.H. Towns* 1: 570–576; *N.H. Prov. Papers* 4: 412–413, 5: 36–40, 63; George Wadleigh, *Notable Events in the History of Dover, N.H.* (Dover, N.H., 1913), pp. 121, 135; John Sibley et al, eds., *Harvard Graduates*, 17 vols. (Boston, 1873–1975), 4: 322–323; *Copy of the Old Records, Town of Duxbury, Massachusetts* (Plymouth, Mass., 1893), pp. 248–262, 264–265, 276–277, 279, 302, 305, 315, 317, 319; Samuel Dexter, *Some Serious Thoughts on the Foundation, Rise and Growth of the Settlements in New England* (Boston, 1738), p. 250; *Mass. House Jour., 1738–1739*, pp. 211–212, 259.

56. Matt B. Jones, "Thomas Maule, Salem Quaker," *Essex Institute Historical Collections* 72 (January 1936): 1–42; Sewall, *Diary*, 1: 341; Duniway, *Development of Freedom of the Press in Massachusetts*, pp. 84–86, 98, 101, 108–109; Kimball, *Providence in Colonial Times*, p. 173.

57. Samuel Dexter, *Sermon Preached in 1728, in Dedham Pulpit* (Boston, 1840), pp. 240–241; Jonathan Edwards, *A Life of David Brainerd*, ed. Norman Pettit (New Haven, Conn., 1985).

58. Frank E. Halliday, *A History of Cornwall* (London, 1975), pp. 265 ff.; Candler et. al., eds., *Colonial Records of the State of Georgia* 4: 18–19, 24; *Dorchester Historical and Antiquarian Society Collections* 1–3 (1846): 54–55.

59. *Dorchester Historical and Antiquarian Society Collections* 1–3 (1846): 58–59, 63–65; Mitchell, *History of the United Church of New Haven*, pp. 12–14, 17.

60. Parker, *History of Londonderry*, pp. 150–151; Nelson et al., eds., *Documents Relating to the Colonial History of the State of New Jersey* 12: 139.

61. *Dorchester Historical and Antiquarian Society Collections* 1–3 (1846): 54–55; Miller, *Jonathan Edwards*, p. 22.

62. Miller, *Jonathan Edwards*, p. 173.

63. Herman Mann, *Historical Annals of Dedham* (Dedham, Mass., 1847), p. 28.

64. Louis K. Wechsler, *The Common People of Colonial America* (New York, 1978), p. 78; *New England's Misery*, p. 13.

65. Charles S. Grant, *Democracy in the Connecticut Frontier Town of Kent* (New York, 1961), p. 166.

VI. THE GOVERNMENT OF FAMILIES, 1600–1760

1. Charles H. And Katherine George, *The Protestant Mind of the English Reformation, 1570–1640* (Princeton, N.J., 1961), p. 272; Perry Miller, *The New England Mind: The Seventeenth Century* (Cambridge, Mass., 1954), pp. 40 ff.

2. *Va. Co. Recs.* 4: 231–232.

3. Cotton Mather, *A Family Well-Ordered, Or an Essay to Render Parents and Children Happy in One Another* (Boston, 1699), pp. 65, 66; see also Larzer Ziff, *John Cotton* (Cambridge, Mass., 1968).

4. Charles Hoadly, ed., *Records of the Colony and Plantation* (Hartford, Conn., 1857), p. 47; *Mass. Bay Co. Recs.* 5: 63; Zara Jones Power, ed., *Ancient Town Records* (New Haven, Conn., 1962), p. 193.

5. Mather, *A Family Well-Ordered,* pp. 3, 4.

6. *New Plym. Recs.* 3: 22, 97; Susie M. Ames, ed., *County Court Records of Accomack-Northampton, Virginia, 1632–1640* (Washington, D.C., 1954), pp. 20, 22, 25; William Bradford, *Of Plymouth Plantation,* ed. Samuel E. Morison (New York, 1952), pp. 316, 317.

7. Samuel Dexter, *Some Serious Thoughts on the Foundation, Rise and Growth of the Settlements in New England* (Boston, 1738), p. 269.

8. Constantia Maxwell, *Irish History from Contemporary Sources, 1509–1610* (London, 1932), pp. 353 ff.; Thomas I. Rae, *The Administration of the Scottish Frontier, 1513–1603* (Edinburgh, 1966), p. 125; *Historical Magazine* 4 (August 1868): 120–122; also Cotton Mather, *Diary,* 2 vols., ed. Worthington C. Ford (New York, 1974), 2: 447; Emile Benveniste, *Le Vocabulaire des institutions indo-européenes,* 2 vols. (Paris, 1969), 1: book 2.

9. Mather, *A Family Well-Ordered,* p. 6; Gordon J. Schochet, *Patriarchalism in Political Thought* (New York, 1975), pp. 83–84.

10. Louis B. Wright, ed., *The Letters of Robert Carter, 1720–1727* (San Marino, Calif., 1940), pp. 80–81; Samuel Sewall, *Diary,* 2 vols., ed. M. Halsey Thomas (New York, 1973), 1: 496; William A. Crozier, ed., *Spotsylvania County Records, 1721–1800* (Baltimore, 1955), p. 4.

11. Robert Beverly, *History and Present State of Virginia,* ed. Louis B. Wright (Chapel Hill, N.C., 1947), p. 287; Amandus Johnson, *The Instruction for Johan Printz* (Philadelphia, 1930), pp. 161–162; *N.H. Hist. Soc. Colls.* 4 (1834): 248.

12. *Va. Co. Recs.* 3: 493–494, 4: 231–232; Basil Sollers, "Transported Convict Laborers in Maryland during the Colonial Period," *Maryland Historical Magazine* 2 (1907): 23–25.

13. John Winthrop, *History of New England from 1630 to 1649,* 2 vols., ed. James Savage (Boston, 1825), 2: 216, 217; Clayton H. Chapman, "Benjamin Colman's Daughters," *New England Quarterly* 26 (1953): 187 ff.

14. Bradford, *Of Plymouth Plantation,* p. 86; Winthrop, *History of New England,* 2: 313; *Va. Co. Recs.* 3: 171; *Hening Statutes* 3: 444–445, 4: 244–246.

15. Berthold Fernow, ed., *The Records of New Amsterdam 1653–1655* (New York, 1897), pp. 199–200; Conyers Read, ed., *William Lambarde and Local Government* (Ithaca, N. Y., 1962), pp. 18, 19, 30, 32, 37, 41, 51; Berthold Fernow, ed., *The Records of New*

Amsterdam 1658–1661 (New York, 1897), pp. 189–190, 297–298, 379, 427–429; Berthold Fernow, ed., *The Records of New Amsterdam 1662–1663* (New York, 1897), p. 105; *New Plym. Recs.* 3: 83, 7: 111; Alan Macfarlane, "The Informal Social Control of Marriage in 17th Century England," in Vivian C. Fox and Martin H. Quitt, *Loving, Parenting and Dying* (New York, 1980), p. 113; Wallace Notestein, *English People on the Eve of Colonization* (New York, 1962), p. 57.

16. Fernow, ed., *Records of New Amsterdam 1653–1655,* pp. 37–38, 155, 156; Joshua Hempstead, "Diary," *New London County Historical Society Collections* 1 (1901): 59.

17. *Md. Archives* 54: 45–46.

18. *Md. Archives* 53: 599; Hoadly, ed., *Records of the Colony and Plantation,* p. 78; John Cox, ed., *Oyster Bay Town Records,* 6 vols. (New York, 1916–1931), 1: 669.

19. Arnold J. F. Van Laer, ed., *Minutes of the Court of Fort Orange and Beverwyck, 1652–1660,* 2 vols. (Albany, 1920), 1: 188–190.

20. *Conn. Hist. Soc. Colls.* 21 (1924): 360.

21. *Md. Archives* 54: 395; 49: 217–218, 232–236; *New Castle Recs.* 2: 289, 390.

22. *R.I. Hist. Soc. Colls.* 5 (1843): 123–124; *Md. Archives* 54: 28–29; Cox, ed., *Oyster Bay Town Records,* 1: 3–4, 205; *Pa. Prov. Coun. Mins.* 1: 207; *N.Y.C. Mayor's Ct., Select Cases,* p. 185; *Mass. House Jour., 1738–1739,* p. 135.

23. Wright, ed., *Letters of Robert Carter,* p. 18; Henry C. Murphy, *Anthology of New Netherland* (New York, 1865), p. 165; Erastus Worthington, *History of Dedham* (Boston, 1827), p. 52.

24. Samuel Sewall, *Diary,* 2 vols., ed. M. Halsey Thomas (New York, 1972), 2: 885, 911, 933.

25. Sewall, *Diary,* 2: 990; Thomas M. and Virginia L. Davis, *Edward Taylor's Church Records and Related Sermons,* 2 vols. (Boston, 1981), 1: 188; Ashley Bowen, *The Journals of Ashley Bowen, 1728–1813, of Marblehead,* ed. Philip C. F. Smith (Portland, Me., 1973), pp. 8–9.

26. *Mass. Bay Co. Recs.* 3: 212; Van Laer, ed. *Minutes of the Court of Fort Orange and Beverwyck,* 1: 248; Fernow, ed., *Records of New Amsterdam 1656–1658,* pp. 335, 338; Mattie Parker, ed., *North Carolina Higher Court Records, 1670–1696* (Raleigh, N.C., 1968), pp. 429–430; Mattie Parker, ed., *North Carolina Higher Court Records, 1697–1701* (Raleigh, N.C., 1971), p. 26; Steven Ozment, *When Fathers Ruled* (Cambridge, Mass., 1983).

27. Arnold J. F. Van Laer, ed., *New York Historical Manuscripts—Dutch,* 4 vols. (Baltimore, 1974), 1: 46–47, 67; *New Plym. Recs.* 3: 75; William R. Staples, *Annals of the Town of Providence* (Providence, R.I., 1843), p. 24; Joseph H. Smith, *Colonial Justice in Western Massachusetts, 1639–1702,* pp. 235–236; William S. Holdsworth, *History of English Law,* 14 vols. (London, 1966), 5: 442–443; *Historical Magazine* 4 (August 1868): 120–122; Alexander S. Salley, ed., *Journal of the Grand Council of South Carolina, 1692* (Columbia, S.C., 1907), pp. 17, 30–31, 33.

28. *New Plym. Recs.* 3: 66; *N.H. Prov. Papers* 3: 272–279; *N.H. Hist. Soc. Colls.* 8 (1866): 68, 118.

29. *New Castle Recs.* 2: 289, 304; *Md. Archives* 54: 10.

30. Parker, ed., *North Carolina Higher Court Records, 1670–1696,* p. 379; Parker, ed.,

North Carolina Higher Court Records, 1697–1701, pp. 90–91, 126–128; Lilian Handlin, "Dissent in a Small Community," *New England Quarterly* 57 (1985); Kenneth Silverman, *The Life and Times of Cotton Mather* (New York, 1984).

31. Winthrop, *History of New England,* 2: 229 ff., 249, 250.

32. Cotton Mather, *Magnalia Christi Americana,* ed. Kenneth B. Murdock (Cambridge, Mass., 1977), p. 278.

33. Perry Miller, *Jonathan Edwards* (New York, 1949), p. 15; *N.H. Hist. Soc. Colls.* 8 (1866): 42–43; Edwin Hall, ed., *The Ancient Historical Records of Norwalk* (Norwalk, Conn., 1847), pp. 110–111; Philip A. Bruce, *Institutional History of Virginia in the Seventeenth Century,* 2 vols. (New York, 1910), 1: 311 ff.; Chapman, "Benjamin Colman's Daughters," loc. cit. 26: 171 ff.

34. Smith, *Colonial Justice in Western Massachusetts,* p. 234; David T. Konig, *Law and Society in Puritan Massachusetts* (Chapel Hill, N.C., 1977), p. 176; Samuel Sewall, "Selections from the Letter Book," *Massachusetts Historical Society Proceedings* 12 (1873): 359; Edward L. Parker, *The History of Londonderry* (Boston, 1851), p. 134; *N.H. Prov. Papers* 3: 727–728; Davis and Davis, *Edward Taylor's Church Records,* 1: 205, 210–211; Sewall, *Diary,* 1: 355, 2: 975.

35. Peter H. Brown, ed., *Scotland before 1700* (Edinburgh, 1893), p. 199; Thomas Whythorne, *Autobiography,* ed. James M. Osborn (London, 1962), p. 3; Roger Williams, "A Key Into the Language of America" (1647), *R.I. Hist. Soc. Colls.* 1 (1827): 118.

36. Mather, *A Family Well-Ordered,* p. 10.

37. Wright, ed., *Letters of Robert Carter,* p. 25; *New York Historical Society Collections for the Year 1918* (1919): 262–263.

38. Sewall, *Diary,* 1: 449; Fernow, ed., *Records of New Amsterdam 1653–1655,* p. 33; Watertown Historical Society, *Watertown Records,* 8 vols. (Watertown, Mass., 1894–1939), 1: 135–136; Parker, ed., *North Carolina Higher Court Records, 1670–1696,* pp. 196–197; Van Laer, ed., *New York Historical Manuscripts—Dutch,* 1: 502–506; *Mass. Bay Co. Recs.* 2: 217; *Md. Archives* 54: 393.

39. William Armstrong Crozier, ed., *Spotsylvania County Records 1720–1800* (Baltimore, 1955), p. 6; Joyce Youings, *Sixteenth Century England* (London, 1984), pp. 154–155; Fernow, ed., *Records of New Amsterdam 1656–1658,* pp. 425, 426; Sewall, *Diary,* 2: 804.

40. Sewall, *Diary,* 1: 300, 329, 343, 346, 348, 349, 359; Mather, *Diary,* 2: 187, 611, 612; Landon Carter, *Diary,* 2 vols., ed. Jack P. Greene (Charlottesville, Va., 1965), 1: 185.

41. Marion D. Learned, *The Life of Francis Daniel Pastorius* (Philadelphia, 1908), pp. 176–177; *Massachusetts Historical Society Proceedings* 12 (1873): 369; Joseph Green, "Common Place Book," ed. Samuel E. Morison, in *Colonial Society of Massachusetts Publications* 34 (1943): 192; *Colonial Society of Massachusetts Publications* 14 (1913): 192–198.

42. Sewall, *Diary,* 1: 347.

43. Horatio Rogers et al., eds., *The Early Records of the Town of Providence,* 20 vols. (Providence, R.I., 1892–1915), 9: 12–14.

44. Arthur B. Tourtellot, *Benjamin Franklin: The Shaping of Genius* (Garden City, N.Y., 1977), pp. 117 ff.; Philip J. Greven, *Four Generations: Population, Land, and Family in Colonial Andover, Massachusetts* (Ithaca, N.Y., 1970), pp. 103 ff., 175 ff.

45. Winthrop, *History of New England*, 2: 265; Sewall, *Diary*, 1: 4; *N.H. Prov. Papers.* 3: 254, 686; *New Plym. Recs.* 3: 201; Watertown Historical Society, *Watertown Records* 1: 105; Fernow, ed., *Records of New Amsterdam 1662–1663*, p. 205; *Mass. Bay Co. Recs.* 3: 140; 4: pt. 1, 247; Gibson C. Chamberlayne, ed., *The Vestry Book of St. Paul's Parish, Hanover County* (Richmond, Va., 1940), p. 103.

46. Hugh Talmage Lefler, ed., *North Carolina History as Told by Contemporaries* (Chapel Hill, N.C., 1965), pp. 43–44; Henry Onderdonk, Jr., *The Annals of Hempstead* (Hempstead, N.Y., 1878), p. 66.

47. Mather, *A Family Well-Ordered*, p. 8; Schochet, *Patriarchalism in Political Thought*, pp. 67–68.

48. Smith, *Colonial Justice in Western Massachusetts*, pp. 224–227; *Hening Statutes* 3: 444–445; *Md. Archives* 57: 426; Rogers et al., eds., *Early Records of Providence*, 9: 5–6.

49. *Md. Archives* 54: 659, 671–672, 686, 53: 133–134, 224–225, 355–357, 387–391; *New Plym. Recs.* 3: 75; Ames, ed., *County Court Records of Accomack-Northampton*, pp. 20, 32.

50. Lefler, ed., *North Carolina History*, p. 42; Van Laer, ed., *New York Historical Manuscripts—Dutch*, 1: 88; *Va. Co. Recs.* 3: 169; *New Castle Recs.* 1: 61; *Md. Archives* 49: 166–168, 230–235, 453, 53: 431, 54: 8, 9, 239, 418, 529, 57: xxviii; *Hening Statutes* 4: 482.

51. *Md. Archives* 54: 167–169, 224–226.

52. Chamberlayne, ed., *Vestry Book of St. Paul's Parish*, pp. 136, 138.

53. Abbott E. Smith, *Colonists in Bondage* (Chapel Hill, N.C., 1947); David W. Galenson, *White Servitude in Colonial America* (Cambridge, Mass., 1981).

54. *Mass. Bay Co. Recs.* 5: 62–63; Hoadly, ed. *Records of the Colony and Plantation*, pp. 118–119, 129; *Md. Archives* 54: 527; *No. Car. Col. Recs.* 1: 517.

55. Jasper Dankers and Peter Sluyter, *Journal of a Voyage to New York, 1679–1680*, ed. Henry C. Murphy (Brooklyn, N.Y., 1867), p. 217; *Md. Archives* 49: 88, 113, 215, 374–375, 53: 501, 502; Salley, ed., *Journal of the Grand Council of South Carolina*, pp. 14, 31–32, 45, 47, 48, 55–56; *Hening Statutes* 3: 447 ff.; *Md. Archives* 54: 490–493.

56. William Whitehead et al., eds., *Documents Relating to the Colonial History of the State of New Jersey*, 30 vols. (Newark, N.J., 1881), 2: 28–29; *Md. Archives* 49: 8–10, 54: 372–373.

57. Fernow, ed., *Records of New Amsterdam 1658–1661*, pp. 386–387; Fernow, ed., *Records of New Amsterdam 1662–1663*, pp. 184–185; *Md. Archives* 53: 410–411.

58. *Va. Co. Recs.* 4: 58–62; George Alsop, *A Character of the Province of Maryland* (New York, 1869), p. 58; James C. Ballagh, *White Servitude in the Colony of Virginia* (Baltimore, 1895), pp. 81 ff.; Winthrop, *History of New England*, 2: 220; Wright, ed., *Letters of Robert Carter*, p. 92.

59. Ames, ed., *County Court Records of Accomack-Northampton*, p. 1.

60. *Va. Co. Recs.* 4: 236; Beverly, *History and Present State of Virginia*, pp. 271–272; *Hening Statutes* 3: 447–462; Cox, ed., *Oyster Bay Town Records*, 1: 83; Jeremias Van

Rensselaer, *Correspondence, 1651–1674,* ed. and trans. Arnold J. F. Van Laer (Albany, 1932), p. 167.

61. Charles Street, ed., *Huntington Town Records* (Huntington, N.Y., 1888) 2: 419–420; Onderdonk, *Annals of Hempstead,* p. 75; John Russell Bartlett, ed., *Records of the Colony of Rhode Island and Providence Plantations,* 10 vols. (Providence, R. I., 1856–1865), 4: 415–416; *Mass. House Jour., 1715–1717,* pp. 134–135; *Mass. House Jour., 1737–1738,* pp. 174–175; *Records of ye Towne Meetings of Lyn, 1717–1730* (Lynn, Mass., 1960), pp. 43–45; Rogers et al., eds., *Early Records of Providence,* 9: 40–41.

62. *Va. Burgesses Jour., 1702–1712,* pp. 240, 264, 270; Daniel Horsmanden, *The New York Conspiracy* (New York, 1810), pp. 93, 94; Hugh Jones, *The Present State of Virginia* (New York, 1865), pp. 114, 115; *N.Y.C. Comm. Coun. Mins.* 3: 28, 88, 89; *Hening Statutes* 3: 537–538.

63. Parker, ed., *North Carolina Higher Court Records, 1670–1696,* p. 378; *Hening Statutes* 3: 333–334, 4: 222–223; *Va. Burgesses Jour., 1702–1712,* pp. 147–148; *Va. Burgesses Jour., 1752–1758,* p. 138; Bartlett, ed., *Records of Rhode Island and Providence Plantations,* 4: 179; *Va. Burgesses Jour., 1742–1748,* pp. 28, 51, 84, 94; *Pa. Prov. Coun. Mins.* 2: 405.

64. Michael Kammen, *Colonial New York* (New York, 1975), pp. 58–60; *Hening Statutes* 3: 447–462; *Pa. Prov. Coun. Mins.* 2: 112, 120.

65. Sewall, *Diary,* 1: 433, 435, 2: 612, 822, 1120; David Levin, *Cotton Mather: The Young Life of the Lord's Remembrancer* (Cambridge, Mass., 1978), pp. 235–236.

66. *Va. Burgesses Jour., 1702–1712,* p. 302; *Va. Burgesses Jour., 1752–1758,* p. 5; *Historical Records of North Castle, New Castle* (Armonk, N.Y., 1975), p. 50.

67. *Mass. Bay Co. Recs.* 5: 25; Staples, *Annals of the Town of Providence,* p. 171; Bartlett, ed., *Records of Rhode Island and Providence Plantations,* 4: 193; *New Plym. Recs.* 3: 57–58; *Hening Statutes* 4: 405–406.

68. *Mass. House Jour., 1761,* Pt. 1: 322–323; *Va. Burgesses Jour., 1702–1712,* pp. 56, 97–98.

69. Murphy, *Anthology of New Netherland,* pp. 88–89.

VII. ENTERPRISE AND MOBILITY, 1600–1760

1. Amandus Johnson, *The Instruction for Johan Printz* (Philadelphia, 1930), pp. 111–112.

2. William Perkins, "A Treatise of the Vocations or Callings of Men," *Workes,* 2 vols. (Cambridge, 1608), 1: 727; John Cotton, *The Way of Life or God's Way and Course* (London, 1641), p. 437; Sir Thomas Smith, *De Republica Anglorum,* ed. Mary Dewar (Cambridge, 1982), pp. 46–49.

3. Perry Miller, *The New England Mind: The Seventeenth Century* (Cambridge, Mass., 1954), p. 44; Robert S. Michaelson, "Changes in the Puritan Concept of Calling or Vocation," *New England Quarterly* 26 (1953): 328 ff.

4. Arnold J. F. Van Laer, ed., *New York Historical Manuscripts—Dutch,* 4 vols. (Baltimore, 1974), 4: 558; *New York Historical Society Collections for the Year 1918* (1919): 32; *Va. Co. Recs.* 3: 245; Johnson, *Instruction for Johan Printz,* pp. 140–141; *Md. Archives* 54: 170.

5. George Sheldon, *History of Deerfield*, 2 vols. (Deerfield, Mass., 1895–1896), 1: 266; Henry A. Hazen, *History of Billerica* (Boston, 1883), p. 216; David T. Konig, *Law and Society in Puritan Massachusetts* (Chapel Hill, N.C., 1979), pp. 35–57; Horatio Rogers et al., eds., *The Early Records of the Town of Providence*, 20 vols. (Providence, R.I., 1892–1915), 17: 219–220.

6. *Va. Co. Recs.* 2: 94–95, 3: 160–161; *Mass. House Jour., 1732–1734*, pp. 31–32; *Mass. House Jour., 1734–1735*, p. 150; *Mass. House Jour., 1735–1736*, p. 293; James T. Lemon, *The Best Poor Man's Country* (New York, 1972), p. xiii; Stephanie G. Wolf, *Urban Village* (Princeton, N.J., 1976), pp. 60–65, 72.

7. Edwin Hall, ed., *The Ancient Historical Records of Norwalk, Connecticut* (Norwalk, Conn., 1847), p. 111; *Records of the Towne Meetings of Lyn, 1730–1742* (Lynn, Mass., 1964), pp. 3–4; Edmund B. O'Callaghan, ed., *The Documentary History of the State of New York*, 4 vols. (Albany, 1849–1851), 3: 365–366, 384; *Va. Co. Recs.* 4: 230; Sylvia J. Turner, ed., *Journal Kept by William Williams of the Proceedings of the Lower House of the Connecticut General Assembly, May 1757* (Hartford, Conn., 1975), p. 29.

8. William Holdsworth, *A History of English Law*, 14 vols. (London, 1966), 4: 317–318; *Hening Statutes* 4: 294–296, 6: 101.

9. John Winthrop, *The History of New England from 1630 to 1649*, 2 vols., ed. James Savage (Boston, 1825), 1: 312 ff.; *New Castle Recs.* 2: 290–291, 302; Bernard Bailyn, "Apologia," Colonial Society of Massachusetts, *Transactions* 42 (1952–1956): 294 ff., 300 ff.; *N.Y.C. Comm. Coun. Mins.* 4: 84, 85; Peter H. Brown, ed., *Scotland Before 1700* (Edinburgh, 1893), p. 198.

10. Henry Burt, *The First Century of the History of Springfield*, 2 vols. (Springfield, Mass., 1899), 1: 359; *Va. Co. Recs.* 2: 82; *Hening Statutes* 6: 51–52; *Mass. House Jour., 1731–1732*, p. 5; Konig, *Law and Society in Puritan Massachusetts*, p. 120.

11. William Nelson et al., eds., *Documents Relating to the Colonial History of the State of New Jersey*, 40 vols. (Paterson, N.J., 1880–1949), 20: 200; *Va. Co. Recs.* 4: 428; William Hubbard, *The History of the Indian Wars in New England*, 2 vols., ed. Samuel G. Drake (Roxbury, Mass., 1865), 2: 252; Van Laer, ed., *New York Historical Manuscripts—Dutch*, 4: 521 ff., 532 ff.; Alexander S. Salley, ed., *Journal of the Grand Council of South Carolina* (Columbia, S.C., 1907), pp. 8, 27, 46, 51; *Mass. House Journ., 1755*, pp. 61, 67, 98.

12. Perez Zagorin, *The Court and the Country: The Beginning of the English Revolution* (New York, 1970), p. 113; Burt, *First Century of Springfield*, 2: 167, 289; Michael Dalton, *Country Justice* (London, 1697), pp. 33, 49, 54, 55; Winthrop, *History of New England*, 2: 160, 349; *Mass. Bay Co. Recs.* 5: 230; *Pa. Prov. Coun. Mins.* 3: 18–19; *N.H. Prov. Papers* 4: 596; Pierre Deyon and Philippe Guignet, "The Royal Manufacturers and Economics and Technological Progress in France," *Journal of European Economic History* 9 (1980): 611–631.

13. *Mass. Bay Co. Recs.* 3: 144; *Va. Burgesses Jour., 1727–1740*, p. 9; *Va. Burgesses Jour., 1742–1748*, p. 262; *Va. Burgesses Jour., 1752–1758*, pp. 123, 245; *Va. Co. Recs.* 4: 55; *Hening Statutes* 6: 118–120; John G. Reid, *Maine, Charles II and Massachusetts* (Portland, Me., 1977), p. 4.

14. Winthrop, *History of New England,* 1: 193, 196.

15. Arnold J. F. Van Laer, ed., *Minutes of the Court of Fort Orange and Beverwyck,* 2 vols. (Albany, 1923), 2: 255–256, 266–270, 278–286, 291–292, 297.

16. *Mass. Bay Co. Recs.* 3: 153; Louis B. Wright, ed., *The Letters of Robert Carter, 1720–1727* (San Marino, Calif., 1940), p. 9; Landon Carter, *Diary,* 2 vols., ed. Jack P. Greene (Charlottesville, Va., 1965), 1: 93, 101; Charles Webster, *The Great Instauration: Science, Medicine and Reform 1626–1660* (New York, 1975), pp. 256–257; *Hening Statutes* 4: 509–510; Nelson et al., eds., *Documents Relating to the Colonial History of the State of New Jersey,* 25: 21; Maurice B. Gordon, *Aesculapius Comes to the Colonies* (Ventnor, N.J., 1949), pp. 32–33.

17. Winthrop, *History of New England,* 1: 31, 116, 2: 25; *Mass. Bay Co. Recs.* 3: 376; Charles J. Hoadly, ed., *Records of the Colony and Plantation* (Hartford, Conn., 1857), p. 51; *Va. Co. Recs.* 4: 146; Van Laer, ed., *New York Historical Manuscripts—Dutch,* 4: 61, 589; Burt, *First Century of Springfield,* 1: 166, 168, 169, 171, 204, 246, 247, 301; Van Laer, ed., *Minutes of Fort Orange and Beverwyck,* 2: 234; Ernest S. Griffith, *History of American City Government* (New York, 1938), p. 146; Hugh Rockoff, *Drastic Measures: A History of Wage and Price Controls in the United States* (Cambridge, Mass., 1984); Michael Kammen, *Colonial New York* (New York, 1975), p. 57.

18. *Hening Statutes* 3: 404–419; *Va. Burgesses Jour., 1702–1712,* pp. xxix–xxx, 147; Berthold Fernow, ed., *The Records of New Amsterdam 1658–1661* (New York, 1897), pp. 142–143; *N.Y.C. Comm. Coun. Mins.* 3: 96–97; Milton M. Klein, "Democracy and Politics in Colonial New York," *New York History* 40 (July 1959): 233; Griffith, *History of American City Government,* pp. 35–36, 54, 138–140.

19. Jeremias van Rensselaer, *Correspondence 1651–1674,* ed. and trans. Arnold J. F. Van Laer (Albany, 1932), p. 172; Edmund B. O'Callaghan, *History of New Netherland,* 2 vols. (New York, 1846–1848), 2: 111; Robert Beverly, *History and Present State of Virginia,* ed. Louis B. Wright (Chapel Hill, N.C., 1947), pp. xxxi, 292, 295–297, 319; Griffith, *History of American City Government,* p. 68.

20. William Bradford, *Of Plymouth Plantation, 1620–1647,* ed. Samuel E. Morison (New York, 1952), p. 253; Winthrop, *History of New England,* 2: 239.

21. Van Laer, ed., *New York Historical Manuscripts—Dutch,* 4: 492–493.

22. Konig, *Law and Society in Puritan Massachusetts,* pp. 74–76; Burt, *First Century of Springfield,* 1: 131.

23. Thomas Morton, *New English Canaan,* ed. Charles F. Adams, Jr. (Boston, 1883), p. 239.

24. *Va. Co. Recs.* 1: 413, 433, 528–529, 532, 2: 36, 336–337; Edmund and Dorothy S. Berkeley, *The Reverend John Clayton* (Charlottesville, Va., 1965), pp. 79, 80.

25. *R.I. Hist. Soc. Colls.* 5 (1843): 152–154.

26. Manasseh Minor, *Diary,* ed. Frank Denison Miner (Stonington, Conn., 1915), pp. 45, 55, 68; Stephen Innes, *Labor in a New Land* (Princeton, N.J., 1983), p. 81.

27. Francis Mamekie, *A Plain and Friendly Perswasive* (London, 1705), pp. 6, 7.

28. *New Castle Recs.* 1: 234; Johnson, *Instruction for Johan Printz,* p. 243.

29. Patricia U. Bonomi, *A Factious People: Politics and Society in Colonial New York* (New York, 1971).

30. Winthrop, *History of New England,* 2: 31; Massachusetts Historical Society, *Proceedings* 12 (1871): 113 ff.; *No. Car. Col. Recs.* 1: 467, 527.

31. John Cox, ed., *Oyster Bay Town Records,* 6 vols. (New York, 1916–1931), 1: 661; Burt, *First Century of Springfield,* 1: 355; *Mass. House Jour., 1732–1734,* pp. 55–56; *Mass. House Jour., 1737–1738,* pp. 214–215, 224, 229, 248; Konig, *Law and Society in Puritan Massachusetts,* pp. 78–82; Innes, *Labor in a New Land,* p. 18.

32. Alexander Brown, *The Genesis of the United States,* 2 vols. (New York, 1964), 1: 58; Van Laer, ed. *New York Historical Manuscripts—Dutch,* 4: 107; Berthold Fernow, ed., *The Records of New Amsterdam 1653–1655* (New York, 1897), pp. 40–42; Fernow, ed., *Records of New Amsterdam, 1658–1661,* pp. 16–17.

33. John Russell Bartlett, ed., *Records of the Colony of Rhode Island and Providence Plantations, 1636–1792,* 10 vols. (Providence, R.I., 1856–1865), 4: 517; *Mass. House Jour., 1734–1735,* p. 185; Joseph J. Kelley, Jr., *Pennsylvania: The Colonial Years, 1681–1776* (Garden City, N.Y., 1980), pp. 126, 160–161; *Va. Burgesses Jour., 1712–1726,* pp. 137–138.

34. Peter M. G. Harris, "The Social Origins of American Leaders," *Perspectives in American History* 3 (1969): 159 ff.

35. Christopher Morris, ed., *The Journeys of Celia Fiennes* (London, 1947), p. 7; John Selden, *Table Talk* (London, 1798), pp. 43, 44.

36. Robert Crowley, *Select Works,* ed. Joseph M. Cowper (London, 1871), pp. 57, 63, 87–89, 163, 165; Peter Laslett, *The World We Have Lost* (London, 1965), pp. 22, 26, 27.

37. *Va. Co. Recs.* 4: 230; *New England Courant,* June 11, 1722; Zara Jones Powers, ed., *Ancient Town Records* (New Haven, Conn., 1962), p. 172; Hall, ed., *Ancient Historical Records of Norwalk,* pp. 99, 100; Charles M. Taintor, ed., *Extracts from the Records of Colchester* (Hartford, Conn., 1864), pp. 15, 25; Hugh Jones, *The Present State of Virginia* (New York, 1865), p. 43; Lawrence Shaw Mayo, *The Winthrop Family in America* (Boston, 1948), pp. 118–119; Michael Zuckerman, *Peaceable Kingdoms: New England Towns in the Eighteenth Century* (New York, 1970), pp. 217–218; Massachusetts Historical Society, *Proceedings,* 2 Series, 9 (1894–1895): 6.

38. Olwen Hufton, "Towards an Understanding of the Poor of Eighteenth-Century France," in *French Government and Society, 1500–1850,* ed. John F. Bosher (London, 1975), pp. 145 ff.

39. Frances M. Caulkins, *History of New London, Connecticut* (New London, 1852), p. 382.

40. Beverly, *History and Present State of Virginia,* p. 275; Carl J. Vipperman, *The Rise of Rawlins Lowndes, 1724–1800* (Columbia, S.C., 1978), p. ix.

41. *No. Car. Col. Recs.* 1: 764–765.

42. New York Historical Society, *Collections for the Year 1918* (1919), p. 84.

43. Beverly, *History and Present State of Virginia,* pp. xxxi, 292, 295–297, 319; William Byrd II, *Histories of the Dividing Line,* ed. William K. Boyd (Raleigh, N.C., 1929), p. 92; Hugh T. Lefler, *North Carolina History as Told by Contemporaries* (Chapel Hill, N.C., 1965), p. 57; Jones, *Present State of Virginia,* p. 48.

44. Bartlett, ed., *Records of the Colony of Rhode Island,* 4: 58.

45. John F. Bosher, "Writing Early Canadian History," *The Written Word* (Ottawa, 1980), p. 33.
46. Cotton Mather, *Magnalia Christi Americana,* ed. Kenneth B. Murdock (Cambridge, Mass., 1977), 1: 278–280; Perry Miller, *The New England Mind from Colony to Province* (Cambridge, Mass., 1953), pp. 42 ff.; William T. Baxter, *The House of Hancock: Business in Boston, 1724–1775* (Cambridge, Mass., 1945).
47. *Va. Co. Recs.* 4: 408–435.
48. Peter Spierenburg, "Elites and Etiquette," *Centrum voor Maatschappijgeschiednis* (Rotterdam, 1981), pp. ix, 27; Jan Bazant, "The Basques in the History of Mexico," *Journal of European Economic History,* 12 (1983): 8, 9.
49. William D. Miller, "The Narragansett Planters," American Antiquarian Society, *Proceedings* 43 (1933): 49 ff.; Jere R. Daniell, "Politics in New Hampshire under Governor Benning Wentworth, 1741–1767," *William and Mary Quarterly* 23 (1966): 76 ff.
50. *N.H. Towns* 2: 115; New York Historical Society, *Collections for the Year 1918* (1919): 95; Edward P. Alexander, ed., *The Journals of John Fontaine, 1710–1719* (Charlottesville, Va., 1972), p. 86; Miller, "Narragansett Planters," loc. cit., 43: 107 ff.; Samuel A. Drake, *The History and Antiquities of Boston* (Boston, 1856), p. 554; David Pulsifer, "Thomas Rumsey," *New England Historical Genealogical Register,* 15 (1861): 60.
51. Wright, ed., *Letters of Robert Carter,* pp. 81–82, 84–85.
52. *Mass. House Jour., 1760–1761,* p. vii.
53. Samuel Sewall, *Diary,* 2 vols., ed. M. Halsey Thomas (New York, 1973), 1: 534 ff., 540, 547.

VIII. RIGHTS, 1600–1760

1. John Locke, *Two Treatises of Government,* ed. Peter Laslett (Cambridge, 1960), p. 443; Émile Benveniste, *Le Vocabulaire des institutions indo-européennes,* 2 vols. (Paris, 1969), 2: 99 ff.; also, Vilma Fritsch, *Left and Right in Science and Life* (London, 1968), pp. 28 ff.
2. Edmund B. O'Callaghan, ed., *Documents Relative to the Colonial History of the State of New York,* 15 vols. (Albany, 1853–1857), 2: 155; Peter N. Carroll, *Puritanism and the Wilderness* (New York, 1969), p. 88; George H. Haynes, *Representation and Suffrage in Massachusetts, 1620–1691* (Baltimore, 1894), p. 33.
3. Patricia U. Bonomi, *A Factious People: Politics and Society in Colonial New York* (New York, 1971), p. 78.
4. Everett Kimball, *The Public Life of Joseph Dudley* (London, 1911), pp. 182–183; Edwin S. Gaustad, *The Great Awakening in New England* (New York, 1957), pp. 108–110; Joseph J. Kelley, Jr., *Pennsylvania: The Colonial Years, 1681–1776* (Garden City, N.Y., 1980), pp. 158–160.
5. James H. Hutson, "Benjamin Franklin and Pennsylvania Politics," *The Pennsylvania Magazine of History and Biography* 93 (July 1969): 313 ff.
6. Bonomi, *Factious People,* pp. 168–171.
7. Bonomi, *Factious People,* pp. 280–282; Ernest S. Griffith, *History of American City Government* (New York, 1938), pp. 366–367; Kelley, *Pennsylvania,* pp. 228 ff.

8. Edmund S. Morgan, *American Slavery, American Freedom* (New York, 1975), pp. 288–289.

9. Henry M. Burt, *The First Century of the History of Springfield: The Official Records, 1636 to 1736,* 2 vols. (Springfield, Mass., 1899), 1: 268; Michael Zuckerman, *Peaceable Kingdoms: New England Towns in the Eighteenth Century* (New York, 1970), pp. 169–170, 177–178; Samuel Greene Arnold, *History of the State of Rhode Island and Providence Plantations,* 2 vols. (New York, 1860), 2: 52–57; William Willis, ed., *Journals of the Rev. Thomas Smith and the Rev. Samuel Deane* (Portland, Me., 1849), pp. 67–71; Joshua Hempstead, "Diary," *New London County Historical Society Collections* 1 (1901): 178, 267, 362, 419; Francis M. Caulkins, *History of New London, Connecticut* (New London, Conn., 1852), p. 385; Oscar Zeichner, *Connecticut's Years of Controversy, 1750–1776* (Chapel Hill, N.C., 1949), p. 9; John Russell Bartlett, ed., *Records of the Colony of Rhode Island and Providence Plantations,* 10 vols. (Providence, R.I., 1856–1865), 4: 195–196, 207–208.

10. *Conn. Pub. Recs.* 8: 512; *The Law Papers, Correspondence and Documents during Jonathan Law's Governorship of the Colony of Connecticut, 1741–1750, Conn. Hist. Soc. Colls.* 11 (1907): 140; Zeichner, *Connecticut's Years of Controversy,* pp. 24, 26; Clarence C. Goen, *Revivalism and Separatism in New England, 1740–1800* (New Haven, Conn., 1962), pp. 62, 195–196, 200, 267.

11. Ellen D. Larned, *History of Windham County, Connecticut,* 2 vols. (Worcester, Mass., 1874), 1: 273, 409, 415–416, 480, 482; see also Christine L. Heyrman, *Commerce and Culture: The Maritime Communities of Colonial Massachusetts* (New York, 1984), pp. 182–204, 366–405.

12. *The Law Papers, Conn. Hist. Soc. Colls.* 15 (1914): 440, 441; Kenneth A. Lockridge, *A New England Town: The First Hundred Years; Dedham* (New York, 1970), pp. 119 ff.; Zuckerman, *Peaceable Kingdoms,* pp. 99 ff.; Griffith, *History of American City Government,* p. 366; Robert J. Dinkin, *Voting in Provincial America* (Westport, Conn., 1977), p. 139.

13. New York Historical Society, *Collections for the Year 1918* (1919): 179; William Nelson et al., eds., *Documents Relating to the Colonial History of the State of New Jersey,* 40 vols. (Paterson, N.J., 1880–1949), 20: 24; Burt, *First Century of Springfield,* 1: 267; Griffith, *History of American City Government,* pp. 142, 209, 212, 373; Kelley, *Pennsylvania,* p. 237.

14. Nelson et al., eds., *Documents Relating to the Colonial History of New Jersey,* 19: 47–50; William Livingston et al., *The Independent Reflector,* ed. Milton M. Klein (Cambridge, Mass., 1963), p. 282.

15. *No. Car. Col. Recs.* 3: 560; Nelson et al., eds., *Documents Relating to the Colonial History of New Jersey,* 11: 550; *A Report of the Record Commissioners of the City of Boston Containing the Boston Records from 1729 to 1742* (Boston, 1885), pp. 260–261; Zuckerman, *Peaceable Kingdoms,* pp. 173–175.

16. Landon Carter, *Diary,* 2 vols., ed. Jack P. Greene (Charlottesville, Va., 1965), 1: 117, 119.

17. *Mass. House Jour., 1729–1731,* pp. 194, 377; Hutson, "Benjamin Franklin and Pennsylvania Politics," loc. cit., 93: 309.

18. Jacob Haven, *A Discourse Delivered November 23, 1758* (Boston, 1759), pp. 292, 294; New York Historical Society, *Collections for the Year 1919* (1920), pp. 326–328;

Edmund and Dorothy Berkeley, eds., *The Reverend John Clayton* (Charlottesville, Va., 1965), pp. 33–39.

19. Arnold J. F. Van Laer, ed., *New York Historical Manuscripts—Dutch,* 4 vols. (Baltimore, 1974), 4: 103.

20. *Mass. House Jour., 1715–1717* (Boston, 1919), p. 195; *Mass. House Jour., 1718–1720,* p. 219.

21. Nelson et al., eds., *Documents Relating to the Colonial History of New Jersey,* 20: 18.

22. Roger Williams, *Complete Works,* 7 vols., ed. John Russell Bartlett (New York, 1963), 6: 14–15; David Levin, *Cotton Mather: The Young Life of the Lord's Remembrancer* (Cambridge, Mass., 1978), p. 248.

23. Preston W. Edsall, ed., *Journal of the Courts of Common Right and Chancery of East New Jersey, 1683–1702* (Philadelphia, 1937), pp. 105–108, 273; John Winthrop, *The History of New England from 1630 to 1649,* 2 vols., ed. James Savage (Boston, 1825), 2: 56 ff.; *Mass. House Jour., 1734–1735,* p. 35.

24. Robert E. Moody, ed., *The Letters of Thomas Gorges, Deputy Governor of the Province of Maine 1640–1643* (Portland, Me., 1978), p. 121; *New Castle Recs.* 1: 38, 100, 232.

25. Winthrop, *History of New England,* 2: 35, 167; Moody, ed., *Letters of Thomas Gorges,* p. 55.

26. Burt, *The First Century of Springfield* 1: 200, 2: 49; Joseph H. Smith, *Colonial Justice in Western Massachusetts, 1639–1702* (Cambridge, Mass., 1961), p. 219; John D. Cushing, ed., *The Laws of the Pilgrims* (Wilmington, Del., 1977); Julius Goebel, Jr., "King's Law and Local Custom in Seventeenth Century New England," in Lawrence M. Friedman and Harry N. Scheiber, eds., *American Law and the Constitutional Order* (Cambridge, Mass., 1979), pp. 32, 34; Lawrence M. Friedman, *A History of American Law* (New York, 1973), pp. 78–80; Bartlett, ed., *Records of the Colony of Rhode Island,* 5: 277, 289 ff.

27. Charles A. W. Pownall, *Thomas Pownall* (London, 1908), p. 84, 97; Edsall, ed., *Journal of the Courts of East New Jersey,* p. 34; *No. Car. Col. Recs.* 1: 462–464; *Mass. Bay Co. Recs.* 5: 200; Richard R. Johnson, *Adjustment to Empire: The New England Colonies, 1675–1715* (New Brunswick, N.J., 1981), p. 371; Stephanie G. Wolf, *Urban Village* (Princeton, N.J., 1976), pp. 139, 140, 169.

28. *A Report of the Record Commissioners of the City of Boston Containing the Boston Records from 1729 to 1742,* pp. 116–117; Julius Goebel and T. Raymond Naughton, *Law Enforcement in Colonial New York* (Montclair, N.Y., 1970), pp. xxv ff., 27.

29. Moody, ed., *Letters of Thomas Gorges,* p. 75; Wolf, *Urban Village,* p. 206; Michael Dalton, *Country Justice* (London, 1697), p. 1; Goebel and Naughton, *Law Enforcement in Colonial New York,* p. 57; Winthrop, *History of New England,* 2: 118, 208.

30. *Md. Archives* 10: 522, 534–545, 41: 385.

31. Ebenezer Cook, *The Sot Weed Factor,* in Edward C. Steiner, ed., *Early Maryland Poetry* (Baltimore, 1900), p. 30; Robert Crowley, *Select Works,* ed. Joseph M. Cowper (London, 1871), pp. 82, 83; John Selden, *Table Talk* (London, 1798), p. 57; Mattie Parker, ed., *North Carolina Higher Court Records, 1670–1696* (Raleigh, N.C., 1968), pp. 204–205.

32. *A Report of the Record Commissioners of the City of Boston Containing the Selectmen's*

Minutes from 1754 to 1763 (Boston, 1887), p. 94; Selden, *Table Talk*, p. 58; Winthrop, *History of New England*, 2: 205; Julius Goebel, "King's Law and Local Custom in Massachusetts," *Columbia Law Review* 31 (March 1931): 416 ff.

33. Alexander Brown, *The Genesis of the United States*, 2 vols. (New York, 1964), 1: 69–70; *Hening Statutes* 6: 403–405; John Wise, *The Churches Quarrel Espoused* (New York, 1713), pp. 55–56.

34. *N.H. Hist. Soc. Colls.* 8: 321; *Md. Archives* 7: 201–203, 17: 36; 41: 207–213, 221–223, 255, 258, 259, 457, 458; *New Castle Recs.* 2: 440; *Pa. Prov. Coun. Mins.* 3: 110; Bartlett, ed., *Records of the Colony of Rhode Island*, 4: 27.

35. Winthrop, *History of New England*, 2: 87; *Mass. Bay Co. Recs.* 5: 81; *Report of the Record Commissioners of Boston: Selectmen's Minutes from 1754 to 1763*, p. 188; Alan Heimert and Andrew Delbanco, *The Puritans in America* (Cambridge, Mass., 1985), p. 166; Haynes, *Representation and Suffrage in Massachusetts*, p. 27; Raphael Semmes, *Crime and Punishment in Early Maryland* (Baltimore, 1939), pp. 48–49; *Va. Co. Recs.* 3: 68–69; Carl N. Everstine, *The General Assembly of Maryland, 1634–1776* (Charlottesville, Va., 1980), p. 76; Jean R. Soderlund, ed., *William Penn and the Founding of Pennsylvania* (Philadelphia, 1983), p. 74.

36. *Conn. Pub. Recs.* 7: 44; Lawrence Shaw Mayo, *The Winthrop Family in America* (Boston, 1948), p. 131; *Law Papers, Conn. Hist. Soc. Colls.* 13 (1911): 27–28, 69, 354–357; Arnold, *History of Rhode Island*, 2: 61.

37. *Mass. House Jour., 1737–1738*, pp. 10, 207–208; *Mass. House. Jour., 1748–1749*, p. 244.

38. Dalton, *Country Justice*, pp. 446, 519; W. S. Holdsworth, *A History of English Law*, 14 vols. (London, 1966), 6: 38.

39. *Mass. House Jour., 1718–1720*, pp. 192–193; *Mass. House Jour., 1747–1748*, pp. 66, 71–72, 74, 82, 97.

40. David John Mays, *Edmund Pendleton*, 2 vols. (Cambridge, Mass., 1952), 1: 134; *N.H. Town Recs.* 1: 226; *Pa. Prov. Coun. Mins.* 2: 20; *N.H. Prov. Papers* 3: 342–343, 392; Charles S. Grant, *Democracy in the Connecticut Frontier Town of Kent* (New York, 1961), p. 7; Bartlett, ed., *Records of the Colony of Rhode Island*, 5: 114.

41. *N.H. Prov. Papers* 3: 516–517; *Mass. House Jour., 1718–1720*, p. 301; Philip C. F. Smith, ed., *The Journals of Ashley Bowen 1728–1813* (Portland, Me., 1973), p. 10; *Mass. House Jour., 1746–1747*, p. 555; *Mass. House Jour., 1747–1748*, p. viii; *A Report of the Record Commissioners of the City of Boston Containing the Boston Town Records, 1742 to 1757* (Boston, 1885), p. 85; *Report of the Record Commissioners of Boston: Selectmen's Minutes from 1742 to 1743* (Boston, 1887), pp. 115–116, 125–126; *Report of the Record Commissioners of Boston: Selectmen's Minutes from 1754 to 1763*, pp. 96–97.

42. Van Laer, ed., *New York Historical Manuscripts—Dutch*, 4: 235; *R.I. Hist. Soc. Colls.* 5: 98, 108.

43. *Boston Town Records, 1742 to 1757*, pp. 221, 240, 263; Pownall, *Thomas Pownall*, p. 135; *Va. Burgesses Jour., 1727–1740*, pp. 241–242; *Va. Burgesses Jour., 1742–1749*, p. 4; *Va. Burgesses Jour., 1752–1758*, pp. xviii, 141, 143, 154, 299; Mays, *Edmund Pendleton*, 1: 72; *Report of the Record Commissioners of Boston: Selectmen's Minutes from 1742 to 1753* (Boston, 1887), pp. 99, 105.

44. *N.H. Prov. Papers* 3: 292, 4: 277, 678.

45. Clarence L. Ver Steeg and Richard Hofstadter, eds., *Great Issues in American History* (New York, 1969), pp. 241–242, 249–250.
46. Oscar Handlin, "The Eastern Frontier of New York," *New York History* 18 (1937): 50 ff.; Goebel and Naughton, *Law Enforcement in Colonial New York,* pp. 87 ff., Walter A. Knittle, *The Early Eighteenth Century Palatine Emigration* (Philadelphia, 1936); Edgar J. Fisher, *New Jersey as a Royal Province, 1738 to 1776* (New York, 1911); Eugene R. Sheridan, *Lewis Morris* (Syracuse, N.Y., 1981), pp. 198, 199.
47. *N.H. Hist. Soc. Colls.* 8 (1866): 321.
48. *New York Weekly Journal,* January 21, 1734.
49. Joel Hurstfield, *Freedom, Corruption and Government in Elizabethan England* (Cambridge, Mass., 1973), pp. 70 ff.; Dalton, *Country Justice,* p. 258; *R.I. Hist. Soc. Colls.* 5 (1843): 146–151.
50. *Mass. House Jour., 1718–1720,* p. 369; *Mass. House Jour., 1722–1723,* p. 72; *Pa. Prov. Coun. Mins.* 3: 370; John Blair, ed., *Charter to William Penn and Laws of the Province of Pennsylvania* (Harrisburg, Pa., 1879), p. 35; Helen Hill Miller, *The Case for Liberty* (Chapel Hill, N.C., 1965), pp. 30, 32.
51. *Mass. House Jour., 1750–1751,* pp. 181–182, 209; *Mass. House Jour., 1755,* pp. 58–59; Caulkins, *History of New London,* p. 458.
52. *New England's Mis'ry, the Procuring Cause and a Remedy Proposed* (Boston, 1758), pp. 8–9; Nelson et al., eds., *Documents Relating to the Colonial History of New Jersey,* 19: 56; Clyde A. Duniway, *The Development of Freedom of the Press in Massachusetts* (New York, 1906), p. 120; Louis K. Wechsler, *The Common People of Colonial America* (New York, 1978), p. 124.
53. Livingston Rutherfurd, *John Peter Zenger* (New York, 1904); Duniway, *Freedom of the Press,* p. 113. See also Leonard W. Levy, *Legacy of Suppression: Freedom of Speech and Press in Early American History* (Cambridge, Mass., 1960); Stanley M. Katz, ed., *A Brief Narrative of the Case and Trial of Peter Zenger* (Cambridge, Mass., 1963).
54. *Mass. House Jour., 1729–1731,* pp. 153–154; Locke, *Two Treatises,* p. 46; Isaac Kramnick, *Bolingbroke and His Circle* (Cambridge, Mass., 1968), pp. 166 ff.
55. *Va. Co. Recs.* 1: 400, 633–644, 2: 14; Arnold, *History of Rhode Island* 2: 61; Carter, *Diary,* 1: 107.
56. Berthold Fernow, ed., *The Records of New Amsterdam 1653–1655* (New York, 1897), pp. 252, 254, 291, 368–375, 388; Berthold Fernow, ed., *The Records of New Amsterdam 1656–1658* (New York, 1897), pp. 67, 76, 80–81, 97–98, 120–123, 130, 141–147; Berthold Fernow, ed., *The Records of New Amsterdam 1658–1661* (New York, 1897), p. 424; *Pa. Prov. Coun. Mins.* 2: 385–390; Roger Sherman's and Thomas Moore's almanacs, Wechsler, *The Common People,* p. 122.
57. Holdsworth, *History of English Law,* 6: 61; see also James H. Kettner, *The Development of American Citizenship* (Chapel Hill, N.C., 1978).
58. Richard Brown, *Modernization: The Transformation of American Life, 1600–1865* (New York, 1976); Timothy H. Breen, *Puritans and Adventurers: Change and Persistence in Early America* (New York, 1980); Joyce Appleby, "Value and Society," in Jack P. Greene and J. R. Pole, eds., *Colonial British America* (Baltimore, 1984), pp. 290 ff.
59. *Mass. House Jour., 1760–1761,* pp. 90, 100.

60. Winthrop, *History of New England*, 2: 229 ff.; *R.I. Hist. Soc. Colls.* 5 (1843): 128; Maurice Pollet, *John Skelton, Poet of Tudor England*, ed. John Warrington (London, 1971), pp. 85, 97.
61. Livingston et al., *Independent Reflector*, p. 330.
62. Nelson et al., eds., *Documents Relating to the Colonial History of New Jersey*, 12: 36, 37, 39–40.
63. New York Historical Society, *Collections for the Year 1919* (1920), pp. 203–204.
64. Nelson et al., eds., *Documents Relating to the Colonial History of New Jersey*, 11: 231.

INDEX

269

ABOUT THE AUTHORS

OSCAR HANDLIN taught at Harvard University for almost fifty years; there his seminars helped train a whole generation of social historians and his lecture courses left a significant impression upon class after class of undergraduates. Addressing both students interested in professional careers as historians and those who turned to the subject as part of a liberal education, he learned the value of technical competence and also of clear expressive communication. The original scholarship that informed his instruction at every level also found expression in many books and articles, each grounded on careful research and each written in a style direct, eloquent, and accessible to every reader. The Pulitzer prize in history and numerous other awards and honorary degrees recognized his work.

Among his related activities were service as director of the Harvard University Library, as chairman of the United States Board of Foreign Scholarships, as editorial director of Channel 5-TV (Boston), and as author of a monthly column on books for *The Atlantic*.

LILIAN HANDLIN is a graduate of Queens College and Brown University, and received her Ph.D. at the Hebrew University of Jerusalem, where she was an instructor in the Department of History. She is author of *George Bancroft: The Intellectual as Democrat* (1984) and coauthor of *Abraham Lincoln and the Union* (Boston, 1980) and *A Restless People* (New York, 1982).